Pavel Kann

KU-733-989

LENINGRAD

A Guide

Planeta Publishers
Moscow

П. КАНН

Л Е Н И Н Г Р А Д

Путеводитель

на английском языке

Translated from the Russian

Editor of the Russian text Yakov Brodsky
Editor of the English text Alexandra Buyanovskaya
Designed by Eteri Simanovich
Art editor Alla Tomchinskaya
Maps by Lyubov Cheltsova
Layout by Nina Dolzhikova
Photos by Boris Manushin

First edition 1984
Second edition 1988, 1990
© Planeta Publishers, 1990
English translation © Raduga Publishers 1984

К $\dfrac{4911020000\text{-}245}{027(01)\text{-}90}$ без объявл.

ISBN 5-85250-204-9

CONTENTS

Dear Reader! This book is a guide to Leningrad, one of the most beautiful cities in the world. We invite you to walk along its streets and embankments, to admire exquisite architectural ensembles created by master architects of former and of Soviet times, to become acquainted with the history and contemporary life of this city of many millions, with this leading cultural, scientific and industrial centre of the USSR.

A relatively young city, Leningrad can lay no claims to a history spanning more than a few centuries. You will find neither ancient ruins nor exotic architecture, but we are convinced that your visit to Leningrad will become an unforgettable experience. Tourists often find certain aspects of Leningrad reminiscent of other famous European cities. Its quiet embankments and steeply sloping roofs remind one of Paris; its canals and arched bridges, of Venice; its shady parks and grand palaces, of Prague ... However, these are only first, superficial impressions. For Leningrad is truly a unique city.

Leningrad is known the world over as the cradle of the Great October Socialist Revolution of 1917 and as a city that bravely withstood the 900-day siege laid by the Nazis, during the Second World War. Leningrad is a city of Revolution, a heroic city, a hard-working city.

The life and work of Lenin are closely linked to the city of Leningrad. It was here that he began his revolutionary activities at the turn of the 20th century and later laid the foundations of the Communist Party of the Soviet Union. In the working-class districts of the city he headed Marxist circles and trained workers to become professional revolutionaries. Here, in this city on the Neva, in October of 1917, Lenin uttered his historic words on the victory of the Socialist Revolution, on the birth of the world's first workers' and peasants' state; namely here Lenin proclaimed the peaceful policy of Soviet power that has continued to be carried out by the Communist Party and the Soviet government.

Leningrad may truly be called a centre of Russian culture. Among those who lived and created many of their immortal works here were Alexander Pushkin, Pyotr Tchaikovsky, Fyodor Dostoyevsky, Giacomo Quarenghi, Nikolai Gogol, Ilya Repin, and Dmitri Shostakovich ... Leningrad was the birthplace of the Russian Academy of Sciences and a home to many of Russia's most gifted minds: the encyclopedic scholar Mikhail Lomonosov and the chemist Dmitri Mendeleyev, the inventor of the radio Alexander Popov and the creator of synthetic rubber Sergei Lebedev, the astronomer Vasili Struve, the physicists Vasili Petrov, Pavel Yablochkov and Abram Ioffe, the explorers Pyotr Semyonov-Tien-Shansky and Nikolai Przhevalsky, the shipbuilding theoretician Alexei Krylov and the physiologist Ivan Pavlov, founder of the doctrine on conditioned reflexes.

Interesting encounters with the creations of world-famous architects, artists, and sculptors await you in the streets, squares, and museums of Leningrad. You will become involved in the history of the city.

We believe that this guide will serve as a good companion and adviser during your stay in Leningrad, and that upon leaving the city you will carry away in your heart the cordial warmth that will be extended to you by the Leningraders.

SOME ADVANCE TIPS AND INFORMATION

A Bit of Georgraphy

One of the largest northern cities in the world, Leningrad lies near the Arctic Circle, on the same latitude as the southern part of Alaska and the southern tip of Greenland. However, despite its northern location, Leningrad has a fairly mild climate: on the average, the temperature is above the freezing point 222 days a year. This is mainly owing to the warm air masses brought to the city by winds from the Atlantic Ocean.

When preparing for a trip to Leningrad it is useful to know approximately when the seasons begin and end.

Season	Begins	Ends	Duration in Days
Winter	December 5	March 16	102
Spring	March 17	June 1	77
Summer	June 2	September 11	102
Autumn	September 12	December 4	84

The following data on the mean monthly temperature (Centigrade) in Leningrad will also prove useful:

January	$- 7.9°$	July	$+17.7°$
February	$- 8.4°$	August	$+16.1°$
March	$- 4.7°$	September	$+10.8°$
April	$+ 2.1°$	October	$+ 4.5°$
May	$+ 8.7°$	November	$- 1.6°$
June	$+14.8°$	December	$- 6.6°$

It is hard to say what time of the year is best for a visit to Leningrad, for each season has its own charm.

Winter is a rather fitful season. Cold days often alternate with warmer temperatures bringing heavy snowfalls. But how truly beautiful the winter-time city looks with its gardens and parks blanketed in snow, and the granite embankments of the Neva and the palaces glittering with hoarfrost. All this creates an indefinable, fantastic impression.

Spring does not arrive all at once. Its first month, March, is very unstable. Only after around April 3 does the temperature consistently stay above freezing. If you come to Leningrad in April or early May, you will be able to see a most thrilling sight—the ice-drift on the Neva. Enormous ice floes, hurried on by the wind and a strong current, race down the river to the Gulf of Finland.

Summer in Leningrad is moderately warm. There is less rainfall in July than in June or August, while August is almost 2 °C cooler than July. This can vary, of course, with some years bringing higher temperatures in June than in July or August.

Leningrad is famous for its White Nights. They begin after the 10th of June; by this time the sun sets only 9 degrees below the horizon. By June 21 the length of the day has increased to 18 hours 53 minutes.

During White Nights, when a faint twilight takes the place of night darkness (and then not even for more than 30-40 minutes), the streets, squares, and embankments acquire a unique charm. The White Nights come to an end around July 2.

Autumn really takes over in the middle of September, which is usually a mild month in Leningrad. Only towards the end of the month does the temperature fall below 10 °C. In October, however, freezing weather becomes more common, though there may still be some unexpectedly warm and sunny days. On such days Leningrad is particularly impressive. The gentle rays of the sun play on the gilded steeples and domes, the warm, brilliant colours of the northern autumn paint the gardens, parks and streets of the city.

Indeed, Leningrad is magnificent at any time of the year. But this you will discover for yourself.

How to Get to Leningrad

Leningrad is a major transport junction with two airports, five railway stations servicing twelve separate lines, three seaports, one river port and two interurban bus stations.

Since the Volga-Baltic Canal was built in 1964 Leningrad has become a port of five seas: its waterways extent to the Baltic, White, Caspian, Azov and Black seas.

Soviet **railways** are known for their efficiency and high standard of technical equipment. Comfortable air-conditioned coaches and compartments, restaurants and snack-bars, good food, and obliging conductors will make travelling easy and enjoyable.

The following table provides useful information for those planning to travel to Leningrad by rail.

International Railway Lines to Leningrad

Point of Departure	Point of Entry into the USSR	Travel Time (hrs., mins.)	Major Stops in the USSR
Moscow		8-00	
Warsaw	Grodno	22-39	Grodno, Vilnius Daugavpils, Pskov
Berlin	Grodno	32-35	Grodno, Vilnius Daugavpils, Pskov
Paris	Grodno	48-00	Grodno, Vilnius Daugavpils, Pskov
Prague	Chop	48-59	Lvov, Vilnius Pskov
Budapest	Zakhon	44-05	Lvov, Vilnius Pskov
Sofia	Vadul-Siret	30-42	Lvov, Vilnius Pskov
Helsinki	Luzhaika	12-40	Vyborg

Leningrad is connected to 19 countries, 25 European cities and 200 cities in the Soviet Union by **35 Soviet airline flights and 26 foreign airline flights**.

Flying into Leningrad, one sees from afar the glass towers of the Pulkovo Airport. Moving sidewalks (170 metres long each) and comfortable, spacious vestibules and waiting-rooms provide maximum convenience for passengers.

We now follow with information on air-travel time from a number of European cities to Leningrad:

Point of Departure	Flight Time in hrs. and mins.
Moscow	1-00
Warsaw	1-55
Berlin	2-35
Budapest	2-40
Prague	2-40
Belgrade	3-15
Burgas	3-10
Sofia	3-10
Helsinki	1-00
Amsterdam via Stockholm	4-45
Stockholm	1-25
Copenhagen via Stockholm	3-55
Oslo via Stockholm	3-35
London via Copenhagen	5-45
Paris	3-45
Hamburg	2-30
Zurich	3-30

Four to five thousand ships from over 50 countries of the world call at the **Leningrad seaport annually**. The city is linked by regular passenger lines with such cities as Montreal (via Le Havre, London, Bremerhaven), Le Havre (via London and Helsinki), Stockholm, Lappeenranta, and others. Those visiting Leningrad on cruises live on board ship during their stay in the city.

How to Pack

First of all, make sure you have your passport (check its validity), a Soviet entrance visa, tourist vouchers, travel tickets, and money. If you do not know where you will be staying in Leningrad, your correspondents may write to you at the following address: USSR, 190000, Leningrad, General Post Office, Poste restante (your name).

Do not overload your suitcase with things unnecessary for the trip. If you are to travel in winter, then, of course, take warm underwear, woollen stockings or socks, warm waterproof footwear, a winter overcoat and a fur or woollen cap.

We advise you to take along your usual toiletry items, and if you plan to pack any electric appliances—shavers, hair-dryers, etc.—keep in mind that the city's voltage is 220 v a.c. You may need to obtain a converter and/or plug adapter.

The Leningrad pharmacies (drugstores) offer a wide range of medicines (of both Soviet and foreign manufacture), but if you are on any kind of medication we recommend that you take along a supply to last you the duration of your trip.

The same goes for print, slide and cinema film. It is advisable to pack enough film of various degrees of sensitivity with your photo- and cine-cameras.

It is not necessary to take along food of any kind: Intourist is a good host and feeds its guests lavishly.

Time Zone

Should you wish to telephone from Leningrad to another country, you must remember that Leningrad time is two hours ahead of Central European time. Thus, when it is 12 noon in Leningrad it is 10 a.m. in Paris, Prague, Rome, Stockholm, Warsaw, Vienna, and Berlin. At the same time it is 11 a.m. in Helsinki, Sofia, Athens, Bucharest, and Cairo. In London it is 9 a.m., in New York 4 a.m., in Buenos Aires and Mexico City—3 a.m., in Delhi—2.30 p.m., in Tokyo—6 p.m., and in Canberra—7 p.m. From the last Saturday in March to the last Saturday in September, the Soviet Union is on daylight saving time. The "World Clock" on the Leningrad General Post Office at No. 9. Communications Union Street (Ulitsa Soyuza Svyazi) will help you to find the time in different countries.

Some More Advice

Upon your arrival in Leningrad you will be met in the airport, at the railway station, or at the seaport by representatives of Intourist, of the Sputnik Bureau of International Youth Tourism, of the All-Union Central Council of Trade Unions, or of other organisations awaiting you. They will help you with the necessary formalities. However, we advise you to check with your travel agent before your departure to be sure that he or she has notified the Leningrad branch of Intourist, or the organisation at whose invitation you are travelling to Leningrad, of your arrival date and your flight number or the numbers of your train and coach.

However, in the unlikely event that you are not met for whatever reason, you have only to approach any employee of the airport or station and say the word "Intourist". This will suffice to immediately contact an Intourist representative who will render you all the necessary assistance.

There are Service Bureaus in all of Leningrad's foreign-tourist hotels. These Bureaus are designed to help make the visit of our foreign guests as interesting as possible. The employees of the Service Bureaus advise foreign visitors on matters concerning their stay in the USSR and organise additional sightseeing excursions in the city and its environs, as well as visits to museums, exhibitions and concert halls, theatres, and sports stadiums. The Service Bureaus are usually open from 9 a.m. to 10 p.m.

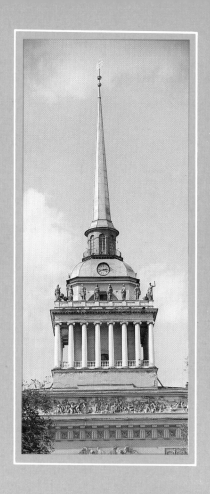

THE CITY'S HISTORY
LENIN MEMORIAL PLACES
BUILDING AND ARCHITECTURE
LENINGRAD MISCELLANEOUS

THE CITY'S HISTORY

Over a thousand years ago the territory of today's Leningrad and the adjacent lands were inhabited by Slavic tribes; subsequently, in the 10th century, these lands became part of Kievan Russia, a feudal state that emerged in Eastern Europe at the turn of the 9th century. The geographic location of these lands was most convenient: the major trade route of the Slavs, "from the Varangians to the Greeks", lay across the Gulf of Finland, along the Neva and Lake Ladoga, linking Northern Russia to Southern, and also the Baltic lands and Scandinavia to Byzantium. Russian merchant ships travelled by this route to the "Varangians" (as the Scandinavians were then known) carrying to the North European ports timber, hemp, furs and other highly prized goods. Vessels with cargoes sold at no meaner profit in Russia sailed in the opposite direction.

In the 12th century, after the break-up of Kievan Russia, this region became a constituent of the Novgorodian land. The region encompassing modern-day Leningrad, the Neva, and the southern coast of the Gulf of Finland was then called Vodskaya Pyatina—a territorial-administrative subdivision of the Novgorodian land, named after the local tribe of Vod.

The convenient location of the Vodskaya Pyatina attracted its northern neighbours. From the 13th to the 16th centuries Sweden repeatedly attempted to annex it. For a long time these attempts were fruitless, until in 1617 the Swedish King succeeded in seizing the banks of the Neva and building a fortress, Nienschantz (Kantsy), at the mouth of the river Okhta.

Russia was thus cut off from the Baltic Sea, an important waterway leading to the countries of Western Europe. This development, of course, greatly affected both the economic and political life of the Russian state.

In 1700, a war broke out between Russia and Sweden for the age-old Russian lands, for an outlet to the Baltic. Known in history as the Northern War, it ended in 1721 with Russia's victory. This renewed access to the Baltic enabled Russia to expand her economic, cultural, and political contacts, to both her own benefit and that of the countries of Western Europe.

On May 16 (May 27, New Style) of

the year 1703, after the Russian troops had captured the Nienschantz Fortress (an important strategic point), Peter the Great ordered the construction of the Peter and Paul Fortress on Zayachi Ostrov (Hare Island) in the widest part of the Neva estuary. This date marks the beginning of the building of a stronghold and a trading port on the Baltic coast—St. Petersburg.

Enterprises, large-scale for those times, were erected in the new city to serve, in the main, the army and navy: the Admiralty Wharf, the Tar Yard (Smolyanoi Dvor), where tar and pitch for calking the ships were prepared and stored, the Foundry (Liteiny Dvor), where gunnery was founded, powder works and tanneries. In 1712, Peter the Great moved the capital of Russia from Moscow to St. Petersburg, establishing it as the main industrial and political centre of the country.

The new capital grew rapidly; it was built according to the plans of prominent Russian and foreign architects (the latter were invited specially for this purpose). The actual builders of the city were soldiers, serfs, and craftsmen, resettled on the banks of the Neva from all parts of Russia. They dug canals, built roads, factories, embankments, palaces and mansions that housed the nobility and courtiers, and the various governmental bodies. These workmen also became the first citizens of the new capital. Many foreigners, too, settled here "for permanent residence"—mostly sailors, craftsmen, physicians, apothecaries and teachers. Many of them soon became Russified and blended in with the city's Russian population almost entirely.

However, St. Petersburg was not only the industrial and political centre of the country. Established educational institutions moved in, and new ones were founded: the Naval Academy, the Artillery and the Engineering schools, and the School of Surgeons. The city was not quite ten years old when printing presses were set up and the publication of books and of the first Russian printed newspaper began. Russia's first museum of natural history (the Kunstkammer) was founded, her first public library and first permanent public theatre were opened. St. Petersburg quickly came to occupy a leading place in the cultural life of the country.

At first the city was built in the area protected by the bastions of the Peter and Paul Fortress, the area of today's Revolution Square (Ploshchad Revolyutsii) (included in sightseeing Excursion No. 1). After St. Petersburg had become the capital, intensive building was begun in the eastern part of Vasilyevsky Island (Excursion No. 2). However, at that time there were no bridges over the Neva, and so the attempt to build the centre of the capital on an isolated island in a deep river failed. Thus, by the middle of the 18th century construction went on mainly on the left bank of the Neva, in the area between the Smolny and Ploshchad Truda (Labour Square).

St. Petersburg was one of the first cities in the world to be built according to preconceived plans envisaging the ensemble principle of construction. Almost all the basic trends in world and Russian architecture of the 18th-20th centuries are represented. Among those who worked here were such outstanding architects as Bartolomeo Rastrelli (the Winter Palace, the Cathedral of the Smolny Convent, the Stroganov Palace); Antonio Rinaldi (the Marble Palace); Alexander Koko-

View of the Admiralty. Engraving. 18th cent.

rinov and Jean-Baptiste Vallin de la Mothe (the Academy of Arts); Ivan Starov (the Taurida Palace); Giacomo Quarenghi (the Smolny Institute, the Academy of Sciences); Andreyan Zakharov (the Admiralty); Andrei Voronikhin (the Kazansky Cathedral, the Mining Institute); Vasili Stasov (Barracks of the Pavlovsky Regiment, the Narva Gate); Carlo Rossi (the General Staff, the Mikhailovsky Palace and the Alexandrinsky Theatre), and many other architects famed for their creations both in Russia and in other countries. Later we shall dwell in greater detail on Leningrad as a unique architectural museum.

The city is interesting not only for its palaces and cathedrals. It is also the site of the first revolutionary movement in Russia against autocracy and serfdom. On December 14, 1825, Russian revolutionaries of noble families marched into Senate Square, leading troops who had refused to swear allegiance to Nicholas I on his accession to the throne. The uprising was quickly suppressed owing to the hesitation of the Decembrists themselves (as the revolutionary nobles came to be known in Russian history) and to their isolation from the popular masses. The events of December 14, 1825, will be dealt with at greater length during your excursion to Ploshchad Dekabristov (Decembrists' Square) (Excursion No. 3).

The highest phase in the revolutionary movement in Russia—the proletarian—is closely related to the history of St. Petersburg, or Petrograd (as the city was renamed on August 18, 1914). The revolutionary activities of Vladimir Lenin unfolded in this city, where he organised the League of Struggle for the Emancipation of the

Construction of the Neva's Embankment. Engraving. 18th cent.

Working Class—the embryo of the Communist Party of the Soviet Union; here the first Russian revolution of 1905-1907 began, and here on February 27, 1917, a bourgeois-democratic revolution overthrew Russian autocratic rule. And it was in this city that a salvo fired by the cruiser *Aurora* on October 25 (November 7), 1917, announced the victory of the Great October Socialist Revolution.

Thus, Soviet rule was established in Russia. However, the overthrown ruling classes could not reconcile themselves to the victory of the proletarian revolution. In the very first days following the October Revolution the former head of the bourgeois Provisional Government, Kerensky, having escaped from Petrograd, launched counter-revolutionary troops against the city. A Junker rebellion took place at the same time (the Junkers were

cadets of military schools). Under the guidance of the Communist Party the Petrograd workers and sailors quelled the first attempt of the counter-revolution to crush the workers' and peasants' rule.

Internal counter-revolution was actively supported by foreign imperialists. On February 18, 1918, the armies of Kaiser's Germany, violating the armistice with Soviet Russia signed on December 2, 1917, launched an offensive along the entire front—from the Baltic to the Black Sea. On February 21, 1918, the Central Committee of the Communist Party and the Soviet government called all workers and peasants to the defence of the revolution. A state of siege was proclaimed in Petrograd. The new-born regiments of the Red Army, unschooled as yet in the military arts, but staunchly devoted to Soviet power, together with units of sailors and armed workers blocked the way to revolutionary Petrograd for Kaiser's troops. Bloody battles were waged on the approaches to the city. During these grim days the Council of Peoples' Commissars (the highest organ of state power) decided to evacuate the government from Petrograd. On the night of March 10-11, 1918, Lenin and other leaders of the Communist Party and the Soviet government left for Moscow. On the 12th of March, on Lenin's order, a red flag was raised over the Kremlin. Moscow had again become a capital, but now it was the capital of the Soviet state.

Up to November of 1919 armed workers, soldiers, and sailors defended Petrograd against Russian counter-revolution and foreign intervention. When the military danger had passed, new troubles befell the city: economic devastation, famine, epidemics. But Petrograd lived, struggled, and survived.

On January 21, 1924, Lenin died. The news of the death of the leader of the Revolution grieved the hearts of peoples around the world. On January 26, 1924, the Second All-Union Congress of Soviets (the supreme organ of state power), at the request of the working people of Petrograd, changed the name of that city to Leningrad in honour of the great leader. Petrograd became Leningrad.

After the victory over the interventionists and internal counter-revolution, the Communist Party and the Soviet government proceeded to restore and rebuild the country's national economy on a socialist basis. In 1925, the 14th Congress of the Communist Party, in accordance with Lenin's behests, set a course for socialist industrialisation. Leningrad played an ex-

Peter and Paul Fortress

ceptionally important part in the solution of this problem.

During the years of World War I and the Civil War (1918-1920) industrial production in the city was diminished eightfold, but by 1926-1927 the Leningraders had already achieved—and in some areas even exceeded—the industrial production level of 1913 (the year when industrial production in tsarist Russia reached its peak). Mass production of tractors, timber haulers, machine tools and machines was launched in subsequent years—before the Revolution such items had to be imported from abroad. Leningrad began to make turbines and generators, diesel and steam engines, optical instruments and tools.

Achievements in the building of socialism and economic growth led to essential improvements in municipal services and the everyday life of the Leningraders. The former royal palaces and mansions of the nobility were turned into holiday homes and workers' clubs. The establishment of communal services and amenities was commenced in the suburbs of the city. The Narva, Moscow, and Neva Zastavy (Gates) and the Vyborgskaya Storona (Vyborg Side) became enormous building sites.

On June 22, 1941, Nazi Germany attacked the Soviet Union without warning, marking the beginning of the Great Patriotic War of 1941-1945. A grim ordeal fell to the lot of Leningrad and its citizens in this war. In East Prussia a group of armies, designated "Nord", was ready for the offensive against Leningrad. Consisting of 42 divisions, "Nord" numbered something like 725,000 officers and men, more than 13,000 guns and 1,500 tanks.

By July 10, 1941, the army group "Nord" had seized almost the entire territory of the Soviet Baltic republics and had broken into Leningrad Region. However, the resistance put up by Soviet troops halted the enemy offensive; the plan of the Nazi high command to take Leningrad "on the rush" was an utter failure. Not only military troops defended the city—at the call of the Communist Party the entire population rose to the defence of Leningrad. People's Volunteer Divisions, partisan units, and special battalions for fighting enemy agents were formed. Some 500,000 Leningraders built the city's defences under enemy machine-gun fire and bombs dropped by planes. A total of over 4,000 steel-and-concrete pillboxes and log-and-earth emplacements, 17,000 embrasures in buildings, 25 kilometres of barricades and many other defences were built in the city.

Evacuation of the population, industrial plants and factories, museums, etc. began as soon as the war broke out. From June through August 70 large industrial enterprises were evacuated, as well as many of the scientific research institutions, schools of higher learning, works of art, etc. Forty-five Pullman cars were provided for evacuating the treasures of the Hermitage. Everything that could not be taken away was safely hidden. Trenches were dug under the great old lindens in the Summer Garden and the 18th-century marble statues adorning the Gardens were buried in them. Sculptor Pyotr Klodt's four bronze horses were taken off their pedestals on Anichkov Bridge and buried in the gardens of the Young Pioneers' Palace. Cliff-scalers and alpinists muffled up in protective covers the golden spires of the Admiralty and the Peter and Paul Fortress,

Archway of the former General Staff. View of the Alexander Column

and coated the dome of St. Isaac's Cathedral with grey paint. The statue of Lenin in front of the Finland Station and the monument to Peter the Great on the Neva embankment were sand-bagged and built over with boards and logs...

The enemy ring around the city was drawn ever tighter. By late August-early September of 1941, the enemy troops had cut off all the railways linking Leningrad to the rest of the country and seized Schlüsselburg (now called Petrokrepost), a town at the outflow of the Neva from Lake Ladoga. This marked the beginning of the 900-day siege of Leningrad. These were 900 days of incredible hardships and privations, 900 days of hunger and cold, 900 days of artillery shelling and air raids.

After the attempts to take Leningrad by storm had failed, the German naval headquarters issued, in September 1941, a secret directive "On the Future of the City of Petersburg". In this document, now a museum exhibit at the Piskaryovskoye Cemetery, it was said: "The Führer has decided to wipe the city of Petersburg off the face of the earth ... It is proposed to tighten up the blockade of the city and level it to the ground by shelling and continuous bombing from the air..."

The realisation of this plan was carried out methodically and ruthlessly. Gunfire was directed not only against defence enterprises. On the maps of the enemy artillerymen such "military" objectives as museums, palaces and schools were pinpointed.

Olga Berggolts, a Soviet poetess who worked throughout the entire siege at Radio Leningrad, wrote on December 20, 1943: "The Germans have lately begun to shell the city at night ever more frequently. With de-vilish cunning the enemy has for two and a half years been incessantly inventing means to destroy civilians ... Sometimes the shelling is like a mad squall of fire—first aimed at one part of the city, then another, then a third, and so forth ... At times as many as eighty batteries hit all parts of the city at once. Sometimes they shoot a tremendous volley from several heavy guns at once, and then there is a long interval—20-30 minutes. The idea behind such intervals is to lure the people out from their shelters after about twenty minutes of quiet, and then start firing on them again. This type of shelling is usually aimed at several districts of the city at once and they sometimes last—as it was at the beginning of December—up to ten and more hours without let-up. This summer there were shellings that lasted 26 hours at a stretch.

"The enemy shells the city in the morning and in the evening, when people are going to work or returning to their homes.

"At this time he uses, mainly, shrapnel shells in order to kill people. Shrapnel is also used frequently on Sundays and holidays, at times when people come out onto the streets for a walk."

The thunder of explosions boomed ceaselessly over Leningrad. The fascists fired a total of about 150,000 shells on the city during the blockade years. Almost simultaneously with the artillery shelling air raids began on September 6, 1941. The fallen walls of No. 119, Nevsky Prospekt, the first war ruins in Leningrad, have been preserved. Disastrous consequences followed the air raid of September 8, 1941. The enemy planes dropped 12,000 incendiary bombs, causing 178 fires in which industrial enterprises and residential buildings were consumed. Over the southern areas of the city clouds of white smoke rose up into the sky: the Badayev Warehouses, the largest food storehouses in Leningrad, were ablaze, burning for more than five hours.

Not all the bombs dropped, however, brought death and destruction. Some of them (so very few) conveyed to the Leningraders signs of workers' solidarity. In 1943 one of these bombs landed in the Peter and Paul Fortress. It did not go off. When sappers opened it up, they found a note with the following message: "The German workers are with you."

During the siege an average of 16 high-explosive bombs, 320 incendiary bombs and 480 shells fell on every square kilometre of the city. All in all over 107,000 high-explosive and incendiary bombs were dropped on the city. As a result of the air raids and shelling over 16,000 civilians were killed and over 33,000 wounded.

However, an incalculably greater number of lives were carried away by hunger. At the beginning of the war food consumption in Leningrad rose somewhat: refugees arrived from the Soviet Baltic republics and Leningrad Region; besides, the garrison increased sharply, more and more troops concentrated in the area.

The Party and State organs were deeply concerned over the food supplies for Leningrad. But it was tremendously difficult to bring supplies to the city: all overland roads had been severed by the ring of the enemy blockade. Only to the east of Leningrad, on the southwestern shore of Lake Ladoga, a tiny tract of land, about 30 kilometres long, remained

unoccupied by the Germans. Here a connection with the eastern shore of Lake Ladoga, which was in Soviet hands, was established through a shipping route. When the navigation season ended food supplies could only be flown in.

Great as these efforts were, they did not provide enough food for the city and the front at even the most modest ration norms. Famine threatened Leningrad. From November 20, 1941, the Leningraders began to receive the lowest bread ration of the entire siege—250 grams per day for factory workers (roughly, one-third of the population) and 125 grams for all others. This dark-brown, sticky stuff containing only 50 per cent of rye flour—the rest consisting of cellulose, malt, soya flour, bran, and similar substances—was the basic food of the city's inhabitants.

Other products, too, were supposed to be issued on the ration cards, but during the grimmest days in the history of Leningrad, the winter of 1941-1942, their distribution was very irregular. Over a long period of time two-thirds of the population received a daily ration equal to 500-600 calories, while the human body expends 3,000-5,000 calories per day. True, additional nutrition was issued to workers at defence enterprises: acorn "coffee", kelp, casein glue, protein yeast, fermented soya milk and other substitutes that somewhat dulled the feeling of hunger.

There were other hardships, too. Owing to the absence of electric power and fuel, neither water-supply lines, sewerage, nor heating systems worked. The unheated homes were dimly lighted by smoky little wicks.

The Leningrad Party Committee and the Executive Committee of the

Leningrad Soviet of Working People's Deputies (the municipal administration) did all they could to help the famished people. Thousands of Party and Komsomol members, despite their own hunger and weakness, patrolled the streets, helping others get to their homes or a hospital. Special "warming up" rooms were set up inside apartment buildings, where hot water could be obtained. Infirmaries of a semi-hospital type were opened for the most weakened citizens.

With the onset of the cold weather it became possible to improve the food situation of Leningrad a little by bringing provisions over the frozen Lake Ladoga. This lake is over 200 km long, and about 125 km wide. Its southern part, however, is considerably narrower, and when the water froze here, a 37-km ice road was laid—the Road of Life, as the Leningraders called it. On November 22, 1941, while the ice was still thin (18 centimetres), lorries carrying supplies set off across it towards Leningrad. On December 25 the bread ration for the inhabitants of the city was slightly increased: 350 grams for workers, 200 for everybody else.

In April 1942, the Road of Life was closed to traffic. The spring ice could no longer withstand the weight of the lorries. During that most trying time for the besieged city suffering from scurvy, two freight cars of onions reached the village of Kobona on the eastern shore of Lake Ladoga. However, transporting this vital cargo to the Leningraders presented a major problem. They tried taking it across on sleds, but the horses refused to step out into the 50–60 centimetres of icy water that covered the frozen lake. Next they loaded the cargo into boats, but the attempt to row across

the shallow water proved futile. Finally the soldiers and civilians servicing the Road of Life decided to carry the onions across on foot, each taking a load of 10–15 kilograms.

These valiant people trudged through knee-high water for over 30 kilometres, when even a short stop for rest was fatal. Nonetheless, Leningraders received life-saving onion on May Day.

Throughout the entire operation of the Ladoga route from the beginning of the blockade (September 1941) to March 30, 1943, almost 1,500,000 tons of supplies and about 450,000 people, mainly servicemen, were conveyed over it to Leningrad. From Leningrad 1,200,000 people, mostly women, old people and children, were evacuated via the ice road. However, famine reaped an abundant harvest of lives. During the siege over 640,000 people starved to death. Among the exhibits in the museum at Piskarevskoye Cemetery (Excursion No. 10) there are photocopies of a tragic document— the diary of eleven-year-old Tanya Savicheva. Virtually every entry records the death from starvation of a member of her large family. And this tragic document ends with the words: "The Savichevs died. They all died."

The famished Leningraders were struck down by death at various times and places—in the street, during their sleep at night, by the workbench or in the laboratory ... Along the deserted, snow-drifted streets, mustering the last of their strength, people hauled away frozen corpses on children's sleds. Later on, when the living had become too weak to haul the dead to the cemetery, lorries drove through the city, picking up corpses in the streets, the yards, the squares.

Neither air raids, shells, nor hunger

House in the Constructivist style. Mid–1930s

could break the spirit of the Leningraders. Nikolai Balyasnikov, a worker of the Kirov plant, wrote in his diary on December 25, 1941, not long before he died: "What hardships we Leningraders must endure! It's hard to imagine how things could be any worse. But the fascists won't take us, won't break us! Not by hunger, or cold, or shelling! We'll die, but we won't let the enemy in."

Under the terrible conditions of siege the city not only fought for its life, it also helped the country rout the fascist invaders. Factories of the besieged Leningrad sent off to the front lines 2,000 new and repaired tanks, 1,500 airplanes, 150 heavy naval artillery pieces and over 4,500 guns of other calibres, 12,000 mortars, 225,000 submachine-guns, 10,000,000 artillery shells and mines. Not only did the inhabitants of the besieged city supply arms and ammunition to the Leningrad Front, but part of the output of the Leningrad munition factories were delivered by air to the troops defending Moscow. In October-December of 1941 alone the defenders of Moscow received from blockaded Leningrad, by air, over a thousand artillery pieces.

Scientists also made no mean contribution to the defence of Leningrad. During the very first days of the war a special committee was formed for the practical realisation of defence proposals and inventions. Among its members were scholars of world fame. Metallurgists worked out new grades of high-quality steel, chemists invented an explosive that was manufactured in Leningrad from local resources, new types of ammunition and new optical instruments for anti-aircraft guns were designed in scientific-research laboratories.

In the heroic chronicles of the Leningrad defence there is a chapter devoted to the feat of the staff of the Vavilov Plant-Breeding Institute that is, probably, the most vivid illustration of the courage and fortitude of the city's scientists. A valuable collection of grain cultures from 118 countries of the world had been collected under

Streets during the siege of Leningrad in 1941–1944

the guidance of the outstanding Soviet scientist Academician Nikolai Vavilov. Just before the war this collection included over 100,000 samples of wheat, rye, rice, maize, and many other cultures. Through the study of these plant samples botany researchers were able to solve some urgent problems in crop development. It had not been possible to evacuate this unique collection, but not a single grain from it was lost. Many of its custodians died of hunger but the collection was saved for science, for humanity.

The war against the Nazi invaders was fought by soldiers, workers, scientists ... by musicians, too. Yes, indeed, by musicians. Dmitri Shostakovich's Seventh (or Leningrad) Symphony was composed in the besieged city; on August 9, 1942, it was broadcasted from Leningrad on all wavelengths and was heard by people not only in the Soviet Union, but in other countries as well, and even on other continents. The concert was conducted by Karl Eliasberg. At the order of the Soviet High Command of the Leningrad Front a barrage of artillery fire was launched against the enemy positions at the moment when the performance of the symphony began in Leningrad's Philharmonic. Not a single enemy shell reached Leningrad.

Two months later, the sounds of Pyotr Tchaikovsky's Fifth Symphony were broadcast from the besieged city directly to London. The broadcast was preceded by twelve air-raid-warning signals. On the thirteenth the performance began. A bomb dropped not far from the radio building, but the conductor, Karl Eliasberg, did not interrupt the concert.

A few days later the following words came to the besieged city over the radio: "Come in, Leningrad! This is London! London is with you. Every gunshot of yours is answered in London. London salutes the heroism of Leningrad."

In 1943 Leningrad cartographers received an unusual order. At the bidding of Supreme General Headquar-

THE CITY HISTORY 27

Victory Square. Monument to the Heroic Defenders of Leningrad

ters, the headquarters of the Leningrad Front assigned them the task of drawing up a large-scale map of Berlin and its suburbs. Within two months of intensive work the cartographers had prepared a map 180 cm × 180 cm which showed the streets and squares of Berlin as well as important military objectives, including the imperial Chancellery and the Reichstag. It was namely this map that the Soviet troops later used in

storming the capital of the fascist Reich.

Soviet troops broke through the blocade in the vicinity of Schlüsselburg in January of 1943, and on February 7 the first train from the Mainland arrived at the Finland Station. This break-through created favourable conditions for the launching of a decisive offensive. In the early hours of January 14, 1944, the Leningraders were awakened by the thunderous boom of artillery fire that marked the beginning of the operation for putting a complete end to the blockade. On January 27 a salute from 324 guns was fired over the city to celebrate the complete defeat of Nazi troops in the environs of Leningrad.

The lifting of the blockade was an event of international significance. The British *Star* stated that the battle of Leningrad had planted misgivings among the Nazis. It made them feel that they were only temporary masters in Paris, Brussels, Amsterdam, Warsaw and Oslo.

For the outstanding services of its inhabitants to the country, for their courage and heroism in the struggle against the fascist invaders, Leningrad was awarded the Order of Lenin in January 1945.

When at last the thunder of artillery fire stopped and silence reigned over Berlin on that long-awaited day in May 1945, among the multitude of inscriptions on the columns of the Reichstag there was this one: "Major Andreyev, Okhrimenko, and Mikhailov from Leningrad were here. We came here so that Germany should not come to us."

In the Museum of the History of Leningrad there is a document sent to the Leningraders by US President Franklin Roosevelt in 1944: "In the name of the people of the United States of America, I present this scroll to the City of Leningrad as a memorial to its gallant soldiers and to its loyal men, women and children who, isolated from the rest of their nation by the invader and despite constant bombardment and untold sufferings from cold, hunger and sickness, successfully defended their beloved city throughout the critical period September 8, 1941 to January 18, 1943, and

thus symbolized the undaunted spirit of the peoples of the Union of Soviet Socialist Republics and of all the nations of the world resisting forces of aggression."

In the postwar period the housing problem became particularly acute in the city. Hundreds of buildings had been destroyed by air raids and shelling. During the years of war Leningrad lost 5.5 million square metres of housing. It was necessary to create, in the shortest possible time, normal conditions for the life, work, and recreation of those people who had survived the horrors of the 900-day siege.

Again the whole country came to the aid of the city. From all parts of the Soviet Union trainloads of building materials, glass (almost all the windows in the houses were covered with plywood) and food arrived in Leningrad. Many Leningraders took crash training courses in which they were taught basic construction skills, and in their free time they worked at the construction sites on a voluntary basis, without pay.

The entire city had suffered from the air raids and shelling, but the greatest damage had been done in the suburbs. In the Kirov and Moscow districts—you will walk along their main thorougfares, Prospekt Stachek (Strikes Avenue) and Moskovsky Prospekt (Moscow Avenue) (Excursions Nos. 6 and 7)—half of the dwelling houses had been reduced to ruins. But even on the central thoroughfare of the city, Nevsky Prospekt (Nevsky Avenue), almost every building had sustained damages. The Admiralty, Gostiny Dvor (a large department store), the Russian Museum, the Lesser Hall of the Philharmonic, the Club of Workers in the Arts, and the

Palace of Young Pioneers had all been destroyed or damaged by high-explosive or incendiary bombs, by artillery shelling...

It seemed that it would take years and years to eliminate these terrible consequences of the war. However, by the end of 1945 one-third of all the ruined buildings of Leningrad had been restored. By 1949–1950 not a single ruin remained in the city. It is noteworthy that not only was the city being built up again—it was being restored to its original beauty. In their reconstruction projects the architects strove to restore each building to its original aspect, to clear the city of haphazard features added at later periods.

Thus, the buildings at the intersection of the Moika and Nevsky Avenue (Excursion No. 5) were given a new colour scheme that is retained to this day. Building No. 30 on Nevsky Avenue (19th century) was restored to its original appearance; since 1949 it has housed the Lesser Hall of the Leningrad Philharmonic. In working on this reconstruction project, architect Valentin Kamensky used the original sketches of Paul Jacquot and succeeded in restoring all the details of the designs conceived by Leonti Benois. The little square on Plekhanov Street near the Kazansky Cathedral underwent a radical alteration. This square is surrounded by a splendid wrought-iron railing created by Andrei Voronikhin (19th century) that was formerly concealed by gawky buildings. The destroyed Gostiny Dvor (18th century) was restored in precise conformance with the drawings made by Jean-Baptiste Vallin de la Mothe, who worked on its façades. The city rose from its ruins rejuvenated, transformed, even more beautiful than it had been before the war.

The master plan for the development of Leningrad and the Leningrad Region for 1986–2005 envisages the concentric growth of the city, though it is to remain primarily within its current boundaries. Large-scale construction work will take place in the Strelna, Petrodvorets, and Lomonosov districts, on the southern bank of the Gulf of Finland and on the northern between Gorskaya and Sestroretsk, where considerable attention will also be given to flood control.

Throughout its history Leningrad has been inundated with floods more than three hundred times. The greatest and most devastating floods were those of 1777, 1824, and 1924, when the water level rose to more than 300 cm. Formerly the explanation for the "mechanism" of the floods was that the force of the wind from the Gulf of Finland blocked up the way for the water of the Neva, turning its flow back onto the city. However, this idea was refuted, for instance, by the flood of 1752, which occurred during complete calm. Recent data give evidence of another cause of the floods. A cyclone forming in the centre of the Baltic Sea creates a vacuum above the surface of the water, as a result of which a giant pillar of water surges upward, then breaks and, falling, pours into the narrow neck of the Gulf of Finland; an enormous wave speeds to the mouth of the Neva and breaks over the city. In order to protect the city against floods it has been decided to build 25.4 kilometres of stone-and-earthen dikes between the northern and southern shores of the Gulf. The project envisages built-in passages for ships and for water as well as a motor highway over the Gulf of Finland.

Leningrad is one of the greatest industrial, scientific, and cultural centres of the Soviet Union. The leading branch in Leningrad's industry is mechanical engineering. The universal machine-tools of the Yakov Sverdlov Machine-Tool Production Association are well known both in our country and abroad. These machines operate automatically on a pre-fixed programme, performing numerous complicated operations.

The Sergei Kirov Association of Industrial Enterprises—Elektrosila—produces powerful turbogenerators. A turbogenerator with a 1,200,000 kwt capacity is in operation at the Kostroma regional electric power station on the Volga. Its capacity is equal to the total output of all the electric power stations of pre-revolutionary Russia. This unit, with no analogues anywhere in the world, was created by the workers and scientists of Leningrad.

A unique telescope with the largest reflector in the world (the diameter of its mirror is six metres) has been created by the Lenin Optical Production Association in Leningrad. Specialists affirm that this telescope is truly a wonder even in our age of scientific and technological revolution. It has been installed at an elevation of two kilometres in the Caucasus. With its aid, in the absence of atmospheric disturbances, it is possible to discern the light of a candle over a distance of 25,000 km.

Leningrad plays an important part in the development of science and culture. A complex of academic institutions conducts fundamental studies in the field of biology, evolutionary physiology and biochemistry, physics, geology, celestial mechanics, astronomy, etc. Extensive work is carried out by the researchers of the Leningrad branches of the Institutes of History, Russian Literature, Archaeology, Oriental Studies, Ethnography, Socio-Economic Studies, etc.

Leningrad is rightly called a city of museums. Some fifty museums devoted to the history of the Revolution and general history, art, and other museums are open to the public. Among them are the Hermitage with its collection of artistic and cultural-historical treasures, one of the greatest in the world, and the Russian Museum—an outstanding collection of Russian works of fine arts. Leningraders and guests of the city take a particular interest in the local branch of the Central Lenin Museum and in the Lenin flat-museums.

The fame of Leningrad's theatres is widespread. Their performances attract many theatre-goers both in the Soviet Union and abroad. A prominent place in world theatrical art is occupied by the Kirov Academic Opera and Ballet Theatre, the Pushkin Academic Drama Theatre, the Maxim Gorky Academic Drama Theatre. We shall not enumerate the other theatres of the city—each one is interesting in its own way.

In 1957 the United Towns Organisation (or World Federation of Twinned Cities) was founded. A non-governmental international organisation, UTO promotes the development of co-operation and friendship among towns of different countries and their populations, irrespective of race, language, religion, and political beliefs. Leningrad is a UTO member. Santiago de Cuba, Dresden, Ho Chi Minh, Gdansk, Plovdiv, Zagreb, Turku, Osaka, Göteborg, Le Havre ... Leningrad is twinned with more than twenty cities.

The Seventh World Congress of

the UTO was held in Leningrad in 1970. Delegations from other countries study with great interest the achievements of the Leningraders in the field of industry, science and culture.

The Leningraders, in their turn, have learned much that is interesting and useful during their visits to Dresden, Santiago de Cuba, and other twinned cities.

Many Leningrad organisations have signed agreements on co-operation and socialist emulation with their counterparts in the twinned cities of socialist countries. Within the framework of such a document, for instance, the Leningrad Production Association Elektrosila and the Dresden Sachsenwerke exchange teams of workers and specialists who work for some time in each other's workshops, sharing experience and skills. The co-operation of specialists from the Leningrad Elektrik Plant and Elektrostahlgeräte (GDR) significantly furthered the creation of new models of modern welding equipment.

The Mikhail Kalinin Polytechnical Institute of Leningrad and the University of Santiago de Cuba are successfully carrying out their mutual educational and scientific-research programme. The Leningrad Institute's specialists helped the Cuban scientists in organising the work of several laboratories, presented them with laboratory equipment and a library, acquainted them with their methods of training post-graduate students.

Contacts between the twinned cities, even when they are of a purely practical nature, help people better understand each other, awaken mutual interests, and promote close ties.

LENIN MEMORIAL PLACES

There are over 270 spots in Leningrad and its environs that are associated with the life and work of Lenin. Here he headed the first Russian Marxist circles, the armed uprising of October 1917, the Communist Party and Soviet State he had founded. After the Soviet government had moved in 1918 to Moscow, Lenin visited the city twice—in 1919 and 1920.

The Leningrad branch of the Central Lenin Museum (we shall dwell upon it in greater detail during your Excursion No. 3) was established in 1937 in one of the finest buildings of the city, the Marble Palace on the Neva Embankment.

The exhibits of the branch of the Central Lenin Museum are supplemented by those of the Lenin memorial flat-museums in Leningrad and its environs.

The building of the **University** at No. 7, Universitetskaya Naberezhnaya (University Embankment)—Excursion N 2—carries a memorial plaque. Lenin first visited the St. Petersburg University in 1890, and then in 1891 when he took examinations as an extramural student for the entire course of law school. Some of the examinations were held in the building of the Academy of Sciences next door (No. 5, University Embankment). Lenin sat for one written and thirteen oral examinations in eighteen subjects and passed with the highest marks. On November 15, 1891, he received a first-class diploma.

Lenin also visited the University building in the years of the first Russian revolution, 1905-1907. In those days the University was a site of endless meetings, a centre of revolutionary propaganda; its premises were frequently used by the Bolsheviks for their revolutionary activities. Here, in May of 1906, Lenin reported to a meeting of Party functionaries on the results of the Fourth (Unifying) Congress of the RSDLP (the Russian Social-Democratic Labour Party). In 1907 Lenin spoke in this building in connection with the elections to the Second State Duma (Parliament).

From February 12, 1894 (after having moved to St. Petersburg in August 1893) until April 25, 1895, during the period of his intensive work for the creation of a revolutionary Marxist party in Russia, Lenin lived at **No. 7, Bolshoi Kazachi Pereulok (now Pereulok Ilyicha—Ilyich Lane)**. Here, on the second floor of a modest house, in flat No. 13, he occupied a small (14 sq. metres) corner room at the end of a corridor. At that time Lenin held a job as a junior lawyer. However, this work was merely a legal front for his revo-

Statue of Lenin at the Finland Railway Station

lutionary activities. He did not occupy himself much with law practice, since all his time and energy were given to the revolutionary cause.

The room was more than modest: a low ceiling, a round stove in the corner, at the window a table with an oil lamp at which Lenin used to work. Between the simple iron bedstead and a chest of drawers stood a low bookstand. On the left side, along the wall, there was a couch on which the comrades who visited him usually sat. Besides this furniture there were also several chairs, a coat-rack by the door, and next to it a wash-stand with a porcelain basin and jug. These were the entire furnishings of the small room.

Lenin's room has been restored to its former appearance, and is now kept as a museum. In this room Lenin worked on writings that were to play a most important part in routing the anti-Marxist ideology of the Narodniks (Populists) and the views of the advocates of the so-called "legal Marxism", and here he was often visited by his comrades of the revolutionary underground.

One of them, Mikhail Silvin, would recall his frequent visits to Lenin, which he made "usually in the evening ... At times of bitter reflections or depression ... seeking moral support." Once in the autumn of 1894, Silvin came here in a gloomy mood. "Shall we ever arouse this great mass?.. Shall we ever break this power, tsarism?" he exclaimed excitedly. "Lenin," recollected Silvin, "reassured me, saying that revolutionary movements always develop faster than people anticipate ... 'You'll see, we'll soon grow up into a true party ... The revolution will come, and we shall come out into the light of day as a communist party ready to fulfil its task.'"

Silvin writes in his memoirs that Lenin "was endowed with the faculty of carrying his listeners away, of im-

pressing them, of inspiring them with faith and loyalty to himself and to the common cause. This faculty of his to carry away, to imbue boundless trust in himself, to inspire people with a feeling of unswerving devotion to the common cause—all this I had many occasions to observe ... This great attraction, this power over the hearts and minds of individuals and of the broad masses were conditioned by a complete oblivion of his own personal interests, an exclusive devotion to one great idea—the liberation of humanity."

In 1924 Bolshoi Kazachi Pereulok was renamed Pereulok Ilyicha. In 1938 the flat in which Lenin had lived was turned into a memorial museum. The furnishings of the room were restored with the aid of Mikhail Silvin and the former landlady of the flat. From this flat, in the spring of 1895, Vladimir Lenin went abroad in order to establish contacts with Russia's first Marxist organisation—the Emancipation of Labour—headed by Georgi Plekhanov. Lenin returned to Russia in September of the same year. In a double-bottomed suitcase he brought back illegal Marxist literature.

After his return to St. Petersburg on September 30, 1895, Lenin moved into **No. 6/44 on the corner of Tairov Pereulok (now Pereulok Brinko) and Sadovaya Ulitsa (Garden Street), flat No. 30**, where he lived until November 22. This was a period of indefatigable work towards the creation of the St. Petersburg League of Struggle for the Emancipation of the Working Class—the first serious inception of a revolutionary party.

The gendarmes succeeded in tracking down the League of Struggle. On the night of December 8-9, 1895, Lenin was arrested. That same night many other members of the League were also arrested. Lenin spent 14 months in solitary confinement awaiting his trial. He decided to use his time in prison to collect material

Leningrad branch of the State Museum of the Great October Socialist Revolution (former mansion of Matilda Kshesinskaya)

for a work he had planned to write—*The Development of Capitalism in Russia*. His family obtained books for him from various libraries. A whole corner in Lenin's prison cell was piled with books. From prison Lenin sent out—illegally—a draft programme for the social-democratic party written in milk between the lines of a medical book, also a popular booklet *On Strikes* and political leaflets.

Lenin carried on a secret correspondence with his comrades from the League of Struggle for the Emancipation of the Working Class who were incarcerated in the same jail, he comforted and encouraged the imprisoned revolutionaries. One of them, Gleb Krzhizhanovsky, who subsequently became a leading Soviet scientist, reminisced: "To receive and read a letter of his was equal to taking some particularly exhilarating tonic, one was immediately stimulated and morally braced up by it."

At the beginning of 1897 an order was issued for Lenin to be exiled to Eastern Siberia, where he was to be under open police surveillance for

three years. He was discharged from prison on February 14, having been given permission to stay in St. Petersburg until the evening of February 17 "to prepare for his journey". These three days Lenin lived in the flat of his mother, Maria Alexandrovna; he used his time for meeting comrades, and for discussing the tasks and methods of social-democratic activities in Russia.

Upon his return from the Siberian exile (in early 1900) Lenin was forbidden to live in St. Petersburg, Moscow, and all the industrial and University centres of Russia. In the summer of 1900 he left the country in order to organise the publication of an all-Russia political newspaper, designated to become the centre of the struggle for setting up a Marxist party in Russia, to be instrumental in the enlightenment of the working class. Such a paper was founded—the *Iskra* (Spark). Under Lenin's leadership it played an important part in the preparation of the first Russian bourgeois-democratic revolution of 1905–1907.

The revolution started on Sunday, January 9, 1905, with a peaceful march of the workers of St. Petersburg (more than 140,000 people) to the Winter Palace (Excursion No. 3). They wanted to submit a petition to the tsar appealing for improvement of the life of the working people in the capital. The tsarist government perpetrated a brutal massacre, opening fire against the unarmed marchers. That same day, known in history as Bloody Sunday, barricades went up in St. Petersburg, a revolution broke out in Russia...

Lenin returned from abroad to revolutionary St. Petersburg on November 8, 1905. After a short rest and meetings with Party workers he visited the Preobrazhenskoye cemetery to pay homage to the grave of the workers shot on January 9, 1905. The next day he went to the office of the first legal Bolshevik newspaper, *No-*

vaya Zhizn (New Life). After his return from emigration Lenin used to come here daily, supervising the work of the newspaper. Anatoli Lunacharsky, a member of the editorial board and subsequently People's Commissar for Public Education in the Soviet government, wrote of Lenin's style of work as editor-in-chief: "There was not a single note or press-cutting of mine that had not been looked through by Lenin. In the majority of cases the entire material except telegrams, news items, etc. was read out loud at a board meeting headed by Lenin. He himself also read his articles to us, and he readily listened to all comments and suggestions." *Novaya Zhizn* became the factual central organ of the Bolshevik Party, an important centre from which Party activities were directed.

For several days in November 1905 Lenin lived illegally at **No. 1/41, Tenth Rozhdestvenskaya Street (today Desyataya Sovietskaya—Tenth Soviet Street), flat No. 3**. This was the home of Pyotr Rumyantsev, a member of the Central Committee of the Russian Social-Democratic Labour Party. Lenin's wife and comrade-in-arms, Nadezhda Krupskaya, later recalled that Lenin was always extremely diffident about staying in other people's homes and this affected his work efficiency. At the end of November Lenin and Krupskaya took up residence in the "San Remo" furnished rooms, at No. 90, Nevsky Avenue. However, after several days they had to move out; Nadezhda Krupskaya's inexpertly forged passport had aroused the suspicion of the police, so Lenin proposed that they move to another place. Lenin's sister Maria Ilyinichna arranged for them to live at the home of her friends at No. 15/8, Grechesky Prospekt (Greek Avenue), flat 9. They moved into this place on December 1. But as soon as they were registered the house was surrounded by police sleuths. The attempt to live openly

was unsuccessful, so it was decided to settle down illegally.

At that time Lenin frequently made speeches before gatherings of St. Petersburg workers, propagandists and Party functionaries, at meetings of the St. Petersburg Soviet of Workers' Deputies. In the spring and summer of 1906 Lenin directed the work of the legal Bolshevik newspapers *Volna* (Wave), *Vperyod* (Onward) and *Ekho* (Echo)—papers that continued the cause of *Novaya Zhizn* after it had been closed down in December 1905.

In December 1907, after the defeat of the revolution, Lenin emigrated from Russia, in compliance with a resolution passed by the Bolshevik centre. Abroad he continued his tireless work as leader of the Bolshevik Party and the Russian working class. No sooner did word come of the February 1917 revolution that had overthrown the Russian monarchy than Lenin made ready to return to his native country.

The square in front of the Finland Station on the evening of April 3 was the scene of the unforgettable welcome given Lenin by the Petrograd workers, soldiers and sailors (this square is included in Excursion No. 4 of this guidebook).

The train pulled into the station at 11.10 p.m. When Lenin, surrounded by his associates, came out onto the square a many thousand-voiced "Hurrah!" resounded; soldiers' and sailors' caps flew into the air; music was struck up by bands and a thunderous rumble of greetings rolled from end to end of the square: "Long live Lenin!", "Greetings to the leader of the working class!" The workers lifted Lenin onto the turret of an armoured car. From this makeshift rostrum he greeted the revolutionary proletariat of Petrograd, closing his speech with a call for socialist revolution. In this armoured car Lenin was driven to the mansion housing the Central and Petrograd Committees of the Bolshevik Party. Today the building houses the Museum of the Great October Socialist Revolution (Excursion No. 1).

After he arrived, Lenin went into a room opening on a balcony; this was the room of the Central Committee secretariat (currently Hall No. 10 of the museum). From the balcony he delivered a short speech to the workers and soldiers outside. Later Lenin participated in a meeting with Party functionaries in the largest hall of the mansion on the ground floor (today this is Hall No. 2 of the museum). Having listened to the welcoming speech of one of the comrades, Lenin said: "Comrades, I think we've done enough congratulating each other on the revolution. I have the following thoughts on the future of the Russian revolution." And he began his speech.

"I remember," recalled Andrei Andreyev, a prominent figure in the Bolshevik Party, "that Lenin spoke for no longer than an hour. But he said a great deal. He spoke of the necessity for a transition into the second phase of the revolution. The first, bourgeois-democratic, phase of the revolution—the overthrow of tsarism—has already been accomplished. We cannot stop at the first phase, or the bourgeoisie will strangle the revolution. We must now proceed to the second phase—the socialist revolution—we must fulfil the tasks of immediate practical work in the Party for its preparation. The Bolsheviks can and should no longer rally round the old slogan calling for a democratic republic. All power must be transferred to the Soviets." The programme for the transition from bourgeois-democratic revolution to socialist revolution was formulated by Lenin for the first time in this speech.

After Lenin's speech, a lively discussion took place. It went on until morning. During the night Lenin spoke from the balcony many times to the delegations of workers, soldiers and sailors that were arriving at the mansion in a continuous stream. Only early in the morning did Lenin go to the home of his elder sister, Anna Ulyanova-Yelizarova, **No. 48/9, Shirokaya Ulitsa (Broad Street), flat No. 24 (today it is 52, Ulitsa Lenina—Lenin Street)**. Here he lived from April 4 to July 5, 1917.

Lenin's relatives and friends often got together in this flat, and conferences and talks with members of the Central Committee and other leaders of the Bolshevik Party took place here. In 1927, the flat was converted into a museum. Its exposition includes documents, photographs and publications that reflect the prodigious activities of the leader of the Revolution in those days. Lenin wrote over a hundred and fifty works in the months of April, May and June of 1917.

The furnishings of the flat-museum were restored under the guidance and with the participation of Anna Ulyanova-Yelizarova. The exposition displays many authentic household articles and pieces of furniture that were in use here in 1917: two simple bedsteads covered with coarse woollen blankets (the bed on the left was Lenin's, on the right—his wife's), a plain desk with a simple inkstand and a table lamp, two bentwood chairs. By the door stands a wardrobe—true, no clothes were kept in it: at Lenin's request it was adapted for holding books. "My own wardrobe isn't large," Lenin used to say, "A coat can be hung on a nail, but I have no place for books and newspapers."

A padded easy chair that belonged to Lenin's mother, Maria Alexandrovna Ulyanova, stands in the room in a glass case. This chair was especially treasured by Lenin.

During the April-July period Lenin made almost daily visits to the **editorial office of the Bolshevik newspaper** *Pravda* (Truth) (No. 32, Moika Embankment), that came out under his direction. Within this period (April 5–July 5) *Pravda* carried over 170 articles and notes written by Lenin and newspaper reports on his speeches. Some editions of the paper carried several items submitted by Lenin.

The successes achieved by the Bolsheviks among the masses frightened the counter-revolutionaries. After the July days of 1917, when, on the order of the reactionary Provisional Government, firing was opened on a peaceful demonstration of workers, soldiers and sailors, the Bolsheviks were subjected to severe persecution. An order was issued to find and arrest Lenin at any cost. A fake document on the alleged ties of the Bolsheviks with Kaiser's Germany was circulated. The commander-in-chief of the Petrograd military district ordered the commander of a detachment specially formed for finding Lenin to shoot the latter on sight.

In this situation the Party decided to hide its leader in a secret place. After changing a number of secret addresses, on July 7 Lenin settled in the flat of a Bolshevik worker, Sergei Alliluyev, at **No. 17, Tenth Rozhdestvenskaya Street** (today Desyataya Sovietskaya—Tenth Soviet Street), **flat No. 20.**

The Alliluyev flat was at the top of a large six-storey building. Lenin occupied a small room, its window overlooking the courtyard. In 1938, a museum was opened here. The appearance of Lenin's room has been carefully restored. The bed, sofa, wardrobe, green baize-covered desk with its electric lamp and a dark lampshade, and a clock—all stand in their former places. Some chairs, a bookstand, the portraits of the poets Nikolai Nekrasov and George Byron—such were the modest furnishings of the room. The exposition of this museum contains thirty authentic objects remaining from the time when Lenin lived here.

The situation in Petrograd was extremely strained. Agents of the Provisional Government were making a rigorous search for Lenin. On the evening of July 7 a meeting in the Alliluyev flat decided to move Lenin to a safer place. In the morning of July 8 Lenin was told that a reliable retreat had been prepared for him not far from the station of Razliv, on the outskirts of Petrograd, with a factory worker, Nikolai Yemelyanov.

A temporary lodging was prepared for Lenin in the loft of a barn in the yard of Yemelyanov's house. This barn is now a museum over which a glass case has been erected. Lenin lived in Razliv from July 10 to August 8. This period of Lenin's life is described in greater detail in the section on the environs of Leningrad.

By the end of July–beginning of August the situation in Petrograd had become still more complicated. Shady-looking characters began to appear in Razliv. On the decision of the Central Committee of the Party, Lenin left Razliv on August 8, and next day illegally departed for Finland under the guise of a stoker on locomotive No. 293. In Finland he stayed in the village of Yalkala, in **the home of a worker, Peter Parviainen**. The latter was told that his temporary tenant was Konstantin Petrovich Ivanov, a writer.

Parviainen's house, restored to its former appearance, was turned into a museum in 1940. It was underpinned with a concrete foundation, the roof was completely repaired. All the wooden parts and the walls were impregnated with special resins. A protective cover was erected over this memorial structure. The restored furnishings of the room in which Lenin lived are extremely modest: a table with a linen table-cloth, and an oil lamp on it, a bed covered with an angora wool blanket, a couch, a round chess-table with a flower vase on it, two bentwood chairs, a coat-rack by the door.

In Yalkala, Lenin wrote assiduously. In his leisure hours he helped Parviainen mow hay, went to the woods for mushrooms and whortleberries, bathed in the lake, angled. His friends were Parviainen's little children for whom he had a touching regard. The company of children was always a source of great delight to Lenin.

Lenin lived for several days in Yalkala, and then, having made himself up as a Finnish pastor, he went to Helsingfors (now Helsinki). There was no need to be afraid of police sleuths in Helsingfors, since Lenin lived in the home of the ... chief of that city's police; this post was then held by a Finnish social-democrat, Gustav Rovio. In order to be closer to Petrograd, to set up a more operative contact with the Central Committee, Lenin soon moved to Vyborg.

In the situation of burgeoning socialist revolution and preparation for an armed uprising, the need for Lenin's personal leadership in the activities of the party became more and more pressing. At the beginning of October 1917 Lenin arrived, in the cab of that same locomotive No. 293, at an outlying northern suburb of Petrograd (Udelnaya station) and was lodged in the home of a Bolshevik Party member, Margarita Fofanova, at **No. 1, Serdobolskaya Ulitsa, flat No. 41 (today No. 180)**.

In this flat Lenin worked out the plan for the armed uprising. Notably, here he wrote his work *The Advice of an Onlooker*. In it he summarised and complemented the statements made by Karl Marx and Friedrich Engels concerning uprising, armed the party with a system of rules and guiding principles for the triumphant conclusion of the uprising. Here, on the evening of October 24, 1917, Lenin wrote a letter to the Bolsheviks participating in the Congress of the Northern Region Soviets. In this letter he warned that to delay the uprising was

to mortally threaten the revolution, and he called for immediate action against the Provisional Government.

Lenin's hiding place was kept a close secret. Besides his hostess, the only persons who visited him were his wife, Nadezhda Krupskaya, and Eino Rahja, whom the Bolshevik Central Committee had assigned to be Lenin's bodyguard when he left the flat to conduct a Central Committee meeting or to meet leading Party members.

In 1938, Margarita Fofanova's flat was converted into a museum. Everything in it is as it was in the October days of 1917. All the objects were selected on the advice of Fofanova herself. For instance, the window curtains are made of coarse printed cloth—an exact copy of those that hung here in Lenin's time. In the archives of the Tryokhgornaya Manufaktura factory Fofanova found the old design of the cloth, and thus a copy of the no longer existing curtains was made.

Visitors to this museum pay particular attention to the plan of Petrograd published in 1915 (Lenin used it while preparing the armed uprising and for charting routes to the places of secret meetings), and to Fofanova's books, some of which were read by Lenin.

The room in which Lenin lived is furnished as follows: by the window stands a desk, on it an oil lamp with a green shade and a metal pen-rack. By the desk is a low bookstand, on its shelves—1917-dated newspapers; by the wall there is a bed, opposite it a small sofa, a chest of drawers and a wash-stand with bowl and jug.

The building housing the museum has been reconstructed: its façade was renovated and two storeys added. But the flat in which Lenin lived remains unchanged. This is one of the most frequented Lenin memorial museums, one of the most notable

Lenin's desk in Anna Ulyanova-Yelizarova's flat

historical-revolutionary sights in Leningrad.

Flat No. 31 at No. 32, Naberezhnaya Reki Karpovki (Karpovka Embankment) was also turned into a museum in 1938. Here, on October 10, 1917, Lenin conducted the historical meeting of the Central Committee of the Bolshevik Party at which the decision for an armed uprising was taken.

The place for this meeting was no random choice; the house was in a locality comparatively distant from the centre of the city, part of it was taken up by furnished rooms usually occupied by pious pilgrims, who travelled to Petrograd to pay their devotions in a monastery situated on the opposite bank of the Karpovka River. The entrances to the house were always open, people arrived and departed at all times of the day or night, so nobody paid any attention to new arrivals.

The room where the historical meeting was held looks the same today as it did in those crucial days of October 1917: an oaken folding table stands in the middle of the room, six chairs surround it, a lamp with a white shade hangs from the ceiling. There

is also a sideboard, a bookstand and portraits of revolutionary democrats on the walls—the poet Nikolai Nekrasov and the satirist Mikhail Saltykov-Shchedrin.

After this meeting, at the proposal of the Central Committee of the Party, a Military Revolutionary Committee was set up under the Petrograd Soviet; this Committee became the legal headquarters of the uprising. Its activities were guided by the Central Committee of the Party. Preparation for armed action went on in all the important areas of the country, a workers' Red Guard was being formed everywhere.

On October 16 an expanded session of the Central Committee of the Party and its most active members was convened. It was held on the outskirts of the Vyborgskaya Storona (or Vyborg Side, as it was called), in the building of the Lesnovsko-Udelninsky District Duma (Council), **No. 13/17, Bolotnaya Ulitsa**. At this meeting a Military Revolutionary Centre was elected, to become the steering nucleus in the Military Revolutionary Committee.

In 1977, a memorial museum was opened in this building. Excursionists may view the rooms in which the expanded session of the Bolshevik Party's Central Committee was held, acquaint themselves with the exposition "The Vyborg Side in the Period of Preparation for and Realisation of the Great October Socialist Revolution". Numerous documents, proclamations, leaflets, and resolutions passed by various meetings, materials from Bolshevik newspapers and photographs bespeak the participation of the workers of the Vyborg Side in the political events of 1917.

On the evening of October 24 Lenin left his last secret lodging on Serdobolskaya Street and, accompanied by Eino Rahja, went to the Smolny building occupied by the Central and Petrograd Committees of the Bolshevik

Lenin's room in Serdobolskaya Street flat

Party and the Military Revolutionary Committee of the Petrograd Soviet. Lenin immediately assumed direct leadership of the uprising.

Late in the evening of October 25 (November 7 New Style), 1917, the Second All-Russia Congress of Soviets opened in the Smolny Assembly Hall. Lenin was unable to be present at its first session, since these were the decisive hours of the armed uprising. It was almost 4 a.m. when the delegates enthusiastically applauded the news of the taking of the Winter Palace and the arrest of the Provisional Government. Only after this did Lenin, who had not slept a wink for two nights and days, go for a short rest to the home of his comrade-in-arms, Vladimir Bonch-Bruyevich **(No. 5, Khersonskaya Ulitsa, flat No. 9)**.

With great difficulty his host persuaded Lenin to go to sleep in a small separate room. Everybody went to bed. In his room Lenin put out the light, too, But not for long. Having made sure that everything was quiet in the house, he noiselessly got out of bed, shut the door tightly, turned on the light, sat down at the table and immersed himself in work. It was already light outside when he lay down for a nap, but very soon, cheerful and energetic he entered the dining-room and greeted everybody: "Congratulations on the first day of the Socialist Revolution!" When everyone had sat down to have tea, Lenin took the clearly written pages he had worked on at night out of his pocket and read the draft of the Decree on Land that announced the confiscation of all the lands from the landowners without any compensation, and the transfer of them to the people.

Bonch-Bruyevich's apartment was turned into a museum in 1938. There are two memorial rooms in it—the dining-room and the study. The large, light dining-room looks just as it did in 1917. In the left corner there is a tall tiled stove faced with ornate tiles, next to it, by the wall, stands a dinner table covered with a white table-cloth, on it are a samovar and a tea-set. Bentwood chairs stand by the table. Against the opposite wall are a sofa, a round table, and a grand piano. Over them hangs a portrait of Bonch-Bruyevich's three-year-old daughter.

In this room, on April 4, 1917, Lenin conducted a joint meeting of the members of the Central Committee who had arrived from emigration abroad, and the members of the Russian Bureau of the Central Committee; here he had meetings with members of the Bolshevik Central and Petrograd Committees, with the editorial staff of the newspaper *Pravda*, and with workers who were active members of the Bolshevik Party.

Bonch-Bruyevich's study was a narrow room with one window adjacent to the dining-room. In this room Lenin wrote the historical Decree on Land.

On the evening of October 26 (November 8)*, the second, concluding

* In contrast to the Julian Calendar (Old Style), the Gregorian Calendar (New Style) was first adopted by a number of European countries in 1582. The USSR adopted it in February 1918.

session of the Congress of Soviets was held in the Smolny Assembly Hall. Welcomed with an enthusiastic ovation, Lenin mounted the rostrum and delivered his speech on peace. The audience stood and listened to him. Noting that the question of peace was the most burning, crucial issue of the day, Lenin read out his draft of the Decree on Peace. This historical document contained an appeal, on behalf of the Second All-Russia Congress of Soviets, to all the peoples and governments participat-

ond was the adoption of Lenin's Decree on Land. Then the Congress founded the world's first workers' and peasants' government, the Council of People's Commissars headed by Vladimir Lenin.

In the early days of Soviet power—from October 27 to November 10, 1917—Lenin had his office on the second floor of the south wing of the former Smolny Institute, in a corner room that then carried the number 67. Today this room is marked by a memorial plaque. The door still carries an

View of Smolny and Proletarian Dictatorship Square

ing in World War I, proposing that negotiations be started immediately for the conclusion of a just and democratic peace—with no annexations or contributions. The Decree denounced war as a means of deciding moot issues and offered a peaceful way of solving them. The possibility of peaceful coexistence of states with different social systems was proclaimed in this Decree.

The Congress accepted Lenin's Decree on Peace—this was the first historic act of the Soviet State. The sec-

enamelled plate with the inscription "Class Mistress" (the Smolny Institute was an educational establishment for young ladies). In January 1974, the room was turned into a museum. Here Lenin signed the first decrees and orders of the Soviet government, here he conducted meetings of the Council of People's Commissars, received workers and soldiers, delegates of the Second All-Russia Congress of Soviets.

Room No. 67 is actually two rooms. In the first, smaller one, stood the

Statue of Lenin at the Smolny

small table at which the Secretary, Nikolai Gorbunov, took down the minutes of the Council's meetings. Room No. 67 has been restored to the way it looked when Lenin worked there.

It soon became clear that larger premises were necessary for the offices of the Chairman of the Council of People's Commissars and the apparatus of the government. So, another corner room on the same second floor became Lenin's new office. Here he worked from November 10,

Lenin's study

desks of Bonch-Bruyevich (who became the Business Manager of the Council of People's Commissars) and of the Council's Secretary Nikolai Gorbunov. This room gave access to the second, larger one; one of its windows opened onto the Neva and two—onto Smolny Avenue. This was Lenin's office. Here, under a low-hanging electric light, stood his desk. Behind a low screen stood a bed where Lenin slept when he was unable to get back to Bonch-Bruyevich's home. By the window there was a

1917, to March 10, 1918. During this period Lenin not only worked, but also lived in Smolny, in one of the rooms on the first floor, in the north wing of the building. This small room, with its single window overlooking the inner courtyard of the Smolny building, divided into two parts by a low wooden partition, served simultaneously as a dining-room, study, and bedroom.

In 1927, the room became a museum. The furnishings were restored to their former appearance under the guidance of Nadezhda Krupskaya. The furniture is authentic.

To the left of the door stands a bookcase with a mirror and a small sideboard. Opposite the door, by the wall, is a small desk covered with green baize, on it an old-fashioned telephone, an inkstand with one inkwell and a wooden penholder, an oil lamp with a glass reservoir. At first, it was really an oil lamp, but at Lenin's request the burner was removed and replaced by an electric bulb in a socket. Krupskaya recalled that, when the electric power failed, they could unscrew the socket, pour kerosene into the reservoir, and put in the burner. Since at that time, owing to the lack of fuel, the power plants operated erratically, Lenin was not infrequently compelled to work by the light of the oil lamp. On the desk are copies of the newspapers of that time, *Pravda* and *Rabochi i Soldat* (Worker and Soldier).

Along the opposite wall stand a couch, cloth-covered armchairs, and a small oval table on carved legs. An electric bulb with a tin shade hangs on a pulley from the ceiling. Behind the partition there is a tiled stove in one corner, and beside it a wardrobe. Here also stand two iron bedsteads, and between them a small table with a mirror. The mirror was a gift to Krupskaya from a soldier, a machine-gunner on guard service at Smolny.

The exposition in the adjacent room reflects the tireless activities of Lenin during the first months of Soviet rule.

After the Soviet government moved to Moscow (March 1918) Lenin visited Petrograd twice. The first time he arrived on March 12, 1918, to attend the funeral of his brother-in-law (his elder sister Anna's husband), the Bolshevik Mark Yelizarov.

On the next day Lenin visited the building of the former Nikolayevsky Palace that had been allotted to the trade unions and renamed the **Palace of Labour** (its address today is No. 4, Ploshchad Truda—Labour Square). Lenin attended a session of the First Congress of the Agricultural Workers of Petrograd Gubernia held in this building, and delivered a speech concerning the organisation of a trade union of agricultural workers.

In the evening of the same day Lenin spoke twice in the **Opera Hall of the Narodny Dom** (People's House) (No. 4, Lenin Park) on the internal and international situation of the Soviet Republic. That same day he left for Moscow.

Lenin came to Petrograd the second time on July 19, 1920, the opening day of the Second Congress of the Communist International—an international organisation founded in accordance with the requirements and tasks of the revolutionary working-class movement (1919-1943). The Congress commenced its work in Petrograd and continued it in Moscow.

In the early morning thousands of people assembled in front of Moscow Station on Ploshchad Vosstaniya (Uprising Square) to welcome the delegates to the Congress and greet Lenin. After this Lenin went to **Smolny**.

In the afternoon Lenin delivered a speech in the **Taurida Palace** on the international situation and the basic tasks of the Communist International (Excursion No. 4). When the first session of the Congress was closed, Lenin, accompanied by a small group of delegates, was driven to **Kamenny Ostrov (Stone Island)** (Excursion No. 1) to look at the first vacation homes for workers and visited several of them.

After this Lenin, together with the delegates to the Second Congress of the Communist International, visited **Marsovo Polye (the Field of Mars)** (Excursion No. 3) and placed wreaths on the graves of the fallen revolutionary fighters. In the evening Lenin spoke from a platform erected near the wall of the **Winter Palace** (Excursion No. 3). The workers, soldiers, and sailors of Petrograd greeted their leader with a stormy ovation. Lenin delivered a speech. From this meeting he went directly to the Moscow Station and left on the 8 p.m. express train for Moscow, where the Congress continued its work. This was the last time Lenin visited Petrograd.

Not only the above-listed, but many other memorial places in Leningrad are connected with the life and work of Lenin. In an endless stream both Soviet people and foreign guests come to the Lenin memorial places. The love of the working people for Lenin, for his genius, is boundless, infinite is their respect for everything connected with his life.

BUILDING AND ARCHITECTURE

Many of the city's buildings are real gems of Russian architecture; the more conspicuous among them may be deservedly regarded as masterpieces of world significance.

The city's overall layout, its skyline and general view began to take shape almost concurrently with the inception of St. Petersburg. A complete innovation in Russian town planning was that instead of taking as its focal point a hill with a citadel, a *kreml*—from which the name of the Kremlin springs—an island in the Neva's estuary was chosen. A fortress totally unlike the medieval Russian citadel was erected there. Moreover, construction did not follow the scheme of concentric circles characteristic of the towns and cities built earlier, but was a more or less free arrangement conforming to the natural pattern of the Neva River with its numerous branches and canals criss-crossing the city's territory.

Aside from the former French royal residence at Versailles, St. Petersburg was the first city built from the very outset according to a preconceived master plan. This allowed for an excellent arrangement of thoroughfares and streets and for those architectural ensembles for which Leningrad is rightly famed.

In the earlier part of the 18th century, when architects of Russian stock were few and far between, it was mostly architects of foreign extraction who built the city. Some were attracted by the high pay, others by simple curiosity, and still others by the great possibilities for construction in Russia's new metropolis. They were received most graciously, learned to speak and write Russian, grew accustomed to the Russian way of life and took an active part in the development of Russian culture. Indeed, many spent the greater part of their lives in St. Petersburg, engaged in the joys of creative endeavour. Thus, the Swiss Domenico Trezzini, the Italians Gaetano Chiaveri and Mario Fontana, the Frenchman Jean-Baptiste Leblond and the German Johann Schlüter, to mention only a few, found a second homeland in Russia. However, such native Russian architects as Mikhail Zemtsov, Timofei Usov, Ivan Korobov and Pyotr Yeropkin, among others, quickly gained prominence. Thus, Pyotr Yeropkin, as a member of the Commission for the Construction of St. Petersburg, set up in 1737 to supervise and direct the planning and building of the city, was responsible for its tri-radial centre, a system of three arterial thoroughfares radiating out from the Admiralty building, a system which remains to this day. The master plan drawn up under his supervision lay at the base of all the urban construction that took place there throughout the 18th century.

In Petrine times the city's architects demonstrated such common stylistic traits as regularity, implying the repetition of certain types of models, linear building and clear-cut planning, and an imposing monumentality coupled with modest exterior decoration.

Characteristic of most of the buildings erected in St. Petersburg over the first twenty to thirty years of its existence were clear silhouette, polychrome decor, grace and excellent landscaping. These features are manifest in such structures as St. Peter and St. Paul Cathedral (Excursion No. 1), the Kunstkammer or Museum of Curiosities and the Twelve Collegiums (Excursion No. 2). They and numerous other structures of the Petrine period may in a way be classified as Baroque style of the first third of the 18th century.

In line with Peter the Great's concept, his new capital was to be unlike Moscow not only in its plan but also in its architecture. Three types of houses were devised and endorsed: one for commoners, another for the well-to-do, and a third type for the nobility. The first was one-storey with but four windows along the front; the second, also one-storey, but with more windows, was topped by an attic storey having three windows, while the last was an opulent two-storey mansion of brick with a sumptuous entrance overhung by a balcony · with ornate wrought-iron railing.

In 1714, Peter issued an edict for-

bidding the construction of stone or brick buildings anywhere in Russia save St. Petersburg, and commanding all stonemasons to report to the new capital for work. However, since the city lacked not only stonemasons but the very stones to build with, the self-same edict obligated every new arrival to bring stones with him—three of at least five pounds each if arriving by cart, and from ten to thirty stones of at least ten pounds each if coming by water. A stiff fine was imposed upon all failing to comply.

Many magnificent imperial residences, palaces and churches appeared in the city and its environs in the mid-18th century. They were characterised by ornate decoration and heavily moulded fronts, and a sumptuous appointments of their interiors. This style came to be known in architectural history as **Russian Baroque**. Its prime exponents were Francesco Bartolomeo Rastrelli and Savva Chevakinsky, two great masters whose prolific talents were worthily translated into stone and mortar by the industry of thousands of regrettably anonymous Russian stonemasons, wood- and stone-carvers, plasterers, and gilders. Outstanding examples of Russian Baroque include the Smolny Convent (Excursion No. 4), the Winter Palace (Excursion No. 3) and the Stroganov Palace (Excursion No. 5), all three built by Rastrelli, and the Cathedral of St. Nicholas with its belfry standing separately (Excursion No. 3), built by Chevakinsky.

For many reasons, by the 1760s, the Baroque style was gradually ousted by **Classicism**. The second half of the 18th century was marked by increasing restrictions placed on the serfs throughout Russia, coupled with the enrichment of the nobility and the wide-scale construction of country estates. The Baroque style was too or-

Kikin Palace. 18th cent.

nate, and a more economical, simpler, less sumptuous style that could be more easily adopted by untrained serf-craftsmen working in the distant provinces was needed. Thus, there was no necessity of hiring celebrated, and naturally, expensive architects and sculptors. Classicism, with its clear-cut rationale, strict symmetry of form and proportion, sparse decoration, and balanced composition fit the bill.

Though Classicism established itself in the domain of Russian architecture, it did not make for monotony in St. Petersburg. The first of its phases (there were several between 1760 and 1830) still incorporated Baroque elements. The Marble Palace (Excursion No. 3) built by Antonio Rinaldi, and the Academy of Arts (Excursion No. 2) designed conjointly by Alexander Kokorinov and Jean-Baptiste Vallin de la Mothe are typical examples.

Strict Classicism, the second phase, reached its high water mark during the late 18th and early 19th centuries and is characterised by faithful adherence to the architectural forms and proportions common in ancient Greece and Rome. Striking examples are afforded by the Taurida Palace (Excursion No. 4) built by Ivan Starov, and the Academy of Sciences and the Smolny Institute (Excursions No. 2 and No. 4), both of which were designed by Giacomo Quarenghi.

The third phase, that of *High Classicism*, is characterised by groups of buildings with sculpted decoration consonant with the purpose of the ensemble in theme. The style is best illustrated by buildings erected in St. Petersburg from 1800 to 1830, including such gems as the Admiralty (Excursion No. 3) built by Andreyan Zakharov, the Stock Exchange (Excursion No. 2) by Jean Thomas de Thomon, the Kazansky Cathedral and the Mining Institute (Excursions No. 5 and No. 2) by Andrei Voronikhin, the Barracks of the Pavlovsky Regiment and the Narva and Moscow Gates (Excursions No. 3, 6 and 7) by Vasili Stasov, and the General Headquarters, Mikhailovsky Palace and the Alexan-

Smolny Cathedral. 18th cent.

drinsky Theatre (Excursions No. 3 and No. 5), all by Carlo Rossi. Some of these structures keynote the overall architecture of the world-famous ensembles grouped around the Palace, Pushkin, Arts and Ostrovsky squares.

By the mid-19th century a decline set in, with many architects indulging in eclecticism and borrowing freely from various styles with evidence of French and Italian Renaissance, Romanesque, Gothic, Early Russian and even Moresque motifs in their work. Examples are furnished by the Mariinsky and Nikolayevsky palaces (Excursion No. 3) built by Andrei Stakenschneider, the Lutheran Church (Excursion No. 5) by Alexander Bryullov, the Mariinsky Theatre (Excursion No. 3) by Albert Cavos, and the palace built by Alexander Rezanov for Grand Prince Vladimir Alexandrovich (Excursion No. 3).

Those years were marked by intensive construction of banks and large emporiums, railway stations, industrial establishments and mansions for wealthy merchants and industrialists, as well as multi-storey tenements with dimly lit inner courtyards designed with the sole purpose of extracting the maximum of profit from each square metre of floor space. This rapid, haphazard construction was often inconsistent with the existing well-integrated groups of structures, their perfect sense of harmony. Thus, next door to the Alexandrinsky (now Pushkin) Theatre and the Public Library (Excursion No. 5), both built by Carlo Rossi in the High Classicist style, a house in the Russian Revivalist style was thrown up. It had small narrow windows and enormous representations of traditional Russian decorative elements on its façade. Those years also witnessed the influence of technological progress on the city's architecture and construction methods, the wider use of ferro-concrete, metal, and large sheets of glass.

At the turn of the century, the **Art Nouveau** movement brought with it asymmetrical proportions, sinuous forms and functional solutions. In Pe-

Sheremetev's Palace on the Fontanka. 18th cent.

tersburgian architecture the style is illustrated by the Yeliseyev Store at No. 56, Nevsky Avenue (Excursion No. 5), built by Gavriil Baranovsky; the home built by Alexander Gogen for ballerina Matilda Kshesinskaya (Excursion No. 1); and the house at No. 1/3, Kirovsky Avenue (Excursion No. 1), built by Fyodor Lidval.

Also built around this time and later were edifices whose architecture displayed the coupling of elements of Russian Classicism with Italian Renaissance—such as the building put up by Marian Lyalievich on Nevsky Avenue for the business house of the furrier Mertens (Excursion No. 5), or the country house Ivan Fomin erected for Senator Polovtsov on Stone Island (Excursion No. 1).

In 1919, shortly after the Great October Socialist Revolution, the first two new architectural and town-planning offices, a council and a workshop, were set up. Though funds and manpower for extensive construction were in short supply, due to economic dislocation and the Civil War,

that very year a project was devised under the supervision of the architect Ivan Fomin to renovate the then dusty and ill-appointed Field of Mars and transform it into a public garden. By 1920 the project was completed and an imposing granite memorial, executed by the sculptor Lev Rudnev, had been unveiled over the graves of the revolutionary fighters buried there (Excursion No. 3).

In the 1920s, construction in the city, renamed Leningrad after the death of Lenin, was launched on a much wider scale. In 1925, the plans of architects Vladimir Shchuko and Vladimir Gelfreikh for the Proletarian Dictatorship Garden and Square were executed in front of the Smolny building, while at the entrance to the garden magnificent propylaea were erected, ennobling the entire grouping (Excursion No. 4).

A great deal of construction was under way in the suburbs. The stark contrast between the squalid working-class neighbourhoods on the outskirts of the city and its sumptuous, well-ap-

Corner of Nevsky Avenue and the Moika Embankment

pointed centre was gradually done away with. The elimination of private ownership of the land allowed for more effective city planning. Housing construction was undertaken on a wide scale. In 1925, for example, a new street was built on the vacant plots of land in the former Narva Gate district. This new thoroughfare was named Traktornaya (Tractor) Street in honour of the first tractors manufactured in the Soviet Union.

Moreover, in 1927, to mark the tenth anniversary of the Socialist Revolution, construction was completed on two imposing community centres, one on the Vyborg Side, the other beyond the former Narva Gate. The utterly novel architectural design of their auditoriums set the pace for a new type of theatre, no longer divided into the traditional dress circle and galleries.

In the 1930s several edifices with new social functions were built. They included the premises of the Executive Committees of the Soviets of People's Deputies of the Kirovsky (Ex-

cursion No. 6), Moskovsky (Excursion No. 7) and Nevsky districts, the Lensoviet Community Centre (Excursion No. 1) and the Kirov Community Centre on Vasilyevsky Island. The dominant architectural style of the period came to be known as **Constructivism**, which emphasised the structural elements of a building along with its functional purpose.

In line with the urban development programme for the city charted by the Communist Party and Soviet Government, the construction of housing, public buildings and factory premises was launched on a wide scale, as a result of which the former squalid working-class neighbourhoods, wastelands and garbage dumps on the outskirts of the city were transformed into modern residential areas with all the necessary utilities, consumer services, educational, recreational and other facilities.

In the process many unforeseen contingencies arose. The city's utilities and public services were in a terrible state: underground water and

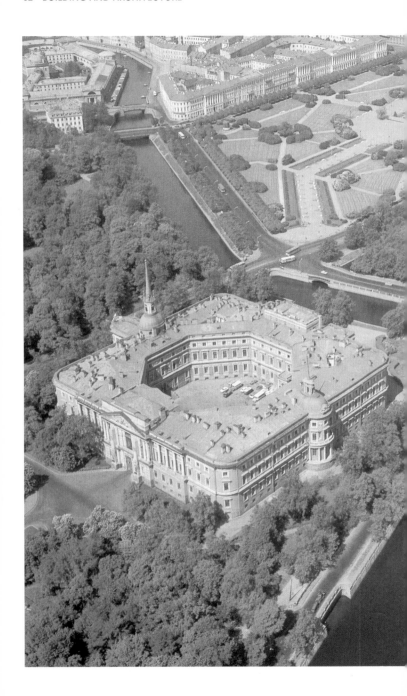

Mikhailovsky Castle. 1797–1800

Kirov Palace of Culture. Mid–1930s

electric mains, sewers, gas lines were all laid at different levels to form a huge labyrinth, all due to the haphazard manner in which the "city fathers" conducted public affairs before the Revolution. Completed in 1932 was a document of vital importance for Leningrad—a master plan for the reconstruction of its underground mains, sewers, etc.

Nazi Germany's attack in 1941 caused untold damage to the great city. Not a single building in it remained intact after the war. Five and a half million square metres of housing were destroyed by enemy shelling and bombing. More than three thousand houses, some four hundred school buildings and hundreds of industrial establishments were gutted. Hundreds of buildings of great architectural value were badly damaged. Yet even during the 900-day siege, the city's architects thought of the postwar recovery. Enfeebled by hunger, they worked on in unheated rooms by the dim light of oil lamps, designing those triumphal arches un-

der which the victorious Soviet troops passed in the summer of 1945 after the rout of Hitler's armies.

The war interrupted the sweeping construction programme designed to extend the city's boundaries as envisaged in the master plan drawn up in the mid-1930s. During postwar reconstruction, architects and builders concentrated on providing housing, rebuilding ruined factories and administrative buildings and restoring damaged architectural monuments. They sought to reflect the Soviet people's heroic victory in their work. To this end, they turned to Russian Classicism and ancient Greek styles, so wonderfully suitable for expressing the heroic motifs in architecture. This trend, which prevailed up to the early 1950s, is illustrated by the design of several stations on the first section of the Leningrad Metro (Excursion No. 11), the colonnaded buildings on the east side of Ploshchad Revolutsii (Revolution Square) (Excursion No. 1), and the façade of the residential block on Ploshchad Mira (Peace Square) at

Sverdlov Embankment

the end of Moskovsky Avenue (Excursion No. 7).

Likewise, the Moscow and Seafront Victory Parks (Excursions No. 7 and No. 1) were laid out shortly after World War II. The main thoroughfares in the city's south and north were lengthened, and Kirov Stadium, a truly grandiose affair for that time, was built.

Starting in the 1950s, the application of standardised, prefab construction methods boosted the housing programme. This naturally speeded up construction rates and cut down on costs.

The Soviet Constitution gives citizens of the USSR a legal right to the indefinite lease of housing, whether state- or public-owned. All families in need of better living conditions are, as a rule, provided with flats, with priority granted in this respect to disabled war veterans, the families of servicemen killed in action, families with many children, single mothers and labour veterans.

The Soviet authorities would not even consider recouping the huge investments in housing through rents, which have remained at the 1928 level; in fact, rents do not even cover a third of maintenance costs.

More high-rise buildings are appearing. In 1973, construction of five-story walkups, which but ten years earlier, in 1963, had accounted for 82 per cent of all the housing built, was discontinued. Blocks of apartment buildings, ten-storeys and more, are now common.

The new master plan for the development of the city and the region from 1986 to the year 2005 does not envisage a "sprawl" in Leningrad's territory; it will extend only slightly beyond the city's current boundaries. This is in accordance with the city's estimated population at the end of the given period, expected by demographers to reach 5,500,000. Within the city limits there remains a considerable number of unoccupied areas. This reserve has been retained thanks to the fact that from 1970 on, the city has been built up much more densely.

Yubileiny Sports Palace

Another, though less significant reserve lies in the elimination of "blank spots" left in large-scale construction projects for public buildings. These will add the final touches to the area along the city's arterial roads.

The focal points of construction in the coming years will be the city's northwestern and southwestern districts. Nine- and ten-storey buildings will make up the majority of dwellings, accented by occasional sixteen- and eighteen-storey structures.

There is no doubt that the attractive new high-rise buildings, beautiful avenues and lush parks will enhance the loveliness of the unique open-air museum that is Leningrad.

LENINGRAD MISCELLANEOUS

■ The Neva is a comparatively young river—no more than 2,500 years old. Its total length is 74 km, 32 km of which flow within the boundaries of Leningrad. For the volume of water it carries it takes fifth place among the rivers of the European part of the USSR (after the Volga, Pechora, Kama, and Northern Dvina). The mean velocity of its current is 0.9-1.2 m/sec (3.2-4.3 km/hr). The Neva pours 9,000,000 cu m of water into the sea per hour.

■ Leningrad is often called the Northern Venice. This is not too great an overstatement. Venice lies on 118 islands, Leningrad on 44. The largest island of the Neva delta is Vasilyevsky Island (1,050 hectares).

■ Within its present-day boundaries Leningrad includes 86 rivers, brooks, channels and canals.

■ Of the largest cities in the world (with populations over one million) Leningrad is nearest to the North Pole. It is situated only six degrees south of the Arctic Circle, on the same parallel as the northern part of the Kamchatka Peninsula and the southern part of Alaska. The White Nights period sets in on June 11 and lasts till July 2.

■ In 1815, the first Russian steamboat, the *Yelizaveta*, was built in St. Petersburg, a wooden vessel 18.3 m long and 4.6 m wide. Its steam-engine had a 4 hp capacity.

■ Leningrad is the birthplace of Russian porcelain. Porcelain first appeared in China between the 4th and 6th centuries, in 1710 the first porcelain works in Europe was opened in Meissen (Saxony). The technology involved in the manufacture of chinaware in Meissen was, as in China, a close-locked secret. Dmitri Vinogradov, a Russian scientist, discovered the secret of the manufacture of porcelain in 1746. The pottery shop where Vinogradov worked was expanded and reconstructed. Today it is the Mikhail Lomonosov Porcelain Factory.

■ The first system for the televised reproduction of images by means of a cathode tube was invented by Professor Boris Rosing of the St. Petersburg Technological Institute. In 1907 he took out a patent for a method of electrical telescopy—the transmission of an image over a distance. On May 9, 1911, Rosing demonstrated, for the first time in the world, geometrical figures on the screen of a cathode tube. Rosing's works were the basis for the subsequent development of electronic systems of television.

■ In 1926, the Supreme Council of the National Economy of the USSR (the central organ managing the key branches of the national economy from 1917 through 1932) announced a competition for the development of an industrial method for obtaining synthetic rubber. First place in this competition was awarded to Sergei Lebedev, a chemist who produced a two-kilogram sample of synthetic rubber and a full description of the technology of its manufacture. Up till then the problem of synthetic rubber production had seemed unsolvable.

The first batch of synthetic rubber,

weighing 265 kg, was produced by the Lebedev method in Leningrad on February 15, 1931. In 1932 (five years earlier than in Germany and ten years earlier than in the USA), the first specialised plant for the production of synthetic rubber was commissioned in Yaroslavl, a city on the Volga.

■ The streets of St. Petersburg were first officially named in 1738. The names of the streets, squares and embankments were written on small boards fastened to special posts. At that time 732 such posts were set up. Thirty years later Empress Catherine the Great ordered the police to remove the posts and have the names of the streets inscribed on marble tablets to be attached to the walls of houses at the end of each street. In 1803, the marble tablets were replaced by tin plates. One of the marble tablets may still be seen on the wall of the Hermitage Museum at the corner of Zimnyaya Kanavka (Winter Ditch) and the Neva Embankment—Excursion No. 3. In 1896 and later, enamelled plates were introduced.

House numbers were introduced in St. Petersburg in 1834: the houses from one end of the street to the other were given a single system of increasing numbers. The currently functioning system was implemented in 1858: the even numbers on the left side of the street, the odd numbers on the right side.

■ At the beginning of the 19th century an edict forbidding smoking in the streets was issued in St. Petersburg. It was rescinded in July 1865.

■ In 1857, a governmental decree was issued concerning the height of private houses built in the city. No matter how many storeys were to be built, the height of the house was not to exceed the width of the street in which it was being erected, and its total height was not to be more than 11 sazhens (1 sazhen = 2.13 m) or less than 5.5 arshins (1 arshin = 71.12 cm); in other words, the houses could be no more than 23.5 m and no less than 4 m in height.

■ Several sundials set up in the 18th century have been preserved in Leningrad. They can be seen near the Menshikov Palace, at the corner of University Embankment and Syezdovskaya Liniya (Congress Row), on one of the towers of the Lutheran Church (No. 22, Nevsky Avenue), on the stone posts standing on Moskovsky Avenue at the Fontanka Embankment, and on Repin Square.

■ The longest streets in Leningrad are Prospekt Obukhovskoi Oborony (Obukhov Defence Avenue) at 9,760 m, Moskovsky Prospekt (Moskovsky Avenue) at 9,265 m, Leninsky Prospekt (Lenin Avenue) at about 9,000 m, and Prospekt Stachek (Strikes Avenue) at 8,471 m.

■ By 1750 there were about 150 streets in St. Petersburg; in 1815, 431; and in 1903—681. Now Leningrad has more than 1,800 thoroughfares, streets, avenues, lanes and embankments with a total length of more than two thousand kilometres.

■ The distant precursor of the present-day General Post Office was the Postal Yard founded in 1714. It stood on the bank of the Neva, on the site where the Marble Palace (Excursion No. 3) stands today. Postal correspondence was accepted here and then dispatched to other cities of the country and abroad. The Postal Yard did not make postal deliveries to addresses in St. Petersburg. There were no postmen on its staff. Business offices and private individuals had to send someone to the Postal Yard or go themselves for their letters.

In 1833, the first city postal service was set up in St. Petersburg. Letters were accepted from the population in 45 shops; payment was according to the weight of the letter. These shops were visited three times a day by postmen who delivered the letters to the Post Office, where they were sorted, and then delivered by the postmen to the addresses. The shopkeepers profited from this arrangement: they were paid ten per cent of the money received for the letters they accepted.

Envelopes with postmarks confirming payment for postage were introduced in 1848. In that same year letter-boxes appeared in St. Petersburg. Stamps were put into circulation in 1858, and the issue of postcards was commenced in 1872.

■   Street-lights appeared in St. Petersburg in 1718. Four lamp-posts were set up at that time on the Neva embankment, near the Winter Palace. In 1723, there were already 595 lamp-posts on the central streets of the city; they burned hempseed oil. In 1770, there were already 1,257 lamp-posts in St. Petersburg; in 1794, 3,400; and in 1858, 8,494. They emitted a dim light and spattered oil on passers-by. In his story *Nevsky Prospekt* the famous Russian author Nikolai Gogol wrote: "Keep your distance, I implore you, from the street lamps! And hurry past them quickly, as quickly, as possible. You'll be lucky if you get off with the light no more than spilling its foul-smelling oil over your smart frock-coat."

In 1821, the first gas-lights appeared; in 1863, the first kerosene lamps. An experimental electric street illumination was demonstrated to the residents of St. Petersburg on July 11, 1873. The short Odesskaya Ulitsa (Odessa Street) was flooded with bright electric lights. However, the inventor of the incandescent lamp, Alexander Lodygin, receiving no help from either the government or the city authorities, could not organise the mass production of electric bulbs. In 1876, Pavel Yablochkov, an electrical engineer, took out a patent in Paris for the electric bulb he had invented—the "Yablochkov candle". In March 1879, Yablochkov arranged a test illumination of the Liteiny Bridge, and in April of the same year illuminated the square in front of the Alexandrinsky Theatre (Excursion No. 5) with his lamps.

In 1914, the streets of St. Petersburg were lighted by 13,950 street-lamps. Among them 2,505 burned kerosene, 8,425, gas, and 3,020 operated on electricity. Today the streets of Leningrad are lighted by more than 150,000 electric lights.

■   The first public conveyances were horse-driven cabs. At the turn of the 20th century special two-and-a-half year courses were opened for training "learned cabmen". At graduation they took exams in the geography of St. Petersburg and its environs, French, driving horses, astronomy (specially for night cabbies), and polite manners. In 1901, 55 cabbies graduated with good marks in all the subjects; 60 failed French and had to sit for the exam a second time; 20 failed geography; and 15, astronomy.

In 1847, the first omnibuses appeared, and, in 1863, a horse-drawn tramline was opened. It was owned by a joint-stock company that signed a contract with the city council for the monopoly of passenger traffic in the streets of St. Petersburg. In 1907 electric trams appeared in the city.

■   The first public railway in Russia—between St. Petersburg and Pavlovsk—was opened on October 30, 1837. One of the passengers on its maiden journey wrote of his impressions in one of St. Petersburg's newspapers, saying that on the return run the train made "almost a verst (1 verst = 1,0668 km) a minute ... 60 versts per hour: horrible thought! Meanwhile, you sit calmly, you do not notice this speed that terrifies the imagination, only the wind whistles, only the 'steed' breathes fiery foam, leaving a white cloud of steam in its wake ..."

The railway tickets were punch-stamped brass plates. During the first months the steam-powered trains ran only on Sundays and holidays. On weekdays the locomotives "rested" and the coaches were pulled along by horse teams. Only in April 1838, did steam become the only traction employed on the railway.

■   In the middle of the 19th century three large-scale projects were under construction in Russia: it took forty years to build St. Isaac's Cathedral (begun in 1818), the Blagoveshchensky Bridge was built between 1842 and 1850, and the St. Petersburg-Moscow railway, from 1843 to August 1851. Skeptics affirmed that the bridge would fall after it was completed, that the railway would take many more years to build, and that there would actually be no end to the construction of St. Isaac's. Wags joked that "the bridge over the Neva will be seen by us, but not by our children, we won't see the railway, but our children will, while neither we nor our children will ever see St. Isaac's completed". The railway tracks between Moscow and St. Petersburg were laid down in an almost perfectly straight line. This 656 km railway was at that time the longest double-track line in the world.

■ Peter the Great permitted no bridges to be built over the Neva, since he feared that they would obstruct shipping traffic. The first bridge was built in 1727, after Peter's death. This was a floating bridge, its deck mounted on anchored barges—actually it was a pontoon bridge. It connected the present-day Decembrists' Square with the area of the Alexander Menshikov Palace (Excursion No. 3). For boats passing along the Neva the bridge swung open in two places. A toll was charged for the use of the bridge. Pedestrians paid one kopeck, the charge for a cart was two kopecks, for a carriage drawn by two horses five kopecks, for driving a flock of sheep or goats over the bridge the charge was two kopecks for every ten animals, and one rouble was charged for opening the bridge for a vessel. Only carriages from the royal palace, palace messengers, participants in official ceremonies, and fire brigades were given free passage over the bridge.

The bridge toll was abolished in 1755. After the Blagoveshchensky Bridge was built the old pontoon bridge lost its importance and it was moved towards the Winter Palace, and later returned to its former site. In June 1916, the wooden pontoon bridge caught fire from sparks sprayed by a passing tugboat and was completely burned up. However, to this day one may see the granite abutments—the old approaches to the burnt first bridge over the Neva—on University Embankment at the Menshikov Palace and on the Decembrists' Square by the monument to Peter the Great.

■ A talented Russian self-taught mechanic, Ivan Kulibin (1735-1818), lived and worked in St. Petersburg in the 18th century. He made the unique egg-shaped clock (on display in the Hermitage Museum), constructed the "mirror lanterns"—a prototype of lighthouse beacons, invented excellent prosthetic limbs, and also an optical semaphore telegraph.

In 1776, Kulibin worked out a project for the construction of a gigantic one-span wooden bridge, 298 m long, to cross the Neva. The height of this bridge would permit the passage of large sail-rigged vessels under it. At that time the span of the largest wooden bridge in the world (over the river Limmat in Switzerland) was only 119 m. Kulibin built a model of this bridge, one-tenth of its full size, and this model was successfully subjected to the most complicated tests. However, the project sunk into oblivion. In 1793, the model was placed in the Taurida Gardens, serving as a small bridge over a canal. In 1816, the neglected model fell into complete decay.

■ In the 18th century, the wooden bridges over the Moika were painted different colours. Today, even though those wooden bridges no longer exist, old-timers still remember their previous names. Thus, what was once the Yellow Bridge is now called the Pevchesky (Choristers'—because it spans the river at Palace Square, where the Choristers' Capella is), the Green Bridge (on the axis of Nevsky Avenue) is now the Narodny (People's) Bridge. Two bridges have retained their old names: the Red Bridge (Dzerzhinsky Street), and the Blue Bridge (St. Isaac's Square). The railings and arches of these bridges are today, too, painted in their traditional colours—red and blue.

■ The widest of Leningrad's bridges is the Blue Bridge—99.95 m. This great width makes the bridge almost imperceptible in the ensemble of St. Isaac's Square, being perceived as the square's continuation (Excursion No. 3).

■ The longest bridge in Leningrad is the Alexander Nevsky Bridge—909 m. The width between its railings is 35 m. This bridge connects Ploshchad Alexandra Nevskogo (Alexander Nevsky Square) (Excursion No. 5) with the area of the Zanevsky Prospekt on the right bank of the Neva. The bridge was built in 1960-1965. Its 50-metre middle section can be drawn apart to let heavy ships through—the designers of the bridge took into account the fact that the Neva had become a part of the Volga-Baltic waterway.

■ The first motion picture in Russia was shown in St. Petersburg on May 4, 1896. Advertisements in the city's newspapers promised that in the premises of the Aquarium Theatre (today the Lenfilm Studios, Excursion No. 1) there would take place a "showing of the latest miracle of science—live images moving on the screen of the Lumière cinematograph". A newspaper review noted that "the enthusiasm of the viewers was stupendous, so that at the demand of the audience the picture, showing the arrival of a train, had to be run through a second time".

The famous Russian art critic Vladimir Stasov visited the Aquarium Theatre and then wrote a letter to Lev Tolstoy's elder daughter, in which he said: "Do you in Moscow now have the same thing we have in St. Petersburg, the thing that simply boggles the mind?.. It's, you know,—motion photography! Good Lord, what heights can be reached by the genius of invention in our time! How great is the greatness of today's people!"

The first stationary sound-film theatre in the USSR was opened on October 5, 1929 at No. 72, Nevsky Avenue (Excursion No. 5). Today this building houses the Znaniye cinema theatre.

■ Every day, at exactly 12 noon, a cannon is fired from the bastion of the Peter and Paul Fortress. Leningraders check their watches by it. This volley is a long-established tradition. Back in the early days of the city's existence gunfire volleys from the Peter and Paul Fortress informed the inhabitants of the city of the beginning and end of the working day, notified people who had been invited to the royal residence— the Summer Palace—that it was time to set out for the journey, gave the signal that a new ship was about to be launched from the slipways of the Admiralty, that the Neva had become clear of ice, etc.

From 1865 on, a cannon stationed by the Admiralty walls was fired at midday on a signal sent by telegraph from the Pulkovo Observatory. Soon afterwards it was decided to fire the cannon from the Naryshkin (southern) Bastion of the Peter and Paul Fortress. The first midday volley was fired here on September 24, 1873. These cannon signals were fired until June 1, 1934, after which the bastion was silent for over twenty years. During preparations for the festivities to be held in commemoration of the 250th anniversary of the city it was decided to revive the ancient tradition. Two 152-millimetre howitzers, relics of the Great Patriotic War of 1941-1945, were mounted on the Naryshkin Bastion. On June 23, 1957 they were fired at noon.

■ Leningrad is one of the leading book-printing centres in the Soviet Union. There are over 30 publishing houses in it, among them Lenizdat, publisher of the Leningrad regional CPSU Committee, holder of the Order of the Red Banner of Labour. Lenizdat annually prints over 250 books in a total edition of some 10 million copies. Over 150 newspapers come out in Leningrad (including factory and college papers), and seven magazines. The central and republican newspapers, the Telegraph Agency of the Soviet Union (TASS), and the Novosti Press Agency (APN) maintain 35 branches and correspondent's offices in Leningrad.

■   In 1917, the daily output of the two waterworks of Petrograd was 360,000 cu m of water. In our time the Leningrad waterworks supply the city with over 2,000,000 cu m of water every day. Half of this is utilised for the domestic needs of the Leningraders.

SIGHTSEEING EXCURSIONS

Revolution Square—Peter and Paul Fortress—Lenin Park—Kirov Avenue—Kirov Islands. The Spit of Vasilyevsky Island—University Embankment—Lieutenant Schmidt Embankment. The Summer Garden—The Field of Mars—Palace Square—Decembrists' Square—St. Isaac's Square—Labour Square—Theatre Square. Lenin Square—The Taurida Palace—The Smolny. Nevsky Avenue—Arts Square—Ostrovsky Square—Uprising Square—Alexander Nevsky Square. Strikes Avenue—Strikes Square—Kirov Square—Komsomol Square. Moscow Avenue—Peace Square—Moscow Gate Square—Moscow Square—Victory Square. The Hermitage. The Russian Museum. Piskaryovskoye Memorial Cemetery. The Leningrad Metro

1

REVOLUTION SQUARE—PETER AND PAUL FORTRESS—LENIN PARK—KIROV AVENUE—KIROV ISLANDS

The excursion lasts approximately 4 hours (excluding visits to the museums en route). The nearest metro station is Gorkovskaya. *We recommend that you divide this walk into two parts: Revolution Square, the Peter and Paul Fortress and Lenin Park before lunch; and the sites of Kirov Avenue and Kirov Islands after lunch.*

Tourist attractions: Peter the Great's Cottage (18th century), the cruiser *Aurora*, the Museum of the Great October Socialist Revolution (the former residence of Matilda Kshesinskaya), the Peter and Paul Fortress (18th century), the Kirov Memorial Museum, the Botanical Gardens, the Stone Island Palace (18th century), the Yelagin Palace (19th century), and the Esplanade Victory Park.

The waters of the beautiful River Neva flow quietly to the sea. The widest part of the river divides the left bank of the Neva, the city centre, from the Petrograd Side which lies in the greenery of gardens and parks.

The austere bastions of the Peter and Paul Fortress break up the green frame of the banks. The contrast of the greenery and stonework, the horizontal lines of the fortress walls and the vertical lines of the bell-tower determine the landscape in this old part of the city.

You begin to get to know Leningrad on the right bank of the Neva in **REVOLUTION SQUARE** (Ploshchad Revolyutsii), formerly Trinity Square, which dates back to the early days in the city's history. Here in the years of the Northern War (1700–1721), under the protection of the then earthen bastions of the Peter and Paul Fortress, the first buildings of Russia's future capital—the Senate, the Shopping Arcade, a church, the Custom's House, and an inn—went up.

Today a large public garden lies in the centre of the square. In the northern part of the square stands the group of buildings of the Museum of the Great October Socialist Revolution; in the eastern part, the buildings of the Lenproekt Institute and a home erected for veterans of the revolutionary struggle; in the west the square is bounded by the walls of the Peter and Paul Fortress and in the south by the embankment of the Neva.

1

Near Revolution Square, on the quiet Peter's Embankment (Petrovskaya Naberezhnaya), stands **Peter the Great's Cottage**, the only building to survive to our time from the early years of the city's existence. The cottage was built in three days at the end of May 1703. It is a small (approximately 12 m long, 5.5 m wide and some 2.5 m high) single-storey wooden structure which did not originally have a stone foundation, nor were there stoves or flues in it. Peter the Great lived here only in the summer.

The cottage was built of rough-finished pine logs painted to look like bricks (this type of decoration was frequently employed when construction of the city began in order to give the hastily erected wooden buildings the appearance of brick structures). It has seven windows, is roofed with little boards to look like tiles, plain furniture graced the rooms and all sorts of tools hung on the walls. Peter the Great mastered 14 skills professionally.

After the Summer Palace in the Summer Garden was built, Peter moved there, but the cottage was preserved as a historical sight of St. Petersburg. The thorough restoration work carried out in the years of Soviet rule has largely returned the cottage to its initial appearance, and since 1930 it has been a museum.

Under the vaults of the stone tent roof with the glazed arches erected over the cottage in 1844, an exhibition devoted to the victory of Russia in the Northern War and to the early years of the city's construction has been set up. Here you can see the boat which was, according to legend, built by Peter himself. In 1875, a garden was laid out round the cottage and a bronze bust of Peter was erected, cast from a model by Parmen Zabello. This bust is a simplified copy of the one made by Carlo Rastrelli (the father of the famous architect), for whom Peter the Great sat in person, and now kept in the Hermitage.

Opposite the cottage by the stairs descending to the Neva, two striking sculptures stand on granite pedestals; these are the fairy-tale creatures **Shih Tze**, carved in granite and looking like a cross between a lion and a frog. In ancient China such sculptures guarded the entrances to palaces and burial vaults. These Shih Tzes were erected here in 1907.

Not far away, at the point where the arm of the Neva, the Greater Nevka (Bolshaya Nevka), flows out of it, the legendary **cruiser *Aurora*** lies at anchor. The cruiser was named after the frigate *Aurora*, which became famous during the Crimean War (1853–1856).

Built at the St. Petersburg shipyard, the cruiser was launched in 1903 and fought in the battles of the Russo-Japanese War (1904–1905). Not long before the February Revolution of 1917 it was placed in dock for a general overhaul. In October 1917 the sailors of the *Aurora* joined the insurgent people. On the night of October 25 (November 7), on the orders of the Military Revolutionary Committee, the cruiser sailed into the Neva and dropped anchor by the middle span of the St. Nicholas Bridge (now the Lieutenant Schmidt Bridge) and trained its guns on the brightly illuminated windows of the Winter Palace, the seat of the Provisional Government. At 21 hours 45 minutes the *Aurora* gave the signal for the storming of the Winter Palace.

The crew of the *Aurora* fought heroically in the Civil War and the Great Patriotic War (1941–1945). In November 1948 the ship was allotted a permanent mooring near the building of the Nakhimov Military Naval College as a monument to the Great October Socialist Revolution. In 1957 a branch of the Central Naval Museum was set up on the *Aurora*. The six-inch gun from which the legendary shot was fired is carefully preserved on the

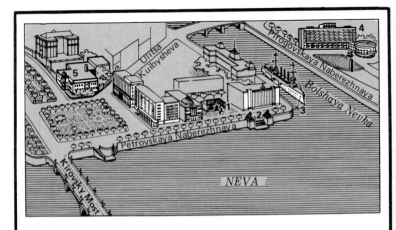

PLOSHCHAD REVOLUTSII—PETROVSKAYA NABEREZHNAYA

1. *Peter the Great's Cottage*
2. *The granite sculptures Shih-Tze*
3. *The Cruiser* Aurora, *branch of the Central Naval Museum*
4. *Hotel Leningrad*
5. *Museum of the Great October Socialist Revolution*

ship, as is the radio-room, the first radio station of the proletarian revolution. From this station Lenin's appeal "To the Citizens of Russia" was broadcast, announcing the overthrow of the bourgeois Provisional Government and the victory of the proletarian Revolution in Russia.

In a special room on the ship you can see the gifts presented to the *Aurora*, such as a memorial medal presented by French pilots of the Normandy-Niemen Regiment, which fought on the Soviet-German front in 1943–1945; the banners of the Italian partisans of the Second World War period; a model of the schooner *Granma*, which the Cubans call the little sister of the *Aurora*; a portrait of Pierre Degeyter, the composer who

wrote the music to the *Internationale*, a gift from the major of the French town of St. Denis; a portrait of Ernst Thälmann, brought from the German Democratic Republic; and other mementoes presented by English, Bulgarian, American, Indian, and numerous other well-wishers from different countries.

After visiting the cruiser, we suggest that you return along Peter's Embankment to Revolution Square and visit the mansion that formerly belonged to the mistress of the last Russian tsar, Nicholas II, the ballerina Matilda Kshesinskaya, at No. 1/2, Maxim Gorky Avenue (Prospekt Maksima Gorkogo).

This mansion faced with light-coloured ceramic tiles, built in 1902 by the architect Alexander Gogen, and now housing the **State Museum of the Great October Socialist Revolution**, is one of the important historical attractions of Leningrad. From March to July 1917 this was the seat of the Central and Petrograd Committees of the Bolshevik Party. In the Greater Hall of the mansion, on the night of April 4, 1917, Lenin gave an account of his famous *April Theses*, which provided the Party with a concrete programme for turning the bourgeois-democratic revolution of February 1917 into a socialist revolution. Lenin worked here for three months, participating in the meetings of Party's directive organs, receiving delegations of workers and peasants. On July 4 (17), Lenin spoke from the balcony of the Kshesinskaya mansion for the last time. On July 6 the troops of the Provisional Government seized and vandalized the house.

In a memorial room of the museum stands an exact replica of the desk Lenin worked at, as well as other furniture that was here between April and July of 1917. The interiors of the offices of the leadership of the Secretariat of the Central Committee of the Bolshevik Party have also been reproduced as they were at that time.

Next to the museum stands the **Mosque** with two minarets decorated with multi-coloured tiles. Its builder (architect Stepan Krichinsky, 1912) used the architectural forms of the Gur Emir Mausoleum of Tamerlane erected in Samarkand at the beginning of the 15th century.

Your next stop will be the **PETER AND PAUL FORTRESS**. Cross Kirov Avenue (Kirovsky Prospekt) and return to the embankment where the small Kronwerk Strait branches off from the Neva by Kirov Bridge, separating Hare Island (Zayachi Ostrov), on which the fortress stands, from the ancient earthern fortification protecting the fortress on the northern side. The path along the right bank of the

Peter the Great's Cottage

strait leads to a huge horseshoe-shaped building situated on the Kronwerk (architect Pyotr Tamansky, 1860s), the famous **Artillery, Engineering and Signals Museum**. In a number of foreign reference books it is described as one of the biggest military museums in the world.

In the museum you can see numerous military objects of the Russian and Soviet armies, ranging from an ancient sword and arquebuses (firearms) of the 13th century to modern ballistic missiles; military standards, medals, ammunition, uniforms of Russian soldiers, unique samples of weapons and firearms of the 14th century to the present day; trophy weapons and documentary materials and items of engineering equipment and signals.

The exhibition acquaints you with the military past of the Russian people and the fighting traditions of the Russian Army. Many of the exhibits are devoted to the Soviet period in the development of the artillery, the engineering and signals corps.

The final section of the exposition tells about the Soviet Armed Forces enhancing their battle readiness, the strengthening of fraternal friendship with the peoples and armed forces of the socialist countries, the joint exercises performed by the armies of the Warsaw Treaty countries, as well as the growth of the might and battle co-operation of these armies.

Your itinerary will now take you across the bridge over the Kronwerk Strait (Kronverksky Proliv), the city's first bridge. You are now near the walls of the Peter and Paul Fortress, the city's initial nucleus.

You already know that St. Petersburg began to be built in 1703 as a fortress to defend the outlet to the Baltic Séa which Russia had reconquered from the Swedes. The fortress went up quickly, as an attack was expected by Swedish ships from the Gulf of Finland and by the Swedish infantry, which had occupied the northern reaches to the city. Peter's choice of the site for a fort was a fortunate one, for the guns on its bastions prevented the enemy fleet from entering not only the Greater Neva but also its main arms, the Little Neva and the Great Nevka.

Initially the fortress was built of earth and wood. In 1706 work began on replacing the earthen walls with stone ones. It took approximately 35 years to erect the new brick walls, which towered above the Neva to a height of almost 12 metres. In the 1780s the walls were faced with granite slabs.

When you pass the **St. John's Gate**, erected in 1740, you will find yourself in front of an extremely interesting old structure, the **St. Peter Gate**. Built by Domenico Trezzini in 1717–1718, this is the only historical and architectural monument that has come down to us almost unchanged (only the figure of St. Peter that stood above the gate has not remained). Until 1740 the St. Peter Gate was the fortress's main entrance. Of the initial decoration on the gate the wooden bas-relief (sculptor Niccolo Pineau) depicting armour and the god of Sabaoth in the clouds, has been preserved.

The wooden bas-relief (sculptor Konrad Osner, circa 1708) depicting a

Cruiser Aurora *lying at anchor in the Bolshaya Nevka*

pagan priest prostrated by the strength of the prayer of the Apostle Peter, is quite intriguing. The allegorical bas-relief was called upon to instil thoughts of the omnipotence of the tsar Peter the Great. Below the bas-relief, a lead effigy (1720) of a two-headed eagle, the coat of arms of the Russian Empire, guards the archway of the gate.

Before the end of the 15th century, when the Russian centralised state was founded, there was no single state coat of arms in Russia. The seals of the Moscow princes and the coins more often than not bore the image of St. George the Dragon Slayer, the hero of Christian mythology. The state coat of arms, the two-headed eagle had appeared in Russia by 1497. The two-headed eagle on the coat of arms of ancient Rome symbolised the equal status of Rome and Constantinople, the two capitals of the Roman Empire. After the Turks had seized Constantinople in 1453, the Grand Prince Ivan III believed that Moscow was fated to take upon itself the splendour and magnificence of fallen Byzantium. In Ivan III's mind, this would be stressed by depicting the two-headed eagle on the coat of arms of Russia, where it remains for the next 420 years. Since the 16th century St. George the Dragon Slayer has been depicted on the shield on the eagle's body as you will see on the St. Peter Gate.

Statues of ancient Roman goddesses stand in the niches of the gateway; on the right there is the **goddess of war, Bellona**, and on the left the **patroness of arts and crafts, of schoolteachers and doctors, Minerva**. These sculptures glorified in allegorical form Peter the Great's wisdom as a military leader and statesman. The St. Peter Gate is the only example of a triumphal structure in Leningrad dating from the beginning of the 18th century.

From the gate an alley lined by squat little houses will take you straight to the cathedral. The building on the left is the **Engineers' House**, erected in the 1740s for the team of engineers building the fortress, and on the right is the **Artillery Arsenal**, built at the beginning of the 19th century.

Rising up in the middle of the fortress is its most valuable architectural monument, the **Cathedral of St. Peter and St. Paul**, the foundations of which were laid in 1712. The Cathedral was built by the architect Domenico Trezzini. The golden spire of the bell-tower, rising high above the Neva and marking Russia's exit to the Baltic Sea, dominates the architectural ensembles on the banks of the Neva.

The cathedral, 121.8 m high, was the tallest building in Leningrad before the television tower was erected. Interesting pages in the history of Russian building techniques are connected with the spire of the cathedral.

During a storm in October 1830, the spire was struck by lightning. The cross crowning it and the angel weather-vane tilted and threatened to fall. It would have required tremendous expense to erect scaffolding up to the very top of the spire.

The roof-builder Pyotr Telushkin offered his services. The main difficulty was to climb up to the foot of the weather-vane and attach a rope-ladder to it so that the materials needed for the repairs could be taken up. Telushkin solved the problem brilliantly. He took into consideration that the spire of the bell-tower was faced with sheets of gilded copper. The horizontal seams between these sheets were smooth, but the vertical edges were bent out slightly, forming ridges that protruded about 9 cm from the surface of the spire. With a rope round his waist and the other end attached to the internal framework of the spire, Telushkin climbed out through an opening cut 20 metres from the base of the spire. Clutching the vertical bends in the facing solely with his fingers, Telushkin moved around the steeple spirally, towing the rope behind him. Enduring the pain and mustering all his strength, he was able to make a loop around the spire. But, when the brave man reached the golden ball forming the base of the weather-vane, it became clear that he would not be able to throw a rope around the globe—284.5 cm in diameter—to the foot of the cross. Then

Cruiser Aurora *(Branch of the Central Naval Museum)*

Telushkin, tying his legs right undernearth the ball leaned back so that he was suspended in the air almost horizontal to the ground. In this position he threw the rope round the base of the cross and climbed up onto the top of the ball to the foot of the weather-vane. Telushkin was rewarded with money and a medal for his brave feat.

The bell-tower crowned with the spire and the main building of the cathedral were not erected simultaneously. Peter the Great ordered that

the bell-tower should be built first and then, after the ground had settled under its enormous weight, the cathedral should be erected. If this had not been done, cracks would have appeared in the places where the walls of the cathedral were joined to the bell-tower.

Especially noteworthy in the cathedral's interior decoration is the **iconostasis of gilded wood** carved in the 1720s. Almost all the Russian tsars, from Peter the Great to Alexander III,

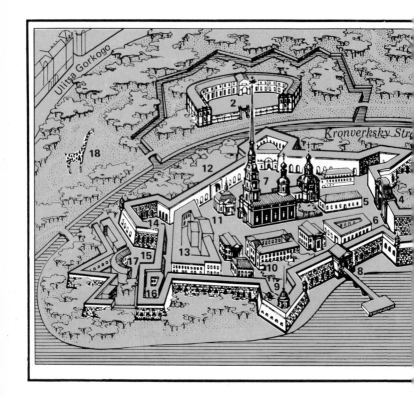

are buried in the Cathedral of St. Peter and St. Paul. The gravestones marking the **graves of Alexander II and his wife** are particularly remarkable. These sarcophagi took 17 years to carve from whole slabs at the Peterhof lapidary workshop: the first from Altai jasper (weighing approximately five tons), the second from rhodonite from the Urals (weighing more than 6.5 tons).

The place where Peter is buried, to the right of the cathedral's southern entrance, was chosen by him personally. In the grave-side oration over the body of Peter the Great, his eminent associate the Archbishop Theophanes Prokopovich said on March 1, 1725: "Russia will be just the way he made it: he made it loved by good people, and it will be loved; he made it fearful for his enemies, and it will be feared; famed throughout the world, it shall not cease to be famed."

The restoration work carried out in the cathedral has returned the walls to their original colour and renovated the paintings above the windows (18th century), which were concealed by soot and dust for many decades.

On the left (southern) side of the cathedral you will see an archway in the fortress wall beyond which there stands one of the finest architectural structures in the fortress, the **Neva Gate** (architect Nikolai Lvov, 1787). The gate is faced with granite and built in the form of a classical portico

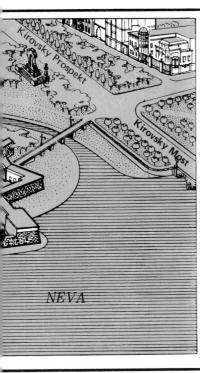

PETER AND PAUL FORTRESS

1. Gorkovskaya *Metro Station*
2. *Kronwerk; Artillery, Military Engineering and Signals Museum*
3. *St. John's Gate, the fortress's main entrance*
4. *St. Peter's Gate*
5. *Artillery Arsenal*
6. *Engineers' House*
7. *Cathedral of St. Peter and St. Paul*
8. *Neva Gate, the Commandant's Pier*
9. *Naryshkin Bastion and the Signal Cannon*
10. *Former Commandant's House*
11. *Pavilion where Peter the Great's boat is kept*
12. *Nikolsky Gate*
13. *Mint*
14. *Zotov Bastion*
15. *Vasilyevsky Gate*
16. *Trubetskoi Bastion; former prison of the Trubetskoi Bastion*
17. *Alexeyevsky Ravelin*
18. *Zoo*

on double columns, which are joined together by sturdy blocks of stone. Through these gates you can go out onto the Commandant's Pier from which a cannon fires at exactly midday according to old tradition.

The **Mint** in the centre of the fortress, is sure to attract your attention. Founded in 1724, its workshops were originally housed in the Trubetskoi Bastion. The building you see today (probably designed by Antonio Porto) was built in about 1802. From 1876 the St. Petersburg Mint became the only place in Russia where metal money was coined. Soviet coins began to be minted there in 1921. Today the Mint not only makes coins but also medals and orders of the Soviet state, memo-

rial and jubilee medals and so forth. The staff of the Mint made the emblems delivered to the Moon, Venus, and Mars by Soviet rockets.

Back in the 18th century the Peter and Paul Fortress was converted into a jail, where the best men of the Russian people who fought against the autocracy were incarcerated. In 1790, on the orders of Catherine the Great, Alexander Radishchev, the first Russian revolutionary aristocrat and author of a book condemning the autocracy and serfdom entitled *A Journey from St. Petersburg to Moscow*, was imprisoned in the fortress.

In 1825, the leading participants in the uprising of December 14, 1825, the Decembrists were thrown into the

View of Peter and Paul Fortress

St. Peter's Gate

prison of the Alexeyevsky Ravelin (the western part of the fortress). Most of them were sentenced to hard labour in Siberia, and five of them, Pavel Pestel, Kondrati Ryleyev, Sergei Muravyov-Apostol, Mikhail Bestuzhev-Ryumin, and Pyotr Kakhovsky were executed on July 13, 1826, on a site adjacent to the fortress in the north.

In the 1860s prominent figures in the Russian revolutionary-democratic movement languished in the dungeons of the Peter and Paul Fortress. In July 1862 the doors of the Alexeyevsky Ravelin prison closed behind the Russian revolutionary, writer, and philosopher, Nikolai Chernyshevsky, who spent two years there before being sentenced to hard labour.

In 1884 the Alexeyevsky Ravelin prison was demolished and a new building erected on its site, but the Peter and Paul Fortress continued to serve as a jail for those who opposed the autocracy. A new prison was constructed inside the Trubetskoi Bastion in 1870–1872. Most of the members of the revolutionary organisation the People's Will, condemned by a court of law, were imprisoned in the cells of the Trubetskoi Bastion. Here Alexander Ulyanov, Lenin's elder brother who was sentenced for his part in the assassination of Alexander III was held (in cell No. 47) before being executed.

At the end of the 19th century prominent revolutionaries, the associates of Lenin — Panteleimon Lepeshinsky (cells No. 23 and 54), Mikhail Olminsky (cell No. 53), Nikolai Bauman (cell No. 56), and many others — were imprisoned in the Trubetskoi Bastion.

In January 1905, the eminent Russian writer Maxim Gorky was thrown into the Trubetskoi Bastion prison (cell No. 60) for a political leaflet he had written. Gorky was suffering from tuberculosis and an acute form of rheumatism. In his first few days in the cell his temperature soared and he was tormented by a hacking cough. The progressive organs of the European press published articles in defence of the writer. The appeal of the great Frenchman, Anatole France, to educated people and scholars in Russia, Germany, Italy, France, and other European countries to unite their efforts to save Gorky resounded throughout the world. The tsarist government was forced to free the writer.

But the history of the Peter and Paul Fortress is not just one of gloomy events. The fortress played an important part in the victory of the October armed uprising of 1917. On the very first day of the uprising the fortress's garrison went over to the side of the people. Its arsenal was used to arm the workers. The fortress was the seat of the uprising's field headquarters from which the action was directly controlled. The Provisional Government resisted for a long time, and the Military Revolutionary Committee took the decision to storm the Winter Palace, the hide-out of the bourgeois government. A lamp burned on the flagpole of the Naryshkin Bastion. This was the signal for the cruiser *Aurora* to open fire. Volleys of gun-

Cathedral of St. Peter and St. Paul

Interior of the Cathedral of St. Peter and St. Paul

fire in the Peter and Paul Fortress joined the rifle and machine-gun fire of the workers, sailors and soldiers storming the Winter Palace.

This was the first time in the 214 years of its existence that the fortress had actually been involved in any military operations. However, the artillery fire helped to break down the resistance of the besieged counter-revolutionaries. In 1924, the Peter and Paul Fortress was made into a museum.

Besides the fortress buildings, which are of architectural interest, inside its walls are two **permanent exhibitions**: The History of St. Petersburg and Petrograd, 1703–1917 (located near the cathedral, in the Commandant's House) and The 18th- to Early 20th-Century Architecture of St. Petersburg and Petrograd (in the Engineers' House).

The documents, photographs, engravings, relics, tools and everyday objects in the first exhibition show the visitor what life was like in St. Petersburg, and later Petrograd, from 1703 to February 1917.

The second exhibition displays unique materials that tell about the construction of the city and about its main ensembles.

In 1973 an **exhibition devoted to the history of Soviet rocket engineering** was opened in the St. John's (Ioannovsky) Ravelin (simply follow the signs located throughout the fortress). A memorial plaque on the wall indicates that in 1932–1933 this building accommodated the USSR's first experimental gas-dynamics laboratory for the development of jet propulsion engines.

In the St. John's Ravelin the world's first electrothermal engine and the first Soviet liquid-fueled rocket engine, developed in this gas-dynamics laboratory, were tested. A bust of the pioneer of aerospace engineering, Konstantin Tsiolkovsky, stands by one wall inside the Ravelin, and above it the words of the scientist read: "Our planet is the cradle of reason, but we cannot live in a cradle for ever."

The exhibits on display here tell the visitor about the life and activities of the outstanding Russian and Soviet scientists working in aerospace engineering and aeronautics: Nikolai Kibalchich, Konstantin Tsiolkovsky, Nikolai Zhukovsky, Friedrich Tsander, Sergei Korolyov, and others. Here you can see their portraits, documents, photographs, scientific works. It also presents a panorama of Soviet aerospace engineering—from the first rockets to those modern spaceships with which man is conquering outer space.

After you have looked round the Peter and Paul Fortress, you can leave by the gate of St. John's Ravelin and head for Revolution Square. On the opposite shore of the Kronverksky Strait, on the left, a nine-metre-high **obelisk of pink granite** can be seen. This monument marks the site where the Decembrists were executed and was erected in 1975 to mark the 150th anniversary of the uprising. On the front face of the pedestal there is a bronze medallion on which the profiles of the executed Decembrists are depicted in relief. The inscription below the medallion reads: "On this site, on July 13 (25), 1826, the Decembrists P. Pestel, K. Ryleyev, P. Kakhovsky, S. Muravyov-Apostol and M. Bestuzhev-Ryumin were put to death." On the other side of the monument the lines of Alexander Pushkin's passionate poem addressed to his Decembrist friends serving hard labour sentences in Siberia are inscribed:

Dear friend, have faith: the wakeful skies
Presage a dawn of wonder—Russia
Shall from her age-old sleep arise,
And our names upon the ruins,
Of despotism shall be incised.

At the base of the obelisk on a large granite slab there is a composition in bronze—a sword, epaulettes, and broken fetters.

Continue along the shore of the Kronverksky Strait to **LENIN PARK**, which was founded in 1845 and acquired its present name in 1923. Its mass of greenery stretches between the Kronverksky Strait and Maxim Gorky Avenue (Prospekt Maxima Gorkogo). In 1914–1921 the famous writer lived here at No. 23. In the park by the alley which opened into Kirov Avenue (Kirovsky Prospekt) a **monument** has been erected **to the crew of the torpedo-boat** *Steregushchy* (sculptor K. Izenberg, 1911).

During the Russo-Japanese war, in 1904, this ship was seriously damaged in an unequal combat. The wounded sailors who remained alive decided to scuttle the ship, preferring death to captivity. The monument depicts the ship's armour-plating torn by shells, two sailors opening the kingston valve and the rush of water into the hold. In 1954, when the jubilee of the

Peter and Paul Fortress

feat performed by the sailors of the *Steregushchy* was marked, a bronze memorial plaque was mounted on the back of the monument. This plaque bears a bas-relief depicting the torpedo-boat sinking, surrounded by enemy vessels, and a list of the crew.

Near the corner of Kirov Avenue and Maxim Gorky Avenue among the trees of the park the **Metro station Gorkovskaya** can be seen. Take a quick look at No. 51, Maxim Gorky Avenue, where Dimitr Blagoyev

(1856–1924) lived in 1884, at that time a student of St. Petersburg University and the organiser of one of the first Marxist groups in Russia. Subsequently, Dimitr Blagoyev became the organiser and leader of the Bulgarian Communist Party. Later, before he was banished to Bulgaria in 1885, Blagoyev lived nearby at No. 12, Vvedenskaya Street (now Koshevoi Street). In 1969, a monument to him was unveiled here.

In the grounds of No. 49, Maxim

Gorky Avenue, stands a large building with a round tower mounted on a cube and a high archway serving as a gateway. This edifice was built in 1912–1913. Immediately after the Revolution it housed the **Labour Exchange**. As there is no longer unemployment in the USSR, the former Labour Exchange is currently used as a premises for lectures by one of Leningrad's institutions of higher education.

Opposite the Labour Exchange is the former **People's House**, a sort of club built by the tsarist government to distract the workers from the revolutionary activities. Constructed in 1900–1910, its architects used the iron framework from the dismantled pavilions at the All-Russia Exhibition in Nizhny Novgorod (now the town of Gorky) in 1896. Lenin spoke at the club twice (in 1917 and in 1919).

Next to it stands the **Lenin Komsomol Theatre**, built in 1939. The building suffered severe damage during the blockade of Leningrad but the city's young people helped to restore it quickly. Heroic and romantic plays predominate on the theatre's varied repertoire.

Adjacent to the theatre you will see the **Planetarium**, opened in 1959. An optical apparatus manufactured by the Carl Zeiss enterprise in Jena (GDR) stands in the middle of the circular demonstration hall seating 480 people. This apparatus consists of more than 100 projectors which recreate a picture of the stellar heavens on the semi-spherical dome 25 m in diameter, depicts the rotation of the planets around the sun, the landscapes of the Moon, Mars, and other galactic phenomena. The Planetarium's cupola is made of aluminium plates covered with several layers of fiberglass.

Visitors to the Planetarium can see the exhibition Man Conquers Space, which is devoted to the outstanding achievements of Soviet science and technology in space exploration, a nine-metre Foucault pendulum illustrating the rotation of the Earth, attend lectures, watch popular-science films, and visit a small observatory on the roof of the building. Among the most interesting exhibits are two globes. One of them, a silver globe in relief, approximately one metre in diameter, is a miniature model of the Moon providing a graphic idea of its surface, while the other is a coloured globe of the Earth.

The extensive grounds of the **Zoo** founded in 1865 spread almost next to the Lenin Komsomol Theatre. The Zoo boasts 415 different species and a total of more than 1,000 animals.

The first part of your excursion ends here. The second part will take you to Kirov Avenue and the Kirov Islands. It begins in Revolution Square, a spot you already know, from which one of the most attractive thoroughfares in Leningrad, **KIROV AVENUE**, leads off to the north. Before the 19th century this was the road to Stone Island and was called Stone Island Avenue; it was given its present name in 1934 in honour of Sergei Kirov, the head of the Leningrad Regional Party Organisation.

A **monument to Maxim Gorky** (sculptor Vera Isayeva, 1968) has been erected at No. 2, Kirov Avenue, where it intersects with Maxim Gorky Avenue. The will of the great writer striving in his thoughts for a better future for his people is emphasised by the decisive stance of the shoulders, the lively expression of his face and its carefully defined features.

On the opposite side stands an originally decorated **house No. 1/3** designed by the architect Fyodor Lidval. In the forecourt the main entrance is crowned with a bas-relief in the centre of which is a cartouche bearing the date when the house was built (1902). To the right of the date a woodland bird is perched on a pine branch threatening to peck a hare sitting next to it. On the left are a lynx and an owl. A larger stone owl is depicted under the edge of the roof. To the left of the main entrance are fantastic large-headed fishes. Lion masks are mounted above the right main entrance. This is but a partial list of the realistic and fantastic animals adorning the façade of this house, an example of the Art Nouveau style of architecture which was current in Russia at the beginning of the century.

Further on, at No. 10, Kirov Avenue, are the **Lenfilm studios** founded in 1918 and associated with outstanding figures in Soviet cinematography whose films have a place in the treasure-house of world cinema. The Lenfilm studios boast a museum whose exhibits re-create the history of the country's oldest studio, tell the visitor about Soviet cinematography and about the work of its leading producers and stars.

The crossroads of Kirov Avenue and Peace Street (Ulitsa Mira) has an original octagonal shape. The buildings lining the square call to mind the traditions of Scandinavian architecture. The **Pasteur Institute of Epidemiology and Microbiology** is situated near the square at No. 14, Peace Street.

In its laboratories researchers are seeking new means of combatting the microbes and viruses responsible for infectious diseases. A team of leading Soviet scientists work at the institute and have an outstanding discovery to their credit, namely the creation of a live vaccine against poliomyelitis.

The **oldest building on the avenue** is No. 21. In 1843 the Lycée, attended at various times by many young people who later became outstanding figures of Russia, including the great poet Alexander Pushkin, the Decembrists Ivan Pushchin and Wilhelm Küchelbäker, and the writer Mikhail Saltykov-Shchedrin, was transferred here from Tsarskoye Selo. In 1917 this house was the premises of the Red

Monument to the crew of the torpedo-boat **Steregushchy**

Guard headquarters of the Petrograd Side. Today it houses the artistic vocational college. A **bust of Lenin** (sculptor Vladimir Pinchuk, 1955) mounted on a pedestal of black marble stands in front of its entrance.

Several large buildings were erected on the avenue in the years just before the Revolution, such as No. 26/28 (architect Leonti Benois, 1911–1912), embellished with a colonnade of red granite. The eminent Bolshevik and the head of the Leningrad Regional Party Organisation, Sergei Kirov (1886–1934), lived here in flat 20 from 1926 to 1934. Today this building houses a **memorial museum** whose exhibits point to the erudition of this man, his industriousness, the broadness of his views and interests, and the great respect he enjoyed among the inhabitants of the city. The memorial flat is part of the museum.

The flat consists of a dining-room, a library, a study, and a little parlour, all of which have been preserved just as they were when Kirov lived here. Although there was a study in the flat, in the evenings and sometimes at night Kirov liked to work at the dining-room table. A chess-table, a radiogram, and a gramophone stand by the wall. In the drawers of the table there are Kirov's favourite gramophone records.

Kirov's personal library contains approximately 20 thousand books, newspapers and journals, including the works of Lenin, many books on philosophy, history, political economy, science and technology, works by Russian, Soviet, and foreign writers. There are quite a few books in the study which Kirov referred to every day.

The walls are hung with photographs of Lenin and his Party associates. On the desk there are samples of minerals and metal ingots, telephones for local calls and direct calls to the Central Committee of the Party, to the Leningrad Regional Party Committee, and to other towns in the country. First Secretary of the Leningrad Regional Party Committee, Kirov was also a member of the Politbureau of the Central Committee and Secretary of the Central Committee of the Communist Party.

In the parlour Kirov's carpentry and plumbing tools are displayed and in the cupboard are his hunting and sports accessories.

Behind the building where Kirov lived the avenue widens into Lev Tolstoy Square (Ploshchad Lva Tolstogo). The building known in Leningrad as the **House with Towers**, an interesting example of the pre-revolutionary architecture of St. Petersburg (designed by Andrei Belogrud, 1913–1916), is a prominent feature in the square. Adjacent to the Tower House is Lev Tolstoy Street, where the buildings of the **Pavlov First Medical Institute** are located.

Here on April 15, 1917, Lenin participated in the first session of the Petrograd City Conference of Bolsheviks. On April 24, 1917 Lenin opened the first session of the 7th (April) All-Russia Conference of the Bolshevik Party in one of the institute's buildings and made several speeches and reports.

The students of the institute receive most of their tuition at the Fyodor Erisman Hospital, named after the Russian doctor and hygiene specialist. In the 1840s the outstanding Russian physician Nikolai Pirogov worked at

the hospital as a consultant and surgeon. In 1897 the first women's medical institute in Russia was opened at the hospital and was subsequently reorganised into the Pavlov First Medical Institute. Ivan Pavlov, Vladimir Bekhterev, Leon Orbeli, Konstantin Skrobansky, Georgi Lang, and many other brilliant scientists actively assisted in organising and promoting this institute. Today the surgical clinics of the institute enjoy a good reputation, specialising in surgery of the pectoral organs.

A pedestrian subway will take you from the square to the Metro station *Petrogradskaya*, built into the 1960s structure of the **House of Fashion** at No. 37, Kirov Avenue. A sturdy portal with 16 pylons unites the two ground floors. They are continued by the smooth glazed surface of the main part of the building. The façades are decorated with stone and metal.

Note the building faced with grey stone (No. 42), opposite the House of Fashion. Its original design is emphasised by the wide glazed apertures in the walls, replacing the windows. This is the **Lensoviet Community Centre** (architects Yevgeny Levinson and Vladimir Munts, 1934). Performances by the country's best theatrical troupes and actors from abroad are often given in the centre's auditorium, which seats 2,400. Clubs for young people interested in aeroplane modelling and radio-engineering, theatre, choreography and other amateur activities are run here.

In March 1959, a **monument to the inventor of the radio, Alexander Popov**, was unveiled in the garden opposite the Community Centre. The first public demonstration of the world's first radio receiver took place on May 7, 1895. On March 24, 1896, Popov transmitted the first message by radio from St. Petersburg University over a distance of 250 metres. It consisted of just two words: Heinrich Hertz (the great German physicist).

Within a year radio signals were being transmitted over a distance of five kilometres, and later up to 150 kilometres. Sculptor Vladimir Bogolyubov depicted the scientist holding a telegraph tape, reporting on the world's first experiments in transmitting signals over long distances. The first radio receiver has been cast in bronze for future generations to see.

Not far from the Community Centre, Kirov Avenue crosses the River Karpovka, whose banks were lined with granite back in the 1960s. **No. 13**, Karpovka Embankment, which can easily be seen from Kirov Avenue, is worthy of attention. It is one of the classical works of Soviet architecture (architects Yevgeny Levinson and Ivan Fomin, 1931–1935).

A new ferro-concrete bridge with wrought-iron railings spans the River Karpovka. The part of the Petrograd Side which lies beyond this bridge is called **Apothecary's Island** (Aptekarsky Ostrov). This name dates back to Petrine times when a huge plantation of medicinal herbs, the Apothecary's Allotment, was set up here in 1713–1714.

A hundred years later the plantation was turned into the St. Petersburg Botanical Gardens. In 1931 **Komarov Botany Institute of the USSR Academy of Sciences**, which is today an important world centre of botanical science, was set up on the basis of the Botanical Gardens. The gardens may be reached by turning right off of Kirov Avenue onto Professor Popov Street (Ulitsa Professora Popova).

During the siege of Leningrad the gardens' greenhouses were destroyed by Nazi bombs and shells. Today the Botanical Gardens possess unique collections of plants from all continents of the world. Approximately 3,500 species of plants from the southern regions of the Soviet Union and also from India, Australia, the USA, Brazil, Cuba, Japan, Ethiopia, and other countries, grow in

Statue of Maxim Gorky

the gardens' greenhouses.

In the greenhouses you can see lianas, giant palms, bamboos, upas-tree, and balsa (the wood of this tree is two or three times lighter than cork; the well-known Norwegian traveller Thor Heyerdahl used it in building his raft *Kon-Tiki*). Here American agave, Australian anaphia, Japanese camelias, orchids, lotuses, and other exotic plants bloom. For more than a hundred years now that wonder of nature, the Queen of the Night cactus, has been growing on Apothecary's Island. When the sun sets on warm summer evenings the cactus opens its flowers of unique hue, closing them again at sunrise. The fruits of the cacao-tree, lemons, bananas, and oranges ripen in the greenhouses. A stroll through the dendrarium, covering an area of 16 hectares and exhibiting a collection of 700 species of trees and shrubs, is a most interesting experience.

Connection with the Botany Institute is a **Botany Museum**. Its herbarium, which contains approximately 5,000,000 sheets with preserved plants, is one of the largest in Europe.

Founded in 1823, the museum boasts a fine collection of samples of timber, fruits and seeds, and also plant products. The 60,000 samples of plants from the Soviet Union and all countries of the world make this collection unique. Many eminent Russian and Soviet scientists and travellers took an active part in creating it. While visiting this museum you can learn what dinosaurs ate, take a look at the "Holy of Holies"—secret writings of medieval medicine men and discover what ingredients they used in their "magic potions".

The exposition highlights four principal themes: The History and Evolution of the Plant World, Plant Life of the World by Botanical-Geographic Regions, Plant Reserves of the USSR, and Environmental Protection.

At the place where a section of Professor Popov Street veers off of Kirov Avenue, there stands the **Leningrad Youth Centre** (No. 47). Erected in 1980, it is a cultural centre where the young people of Leningrad can enjoy a variety of recreational activities. This centre includes a high-rise hotel, a concert hall, a cinema and a lecture hall, an exhibition hall, a swimming pool, a disco-bar, and many other club premises. The centre has an international club, a library, and a debating club; it also schedules lectures and exhibitions of painting, works of graphic art and sculpture. In the Grand Concert Hall, sitting 1,200, various performances are given.

As you walk along Kirov Avenue, stop for a moment at the corner of Chapygin Street (Ulitsa Chapygina). The **Hotel Druzhba** is situated at No. 4 on this street where young people from abroad who are visiting their young Leningrad friends usually stay. When the hotel was completed, it was discovered that the blind butt-end of a neighbouring building spoiled the appearance of the entire reconstructed block. The artistic design of this wall was entrusted to the graduates of the Mukhina Higher Industrial Art School, who created the biggest picture in Leningrad, not with a pencil, or a pen, nor with a brush, but with a pneumatic drill. Against the background of the light plaster, contour lines were cut and, where dark patches were necessary, the plaster was chipped off revealing the dark red brick underneath. This is how the picture symbolically depicting the friendship of people of different races was drawn on its huge stone "canvas".

The **Leningrad Television Centre** stands next to the hotel, and beside it is the highest structure in the city, the television tower completed at the end of 1962. The tower is 316 metres high, 15 metres taller than the famous Eiffel Tower, but almost eight times lighter. The tower's foundations consist of 256 ferro-concrete piles sunk into the ground to a depth of 24 metres. The tower is a grille-like welded single construction in which there is not a single bolt. Its 200-metre-high trunk houses premises for radio apparatuses and equipment, for the service personnel and the lifts. The trunk is topped by a 116-metre antenna. It took just a little over a year to build the tower. In windy weather the amplitude of oscillation of the top of the tower is as much as two metres.

On the small stretch of Kirov Avenue between the Karpovka and the Little Nevka, several buildings are noteworthy for their architectural merits, among them **No. 63 and No. 65**, erected (1908–1911) by Vladimir Shchuko in neo-Renaissance style. The façade of one of the buildings is embellished with pilasters and a sculptured ornament of the same style. The façade of the other building is decorated with large Corinthian columns four storeys high.

Among the achievements of Soviet architecture of the pre-war years **No. 69/71** (architect Nikolai Lanseré, 1937), housing workers of the Institute of Experimental Medicine of the USSR

Academy of Medical Science, occupies a worthy place. The façade, revetted with polished labradorite, is decorated with six symmetrically placed medallions bearing portraits of great medical men in bas-relief.

A street named after the Soviet power-engineering specialist, Academician Heinrich Graftio, extends to the right off of Kirov Avenue. At No. 2b, Graftio Street, in the former flat of the famous singer Fyodor Chaliapin, the exposition of a branch of the **Leningrad Museum of Theatre and Music** opened in 1975.

The name of the great Russian singer Fyodor Chaliapin (1873–1938) is inseparably linked with the history of Russian art at the turn of the century. He is justly considered to be a reformer of the opera, who has enriched not only the Russian and Soviet, but also the world stage.

Chaliapin's career is closely connected with St. Petersburg. The singer came here in 1895 as a nameless young man from the provinces. After his first performances he became a member of the troupe of the famous Mariinsky Opera House, and at the same time, in 1899, a soloist of the Bolshoi Theatre in Moscow.

In 1914 St. Petersburg became Chaliapin's permanent home. The singer settled on Perm (now Graftio) Street in a little three-storey house decorated with pilasters bearing elaborate capitals. Two more floors were subsequently built onto the house.

After Chaliapin went abroad in 1922 one of his friends moved into the flat and carefully kept the singer's archives, his personal effects, and his letters.

At the exhibition devoted to the history of the Russian opera, to outstanding Russian composers and singers, you can see rare photographs and unique theatrical costumes (of Mephistopheles and Boris Godunov) in which Chaliapin performed.

Next to the exhibition are several rooms that have been kept just as they were when Chaliapin lived in the house. The furnishings include an armchair of carved walnut (a gift from Maxim Gorky), the singer's personal

Lev Tolstoy Square

belongings, and his collection of old arms and costumes. Chaliapin used the drawing-room as a study where he spent his morning hours at the grand piano rehearsing for concerts or performances. A remarkable portrait of Chaliapin by Boris Kustodiyev hangs on the wall.

There are many paintings in the singer's apartment, including a portrait of his wife, Maria, by Boris Kustodiyev and a splendid self-portrait of Chaliapin in the parlour.

Further on, a quiet street bearing the name of Academician Ivan Pavlov leads off to the right of Kirov Avenue. The **Institute of Experimental Medicine** is situated here at No. 12. For almost half a century (1890–1936) the outstanding Russian physiologist Academician Ivan Pavlov worked here. The scientist's study has been preserved as a memorial museum.

After the October Revolution, work at the institute was conducted on an ever more extensive scale. On the initiative of Lenin, the Soviet government allotted considerable sums of money for the reorganisation of the institute, the expansion of the old laboratories and the building of new ones. The foundations of Pavlov's materialist teaching on the higher nervous activity of animals and human beings were laid here, at this institute. Today the Institute of Experimental Medicine with its departments of microbiology, general physiology, pathological anatomy, pharmacology, and virology is an important centre in Soviet and world medical science.

Kirov Avenue ends at the wide Stone Island Bridge across the Little Nevka which is decorated with granite obelisks and bronze bas-reliefs. Beyond the bridge, to the north of the Petrograd Side, lie the Kirov Islands. This archipelago consists of three islands. The first, **Workers' Island** (Ostrov Trudyashchikhsya), is known for its landscapes, holiday centres and sanatoriums. **Yelagin Island** (Yelagin Ostrov) has a palace ensemble and the Central Recreation Park. The third, **Krestovsky Island** (Krestovsky Ostrov), boasts a huge stadium, the esplanade of Victory Park and numerous sports clubs.

The bridge across the Little Nevka will take you to the holiday centres and sanatoriums of **WORKERS' ISLAND** (the former Stone Island), where thousands of people, not only Leningraders but visitors from all the republics of the Soviet Union, spend their holidays and undergo treatment.

The first owners of this vast (106 hectares) island were Peter the Great's associate, Chancellor Gavriil Golovkin, followed by Chancellor Alexei Bestuzhev-Ryumin, who brought thousands of serfs from the Ukraine to improve the facilities of his estate. The newly-arrived peasants settled near the island, thereby laying the foundations of those parts of the city which were known as the Old and the New Villages.

In the 18th century canals were dug on the island, they were faced with limestone and granite, and hunting lodges and luxurious mansions were built. On the orders of the future Em-

peror of Russia Paul I (who was then heir to the throne), in the eastern part of the island the **Stone Island Palace** was erected (architect unknown) and continues to stand. There are architectural monuments on the island also worthy of attention. Among them is the **former summer residence of Dolgorukov** on the Little Nevka Embankment (Naberezhnaya Maloi Nevki) at No. 11. Erected by Smaragd Shustov in 1831–1832, the house is of an original cubic design topped by a cupola above a circular central hall. In 1827, the wooden building of the **Stone Island Theatre**, designed by that same architect, was built in just 40 days on the Greater Nevka Embankment (Naberezhnaya Bolshoi Nevki). After a fire in the mid-19th century it was restored by Albert Cavos. In the 19th century during summer performances the back wall of the theatre was removed and the actors performed against the background of the greenery of the park.

The beauty of the island attracted Pushkin, who spent the last summer of his life here in 1836. The country cottage where the poet stayed on the bank of the Greater Nevka has not survived; in 1912–1916 the **palace of Senator Polovtsev**, designed by Ivan Fomin, was built on the site. The architect combined the forms of retrospective Classicism and the Art Nouveau style popular at the time. Skilfully using the methods of strict Classicism, he erected a building that enhances the island to this day. The halls of the palace are finished with marble, Italian silks, ornate moulding and gilding. This building houses one of the first holiday homes for the workers of Petrograd.

During his last visit to Petrograd on July 19, 1920, Lenin visited Stone Island and talked to the workers on vacation there.

The **summer residence of Burgaft** on the River Krestovka Embankment (No. 2, Naberezhnaya Reki Krestovki)

was also designed by Ivan Fomin. According to the architect's plan, it was built near an oak-tree planted in 1709 by Peter the Great. By the 1920 decision of the Petrograd Soviet, these and other mansions were made into sanatoriums and holiday homes for the workers.

To the north-west of Workers' Island the waters of the Greater and Middle Nevka wash **YELAGIN IS-LAND**, which is only 12 hectares smaller than Workers' Island. The

first owner of this island was the eminent diplomat of the early 18th century, Pyotr Shafirov. At the end of the 1770s the island became the property of the wealthy aristocrat Yelagin. Yelagin used his serfs for carrying out all the amelioration work on the island. The marshy area was drained, and a wide earthen rampart, still extant, was built along its shore to prevent the destructive effects of flooding. The hollows formed when the soil was taken for the rampart were used for a sys-

Stone Island Palace. Late 18th cent.

tem of ponds, enhancing the island even today.

At the beginning of the 19th century the island became the summer residence of the tsars. On the orders of Alexander I, the architect Carlo Rossi was commissioned to build a palace there. The first large order in Rossi's career, which was just beginning, earned him an outstanding reputation.

In 1818–1822 the architect created a splendid architectural ensemble here, one of the most important achievements of Russian Classicism. The **Yelagin Palace**, erected on a high stone terrace girded by decorative wrought-iron grilles, dominates in this ensemble. The palace's two main façades differ from one another; its finely decorated front façade faces onto the park. A gentle slope and an elegant flight of stairs embellished with sculptures of lions and decorative railings lead up to the main entrance with its six-column portico.

One of the Kirov Islands

The palace's façade looking out over the Middle Nevka is more austere; its central part is emphasised by the protrusion of the oval hall with two rows of windows, and adorned with columns and a graceful frieze above the windows of the ground floor. The white marble vases, sculptured according to Rossi's design, with Tritons depicted in bas-relief add to the building's impressive architecture.

Not far from the palace stands the semi-circular two-storey building of the **kitchens**. Taking into account the nature of this structure, Rossi built it without window apertures in the façade, for the windows look out over the inside courtyard. The outside wall has niches in which statues (the work of Stepan Pimenov) and decorative vases stand. The main entrance, emphasised by a monumental six-column portico bearing a pediment, faces onto an expansive meadow in front of the Yelagin Palace. The kitchens form a component of the palace and park ensemble.

The **stables**, decorated with a Doric colonnade, is an interesting example · of a utilitarian structure built in the style of Russian Classicism.

Of the other buildings in the ensemble worthy of mention are the **pavilion by the granite jetty** (eastern tip of Yelagin Island) and the **Music Pavilion**, which stands out not only for the grace of its architectural forms, but also for the picturesque combination of grey marble columns and the white marble decorative urns.

The far western tip of Yelagin Island, which looks out over the Gulf of Finland, the so-called **Strelka** (Spit), was replanned in 1926 according to the project of Lev Ilyin: it was made attractive by a terrace, faced with pink granite and embellished with stone lions on stone pedestals.

Today the **Kirov Central Recreation Park** is situated on Yelagin Island. It boasts a large open-air theatre, a variety theatre, a cinema, exhibition pa-

vilions, a sports centre, boating stations, a beach, and a children's sports ground. The Yelagin Palace, which was damaged by fire during the blockade, has now been restored to its former appearance. Now it is used as a lecture-hall, and exhibitions are organised here. Carnivals and the traditional festivals of greeting and bidding farewell to the White Nights take place in the park. In the northern part of the island, on the volley-ball and basket-ball courts in the sports grounds and in the aqua-stadium, competitions are held and athletes are trained.

A real sports centre in Leningrad is **KRESTOVSKY ISLAND**, the largest in the group of Kirov Islands, 420 hectares in area. Owing to its closeness to the Petrograd Side, the former workers' district of the city, palaces and mansions were not built on Krestovsky Island before the Revolution; for the most part facilities began to appear on it after 1917. In 1925 the **Dynamo Stadium** was erected here, followed by new sports grounds, rowing clubs, etc. Opposite the Central Recreation Park there is a yacht-club set up as far back as 1860.

In the autumn of 1945 the city began work on laying out another park. It was created by the inhabitants of Leningrad in honour of the victory gained by the Soviet people in the Great Patriotic War (1941–1945). To drain the marshes, powerful machines made canals, dug out ponds and soon the territory of 168 hectares was covered with flower-beds and lawns, golden strips of sandy beaches stretched along the shores, a network of walkways was laid out, and trees were planted by the Leningraders in the **Esplanade Victory Park**. The overall area of the ponds and canals in the Esplanade Park is more than 18 hectares.

An asphalt road twenty metres wide leads to the western part of the island where the **Kirov Stadium** of unusual design (architect A. Nikolsky, 1950) is situated. It is built of neither stone, nor ferro-concrete, but of soil. More than a million cubic metres of soil were raised from the bed of the Gulf of Finland and the rivers washing the island by powerful machines to construct the hill on which the stadium stands. The muddy soil was transported along pipes to the construction site and was gradually formed into the slopes of the oval hill. Yet another million cubic metres was needed to raise the formerly marshy territory of this part of the island and to even out its shoreline.

The hill looks like a huge volcano. The internal walls of its "crater" form the closed amphitheatre for the spectators, while the sports arena lies at its bottom. It consists of a football ground, a running track 400 metres long, and grounds for field and track events. The 20-metre-wide strip skirting the sports ground allows mass-scale parades of sportsmen and festivities to be held. The stands of the stadium seat 75,000 spectators. The square by the stadium's main entrance is embellished with a **monument to Sergei Kirov** (sculptor Vladimir Pinchuk).

In a picturesque corner of the Esplanade Victory Park, on the shore of a lake, the **restaurant Vostok** is housed in a two-storey glass and aluminium building.

To end your walk around the Petrograd Side and Krestovsky Island we suggest you visit the **New Village** (Novaya Derevnya) district. Before the October Revolution this was a remote district on the outskirts of the city which had no water supply and no sewerage system; the unpaved streets and little wooden houses stood in a sea of impassable mud. In the years of Soviet rule this district has changed beyond recognition: comfortable blocks of flats, schools, shops, cinemas, kindergartens and crèches have mushroomed here, and public trans-port connects the New Village district with the centre of Leningrad. In the 1960s a beautiful new thoroughfare, Nikolai Smirnov Avenue, named in honour of a former mayor of the city, was built on the site of the muddy and cramped Lanskoye Highway.

Among the old structures in this district the **Buddhist temple** built at the beginning of the 20th century on Esplanade Avenue (No. 91, Primorski Prospekt) is noteworthy. Gavriil Baranovsky, the temple's architect, worked in conjunction with the prominent Buddhist scholar Agwan-Khamba, who came to Leningrad from Lhasa expressly for this purpose. The outcome is a unique example of Tibetan architecture. The walls of the temple are faced with granite of a lilac hue, and topped by an entablature of red and dark blue glazed bricks with white rings. The abundance and richness of colour is characteristic of medieval Tibetan architecture.

If you proceed past the temple along Kolomyazhsky Highway you will reach the **place where Alexander Pushkin fought his duel and was mortally wounded**.

The life of the great Russian poet Alexander Pushkin (1799–1837) was a short but outstanding one. In the poet's twenty-five years of creative activity, having assimilated the achievements of Russian and world culture, he passed rapidly through several epochs in literature, from the conventional literary systems of the 18th century to realism, re-creating in his works life in its multitude of aspects. Pushkin's language, which combines the literary and the colloquial, remains the basis of the standard Russian language to this day.

His reputation as a free thinker evoked enmity towards him in high society and among high-ranking officials which eventually grew into actual persecution of the poet.

In November 1836, Pushkin received an anonymous letter by post dishonouring the poet and his wife. Georges Dantes, a French emigrant and admirer of the poet's wife, was involved in the intrigue cunningly plotted by society. Pushkin's confrontation with Dantes ended in a duel, which took place on January 27 (February 8), 1837, just outside St. Petersburg on the bank of the Black Stream (Chornaya Rechka). Pushkin suffered a mortal wound in the stomach and died after two days in terrible pain.

On the site of the pine grove which has long been felled, poplars and willows now grow around a small square with a 19-metre-high obelisk decorated with a bas-relief of the great Russian poet in bronze, erected in 1937.

2

THE SPIT OF VASILYEVSKY ISLAND—UNIVERSITY EMBANKMENT—LIEUTENANT SCHMIDT EMBANKMENT

Approximate time of excursion—2 hours. The nearest Metro station is Vasileostrovskaya.

Tourist attractions: the former Exchange, the Rostral Columns, the Institute of Russian Literature of the USSR Academy of Sciences—the Pushkin House (the former Customs House), the Kunstkammer (18th century), Leningrad University (18th century), the Palace of Alexander Menshikov (18th century), the Academy of Arts (18th century), the Egyptian Sphinxes, the Mining Institute.

THE SPIT (STRELKA) OF VASILYEVSKY ISLAND is the name given to the eastern tip of Vasilyevsky Island, the largest of the islands in the Neva delta.

Here the Neva embraces the spit, as it were, washing it with its two powerful streams and emphasising the magnificent beauty of the river banks. The Palace Bridge (Dvortsovy Most) spanning the Greater Neva (Bolshaya Neva) and the Builders' Bridge (Most Stroitelei) built across the Little Neva (Malaya Neva) in 1960 link the Spit of Vasilyevsky Island with the left bank of the Neva and the Petrograd Side.

Our tour of the Spit will begin with the building of the **former Exchange** (architect Thomas de Thomon with the assistance of Andreyan Zakharov, 1805-1810), reminiscent of an ancient Greek temple. A wide staircase leads from the semicircular square up to the main façade, which is adorned with the figure of Neptune, the god of the sea, in a chariot harnessed to sea horses. On either side are symbolic representations of the Neva and the Volkhov rivers.

On the opposite (western pediment) are the goddess of seafaring, Marine Aphrodite, and the patron of trade, Mercury, surrounded by river nymphs.

At the same time that the Exchange was being built, the granite embankment of the Spit was constructed on piles with two gentle slopes descending to the Neva. The semicircular square on the Spit (now Pushkin Square) was replanned, landscaped and given a more modern appearance in 1925-1926.

In Pushkin Square (Ploshchad Pushkina) by the Exchange stand two monumental **Rostral Columns**, 32 metres high, decorated with metal rostrums—the beaks of ships designed for damaging the sides of enemy vessels. Back in the 3rd and 2nd centuries B. C. the Romans erected rostral columns decorated with the beaks (or *rostra*) of Carthaginian ships, the symbols of Rome's sea victory over Carthage. Here, on the Rostral Columns of the Spit we find the decorative prows of ships, reminders of the victories of the Russian fleet. At the foot of the columns stand large figures personifying the Russian trade waterways: the Dnieper, the Volga, the Volkhov, and the Neva (as seen from the Exchange).

The Spit of Vasilyevsky Island was chosen as the site of the Exchange and these columns because the St. Petersburg trade port was located here from 1733 to 1885. When twilight fell, the hemp oil in the bronze bowls on the Rostral Columns was lit, and the columns became huge torches acting as lighthouses, pointing out the way for ships to approach the port's jetties. (Today seven-metre-high gas torches are lit above these columns during festivals held in the city).

The Spit ensemble was completed with the building of the **warehouses** (1826–1832) and the **Customs House** (1829–1832) on the embankment of the Little Neva. The warehouses and the Customs House were designed by the architect Giovanni Lucini, in accordance with Andreyan Zakharov's project. The Customs House is embellished with an austere portico and sculptures of Mercury, the god of trade, Neptune, the god of the sea, and Ceres, the goddess of fertility. The dome of the building served as an observation point from which the signal was sounded when ships arrived in the port. At that time, a forest of masts rose under the walls of the

Exchange, sails billowed, and in the adjacent squares a lively trade in Russian and foreign goods took place.

After the port was moved to the southwestern outskirts of the city, life in the Spit district became much quieter, and many of the buildings, which had previously served the needs of the port, were used for other purposes. The southern warehouse at No. 1, University Embankment (Universitetskaya Naberezhnaya) houses the **Zoology Institute** and the **Zoology Museum**, one of the largest of its kind in the world.

Approximately 40,000 different species of animals from all over the world are on display in the museum. Moreover, the collection includes 10,000,000 insects, 48,000 fishes, 25,000 amphibia and reptiles, 185,000 birds and 88,000 mammals. Among them are several extremely rare and even unique exhibits, for example, a stuffed mammoth 44,000 years old, removed from the permafrost of Yakutia in 1901, and a mummified baby-mammoth found in the summer of 1977 near the town of Magadan on the Sea of Okhotsk.

The wild Przhevalsky horse, the wild camel, and wild yak, brought back from Central Asia by the famous Russian traveller Nikolai Przhevalsky, are of great value. These animals are nearly extinct today. The museum also boasts fine collections of parrots, hummingbirds, marsupials, and monkeys, including many species now on the verge of extinction. In the invertebrate sections there are rare specimens of shells, sponges, corals, and coral polyps.

The Zoology Museum occupies a part of the Zoology Institute, the country's most important fauna centre.

The former Customs House at No. 4, Makarov Embankment (Naberezhnaya Makarova) is now occupied by the **Institute of Russian Literature of the USSR Academy of Sciences**, more commonly known as the Pushkin House.

2

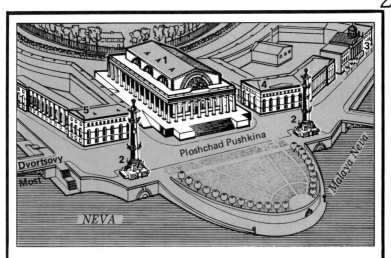

THE SPIT OF VASILYEVSKY ISLAND

1. *Former Exchange, the Central Naval Museum*
2. *Rostral Columns*
3. *Former Customs House, the Institute of Russian Literature of the USSR Academy of Sciences, the Pushkin House*
4. *Former Northern Warehouse, the Dokuchayev Central Soil Science Museum*
5. *Former Southern Warehouse, the Zoology Institute, the Zoology Museum of the USSR Academy of Sciences*

Founded in 1905 as a museum-type depository, in 1930 it became a scientific-research institute and one of the Soviet Union's major literature studies centres. Manuscripts, archives, and letters of almost all the great Russian writers of the 17th to 19th centuries are kept here. The development of Russian literature is illustrated here in the form of manuscripts, printed editions, and works of fine arts, beginning from the 12th century with *The Lay of Igor's Host* up to the present day.

The materials in the exposition tell about the life and work of Mikhail Lermontov, Nikolai Gogol, Ivan Turgenev, Alexander Herzen, Lev Tolstoy, Ivan Goncharov, Fyodor Dostoyevsky, Alexander Blok, Maxim Gorky, and many other Russian and Soviet writers.

The northern warehouse at No. 6, Exchange Passage (Birzhevoi Proyezd) houses the **Dokuchayev Central Soil Science Museum,** the only museum of its type in the world.

The museum comprises four main sections: Soil: An Independent Component of Nature; The Variety of Soils in Nature: From the Arctic to the Subtropics; The Practical Use of Soil and Environmental Protection; The Study of Soil: History and Branches of Development.

In addition to various soil samples (displayed in the form of soil monoliths—in vertical prisms) the museum presents dioramas and pictures that give an idea of the actual environment of soil's existence, as well as samples of all possible kinds of plants and minerals that reflect the conditions of the soil's "life". The natural exhibits are supplemented with illustrative materials—diagrams, maps, posters, photographs, and drawings.

The Stock Exchange at No. 4, Pushkin Square (Pushkinskaya Ploshchad) now houses the **Central Naval Museum**, one of the oldest museums in the country, founded in 1709 by order of Peter the Great.

Today the museum boasts a collection of more than 800,000 exhibits, including an oaken dug-out, raised from the bed of the Southern Bug River, where it had lain for approximately 3,000 years; the boat of Peter the Great, the forefather of the Russian Navy; personal effects of Peter the Great (an axe with which he worked on the slips during the building of the ships, a measuring cane); personal effects of Fleet Admiral Pavel Nakhimov, and many other items. The main sections of the exhibition are devoted to the history of the Russian and Soviet fleet, the feats of the Soviet Navy in the Second World War and the development of the Navy in the post-war period.

Now continue your walk along **UNIVERSITY EMBANKMENT** (Universitetskaya Naberezhnaya), where you will see splendid ensembles created by world renowned architects. But the embankment is famous not only for its architecture. One of the centres of Russian scientific thought took shape here over the course of more than two centuries. Noteworthy in this process is the part played by the **Kunstkammer** (No. 3, Universitetskaya Naberezhnaya), the first Russian natural science museum. The word Kunstkammer comes from the German words *Kunst*, meaning "art", and *Kammer*, meaning a "chamber" or "room".

The private collections of Peter the Great contain all kinds of rare stones, stuffed exotic animals, Buddhist idols, and anatomical preparations.

Spit of Vasilyevsky Island

These collections were made available for the public to see free of charge. When the original premises housing the collections became too cramped, a new building was erected—the Kunstkammer (architects Georg J. Mattarnovi, Gaetano Quiaveri, and Mikhail Zemtsov, 1718–1734)—and was justly referred to as the cradle of Russian science.

For many years (1741–1765) the great Russian encyclopedic scholar, Mikhail Lomonosov, worked here, and the St. Petersburg Academy of Sciences began its activity here (its circular conference hall has retained its original appearance). This building housed the country's first public library and its upper storeys served as an astronomical observatory.

The Kunstkammer building is an interesting example of Russian Baroque. Stretching along the embankment, its façade is divided into three parts—two three-storey buildings linked by a tiered tower. A graceful octagonal turret crowned with a high dome rises above the balustrade of its third tier. This upper part of the building was destroyed by fire in 1747 and restored in 1948–1949, thereby returning the building to its initial appearance.

Today this old building houses the **Miklukho-Maklay Institute of Ethnography**, the **Peter the Great Museum of Anthropology and Ethnography**, based on the collection of Peter's Kunstkammer, and the **Museum of Mikhail Lomonosov**.

Rostral Column

The collections of the Museum of Anthropology and Ethnography tell about the history, economy, architecture, and art of the peoples of Asia, Africa, Australia and the Americas.

The exposition includes tools, utensils, clothing, ornaments, and the musical instruments of the Papuans of New Guinea. Here you will see cloaks and head gear made of bird feathers, the attributes of secret cults, two wooden tablets with the writing of the inhabitants of Easter Island which have yet to be completely deciphered. Only twenty such tablets have been preserved in the world.

The ethnographic expositions demonstrate the traditional culture and way of life of the peoples of Africa, the Americas and Asia (beyond the bounds of the USSR). Single-figure and multiple-figure compositions are widely used in all the expositions, giving an idea of the anthropological and ethnographic appearance of one people or another.

The museum has a rare collection of exhibits devoted to the indigenous population of North America, the Eskimoes, Amugs, and other peoples. The collection was made in the late 18th and early 19th centuries when Alaska was part of Russia. Another exhibition shows the culture and everyday life of the peoples of Latin America (from Mexico to Tierra del Fuego). The museum's exposition ends with a section on the peoples of Africa living beyond the Sahara.

In the circular hall (the eastern gallery of

The exposition in the Mikhail Lomonosov Museum is devoted to the life and work of this outstanding Russian scholar, the founder of the Academy of Sciences, Mikhail Lomonosov (1711–1765). It consists of the following sections: The Life and Scientific Activity of Lomonosov; Lomonosov and 18th-century Russian Astronomy; The Great Academic Globe. The museum contains some of the scholar's personal effects, various types of scientific equipment, geographical

"The Neva" and "The Volkhov" at the Rostral Columns

the building) the Kunstkammer's anatomical curios are on display. Among them is the collection of the so-called "monsters" (physical and physiological anomalies of humans and animals put together by the famous Dutch anatomist Frederik Ruysch and later acquired by Peter the Great. Peter's surgical instruments are on display here as are numerous works of Chinese art preserved from those times—china, lacquered objects, bronzes, and carvings of stone, bone and wood.

maps, astronomical instruments, and books by Lomonosov and his contemporaries.

The museum's main attraction is the Great Academic Globe that was constructed in 1754 with the participation of Lomonosov. A map of the world is depicted on its outer surface and inside is a map of the stellar heavens (corresponding to the data of 18th-century science). This was an original type of planetarium. Ten to twelve

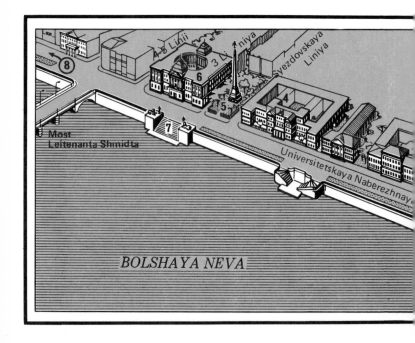

people could stand inside the globe at once, and when it rotated, it created the illusion of movement of the stars. After 1901 the globe was kept in Tsarskoye Selo (now the town of Pushkin). During the war it was stolen by the Nazi invaders. In 1947 it was discovered in the town of Lübeck, was returned to the Kunstkammer and in the autumn of 1963, after it had been restored, put on display.

By the end of the 18th century the old building of the Kunstkammer had become too cramped to house the Academy of Sciences, and it was decided to build new premises. Thus in 1783–1788 the **Main Building of the Academy of Sciences** was erected next to the Kunstkammer. Strictly classical in design this edifice is one of the most prised creations of the architect Giacomo Quarenghi. It is embellished solely with a sturdy eight-column portico with a pediment and a double staircase leading up to the main entrance.

In July 1925, the Russian Academy of Sciences became the All-Union Academy and later the Academy of Sciences of the USSR. In 1934, the Academy's administrative bodies were transferred to Moscow, though many of its scientific institutions continue their work in Leningrad.

A statue of the outstanding Russian scholar Mikhail Lomonosov, executed by the sculptors V. Sveshnikov and B. Petrov, has been erected near the building of the Academy of Sciences.

Behind the statue, Mendeleyev Row (Mendeleyevskaya Liniya) runs perpendicular to the Neva Embankment.

The **USSR Academy of Sciences Library** (No. 1, Birzhevaya Liniya) is situated near the Spit. Today, the

UNIVERSITETSKAYA
NABEREZHNAYA
1. *Former Kunstkammer, the Miklukho-Maklay Institute of Ethnography of the USSR Academy of Sciences, the Peter the Great Museum of Anthropology and Ethnography, and the Museum of Mikhail Lomonosov*
2. *Main Building of the Academy of Sciences*
3. *Leningrad State University*
4. *Former Palace of Prince Menshikov, a branch of the Hermitage*
5. *Obelisk commemorating the victory of Russian troops over the Turks in 1768–1774*
6. *Academy of Arts*
7. *Egyptian Sphinxes*
8. *The Mining Institute and the Mining Museum*

library boasts approximately 17,000,000 books. It exchanges books with almost 3,000 establishments and libraries in more than 100 countries.

In accordance with a mandate introduced by Peter the Great, copies of printed matter from all corners of the country had to be stored here. The library's collection includes *The Apostle*, the first Russian printed book, published by Ivan Fyodorov in 1564; books from the private library of Peter the Great; and some of Mikhail Lomonosov's textbooks, which he referred to as "the gates of my scholarship". The library also has such rare editions as the first publications of Karl Marx's *Capital* in German and French and the first publications of Lenin's works.

The boulevard on Mendeleyev Row (Mendeleyevskaya Liniya) was laid out in the post-war years and separates the buildings of a number of institutions of the USSR Academy of Sciences from the huge edifice that houses the **Leningrad State University.**

This building is one of the oldest in the city and its construction is associated with Peter the Great's desire to have the centre of the city on Vasilyevsky Island. Important administrative reforms were put into effect at that time. The numerous state establishments *(prikazy)* were replaced in 1718 by "collegiums" set up by Peter the Great. (At the beginning of the 19th century they were reorganised into ministries.) The architect Domenico Trezzini was commissioned to design the building for the 12 collegiums, the architecture of which was to reflect the independence of each

Former Kunstkammer

collegium in resolving the problems within its competence and, at the same time, to stress the community of the state tasks set for all these institutions.

The complex of buildings erected according to Trezzini's design in 1722-1741 has survived to the present day, consisting of 12 adjacent structures. Each section is distinguished by a protrusion—a risalit, and a figured pediment. The main façade of this red and white building of tremendous length looks out over the Spit of Vasilyevsky Island and its southern butt-end faces the University Embankment.

In those times there were no permanent bridges spanning the Neva and therefore the government institutions situated on the island were cut off from the main districts of the city by the high waters of the Neva and frequently found themselves in a difficult situation. For these and some other reasons a number of state institutions (including the collegiums) subsequently moved to the left bank of the Neva.

In 1819 the building erected by Trezzini was taken over by St. Petersburg University. Many Russian scholars have made this educational institution famous.

From 1866 to the 1890s, the outstanding Russian chemist, Dmitri Mendeleyev (1834-1907), lived and worked at the University. Mendeleyev is famous for having formulated the Periodic Law and invented the periodic table of elements. Today the apartment in the university where he lived for nearly twenty-five years (1866-1890) is a museum open to the public.

The first sections of the museum are devoted to Mendeleyev's childhood, student years, and his early scientific work. The chemist's study, including his desk, inkstand, paperweight, and ashtray, has remained unchanged. The box on the floor is one he used for transporting books. To the left is a revolving book-stand, to the right an easy chair. By the wall stands a cardboard table, assembled by the chemist himself. The history of the discovery of the Periodic Law of elements figures prominently in the exposition. Instruments from Mendeleyev's laboratory—a barometer and a two-tiered balance for weighing solid and gaseous substances, actually designed by Mendeleyev—are on display here.

In 1891, in the hall of the University Council, Lenin took an examination in an extramural course given by the University's Faculty of Law, writing an essay on criminal law. He received the highest marks in all subjects and was awarded a first-class honours degree.

The part played by the University in the revolutionary movement is also important. One of the early representatives of Russian utopian socialism, Mikhail Butashevich-Petrashevsky, studied here, as did the great Russian revolutionary-democrat Nikolai Chernyshevsky, the founder of the Bulgarian Communist Party, Dimitr Blagoyev, and Lenin's elder brother Alexander Ulyanov.

Leningrad University is one of the larger institutions of higher education in the Soviet Union. Soviet students as well as foreign attend the lectures of its faculties. Just as in other institutions of higher education throughout the country, tuition at Leningrad University is free. Moreover, most of the students receive state stipends. The University's system embraces approximately 150 departments, eight scientific-research institutes, and almost 100 teaching laboratories with the latest equipment. Over 3,000 professors, lecturers, researchers work here.

Adjacent to the University building is a complex of 18th-century houses. The most interesting of them is the **Palace of Alexander Menshikov** (No. 15), the associate of Peter the Great, and an eminent statesman and military figure (1673–1729). Peter's favourite, Menshikov was given the

One of the buildings of Leningrad University

whole of Vasilyevsky Island in 1707. True, later on, in 1714, the tsar took back his present, though in the time that he owned the island, Menshikov managed to build this palace (architects Giovanni Fontana and Gottfried Schädel), the most luxurious building in St. Petersburg at the time.

In the second half of the 18th century the palace housed the First Cadet School. Today, expositions from collections devoted to Russian culture of the early 18th century are mounted in the Menshikov Palace.

The palace was St. Petersburg's first large building of stone. It successfully combines traditional Russian and West European methods and forms of architecture. Dutch and Russian tiles, wooden panelling, carved and gilded decorations, sculptured moulding and monumental decorative painting have been used in its rich and original ornamentation. At present, only a few halls in the palace are open to the public. However, after the current restoration work has been completed, the entire exposition will occupy approximately forty rooms.

Alexander Menshikov's Palace

You are welcome to take a look at this interesting monument of history and architecture.

Passing through the kitchen, with its black and white marble floor, you arrive at the palace's central entrance hall. The walls here are painted to look like marble and in the niches stand Greek and Roman statues, which Menshikov, copying Peter the Great, brought back from Europe. The main oaken staircase leads upward, its railings bearing the intricate monograms of Menshikov and Peter the Great. On display here are various pieces of antique furniture, including a carved 16th-century desk and a wooden travelling trunk with gilded handles—all objects used by Menshikov during military campaigns.

Further on is the secretary's room, containing such noteworthy objects as a carved bureau and medallions on the ceiling bearing representations of the goddesses of fertility and justice, pictures by Dutch landscapists, and astronomical instruments. Next is the palace's state room, the first of those decorated in Dutch tiles. The palace rooms are ornamented with 27,810 tiles. Of them 80 per cent were made by Dutch masters. The white tiles with a cobalt decoration depicting primarily pastoral scenes cover the walls and ceiling.

The stove is faced with tiles of Russian workmanship. Take special notice of the mirror in a silver frame, the early 18th-century oval table, and the portrait of Menshikov. In the next room (the state bedroom) personal effects of the palace's former owner are on display.

The tiles in the chambers of Varvara, the sister of Menshikov's wife, are of particular interest. Here you can see elegant furniture decorated in marquetry, and a cabinet with delftware and Russian glassware.

Menshikov's favourite room was the Walnut Study. Its pilasters topped with gilded capitals and its small lattice-windows looking out over the Neva have recently been restored. Here the restorers made a pleasant discovery: under the canvas of the plafond they found a portrait of Peter the Great in military uniform.

In the exposition in the study take note of the Indian chess pieces, and the mirror in an amber frame hanging on the wall. This mirror belonged to Peter the Great. In pre-Petrine times mirrors were not kept in Russian homes; *Domostroi*, the rules drawn up in the 16th century for social, religious, family and everyday behaviour, forbade people to look at themselves, as this was considered indecent.

The museum's exposition has been expanding of late: several new rooms have been added to those initially on display. The Great Hall has been recreated in all its magnificence, with its moulding, gold leaf, and elegant sconces, hung with the canvases of Dutch painters, and decorated with marble urns. On the first floor you will see the Tapestry Room that served as the main hall when the palace was still one-storey. A small turning room is also displayed. Menshikov equipped his palace with such a room most likely to please Peter, a great lover of the turning trade. Of particular interest in this exposition is a lathe with the inscription: "St. Petersburg 1713". It also includes a shelf with instruments used by Peter the Great, his favourite armchair, antique furniture, books, and prints.

The Menshikov Palace is gradually being restored to its original appearance; the additions made when the building housed the Cadet School are being removed. Among such additions is a **long house** built onto the palace on the Congress Row (Syezdovskaya Liniya) side in the mid-18th century. Here in June 1917 Lenin spoke to the delegates of the First All-Russia Congress of Soviets.

In the garden opposite this building an **obelisk commemorating the victory of Russian troops over the Turks in 1768–1774** under the leadership of Field Marshal Pyotr Rumyantsev, was erected in 1799 by architect Vikenty Brenna.

Next to the garden on the University Embankment stands the **Academy of Arts** (architects Alexander Kokorinov and Jean Baptiste Vallin de la Mothe, 1764–1788). The building with a circular inner courtyard occupies a whole block on Vasilyevsky Island. It is one of the vivid examples of early classicism in Russian architecture. The well-balanced proportions of the main façade are particularly impressive.

Founded in 1757, the Academy of the Three Most Noble Arts (painting, sculpture, and architecture) has played an important part in the development of Russian art. Architects Ivan Starov, Andrei Voronikhin, Andreyan Zakharov; sculptor Mikhail Kozlovsky; painters Alexander Ivanov, Karl Bryullov, Ilya Repin, Valentin Serov, Vasily Surikov, Ivan Shishkin, and others studied and worked here. In the pre-revolutionary years the painters Arkady Rylov, Isaac Brodsky, and the sculptor Matvei Manizer graduated from the Academy. In the years of Soviet rule the Academy has trained more than two thousand artists, among them such outstanding masters as Mikhail Anikushin, Viktor Oreshnikov, and Alexei Pakhomov.

In 1947, by decision of the Soviet government, the All-Russia Academy of Arts became the Academy of Arts of the USSR. This centre of Soviet art has its seat in Moscow. Today the building on University Embankment houses the largest art school in the world, the **Repin Institute of Painting, Sculpture, and Architecture**. This building also accommodates the **Scientific-Research Museum of the USSR Academy of Arts**, one of the country's oldest art museums.

In the museum, works by the greatest painters of the Russian and Soviet art schools are on display.

The section entitled The History of the Russian and Soviet Art School is the country's only special collection of works by students and graduates of the Academy of Arts. Among the exhibits are also several extremely famous works that have long been part of the treasure house of Russian and Soviet fine arts.

Of great interest are various works by graduates of the sculpture class, formed at the end of the 18th and the beginning of the 19th century, as well as reliefs by its former pupils, many of whom have become world famous sculptors.

The section exhibiting moulds from outstanding works of ancient and West European sculpture began its history from the very inception of the Academy of Arts. The copies in this collection, which was formed

in the late 18th and early 19th centuries, were made by eminent masters directly from the originals. The moulds communicate precisely all the plastic features of the originals and comprise the most complete and methodologically selected collections.

In 1964 yet another museum was opened here; the **memorial studio** of the brilliant Ukrainian poet and artist Taras Shevchenko (1814–1861), where he lived and worked from 1858

to 1861. The exposition in the studio reflects the main stages in the life and work of Shevchenko in St. Petersburg, where he spent a total of seventeen years.

On the embankment, before the main façade of the Academy of Arts, a classically austere pier was erected to the design of the architect Konstantin Ton in 1832–1834; the pier is embellished with two **Egyptian sphinxes** on high pedestals, with granite benches

Academy of Arts

bearing images of gryphons and stylised bronze girandoles, each of which stands on four lions' paws.

The gryphons, like the girandoles, were cast in 1834. They adorned the granite pier for several decades, but disappeared at the beginning of this century under inexplicable circumstances. An old lithograph depicting the pier in the mid-19th century allowed Soviet restorers to re-create the gryphons and girandoles. Since

1959 they have again stood guard over the granite steps.

The sphinxes are carved of pink granite obtained from the famous Aswan stone quarries. The hieroglyphic inscriptions on them glorify the Egyptian pharaoh Amenhotep III, who lived in 1455–1419 B.C. and whose palace they embellished. One of the inscriptions reads: "Son of Rah, Amenhotep, ruler of Thebes, the builder of monuments rising to the sky like four pillars

Sphinx

holding up the vault of the heavens." The sphinxes were bought by Russia from Egypt in 1831.

The sculpture is evidently a portrait of Amenhotep, though it is difficult to tell for certain since all the pharaohs of a single dynasty looked very much alike. This is not surprising, given that, according to tradition, they married their own sisters. The depiction of the pharaoh in the form of a sphinx was called upon to instil in people the idea that the ruler of Egypt combined in himself the wisdom of man and the strength and agility of a lion.

Not far from the sphinxes, the Lieutenant Schmidt Bridge, named after the hero of the First Russian Revolution of 1905–1907, spans the Neva. The embankment along the right bank of the Neva, the continuation of University Embankment, is also called **LIEUTENANT SCHMIDT EMBANKMENT** (Naberezhnaya Leitenanta

Shmidta).

Take a look at No. 1 on the corner of the embankment and Seventh Row (Sedmaya Liniya). This old three-storey building, decorated with a Doric portico and graceful window lintels is in its own way a unique sight in the city. Twenty-six bronze memorial plaques are mounted on its façade. In the two and a half centuries that this house has existed more than 80 Academicians have lived and worked in it, thus it is not surprising that Leningraders call it the "Academicians' House".

Residents of the "Academicians' House" have included such outstanding men of science as the geologists Alexander Fersman and Alexander Karpinsky, the linguist Yakov Grot, the physicist Vasily Petrov, the Arabic specialist Ignaty Krachkovsky, and other eminent scientists. Flat 11, where the great physiologist Ivan Pavlov (1849-1936) lived for the last 18 years of his life, has been made into a museum. The furnishings and interior décor of the flat have been left just as they were when Pavlov was alive.

Pavlov's scientific legacy is of tremendous importance. In 1904, he was awarded the Nobel Prize for his research in the field of the physiology of the digestion. The study of conditioned reflexes and types of nervous systems occupy an important place in Pavlov's works. The scientist boldly unravelled the mysteries of the psychic processes, the phenomena of sleep and hypnosis. Revealing the essence of nervous activity, he formulated the idea of the integrity of the organism. In 1935 at the 15th International Congress of Physiologists the Soviet Academician was proclaimed the "doyen of the world's physiologists". The Soviet scientist was elected an honorary member of many Academies, universities and scientific societies of the world. The exhibits in the museum acquaint the visitor with his life and work.

Nearby, at No. 15, Lieutenant Schmidt Embankment, the Swiss-born Academician Leonard Euler, Lomonosov's associate and the author of 756 works, died in 1783.

Behind this house on the bank of the Neva, on a boulevard laid out not long ago, there stands a **monument to Admiral Ivan Krusenstern** (sculptor Ivan Schröder, 1873), the organiser and head of the first Russian round-the-world expedition in 1803-1806, which pioneered a whole series of round-the-world voyages and made a remarkable contribution to Russian and world science. Krusenstern (1770-1846) was a member of a number of scientific institutions in Russia, England, France, and Germany.

The sculptor has depicted the admiral in dress uniform, holding a map of the seas in his left hand. The red polished granite pedestal is decorated with a bas-relief—the bronze coat-of-arms of the navigator with a Negro and a Malayan. The inscription on the monument reads: "To the first Russian to sail round the world, Admiral Ivan Fyodorovich Krusenstern." The overall height of the monument is 5.6 m.

The monument has been erected near the building of the **Frunze Higher Naval College**, the oldest training institution of its kind in the country. In his time, Krusenstern graduated from this college and subsequently became its director. Other graduates were Admiral Fyodor Ushakov, the originator of Russian naval sailing fleet tactics; Pavel Nakhimov, the hero of the defence of Sevastopol (1854-1855) during the Crimean War; Mikhail Lazarev, a participant in the expedition that discovered the Antarctic in 1819-1821, and also many outstanding seamen of the Soviet Navy. Seventy-four graduates of the college have been awarded the supreme title of Hero of the Soviet Union.

In this building, on May 8, 1917, Lenin made a report on the results of the 7th (April) All-Russia Conference

Lieutenant Schmidt Embankment

of the Bolsheviks to a city meeting of the Petrograd Bolshevik Party Organisation. A few days later, on May 14, Lenin gave the lecture *War and Revolution* here.

The panorama along the right bank of the Neva is completed by the building of the **Mining Institute**. Situated between the 21st and 23rd Rows, the institute is named after the revolutionary, theoretician and propagandist of Marxism in Russia, Georgi Plekhanov

(1856–1918), who studied here in 1874–1876. The institute was founded in 1773. The building erected in 1806–1811 to house the institute is an outstanding example of the harmonious synthesis of sculpture and architecture typical of Leningrad's finest ensembles.

The main façade, which overlooks the Neva, has a majestic twelve-column Doric portico topped with a pediment. Andrei Voronikhin designed

Statue of Admiral Ivan Krusenstern

on the Mining Institute seems to stress the fact that the latter is called upon to help penetrate the secrets of the earth's depths and place them at the service of man.

The Mining Institute houses the exhibition of the **Mining Museum**, which was founded at the same time as the institute. The interiors and the furniture were designed under the supervision of the architect Alexander Postnikov. The museum's Hall of Columns, a masterpiece of Russian classicism, is of great artistic value.

Today the Mining Museum boasts one of the world's finest collections illustrating the composition of the earth's crust in all its variety. Its stocks contain tens of thousands of minerals from more than 60 countries; tens of thousands of paleontological remains from geological quarries on different continents, telling about the development of life on earth; hundreds of interesting scale models illustrating the history of mining and mineral processing technology in the 18th and 19th centuries.

the sculptural ornamentation which was executed by Vasily Demut-Malinovsky and Stepan Pimenov. Groups of sculptures have been mounted in front of the main entrance along the edges of the colonnade, as well as bas-reliefs on the frieze with mythological heroes indicating the purpose of the building. One of the sculptures depicts Pluto, the ruler of the underworld, and Cerberus, the fantastic three-headed dog and guard of the underworld, who carried away the splendid goddess, Proserpina, to their domain. The second group depicts the struggle of Zeus' son Hercules with Antaeus, the son of the Earth, symbolising the victory of man over nature, the taming of the forces of the Earth by human reason.

The sculptured frieze, abounding in symbols, circles the building in a 25-metre long band. The subjects are: "Venus comes to the smithy of Vulcan (the god of fire and the patron of blacksmiths) for military accoutrements for Mars" and "Apollo comes to Vulcan for the chariot he made for him". The sculptured ornamentation

You can reach the Grand Avenue (Bolshoi Prospekt) of Vasilyevsky Island on any of the trams passing the Mining Institute. On the left, you will see vessels and the Leningrad passenger seaport. The builders pumped tens of thousands of cubic metres of soil from the bed of the Gulf of Finland onto the low marshy shore and deepened the channel for the passage of ocean-going liners. The granite 270-metre-long wall of the quay allows two passenger vessels to dock simultaneously. The beautiful modern building of the sea terminal houses waiting-rooms, the port's offices and various kiosks. The ground floor is designed for handling incoming passengers. On the first floor, outbound passengers may check in and proceed through customs inspection.

Mining Institute

There is a special auditorium for business meetings and conferences. The three upper storeys make up a hotel with a 600-person capacity. The tower over the building is adorned with a 78-metre spire covered with titanium sheets, which in turn is crowned by a miniature three-masted caravel—the symbol of Russian seafaring (1.2 m in height, 1 m in width).

3

THE EMBANKMENTS AND SQUARES ON THE LEFT BANK OF THE NEVA: THE SUMMER GARDEN—THE FIELD OF MARS—PALACE SQUARE—DECEMBRISTS' SQUARE—ST. ISAAC'S SQUARE—LABOUR SQUARE—THEATRE SQUARE

Estimated time of excursion—4 hours.
We recommend that this excursion also be divided into two parts: the Summer Garden, the Field of Mars, and Palace Square in the first half of the day, and Decembrists' Square, St. Isaac's Square, Labour Square, and Theatre Square in the afternoon.

Tourist attractions: the sculptures of the Summer Garden, Peter the Great's Summer Palace (18th century), the Leningrad branch of the Central Lenin Museum (the former Marble Palace, 18th century), the Engineers' Castle, the monument to the Revolutionary fighters, the Winter Palace, the flat-museum of Alexander Pushkin, the Admiralty, the equestrian statue of Peter the Great (The Bronze Horseman), St. Isaac's Cathedral (19th century), the Mariinsky Palace (19th century), the Musical Instruments Museum, the Kirov Opera and Ballet Theatre (the former Mariinsky Theatre), and the flat of Alexander Blok.

Leningrad's embankments, mostly those of the Neva's left bank, were constructed in 1763–1788, designed and supervised by Yuri Felten (the son of Peter the Great's chef), and are outstanding works of architecture.

Developing the best traditions of Russian architecture and town plan-

ning, the architects of St. Petersburg made expert use of the natural conditions and created architectural ensembles on the Neva which are interlinked by the community of their artistic design. On the Neva's left bank you will see numerous squares and buildings of great historical interest. It was precisely here that many extremely important events in world and Russian history took place.

In the 18th century, the River Fontanka formed the southern border of the city. In the 1760s the city's first stone bridge was constructed at the spot where the Fontanka flowed from the Neva. This steeply arched bridge, which stands to this day, is called Laundry Bridge (Prachechny Most) because the royal laundry was located nearby.

In the foreground lies the **SUMMER GARDEN**, which occupies an area of 11.7 hectares. It is set apart from the embankment by a splendid railing erected in 1770–1784, designed by architect Yuri Felten. The 36 granite columns embellished with alternating vases and urns are united by a light grille which appears to hang in the air. Experts affirm that this is one of the finest examples of artistic wrought-iron work in the world. Interesting evidence has been preserved to the effect that, at the beginning of the 19th century, an English yacht entered the waters of the Neva and dropped anchor by the Summer Garden. The owner of the vessel, a lord and a patron of the arts, admired the open-worked grille of the garden and then, without even going ashore, he ordered the sails raised and returned to England. When asked the reason for this action the lord replied that the goal of his journey had been achieved, that this sight was unsurpassed in splendour.

The work on laying out the Summer Garden began in 1704. It was created in "regular" style, geometrically precise lines dominating in its planning. The garden originally had dozens of fountains depicting subjects from Aesop's fables. It was in those years that

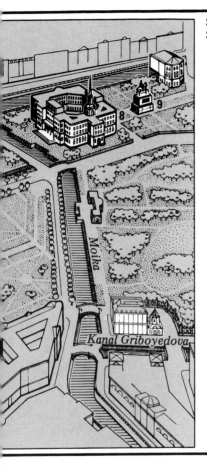

SUMMER GARDEN (LETNY SAD)—MARSOVO POLYE

1. The railing of the Summer Garden
2. Peter the Great's Summer Palace
3. Tea House
4. Coffee House
5. Statue of Ivan Krylov
6. Statue of Alexander Suvorov
7. Marble Palace (Leningrad branch of the Central Lenin Museum)
8. Engineers' Castle
9. Statue of Peter the Great
10. Former barracks of the Pavlovsky Regiment
11. Monument to the fighters for the Revolution

the river feeding these fountains got its name—Fontanka (derived from the Russian word *fontan* meaning fountain). The fountains existed until 1777 when they were damaged by floods and were never restored.

Peter the Great dreamed of creating a garden more beautiful than that at Versailles. To this end he planted the garden with rare trees and flowers, and had marble sculptures brought from abroad.

Many of the sculptures now adorning the Summer Garden date back to the beginning of the 18th century. In the 19th century the intended arrangement of the decorative sculptures in the Summer Garden was forgotten, quite a few of the statues were no longer extant, and those remaining were moved from place to place, thus destroying the original design. In recent years all the sculptures have been rearranged and today they stand in accordance with the aesthetic ideas characteristic of the beginning of the 18th century. Before the northern façade of the Summer Palace, stands the group **Peace and Abundance** (Pietro Baratta, 1722), an allegorical depic-

Summer Garden

tion of Russia's victory in the Northern War. The central figure in the composition is Russia represented as a young woman holding the horn of plenty in her left hand and an upturned torch symbolising the end of war in her right hand. Beside it stands the winged goddess of Victory. With one hand she crowns Russia with a laurel wreath and in the other she holds a palm frond, the symbol of peace; the goddess stands with her foot on a slain lion.

One of the oldest sculptures in the Summer Garden, a **bust of the Polish King Jan Sobieski**, famed for his victories over the Turks, may be found in Palace Alley. Modelled in 1683, the bust is a fair likeness of the king, but bears the somewhat idealised majestic appearance typical of formal portraits of that period.

Do not forget to take a look at the **bust of the Roman Empress Agrippina** in the main alley between the first and the fourth clearings. Dissolute and thirsting for power, this infamous lady murdered her husband, the Emperor Claudius, and placed on the throne her son Nero, expecting

that she would rule the empire. However, Nero, who guessed his mother's designs, ordered his retainers to kill the ambitious empress.

When you look at Agrippina, you feel the emotional tenseness her image harbours. The Baroque style of the bust is emphasised by the ermine mantle. The eyes and the tentacles of an octopus symbolising Agrippina's depravity, can be seen protruding from beneath the folds of the mantle. The empress's countenance is severe and anxious, as though the sculptor were attempting to communicate the sensation of impending death at the hand of her own son.

Among the earliest sculptures of the Summer Garden is the **bust of the Swedish Queen Christina** (17th century). It stands in the main alley between the first and second clearings. The queen's necklace of precious stones is half-concealed by lace. The soft folds in her dress, the ruffles of the lace, the fur on her robes, even her hair, worn in a style typical of that time, are all details highly characteristic of Baroque. Christina's countenance is serene, the mouth only

Railing of the Summer Garden

Cupid and Psyche

twisted in a capricious smile. It should be said that the queen's biography is not a dull one. In her youth she was famous for her fantastic extravagance. The country was poverty-ridden, and a poor country did not suit the queen. She easily renounced Protestantism and became a Catholic, abdicating the throne and leaving Sweden. The Pope welcomed the newly confirmed Catholic, but soon Christina's behaviour shocked him and he expelled the ex-queen from the Vatican.

The sculptural group **Cupid and Psyche** (17th century) situated near the terrace by the Swan Ditch (Lebyazhaya Kanavka) is also worthy of note. One of the myths of Ancient Rome, recounted by Apuleius, holds that Psyche became the wife of the god of love, Cupid, but she only met her chosen one in the dark and never saw his face. Psyche's wicked sisters convinced her that her husband was a repulsive monster. One night Psyche lit a lamp to look at her husband and kill him with a dagger.

Lebyazhaya Kanavka (Swan Ditch)

But on her nuptial couch she saw handsome Cupid and was filled with love. The composition is a typical example of Baroque.

To the side of the main alley, in the northeastern corner of the garden, stands one of the oldest structures in Leningrad—**Peter the Great's Summer Palace**.

The two-storey building of the palace was designed by the architect Domenico Trezzini in 1710–1714. The interior planning of each floor is the same: six halls, a kitchen, a corridor, and a room for the valets or the maids of honour. Peter's apartments were located on the ground floor and those of his wife on the first floor. The kitchen, finished with tiles and the vestibule decorated with elaborate carving on the ground floor, the architectural ornamentation of the Green Study on the first floor, the tiled stoves, and the paintings on the ceilings have been well preserved. The palace has on display genuine articles of Peter the Great's clothing and turner's lathes of Petrine times.

Peter the Great's Summer Palace

There are a number of other buildings of interesting design in the Summer Garden besides the Palace. Among them the Coffee House (architect Carlo Rossi, 1826) and the Tea House (architect Ludwig Charlemagne, 1827) are worthy of attention.

Since 1839 the southern entrance to the garden has been embellished with a decorative vase on a pedestal of dark red porphyry (total height 4,85 m) sculptured in the Swedish town of Alvdalen. This was a gift to Nicholas I from the Swedish King, Karl Johann. In 1855, a statue of the fabulist Ivan Krylov (sculptor Pyotr Klodt) on an interesting pedestal decorated with characters from his fables in high relief, was unveiled in the garden.

Archeological excavations are currently underway in order to determine the appearance of the fountains built in Petrine times.

Next to the Summer Garden stretches the **FIELD OF MARS** (Marsovo Polye). On the way to the field you pass Suvorov Square (Suvorovskaya Ploshchad) with its **statue of the great Russian military leader of the**

18th century, Alexander Suvorov (sculptor Mikhail Kozlovsky). In the statue, one of the masterpieces of Russian monumental sculpture, the sculptor set himself the task of portraying to the greatest possible extent the military genius of Suvorov, his courage and unbending will rather than creating a portrait likeness. On the round pedestal stands a young warrior in a helmet and armour with a drawn sword. With his shield, bearing Russia's coat of arms, the warrior is protecting the sacrificial altar, on which the Neapolitan and Sardinian Crowns and the Pope's tiara lie. This allegory symbolises the victory of Russian arms gained under Suvorov, defending against the French forces the countries that are represented by the emblems on the sacrificial altar. The symbols of human goodness—faith, hope and charity—adorn the three sides of the sacrificial altar. The granite pedestal of the monument (architect Andrei Voronikhin) is embellished with bronze bas-reliefs, allegorical depictions of Glory and Peace, crossed laurel branches and palm fronds above the inscription "Prince of Italy, Count Suvorov-Rymniksky, 1801". The overall height of the monument is 7.9 m.

From the Suvorov monument a panorama of the Field of Mars ensemble opens out. The splendid park stretches for 10 hectares, with valuable monuments of architecture girding its western and southern limits.

In the northwestern corner of the square the **Marble Palace** (No. 5, Ulitsa Khalturina) was erected in 1768-1785, designed by the architect Antonio Rinaldi. It was intended for the eminent nobleman of the 18th century, the favourite of Catherine the Great, Grigory Orlov. This building is regarded as a monument of architecture signifying the transition from Baroque to Classicism. The palace's façades are comparatively modest and laconic in design: the walls are faced with grey granite, the first and second floors are decorated with Corinthian pilasters hewn from pale pink marble. The décor of the main façade, overlooking the forecourt, is largely executed in the Baroque style.

An elegant fence surrounds the forecourt. On the eastern side of the court stands a building erected in the 1780's and rebuilt in the 1840's by Alexander Bryullov. Its western façade is decorated with a frieze by Pyotr Klodt.

Since 1937 the Marble Palace has housed the **Leningrad branch of the Central Lenin Museum**. More than 10,000 exhibits are on display in its 34 rooms, including documents, photocopies of Lenin's manuscripts and his personal effects.

The museum's exposition is dedicated to all the periods in Lenin's life and work, from the first Marxist circles to the last days of his life; the history of his struggle to set up a Marxist party in Russia, to gain the victory of the Great October Socialist Revolution and to form the socialist state; the realisation of his ideas.

The exhibition begins with materials on the childhood and youth of Vladimir Ulyanov (Lenin), on the contribution made by him to revolutionary theory. The exhibits dealing with the period of the preparation for the 2nd Congress of the Russian Social-Democratic Labour Party (1903), at which the Bolshevik Party was set up, evoke great interest. The exposition also throws light on Lenin's theoretical work and organising activity during the first Russian Revolution (1905-1907), his energetic and intensive work in preparing for and executing the October armed uprising in 1917, and, after its victory, in the post of the head of the first workers' and peasants' government.

The materials devoted to the Soviet period reflect the creative activity of the Soviet people under the leadership of the Communist Party in building socialism, the vitality of Lenin's principles and revolutionary traditions today.

The last rooms acquaint the visitor with the great ideological heritage of Lenin. In the rooms on the second floor the permanent exhibition, The Image of Lenin in the Fine Arts is on display.

In front of the museum's main entrance stands an armoured car bearing on its turret the inscription, "The Enemy of Capital". In April 1917, from this armoured car in the square of the Finland Station, Lenin pronounced his historic speech, crowning it with the appeal "Long Live the Socialist Revolution!"

In 1797-1800 on the orders of Tsar Paul I, the **Mikhailovsky Castle** was erected (architect Vasily Bazhenov, with the assistance of Vincenzo Brenna) in the southeastern corner of the Field of Mars (No. 2, Sadovaya Ulitsa). Paul believed that secret passages inside the castle, the earthern ramparts and moats surrounding it and the drawbridges would be reliable protection against the conspiracies budding at court.

Field of Mars

But the emperor resided only some forty days in his new castle. On the night of March 11, 1801, he was strangled by his close associates. A few years later the Central Engineering College was housed in the castle, which has been known since 1819 as **Engineers' Castle**. In the 1830s the future writers Fyodor Dostoyevsky and Dmitry Grigorovich, and later the outstanding Russian electrical engineer and inventor of the arc lamp, Pavel Yablochkov, studied here. Another graduate of the Engineering College was the outstanding Soviet fortifications expert, Hero of the Soviet Union, General Dmitry Karbyshev, who perished in 1945 in the Nazi concentration camp of Mauthausen. On a day when the temperature was below zero the Nazis tortured him to death by dousing him with water until he turned into a pillar of ice. Today the Engineers' Castle houses the Science and Technology Library of the Leningrad Scientific and Technical Information Centre, as well as the depositories of the Central Navy Library.

It is interesting to note that each of the four façades of the castle is of a different design. The main façade faces south. In the late 18th and early 19th centuries there was a square here where parades and changes of the guard were held. The austere façade suited the purpose of the square well.

The northern façade, looking out over the greenery of the Summer Garden, makes quite a different impression. The architect imparted a certain intimacy to it. The protruding risalits are joined up by a terrace resting on pairs of pink marble columns. The wide staircase descending to the garden is adorned with sculptures of Hercules and Flora. The high attic storey embellished with sculptures adds to the ornamentation of the northern façade.

In 1800, a **statue of Peter the Great** (sculptor Carlo Rastrelli) was erected before the main entrance to Engineers' Castle. Peter is depicted as a military leader and victor, powerful and threatening to the external and internal enemies of his state. The pedestal is decorated with bronze bas-reliefs (sculptor Mikhail Kozlovsky) showing the decisive battles of the

Statue of Alexander Suvorov

shown saving their king, Charles XII, who is wounded in the leg. In the clouds, in the upper part of the bas-relief is Cancer the Crab, the sign of the Zodiac for June, i.e. the month when the battle took place, can be seen.

On the left side of the bas-relief devoted to the battle of Gangut, Peter the Great is depicted on the flag-ship overshadowed by the Genius of Victory. On the right side of the bas-relief the capture of a Swedish ship by the Russian forces is shown. In the clouds is Leo the Lion, the sign of the Zodiac corresponding to July. The inscription carved on the pedestal on the orders of Paul I reads: "To my great-grandfather from his great-grandson"

At the turn of the 19th century the square received its present name, the Field of Mars (after the great plain near ancient Rome which served as a ground for military and gymnastic exercises and was named in honour of Mars, the god of war). This name was given in connection with the fact that monuments were erected here to the great Russian military leaders Alexander Suvorov and Pyotr Rumyantsev (the second monument was later moved to Vasilyevsky Island).

After the Patriotic War of 1812 an interesting new structure appeared in the square, the **barracks of the Pavlovsky Regiment** at No. 1, Field of Mars (Marsovo Polye), built by the architect Vasily Stasov in 1817–1820. This tremendously long edifice occupies almost the whole of the western side of the Field of Mars. A tiered attic storey towers above the twelve-column portico of the main entrance, embellished with a composition of banners and armour.

On March 23 (April 5), 1917, 180 people who had perished in the armed struggle against autocracy during the February revolution were buried in a common grave in the middle of the Field of Mars. Since that time the Field of Mars has become an arena for meetings and processions. On April 18 (May 1), 1917, May Day was legally celebrated for the first time in

Northern War (the victory at Poltava in 1709, and the sea victory at the Cape of Gangut in 1714).

In the bas-relief devoted to the battle of Poltava, the Russian troops are depicted on the right. In the foreground Peter the Great stands pointing out with his sword the way to pursue the fleeing Swedes. Next to the tsar is his friend and comrade-in-arms, Alexander Menshikov, who commanded the Russian cavalry. The genii of Victory proclaim the glory of the Russian army. In the left part of the bas-relief the Swedes are

Russia, and tens of thousands of workers gathered on the Field of Mars. One hundred and sixty-seven platforms were set up on lorries and carts. The platform of the Bolshevik Party was situated at the northwestern corner of the square with a red flag flying above it. At two o'clock in the afternoon Lenin mounted the platform. As one of the participants in the meeting recalls, Lenin said that on that day of international proletarian solidarity the workers and soldiers of Petrograd were stretching out their hands in friendship to working people throughout the world, that on that day the slogan "Workers of All Countries, Unite!" would fly round the world and would unite the working people of all countries in their struggle for peace and socialism.

Leningrad branch of the Central Lenin Museum

In 1919, in the middle of the Field of Mars a magnificent granite gravestone, designed by the architect Lev Rudnev, was erected on the graves of revolutionaries. The stone bears lofty epitaphs composed by the eminent figure in the Communist Party, Anatoly Lunacharsky.

One of these texts carved on the granite reads:

By the will of tyrants
peoples have tormented one another.
You arose, the working people
of St. Petersburg,
and, for the first time,
war was started
of all the oppressed
against all the oppressors,
to kill
the very seed of war.

In 1920, work began on landscaping the Field of Mars. In 1957, during the celebrations to mark the 40th anniversary of the Great October Socialist Revolution, the eternal flame was lit in the middle of a granite square. The green carpet covering the square, the age-old trees of the Summer and Mikhailovsky Gardens, the majestic buildings created by famous architects were all harmoniously combined into one impressive and picturesque ensemble.

Extending off the northwestern corner of the square is a street named after the worker and revolutionary Stepan Khalturin. In 1843, the great French writer Honoré de Balzac lived at No. 10, in this street, and here he met Evelina Hanska, whom he married seven years later in the Ukrainian town of Berdichev.

If you walk along the façade of the Marble Palace facing the Neva, you come out onto Palace Embankment (Dvortsovaya Naberezhnaya). Take note of No. 18, built in 1857–1861 by the architect Andrei Stakenshneider for a member of the royal family. Today this building houses a number of the scientific-research institutions of the USSR Academy of Sciences. Nearby at No. 26 is the former palace of the brother of Alexander III, the Grand Prince Vladimir (architect Alexander Rezanov, 1867–1872). This three-storey building with a portal decorated with gryphons is reminiscent

General view of the museum's rooms

in its austere appearance of a Florentine palace of the 15th century. Today this is the **Gorky House of Scientists**, a type of club for Leningrad's scientific intelligentsia.

Further along, the Palace Embankment is intersected by the small **Winter Ditch** (Zimnyaya Kanavka) linking the Neva and the Moika. This name is connected with the early chapters of the city's history. On the orders of Peter the Great, the **first Winter Palace** was built on the section between what

are today Khalturin Street and the Palace Embankment. A canal was dug by its walls in 1718 and came to be known as the Winter Ditch.

On the corner of Palace Embankment and the Winter Ditch take a look at the **Hermitage Theatre**, designed by Giacomo Quarenghi and completed in 1787. The architect built its auditorium in the form of an amphitheatre; there are no boxes, circles, or stalls, and the seats for the audience descend to the stage in wide tiers. The overall appearance and plan of the auditorium is reminiscent of the theatre in Pompeii. Its walls are finished with artificial pink and yellow marble, and embellished with Corinthian columns. In the niches between the columns stand statues of Apollo and nine muses, and the recesses above the niches are adorned with medallions and bas-reliefs of Molière, Racine, Voltaire, and other outstanding men of letters and art. The Hermitage Theatre was in fact the private theatre of Catherine the Great and her descendants. Today this is the lecture hall of the State Hermitage.

The Hermitage Theatre is linked with the building of the **Old Hermitage** (Yuri Felten, 1775–1784) by a small bridge. This bridge over the Winter Ditch affords a scenic view of the Neva and of the slender bell-tower of the Peter and Paul Fortress.

The building of the **New Hermitage**, erected in 1839–1852 to the design of Leo von Klenze by the architects Vasily Stasov and Nikolai Yefimov and intended to house the art collections of the Hermitage, abuts onto the Old Hermitage on the Khalturin Street side. This was the first building in Russia erected expressly for use as a public art gallery. The main entrance to the New Hermitage is decorated with ten huge statues of atlantes made from the model of the sculptor Alexander Terebenev. From the New Hermitage the ensemble of **PALACE SQUARE** (Dvortsovaya Ploshchad), one of Leningrad's largest (59,964 sq m), opens out.

The oldest building here is the **Winter Palace**, a grandiose edifice in the style of Russian Baroque. A variety of the façades is typical of this style; namely, the alternation of the risalits and the recessed sections of the palace's fronts, the extensive use of curvilinear forms, the abundance of decorative ornamentation, and the bicoloured paintwork.

The Winter Palace was built in 1754–1762 by the architect Bartolomeo Rastrelli. Almost 200 m long, 160 m wide and 22 m high, this was the biggest and most elegant building in St. Petersburg. The length of the main cornice encircling the building is almost 2 km. The palace contains 1,057 rooms with a floor area of 46,516 sq m, 117 staircases, 1,786 doors and 1,945 windows. For a long time the Winter Palace was the tallest edifice in the city. In 1844, Nicholas I gave orders to the effect that private houses should be at least one sazhen (2.13 m) lower than the Winter Palace. This rule was effective until 1905. Today the rooms in the Winter Palace house the collections of the Hermitage. You will learn more about this museum in an excursion specially devoted to it (Excursion No. 8).

To complete the architectural planning of the city's central square the government bought up all the private houses lining the square in the south, and in 1819 it commissioned the architect Carlo Rossi to rebuild them for the General Staff of the Russian Army. According to the architect's plan, two grandiose buildings were erected to form an arc opposite the Winter Palace. The buildings were joined up by a majestic triumphal arch, an original monument to Russia's victory over Napoleon in the war of 1812. The sculptors, Stepan Pimenov and Vasily Demut-Malinovsky, decorated it with compositions of armour, and the figures of the genii of Glory. It is crowned with six horses bearing the winged figure of Glory.

In 1829, construction work on the General Staff was completed. Besides the General Staff, the Ministry of Foreign Affairs and the Ministry of Finance were also located here.

The project put forward by the architect Auguste Montferrand for the majestic **Alexander Column**, a monument to the victory of Russia in the Patriotic War of 1812, was approved in September 1829. It took three years

SIGHTSEEING EXCURSIONS 129

3

to hew the shaft of the column from a cliff in one of the bays of the Gulf of Finland. The 704-ton monolith was brought to St. Petersburg in a barge built specially for the purpose. In August 1832, more than 2,000 soldiers, veterans of the 1812 war, and 400 workmen, using a complicated system of pulleys, rolled it onto a high platform, then lowered it onto its pedestal. The final finishing and polishing of the column was carried out after it had been set up. In 1834, it was completed, and on August 30 it was uveiled at a grand ceremony.

The monument is crowned by the figure of an angel sculptured by Boris Orlovsky and symbolising the peace that settled on Europe after the victory over Napoleon. The pedestal is decorated with bas-reliefs, the main one facing onto the Winter Palace, portraying an old water-carrier and a woman leaning on an urn, the symbolic depiction of the Niemen and the Vistula, the two rivers crossed by the Russian army during its pursuit of Napoleon's troops. This composition includes old Russian weapons (precise copies of those kept in the Armoury in the Moscow Kremlin).

The bas-relief on the Admiralty side depicts Peace and Justice. The other two bear Wisdom and Plenty, Victory and Peace recording in the annals of history the memorable years of the Patriotic War of 1812. All the bas-reliefs are the work of the sculptors Pyotr Svintsov and Ivan Leppe based on sketches by Giovanni Scotti.

At 47.5 m, the column is one of the world's tallest monuments of its type. It is not attached to the pedestal in any way; only the force of gravity keeps it in place.

When the work on the General Staff was almost completed, it was decided that the old building on the eastern corner of the square should be given a look more in keeping with the new appearance of the square. Built in the 1840s by architect Alexander Bryul-

lov, the **Guard's Headquarters** merged well with the ensemble in Palace Square. A plaque on the building serves as a reminder that at the end of October 1917 Lenin worked here when he was directing operations against the counter-revolutionary forces attacking Petrograd.

In 1905 and in 1917, this square was the site of extremely important historical events. On January 9, 1905, a peaceful procession of St. Petersburg workers, who were going to the Winter Palace to submit a petition to the tsar regarding their needs, was fired upon. More than a thousand people were killed and more than two thousand wounded. Here in Palace Square the Bolsheviks appealed to the people to take up arms and to fight on the barricades. This day has gone down in the country's history as "Bloody Sunday", and it marked the beginning of the first Russian revolution.

Twelve years later the square witnessed a historical event of paramount importance. On October 25 (November 7), 1917, operating according to a plan worked out under Lenin's guidance, workers, soldiers and sailors stormed the last citadel of counter-revolution, the Winter Palace, where the bourgeois Provisional Government was hiding out.

The first part of your excursion ends in Palace Square. However, if you have the time, you might like to visit the **flat-museum of Alexander Pushkin**, which is not far away from Palace Square at No. 12 on the embankment of the River Moika.

Here the poet lived from September 1836 to the end of January 1837. This was a particularly difficult period in Pushkin's life. He was subjected to increasing persecution on the part of the censors and reactionary circles; his relations with Tsar Nicholas I and high society had become very strained. A humiliating position in court, persecution, and slanderous insults to the honour of the poet and his

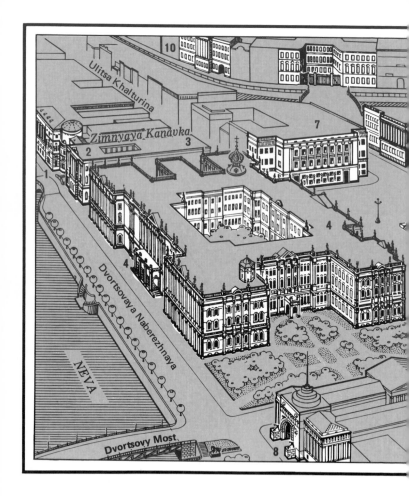

wife ultimately led to the fateful duel with George Dantes on January 27 (February 8) 1837. The mortally wounded Pushkin was brought back to this flat on the embankment of the River Moika, where he died at 2.45 a.m. on January 29 (February 10).

At the time that this book was being made ready for publication, the building was undergoing major repairs and restoration. Upon their completion, the three-storey building facing the Moika and the courtyard wings will house a Pushkin centre for the pur-

poses of study and enlightenment. The memorial flat will be returned to the appearance it knew during Pushkin's time.

The museum's exposition will include the last portrait of Pushkin made in his lifetime—the work of Ivan Linev, a portrait of his wife, painted by Alexander Bryullov; the waistcoat in which Pushkin fought the duel, as well as a locket with a lock of his hair and a death mask of the poet. Among the poet's personal belongings on display are his desk, a bronze ink-stand

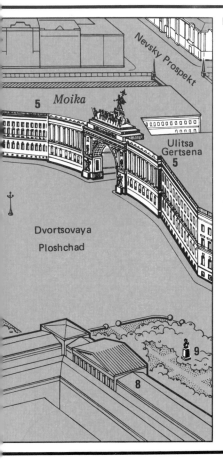

DVORTSOVAYA PLOSHCHAD

1. *Hermitage Theatre*
2. *Old Hermitage*
3. *New Hermitage*
4. *Winter Palace, State Hermitage*
5. *Former General Staff Building and the Triumphal Arch*
6. *Alexander Column*
7. *Former Guards' Headquarters*
8. *Admiralty*
9. *Statue of the poet Vasily Zhukovsky*
10. *Pushkin Flat-Museum*

with the figure of a little African boy, an ivory knife, a bronze bell, a silver sabre, a goose quill, a walking-stick with a button off of Peter the Great's coat inlaid in the handle, and a wooden casket reinforced with iron.

The museum has in its possession Pushkin's personal library, which consists of nearly 4,000 volumes. In addition to classical works of world literature, there are books on geography, astronomy, economics, chess, reference books and dictionaries. Such a variety tells of the remarkable range of the poet's interests. Furthermore, besides his native Russian, Pushkin knew French, Italian, Spanish, Latin, English, and German.

On the first and second floors of the main building is an exposition entitled Pushkin in Russian, World, and Soviet Culture. The side wings serve as the museum's storerooms, while a building in the courtyard contains a library with over 70,000 rare books, a reading-room, and a cinema/lecture hall in which scholars, writers, and artistes lecture and perform.

Zimnyaya Kanavka (Winter Ditch)

The second part of your excursion begins at the **Admiralty**. After the fortifications of the Peter and Paul Fortress had been erected in 1703, yet another defensive outpost of the city was set up in the estuary of the Neva. The building of the shipyard, which later became known as the Admiralty, was used for the purpose. As a fortress, the Admiralty played an important part in the subsequent building up of the city centre. According to the rules of military engineering of that time, it was prohibited to build up the area around a fortress so that the enemy could not approach its walls under cover of the adjacent buildings. Therefore, no buildings were constructed in the area adjacent to the Admiralty. This explains why the expanses of the Palace Square, and Decembrists' Square have remained open, as has Admiralty Square with its garden laid out in the 1870s and now named after the writer Maxim Gorky.

However, in November 1705, an earthern fortress was built on the site of the future Admiralty. Then it was repeatedly reconstructed: the pisé structures were replaced with stone ones, and the stone ones were rebuilt in their turn. In 1738, the main building was rebuilt according to the design of the architect Ivan Korobov, and a tower was raised, crowned with a golden spire. At the beginning of the 19th century a decision was taken to rebuild the Admiralty yet again, and the architect Andreyan Zakharov was commissioned to do the job.

It took from 1806 to 1823 to construct the modern building of the Admiralty. The cubic tower above the building dominates the architecture of the squares adjacent to the Admiralty and can be seen in the distance along the three thoroughfares which converge on it. The main façade, 407 m wide, is divided into six- and twelve-column porticos. Zakharov retained the former planning of the building and the old spire with a weather-vane shaped like a caravel, which rose above the city to a height of 72.5 m. It is cut from gilded sheets of brass, is 192 cm long, 158 cm high and weighs 65 kg.

The building is decorated with 56 large sculptures, 11 reliefs, and 350 moulded ornamentations by eminent Russian sculptors of that time. The sculptures on the façade are based on a common theme—the glory of the Russian Navy.

A high relief above the archway of the main entrance, devoted to the founding of the Russian Navy by Peter the Great, depicts the god of the sea, Neptune, handing over to Peter his trident, the symbol of his power over the sea. Standing next to the tsar is the goddess of wisdom, Minerva, who is appealing to Russia, a young woman sitting under a bay-tree. Russia is resting on the club of Hercules (the symbol of strength) and holds the horn of plenty which is touched by the god of commerce, Mercury, who is standing on bales of goods. Above this high relief, at the corners of the

lower cube of the tower stand the military leaders and heroes of antiquity, Achilles, Ajax, Pyrrhus, and Alexander the Great.

The colonnade of the tower's upper cube is decorated with 28 statues (corresponding to the number of columns). They depict the four elements—Fire, Water, Air, and Earth; the four seasons of the year; the four winds—the South, North, East, and West; and also the mythological patrons of shipbuilding and astronomy, the goddesses Isis and Urania. Each subject is repeated twice.

Two monumental groups 11 m high have been erected along either side of the archway of the main entrance. Each of them, depicting three nymphs, symbolises the mythological goddess Hecate, who personified water, the earth, and the sky.

On the pediments of the side porticos there are high reliefs of "The goddess of justice Themis, blessing labour" (to the right of the tower), "Themis giving rewards for feats in battle and at sea" (to the left of the tower), "Glory blessing military feats" (on the Decembrists' Square side) and "Glory crowning the sciences with laurels" (on the Palace Square side). Eminent sculptors in Russia at the time, such as Feodosy Shchedrin, Stepan Pimenov, Ivan Terebenev, and Vasily Demut-Malinovsky, contributed their works to the Admiralty.

The building opposite the Admiralty, at No. 6, Admiralty Avenue (Admiralteisky Prospekt), housed the **All-Russia Extraordinary Commission for Struggle Against Counter-Revolution and Sabotage** (VeCheKa) from December 7, 1917, to March 10, 1918. The office of the first Chairman of the VeCheKa, Felix Dzerzhinsky, was also here. In 1974, a **memorial museum** containing 43 authentic exhibits connected with the life and work of Dzerzhinsky was opened.

On the eastern side of the Admiralty the **Palace Bridge** (Dvortsovy

Hermitage (Winter Palace)

Most) (architect Robert Melzer, engineer Dmitry Pshenitsky, 1913–1917) spans the Neva, and on the western side lies **DECEMBRISTS' SQUARE** (Ploshchad Dekabristov), formerly known as Senate Square. This square was given its present name in 1925 in honour of the Russian revolutionary gentry who in December 1825 rose up in arms against autocracy for the first time in Russian history.

Life in Russia at that time, with the system of serfdom, the tyranny of the ·autocracy, and the growing anti-serf movement of the peasants, was the main motivating factor in the formation of the Decembrists' world outlook.

The patriotic upsurge of the Russian people during the war of 1812 had a tremendous influence on them. Moreover, the young officers who had taken part in campaigns abroad and become acquainted with the ideas of the French Enlightenment, could not accustom themselves to the fact that the Russian peasantry, the liberators of Europe, remained the "christened property" of the landowners.

The young noblemen set up secret political societies. In time, they gave up peaceful enlightening activity and set out to prepare an armed uprising. However, the Decembrists were not united in their views. The most radical of them were in favour of setting up a republic, while others desired a constitutional monarchy. On December 14, 1825, at a moment when Russia was without a tsar owing to the sudden death of Alexander I, the members of a secret society led some three thousand soldiers and sailors who had refused to take the oath of loyalty to the new tsar, Nicholas I, into Senate Square. The leaders of the uprising thought that they would compel the Senate (the supreme organ of government in Russia) to publish in its name the "Manifesto to the Russian People", compiled by the leaders of

the secret society, and proclaiming the end of the monarchy in Russia, the abolition of serfdom, of class inequality and a reduction in the period of military service. But the plan for the uprising was foiled by unforeseen circumstances. It appeared that the Senate had already sworn loyalty to Nicholas I, and therefore, the hopes placed in the liberation manifesto were groundless. Moreover, Prince Trubetskoi, who had been elected head of the uprising on the previous evening, did not appear in the square. The lack of determination in the Decembrists' tactics prevented them from taking the initiative and going into the attack. Government forces, which were moved to the square, outnumbered those of the rebels four to one.

On the orders of the tsar, the artillery opened fire on the mutinous regiments. In just a few minutes the square was filled with the bodies of the dead and wounded. The uprising had been suppressed by nightfall.

Five hundred and seventy-nine people were brought to trial in connection with the Decembrist affair. Five Decembrists, the leaders of the revolt, were sentenced to death. The rest were sentenced to hard labour or were stripped of their rank and forced to serve as privates.

But the Decembrists' cause did leave its mark. Through their heroism and self-sacrifice these men, the most progressive of the gentry, helped to awaken the people, and the following generations of Russian revolutionaries continued their struggle.

Now that you have acquainted yourself with the main historical events that associated with this square, take the opportunity to admire its sights. The principal architectural attraction in the square is the equestrian statue of **Peter the Great**, the creation of the great French sculptor Etienne Falconet, who embodied in his sculpture the idea of "enlight-

Archway of the former General Staff

ened absolutism" put forward by the French Encyclopaedists: the monarch is directing his country along the path of progress. Peter the Great is depicted as a rider crowned with a laurel wreath; he has halted his galloping steed, forcing it to obey his iron will. The rock is a symbol of the impediments removed and the crushed snake—defeated evil. On the pedestal, a granite rock bearing the outlines of a wave crashing down, in bronze letters in Russian and Latin a laconic inscription reads "To Peter I from Catherine II". The date—1782—signifies the year when the monument was unveiled.

Falconet worked on this sculpture intensively and selflessly. The best horses in the royal stables were placed at the disposal of the sculptor. Day after day riding-masters galloped at great speed onto a specially constructed model of the pedestal of the future monument. Falconet scrupulously copied the movements and the poses of the rearing horses, the tenseness of their muscles. Finally he

Alexander Column

found a way of depicting the horse. One of the generals, an outstanding cavalry officer who was similar in height and figure to Peter the Great, posed for the sculptor.

A word or two must be said about Falconet's assistants: his pupil Marie Collot created the head of the rider, and the outstanding Russian sculptor Fyodor Gordeyev moulded the snake. During the casting of the monument an accident happened: the molten metal poured out of a crack in the clay pipe, causing a fire in the workshop. Falconet, deciding that the product of his many years of efforts would be irrevocably destroyed, ran out of the studio in horror. But Khailov, the founder who was casting the statue, maintained his presence of mind; he tore off his clothes and stuffed them into the crack in the pipe, covering them with clay, and completed the casting.

Considerable difficulties were involved in transporting the granite block for the pedestal to the city from the environs of St. Petersburg, the village of Lahta, where it was found. Legend has it that Peter often climbed this rock to survey the environs of the new city. It seemed it would be impossible to deliver the 1,600-ton monolith to St. Petersburg. However, an unknown Russian blacksmith found a brilliant solution: he suggested that the rock should be raised by levers, mounted on a platform of logs and rolled on copper balls along rails with grooves (more than eight kilometres) to the shores of the Gulf of Finland from whence a specially constructed barge delivered it to the square by the Senate.

In the southwestern corner of the square your eye will be drawn by the **Manège** (architect Giacomo Quarenghi, 1804–1807), a building graced with marble sculptures of Dioscuri.

The myths of the ancient Greeks recount that Zeus sometimes descended from Olympus to enter into nuptial relations with women who did not belong to the realm of the gods. As a result of one such visit the twins Castor and Pollux were born to Zeus and the wife of the Spartan King, Tyndareus. They were so alike that they could not be distinguished from one another. However, Castor was mortal while Pollux had inherited immortality from his father. Both of them were excellent horsemen and brave warriors, and they loved each other and were inseparable. After Castor had perished in battle, Pollux felt so lonely, that he begged Zeus to allow him to die. By decision of the ruler of the gods, the brothers again became inseparable. From then on they would spend one day on Olympus among the immortal gods and the next among the shades of the dead in the underworld.

The Dioscuri in the eight-column portico of the Manège (sculptor Paulo Triscorni, 1810) are miniature marble copies of the statues before the Quirinal Palace in Rome (the residence of the Italian kings from 1870 to 1946).

They were erected in 1817, but in the 1840s the Synod (the supreme organ of administration of the Orthodox Church in Russia) considered it indecent that these naked Dioscuri should stand beside St. Isaac's Cathedral, so they were taken down from the pedestal and mounted on the gate-posts in nearby Horse Guards Lane (Konnogvardeiski Pereulok). In 1954, Castor and Pollux were returned to their former pedestals.

Today the Manège serves as Leningrad's **Central Exhibition Hall** where art exhibitions are organised regularly.

In 1845, on the boulevard near the Manège **two Ionic columns** bearing sculptures of the goddesses of Glory holding laurel wreaths were raised. The columns, made of polished granite from the town of Serdobol, commemorated the feats of the Horse Guards Regiment in battle during the war against Napoleon. The regimental barracks extend along the right side of Trade Union Boulevard (Bulvar Profsoyuzov), which was known as

Alexander Pushkin's Flat-Museum

Pushkin's study

Horse Guards Boulevard at that time. The statues were cast in Berlin from a model by the sculptor Christian Daniel Rauch and presented by the Prussian king to Nicholas I.

In 1763, the **Senate** (the supreme organ of government in tsarist Russia) moved from Vasilyevsky Island to the corner building by the Neva opposite the Admiralty. Early in the 19th century the government bought up a merchant's rooming house next to it and in 1829–1834 it and the Senate were rebuilt by Carlo Rossi and connected by an arch across Galley (Galernaya), now Red (Krasnaya), Street. The buildings of the **Synod and the Senate** are important elements in the appearance of Decembrists' Square. Today these premises house the **Central State History Archives of the USSR**, where millions of volumes of archive documents of the supreme and central organs of state power and government of the Russian Empire are kept. These documents provide a great deal of information about the history of Russia from the beginning of the 18th century to the Great October Socialist Revolution in 1917.

The southern part of Decembrists'

Square is framed by the huge **St. Isaac's Cathedral**. The birthday of Peter the Great (May 30) was marked by the Orthodox Church as the day of St. Isaac, who was considered to be the tsar's patron saint. According to legend, St. Isaac lived in the 4th century A.D. He protected Christians from the Roman Emperor and heretic Valens, for which he was subjected to punishment. The Emperor Theodosius set St. Isaac free from the dungeon. These subjects are depicted in the high reliefs on the eastern and western pediments.

The history of St. Isaac's Cathedral begins in 1710. A small wooden church of St. Isaac of Dalmatia was built near the Admiralty. Later it was replaced with a stone one, which had become dilapidated by the mid-18th century. Finally, at the beginning of the 19th century it was decided to build a cathedral. Many eminent architects of the time took part in the competition; the victor, however, was the talented draughtsman but little experienced architect, Auguste Montferrand. He submitted to Alexander I twenty-four projects for the cathedral bound in a fine album. The next day an order was signed to the effect that Montferrand was to be appointed the court architect.

Lack of experience and knowledge undoubtedly left its mark on Montferrand's work. Several times the construction work had to be halted owing to errors in the project. Vasily Stasov and other famous Russian architects had to correct it.

It took 40 years (from 1818 to 1858) to build this magnificent edifice with its fine colonnades, splendid bronze sculptures and golden dome, which can be seen dozens of kilometres from Leningrad.

When the building was completed, repair work, which lasted many years, was immediately started on the cathedral. Possibly, it was intentionally prolonged, for there was a superstition in court circles that the Romanov dynasty would fall as soon as the repairs on the cathedral were finished.

Forty-three types of stone and marble were used in the ornamentation of St. Isaac's Cathedral. The socle was faced with granite, while the walls, five metres thick in places, were revetted with grey marble. The inside walls and floor of the cathedral were lined with slabs of Russian, Italian, and French marbles, and the columns of the iconostasis were faced with malachite and lapis lazuli. Approximately 100 kg of pure gold were used to gild the grand dome, 21.8 m in diameter. The cathedral is embellished with 382 sculptures, paintings, and mosaics. Many sculptures, for example those on the huge bronze doors, were created with the help of galvanoplastic work. The giant (40 m × 6.5 m) bronze high reliefs on the pediments are bound to attract your attention.

Now let us take a look at the cathedral, beginning with the southern façade (bear in mind that in Orthodox churches the upper tip of the slanting cross-piece of the cross points northwards). On the southern pediment there is a high relief (sculptor Ivan Vitali) on the biblical subject "The Adoration of the Magi". In the centre of the composition Mary sits with the Child surrounded by the Wise Men who are paying tribute to the baby. Figures of the kings of Mesopotamia and Ethiopia can be defined. On the right, near Mary, stands Joseph, his head inclined; in the left part of the high relief an old man embracing a child steps forward towards the central group. The child is holding a small casket containing offerings.

The high relief above the western portico, "The meeting of St. Isaac of Dalmatia with the Emperor Theodosius", is the work of the same sculptor. This composition is called upon to depict the idea of the union of the power of state and church. In the centre of the high relief St. Isaac of Dalmatia is blessing the emperor. Behind St. Isaac warriors are kneeling in worship. Next to Theodosius is his wife Flaxilla (the sculptor imparted to them the features of Alexander I and his wife). In the left corner of the high relief you can see a partially naked man holding a model of St. Isaac's Cathedral. This is the creator of the cathedral, Auguste Montferrand. The high relief above the northern portico depicts "The Resurrection of Christ". On the eastern pediment the meeting of St. Isaac with the Emperor Valens is shown.

Auguste Montferrand lived to see the grand opening of the cathedral (May 29, 1858), though he died a month later. Before his death, Montferrand asked Alexander II for permission to be buried in one of St. Isaac's crypts. The tsar refused his request. The architect's widow, Eliza de Montferrand took her late husband's remains back to Paris.

St. Isaac's Cathedral is one of the most grandiose edifices of its time; even today it stands out for its size (the building is 111.5 m long, 97.6 m wide, and 101.5 m high). The cathe-

Palace Bridge

dral can hold 14,000 people at one time. The building weighs approximately 300,000 tons. It contains 112 polished granite columns of which the 48 lower ones are 17 m high and weigh 130 tons each. It has 562 steps up to its top. Its gilded cross is 30 m higher than the spire of the Admiralty and is only 20 m lower than that of the Peter and Paul Fortress.

Since 1931 St. Isaac's Cathedral has been open as a museum. Noteworthy in the decoration of its interior besides the extremely valuable paintings (some 20 compositions by the eminent Russian masters Karl Bryullov, Fyodor Bruni, and others) are the mosaic pictures made of pieces of smalt in 28,000 hues over an area of 600 sq m. Below the dome hangs the pendulum of Foucault (93 m long).

Next to St. Isaac's Cathedral stands an interesting building at No. 12, Admiralty Avenue (Admiralteisky Prospekt). This triangular building, designed by Auguste Montferrand and erected in 1817–1820, has gone down in the history of architecture as the **residence of Prince Alexei Lobanov-Rostovsky**. The main façade of the house looking out onto the Admiralty is adorned with a fine portico of eight

Corinthian columns mounted on an arcade protruding far enough for coaches to ride right up to the front door along the wide ramp. On granite pedestals white marble lions guard the central archway like sentinels (sculptor Paolo Triscorni, 1810). One of them has placed its paw on a ball, while the other is rolling a ball, which has escaped it. The sculptor did not introduce these balls without reason: the lions, leaning on a round object, had to be at the ready all the time, i.e. to guard their masters.

The southern façade of St. Isaac's Cathedral looks out onto **ST. ISAAC'S SQUARE** (Isaakiyevskaya Ploshchad). The oldest building here, the **Myatlevs' House** at No. 9, was erected in the 1760s in the northwestern corner of the square. Its façades are embellished with large medallions and busts, long reliefs depicting classical processions and compositions of armour. The French philosopher and materialist Denis Diderot lived in this house in 1773–1774 on a visit to St. Petersburg.

At the very back of the square, beyond the Blue Bridge, stands the former **Mariinsky Palace**, built by the architect Andrei Stakenschneider for

Admiralty

Maria, the daughter of Nicholas I, in 1839–1844. In 1884, her descendants sold the palace to the Exchequer, and it became the seat of the State Council, the supreme legislative body of the Russian Empire.

From the vestibule of the palace an elegant white marble staircase embellished with moulding and sculptures of ancient warriors leads to the first floor, to the vast reception room decorated with pilasters of dark crimson Italian marble and a sculptured frieze with episodes from Homer's *Iliad*.

Next to the reception room is the palace's most spectacular room—a rotunda of white marble decorated with Corinthian columns.

In 1917, for some time after the February Revolution, the Mariinsky Palace served as the residence of the Provisional Government. Later on, this was the seat of the pre-parliament, the consultative body under the Provisional Government. On October 25 (November 7), 1917, after seizing the Mariinsky Palace, the insurgents drove out this pre-parlia-

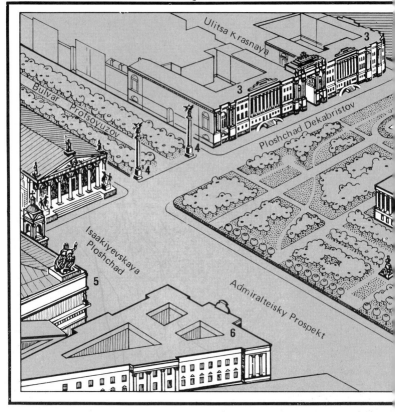

ment. In December 1917, Lenin participated in a meeting of the Bureau of the Supreme Economic Council in this building at which the decree on the nationalisation of the banks was passed.

Today the flag of the Russian Soviet Federal Socialist Republic flies over the former Mariinsky Palace. The façade of the building bears the emblem of the Russian Federation and depictions of the orders Leningrad has been awarded. This is the seat of the Executive Committee (the administrative body) of the Leningrad City Soviet of People's Deputies.

The City Soviet is the organ of state power within the bounds of Leningrad. It manages all the land, all the enterprises of local industry, the trade network, transport, construction work, housing distribution, schools, hospitals, cinemas and theatres, and the militia is subordinate to it.

The Leningrad Soviet is elected by direct and equal elections by secret ballot for a period of two and a half years.

Along the eastern and western sides of the square two identical buildings were erected in 1844–1853, designed by the architect Nikolai Yefimov for the Ministry of State Property. Today the **Vavilov Institute of Plant Breeding** at No. 42 and No. 44, Herzen Street (Ulitsa Gertsena), is housed here. The institute develops new, high yielding and winter-hardy varieties of seeds. In its selection work the institute has at its disposal a

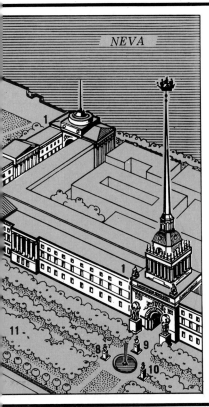

PLOSHCHAD DEKABRISTOV

1. *Admiralty*
2. *Equestrian Statue of Peter the Great ("the Bronze Horseman")*
3. *Buildings of the former Synod and Senate*
4. *Columns bearing sculptures of the goddesses of Glory*
5. *St. Isaac's Cathedral*
6. *Former residence of Prince Lobanov-Rostovsky*
7. *Statue of the geographer Nikolai Przhevalsky*
8. *Statue of the writer Nikolai Gogol*
9. *Statue of the composer Mikhail Glinka*
10. *Statue of the poet Mikhail Lermontov*
11. *Maxim Gorky Gardens*

unique collection of seeds brought from different corners of the world. The institute's numerous experimental stations breed the best sorts of seeds for cereals, beans, oil-bearing plants, vegetable cultures, perennial grasses, and potatoes.

No. 42, Herzen Street is the **Leningrad branch of the Central Scientific Agricultural Library**, which has stocks of 1,000,000 books.

In 1859, a **monument to Nicholas I** (sculptor Pyotr Klodt) was erected in the square, an example of an equestrian statue on two supports. The tsar is depicted in cavalry uniform and a helmet bearing an eagle, in the pose of a rider sitting primly and haughtily. The sculptor conveyed the tsar's love

for military exercises, his vanity, cruelty, and arrogance. The high pedestal is embellished with allegorical figures (Faith, Wisdom, Justice, and Power) whose faces are those of the wife and daughters of Nicholas I. Individual events in his rule, the most flattering for the monarch (according to his close associates) are recorded in the large high relief: Nicholas' speech before his courtiers after the revolt of December 14, 1825 was put down; the suppression of popular unrest in Hay Square (Sennaya Ploshchad, now Peace Square) in 1831; the ceremony of presenting an award to the aristocrat Mikhail Speransky in 1832 for the publication of *A Complete Collection of the Laws of the Russian Empire*

(45 volumes); the tsar examining a bridge on the railway from St. Petersburg to Moscow.

Not long before the First World War a stout building of red granite was built in the square for the German Embassy (architect Peter Berens, 1911–1912). Today this building houses the **Leningrad Amalgamation of the USSR Company for Foreign Travel "Intourist"** which receives and provides foreign tourists with services (No. 11).

Near St. Isaac's Square in an old house at No. 7, Communications Un-

ion Street (Ulitsa Soyuza Svyazi) is the **Popov Central Communications Museum**. Founded in 1877, the museum possesses an extremely valuable collection of exhibits on the history of the development of communications in Russia and the USSR. Here you can see Soviet radio receivers, amplifiers, the latest models of television sets, the latest achievements of Soviet science and technology in the field of high-frequency multi-wave bands and radio-relay communications. Among the museum's exhibits are the world's first telegraph equipment invented by

Decembrists' Square

the Russian scientists Pavel Shilling (1832) and Boris Yakobi (1850), the very first radio receiver, assembled by Alexander Popov in 1895, and also the historical cathode-ray tube of the first television set, constructed back in 1925 by Boris Grabovsky and manufactured at the Svetlana Factory in Leningrad. The museum boasts the USSR state collection of post marks, a unique collection of 4,000,000 stamps and also postcards and stamped envelopes from all over the world beginning from the 1840s.

Opposite the Communications Mu-seum, on the corner of Communications Union Street and Podbelsky Lane at No. 9 is the **General Post Office** (architect Nikolai Lvov, 1782–1789). Originally, there was a courtyard, stables and workshops in the centre of the building, and the upper storeys contained barracks and flats of the post office staff.

In 1801–1803, the post office was partly rebuilt according to the project of the architect Yegor Sokolov. In 1859, the architect Albert Kavos constructed a gallery in the form of an archway, which joins the post office

Equestrian statue of Peter the Great (the Bronze Horseman)

to the house on the opposite side of what is today Communications Union Street. This gallery was built so that the director of the post office could reach his office from his flat without going out into the street. In 1962, the **Clock of the World** was mounted on the archway. The clock has two faces: on the outer, square one, the hands indicate Moscow time, and the inner, round one, shows the time in the world's major cities (the light half is a.m., the dark half p.m.).

In 1903, the post office premises were reconstructed to give them a modern look. The courtyard was roofed with glass, the sheds, stables, and flats were rebuilt to form offices. Thus the extensive inner courtyard has been transformed into the central postal operations room of the present General Post Office.

When you return to St. Isaac's Square, take a look at No. 5—the **State Theatrical, Musical and Cinematography Institute**. The institute houses the **Museum of Musical Instruments**, which has one of the world's largest and most complete collections (approximately 3,000 musical instruments from almost all countries).

In the second half of the last century musical instruments began to be collected at the Moscow and St. Petersburg conservatoires. Similar collections were also accumulated at the Academy of Sciences, and the Ethnographic Department of the Russian Museum. In 1902 these small collections of musical instruments were brought together into a single collection, which became the State Musical Museum in 1918.

The collection contains quite a few exceptionally valuable exhibits: for example, an Italian spinet (one of the precursors of the modern piano) made in 1532, a German spinet of the 17th century richly inlaid with mother-of-pearl; a transverse flute, the work of the well-known musical master Jean Hotteterre who was at the court of the French King Louis XIV; and one of the three surviving guitars of the French master Georges Vauboam, luxuriously decorated with tortoise shell, mother-of-pearl and ivory, created in 1681.

In the Eastern Hall of the museum you will find the creations of Japanese masters: the *samisen*, the *koto*, and the *biva*. There is also a selection of free hanging gongs and exotic instruments made of bird's beaks. Chinese masters are presented by vertical and transverse flutes of bamboo, stringed and bow instruments, and stringed instruments played by plucking including some with snake-skin membranes, various gongs, and drums of various periods in the country's history.

The Indian exhibition has on display a unique instrument in which a thread of real spider's web is used. The collections of folk instruments from Iran, Iraq, and countries of Africa are interesting. Visitors to the museum are also given an opportunity to hear the sounds of these unique instruments.

The museum possesses an extremely well-stocked gramophone record and tape library, which is used during excursions and for recitals held at the museum.

From St. Isaac's Square your excursion continues along Trade Union Boulevard (Bulvar Profsoyuzov) (approximately 650 metres long) begin-ning at the Manège in the northwestern corner of the square and leading to Labour Square (Ploshchad Truda). In the early years of the city's existence these were the outskirts adjacent to the Admiralty's shipyards. One of the auxiliary enterprises, which later became known as the Galley Shipyard, was set up in 1713 to build small and medium-size vessels. A road used to run from the Admiralty to the Galley Shipyard which came to be known as Galley (now Krasnaya) Street. The Admiralty and Galley Shipyard were linked by a waterway. In 1717 the New Admiralty Canal was dug along what is now Trade Union Boulevard to the river Moika and joined the Moika to the Neva at the Galley Shipyard. Soon a canal was built by the contractor Kryukov between the rivers Moika and Neva; it became known as the Kryukov Canal. This canal approached the Neva across the area that is now Labour Square. As a result, a small triangular island has been formed on the edge of the square framed by the Moika, the Kryukov and the New Admiralty (now Krushtein) canals. The islet, called **"New Holland"**, has preserved its name since the beginning of the 18th century.

Surrounded by water, "New Holland" offered a convenient site for storing inflammable materials. In 1730, wooden sheds were built here to store the timber for the ships, and it was later decided to erect large stone buildings on the site of the dilapidated wooden sheds. In 1763, the architect Savva Chevakinsky set out to tackle this task in an original way: he suggested that instead of storing the logs in a horizontal position, it would be easier to season and sort them if they were standing vertically, at a slight incline.

Since timber of different sizes for the shipyards was to be stored, Chevakinsky designed buildings of different heights, rising rhythmically in

Manège (Central Art Exhibition)

steps. The project included a water body in the centre of the islet where more than 30 barges could be unloaded simultaneously. This water body is linked by channels with the River Moika and the Kryukov Canal. The channel linking it with the Moika is spanned by a sturdy arch, one of the most interesting decorative structures in Leningrad.

"New Holland" is not only an architectural monument but also a historical and revolutionary one. From here the navy telegraphists transmitted Lenin's decrees, the appeals of the Bolshevik Party. On November 9 (22), 1917, Lenin came to the radio station "New Holland" and here, in the name of the Soviet of People's Commissars, wrote the appeal in which he suggested that all the revolutionary soldiers and sailors should begin negotiations on a truce with the enemy. This appeal was immediately broadcast.

The buildings along the Moika were completed in 1780, but the building facing onto the Kryukov and New Admiralty canals was finished in the 1840s. Somewhat earlier, at the end of the 1820s, the circular building of the naval prison was built by the architect Alexander Shtaubert on "New Holland" (opposite No. 25 and No. 27 on the embankment of the Krushtein Canal). This is how the overall look of "New Holland" took shape.

There was not a single permanent bridge over the Neva at that time. The need was increasingly felt for better communications between Vasilyevsky Island and the Admiralty Side. In 1842, a project was approved for a permanent bridge across the Neva, designed by the engineer Stanislav Kerbedz. One of his contemporaries wrote about the construction of the bridge in his memoirs that, having approved the project, Nicholas I ordered that the builder's rank should be raised after each subsequent buttress had been completed. After this resolution had been accepted, the writer of the memoirs informs us that Kerbedz introduced a few additional buttresses into the project, and having begun the construction work as an engineer-lieutenant, he completed it as an engineer-general. To check the strength and reliability of this structure, the tsar ordered that a string of heavy carts harnessed to oxen should be drawn across the bridge and that Kerbedz should accompany them. The bridge, soon called the Nicholas Bridge, withstood this test, and the ceremonial opening took place in 1850.

In connection with the building of the bridge, the Kryukov and New Admiralty canals, which run across the square, were enclosed in pipes. The Konnogvardeisky Boulevard (today Trade Union Boulevard), was laid out where the New Admiralty Canal used to flow.

The bridge immediately turned the former outskirts of the city into one of its central squares. In 1853–1861, a palace, a monumental building girded by a wrought-iron railing on a granite foundation was erected here by Andrei Stakenschneider for the eldest son of Nicholas I. The main staircase

Building of the former Senate

and the vestibule of the palace decorated with stucco moulding and columns of grey marble are outstanding achievements of the architect.

Later on, the palace became the home of Xenia, the daughter of Alexander III, and in 1895, the Xenia Institute for Noble Young Ladies (an educational institution where daughters of the gentry could obtain an education) was opened here. In December 1917, by decree of the Soviet of People's Commissars, signed by Lenin, the palace was handed over to the Petrograd Trade Union Council and named the **Palace of Labour** and the former Annunciation Square became **LABOUR SQUARE** (Ploshchad Truda).

During one of his last visits to Petrograd on March 13, 1919, Lenin looked round the Palace of Labour and addressed the First Congress of Agricultural Workers of the Petrograd Province convened in the palace's assembly hall.

Today this building houses the Leningrad Regional Trade Union Council, which has a membership of more than 3,000,000 people.

In the USSR vitally important questions concerning the people are resolved with the direct participation of the trade unions. The trade unions ensure adherence to the labour laws. No person can be dismissed from his job without the written permission of the trade union committee. The trade unions take part in the management of production, being involved in all aspects of it such as planning, the cost and quality of output, the distribution of profits, rate-setting, and so forth. They make sure that the management observes safety regulations. In particular, the board of inspectors of trade unions has the power to close departments, workshops or even enterprises in the event of serious violations of the regulations. The trade unions play a decisive part in distributing housing, are in charge of all the funds allotted for social insurance in the state budget, and manage an extensive network of holiday homes, boarding houses, sanatoriums and check-up centres; they organise activities for children at summer camps during the summer holidays; they have at their disposal thousands of clubs, large and small community centres, and amateur sports societies.

Not far from Labour Square is the only **Higher Trade Union School of Culture** in the country at No. 22, Red Street. This institution trains special-

ists for work in cultural and educational institutions.

Near the Palace of Labour on the embankment of the Neva a granite stele has been erected. It marks the historical mooring of the cruiser *Aurora* on the memorable night in October 1917.

In the years of Soviet rule old Galley Street has been renamed Red Street and the Nicholas Bridge built across the Neva by Kerbedz, is now the Lieutenant Schmidt Bridge, named after the legendary revolutionary who headed the uprising in the Black Sea Fleet in October 1905. In the 1930s, this bridge had to be dismantled, since it could no longer accommodate the increasingly heavy traffic. The bridge was moved from the Neva to the Volga to the town of Kalinin. In 1938, the construction of the new Lieutenant Schmidt Bridge was completed.

You will find the old house near Labour Square (No. 44, Naberezhnaya Krasnogo Flota), now the **State History Museum of Leningrad**, of great interest. The building was erected in the 18th century, and in 1826–1827 it was reconstructed by the architect Vasily Glinka. The main entrance to the museum is decorated with a 12-column Corinthian portico, supporting a triangular pediment, on which there is a high relief of *Apollo in Parnassus* by the sculptor Ivan Martos.

The museum was founded in 1918 and contains some 2,000 mementos, drawings, documentary photographs, and other items of historical value. There are numerous models and dioramas depicting various districts of the city with documentary accuracy.

The display Leningrad in the Years of Soviet Rule opens with documents describing the struggle of the working people, headed

SIGHTSEEING EXCURSIONS 153

ISAAKIYEVSKAYA PLOSHCHAD

1. St. Isaac's Cathedral
2. Museum of Musical Instruments
3. Leningrad Amalgamation of the USSR Company for Foreign Travel "Intourist"
4. Former Mariinsky Palace. The Executive Committee of the Leningrad City Soviet of People's Deputies
5. and 6. Vavilov Institute of Plant Breeding
7. Monument to Nicholas I
8. Blue Bridge
9. Astoria Hotel
10. The General Post Office and the Popov Central Communications Museum

by the Bolshevik Party, for the victory of the Socialist Revolution and the establishment of Soviet rule (you can learn about the history of St. Petersburg and Petrograd from 1703 to 1917 at the branch of the History Museum of Leningrad located in the Peter and Paul Fortress).

A focal point in the exposition is occupied by the materials on the victorious October armed uprising in Petrograd, the culminating stage of the Great October Socialist Revolution. The expositions in the following sections tell about the radical changes that took place in the city after the establishment of Soviet power, in the period of peaceful socialist construction, when Leningrad became one of the most important country's scientific and technological centres. Documents, models, and photographs vividly recount the development of Leningrad's industry, the municipal economy, and the development of science, culture, and art.

A large section in the museum (13 rooms) is devoted to the 900-day siege of the city in the years of the Great Patriotic War of 1941–1945. Documents, photo-

graphs, relics, paintings, sculptures, and graphics impressively depict the fortitude and courage of the people of Leningrad during the blockade.

Maps, diagrams, models, photographs, and documents tell about the heroism of the soldiers on the Leningrad Front and the sailors of the Baltic Fleet, about the feats of the divisions of the People's Volunteers and the partisan detachments, about the fighting and patriotic unity of the inhabitants of the city and the warriors who defended Leningrad from the Nazi invaders.

The exhibits in the next rooms are devoted to the heroic efforts of the people of Leningrad in rebuilding the city.

The exposition devoted to present-day Leningrad gives an idea of the city's tremendous scientific and technological, production and cultural potential. Everything here is evidence of dynamic progress: the plans for the development of the city, the models of new architectural ensembles, the details of space apparatuses, samples of goods produced by Leningrad's enterprises, photographs of the world's largest telescope, the Kirovets tractor, gas- and hydro-turbines, atomic vessels, and much more.

The city's social and intellectual life, its culture and art, and the services provided for the population are also represented at the museum.

From Labour Square the short Labour Street (Ulitsa Truda) leads to Potseluyev Bridge. When you cross this small bridge embellished with granite obelisks, take note of the **yellow building with white columns** on the opposite bank of the River Moika (architects Jean-Baptiste Vallin de la Mothe and Andrei Mikhailov Junior). The building acquired its appearance mainly in the 1760s, but was later subject to reconstruction. Especially noteworthy in its architecture and design is the luxurious hall with white columns and sophisticated interior décor: a light colonnade running round the sides of the hall, the finely worked gilded chandeliers, the decorative moulding, and the murals on the walls and the ceiling. This interior was created in the 1830s by the architect Andrei Mikhailov Junior.

In the years before the Revolution the palace belonged to Prince Felix Yusupov, one of the richest men in Russia. He was thought to be even as rich as the tsar. In Russia Yusupov owned 57 palaces, including four in St. Petersburg. The palace on the Moika was the prince's favourite residence in the capital. Yusupov was known not only for his wealth but also for his eccentricity. Once when he was in Italy he admired a marble staircase in one of the palaces. When the owner refused to sell the staircase, the prince promptly bought the entire residence for a fabulous sum but took from it only the staircase of white Carrara marble which leads up to Yusupovs' private theatre. In this theatre many outstanding Russian and foreign artistes gave performances. In the spring of 1836, the première of the first act of Mikhail Glinka's opera *Ivan Susanin* took place here with the

St. Isaac's Square

St. Isaac's Cathedral

composer himself singing one of the parts.

After the assassination in this palace of the retainer of Nicholas II, the adventurer Grigory Rasputin (December 1916), Yusupov emigrated from Russia. After the October Revolution the palace became the property of the people. Today the palace houses the **Community Centre of Workers in Education**. Hundreds of Leningrad teachers visit the centre every day, exchange experience in the upbringing and tuition of schoolchildren, attend various courses and lectures,

and take part in amateur activities. The centre's amateur dramatic society puts on plays in English and French.

The Potseluyev Bridge leads out into **THEATRE SQUARE** (Teatralnaya Ploshchad), which took on its present appearance primarily in the second half of the 19th century. Of the buildings erected at an earlier period, noteworthy is the **Cathedral of St. Nicholas** (1753–1762) on Glinka Street. This exquisite Baroque cathedral was designed by the architect Savva Chevakinsky. It is an elegant turquoise and white building with a light bell-tower that appears to soar upwards. But the fame of Theatre Square does not lie solely in its works of architecture. It has a place of honour in the development of Russian and Soviet musical art. The **Kirov Opera and Ballet Theatre** and the **Rimsky-Korsakov Conservatoire** are located here.

This square has long been the home of the stage. Back in 1765, a wooden theatre was built here where carnivals took place and amateur troupes performed. Seventeen years later a stone theatre mushroomed on its site and was rightly called the Bolshoi (Grand) Theatre, since it remained the largest theatre in Europe for a long time. The building was many times rebuilt, was burned down and rose again from the ashes. Operas and ballets as well as plays were staged at the Bolshoi Theatre. The stars of the Russian stage appeared there.

In the 1880s the Bolshoi Theatre was rebuilt as the St. Petersburg Conservatoire, the first institution of higher musical education in Russia, founded in 1862 on the initiative of the composer Anton Rubinstein. The lists of its first graduates are enhanced by the name of Pyotr Tchaikovsky.

After the Revolution of 1917 the graduates of the Conservatoire made a great contribution to the development of Soviet musical culture. The outstanding Soviet composer, Dmitri Shostakovich, also a graduate of the Conservatoire, taught there. In 1937, the Leningrad Conservatoire was awarded the Order of Lenin, and since 1944 it has borne the name of the eminent Russian composer Rimsky-Korsakov. An opera studio and a secondary music school have been set up at the Conservatoire.

Up until the mid-19th century a two-storey stone house stood opposite the Bolshoi Theatre. It was used primarily for circus performances. Af-ter the fire of 1859 this building was reconstructed according to the design of the architect Albert Kavos and in 1860 it was handed over to the **Mariinsky Theatre** which was named after the wife of Alexander II, Maria. In the early years of its existence the theatre staged only operas and it did not begin to stage ballet until 1880. In 1919, the Mariinsky Theatre was renamed the State Academic Opera and Ballet Theatre, and in 1935 it was called the Kirov Theatre.

Appearing on the stage of the Mariinsky and later the Kirov Theatre, have been such great masters of Russian and Soviet vocal and choreographic art as Fyodor Chaliapin, Leonid Sobinov, Anna Pavlova, Galina Ulanova, Vakhtang Chabukiani, and many other outstanding artistes. Today the Kirov Theatre is one of the country's leading theatres, its repertoire including approximately 50 operas and ballets by Russian, Soviet, and foreign composers.

This building also houses a museum whose exhibits tell about the theatre's past and present. In the so-called Glass Gallery is an exposition devoted to the life and work of the outstanding singer Fyodor Chaliapin. The exposition contains numerous photographs, documents, and various mementoes. Among them is a piece of plaster taken from the wall on which Chaliapin had drawn Dosifeus, one of the heroes from Modest Moussorgsky's opera *Khovanshchina*, and the costume in which Chaliapin sang in *Boris Godunov* (the opera by the same composer). Godunov's attire of golden brocade studded with sparkling jewels weighs almost 16 kg.

In Theatre Square **monuments to Mikhail Glinka** (sculptor Robert Bakh, 1906) and **Nikolai Rimsky-Korsakov** (sculptors Veniamin Bogolyubov and Victor Ingal, 1952) have been erected.

In the years since the Revolution the architectural complex of old Theatre Square has been enriched. The

Interior of St. Isaac's Cathedral

muddy market place in front of the Mariinsky Theatre, on the corner of Decembrists' Street and Kryukov Canal Embankment, was replaced by the **Community and Technological Centre** with an auditorium seating 1,200 people. In November 1980, the centre marked its 50th anniversary. Opposite it, on the left side of Decembrists' Street, on the site of the prison burned down during the February Revolution of 1917, modern blocks of flats have risen. Beyond them stretches the complex of educational buildings and sports grounds of the **Institute of Physical Education**, the oldest institution of higher learning in the USSR training P.E. teachers and serving as an important centre of scientific-research work. In 1919, the Institute was given the name of its founder, one of the creators of theoretical anatomy, the author of the scientific system of physical training, Pyotr Lesgaft (1837–1909). Among the graduates of the Institute are outstanding sportsmen, champions of the USSR, Europe and the world, and Olympic champions.

At No. 57, behind the Lesgaft Insti-

Executive Committee of the Leningrad Soviet of People's Deputies (former Mariinsky Palace)

tute, the great Russian poet Alexander Blok (1880-1921) lived from 1912 to the end of his days. In 1980, a memorial museum was opened here. Flat No. 21 where the poet lived had been restored in detail. In the study by the left window stands the desk at which the poet's most remarkable works were written. On the desk is a glass ink-pot, a black pen, a crystal stamp bearing the sign of the zodiac, a china ashtray shaped like a dachshund with red eyes. On the wall above a walnut divan hangs a picture by Nikolai Roerich, *The Towns of Italy*; on the floor is an oriental carpet. The dining-room is furnished with a table, bentwood chairs, and a what-not stand of mahogany. The lampshade on a standard lamp by the couch was made by the poet's wife, the daughter of the famous chemist Dmitry Mendeleyev. Here you will see a Schröder grand piano on which there is a lorgnette in a tortoise-shell frame, and a bronze incense-burner; a fan of black ostrich feathers lies on the couch.

In these rooms the poet spent seven of the most active and fruitful years of his life. Here, having completed the poem, *The Twelve*, Blok wrote in his diary, "Today I am a genius ..."

Flat No. 23 on the first floor, where Blok died, houses the literary part of the museum. In the four exhibition rooms you can learn about the life and work of the poet: 1880-1904—the period of symbolism and abstract romanticism; 1905-1907—the emergence of social themes and life-asserting motifs reflecting the sympathetic attitude of Blok to the revolutionary liberation movement; 1908-1916—the period of the poet's increasing recognition of his personal involvement in the fate of Russia, eventually leading him to recognition of the Great October Socialist Revolution and confidence in its triumph. The years 1917-1921 form the Soviet period in Blok's creative work, and are dealt with in a special room. In one of the rooms the visitor can see the poet's death mask.

Not far away from Blok's house Decembrists' Street is intersected by Maklin Avenue (Prospekt Maklina) where you will find two houses connected with Lenin. In 1905-1906 he frequently visited No. 27/27 on English Avenue (as Maklin Avenue was

Kirov Opera and Ballet Theatre

called at the times), where there was a private secondary school. Lenin frequently attended illegal meetings of the Central and St. Petersburg Committees of the Bolshevik Party and also various party meetings, sessions and conferences in this house. Almost directly opposite the school stands No. 32, which in those years housed the higher courses of Pyotr Lesgaft. Lenin attended various party meetings there as well.

Your excursion ends here near the embankments of the Neva's left bank.

4

LENIN SQUARE—THE TAURIDA PALACE—THE SMOLNY INSTITUTE

*Estimated time of the excursion—two and a half hours. Nearest Metro station—*Ploshchad Lenina.

Tourist attractions: the Finland Station, the statue of Lenin, the former barracks of the Cavalry Guards' Regiment (19th century), the Taurida Palace (18th century), the Taurida Garden, the Smolny Convent, the Smolny (18th century).

This excursion will not only take you through the squares and streets of Leningrad but you will trace the path traversed from the February bourgeois-democratic revolution of 1917 to the Great October Socialist Revolution (1917), when the rule of the working people was established in Russia under the leadership of the Bolshevik Party.

The excursion begins at **LENIN SQUARE** (Ploshchad Lenina) in front of the Finland Station.

At the time of the February revolution, Lenin was living in emigration in Switzerland, and from here he guided the activities of the Bolshevik Party in Russia. When news reached him that the tsar had been overthrown, in spite of the difficulties connected with travelling in wartime, Lenin returned to Russia.

On April 3 at 23.10 Lenin's train pulled into the Finland Station, where a guard of honour of sailors and soldiers had already been formed. When Lenin stepped out of the train numerous voices were raised in the shout of hurrah. After the band had finished playing the *Marseillaise*, Lenin made several short speeches of greeting on the platform. Then he was accompanied into the station, where delegations from Bolshevik Party organisations, representatives of the Petrograd Soviet of Workers' and Soldiers' Deputies were awaiting the leader of the Revolution. Lenin greeted them.

In the square in front of the station Lenin was met by the cheers of many thousands of workers, soldiers, and sailors. They lifted him onto an armoured car. The silhouette of Lenin lit by floodlights could clearly be seen against the dark background of the night sky.

The correspondent of the Bolshevik newspaper *Pravda* wrote in his report on the meeting: "Standing on the armoured car, Comrade Lenin greeted the revolutionary Russian proletariat

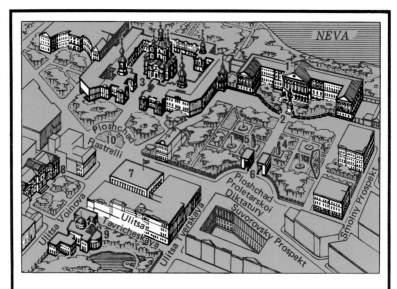

SMOLNY DISTRICT

1. *Smolny Institute*
2. *Monument to Lenin*
3. *Smolny Convent*
4. *Monument to Karl Marx*
5. *Monument to Friedrich Engels*
6. *Propylaea*
7. *House of Political Education of the Leningrad Regional and City Committees of the CPSU*
8. *Kikin Palace*
9. *Taurida Palace*
10. *Monument to Felix Dzerzhinsky*

and the revolutionary Russian army, who have not only liberated Russia from tsarist despotism but also laid the foundations for a social revolution on an international scale ..."

Lenin concluded his speech to the workers and soldiers of Petrograd with the fiery appeal: "Long Live the Socialist Revolution!"

The square in front of the Finland Station and the station building looked quite different in 1917 than they do today. The railway went right down to the bank of the Neva. On the spot where an alley and fountains have been laid out stood warehouses, piles of sleepers and dingy railway buildings.

After Lenin's death (January 21, 1924), at the request of its inhabitants, the city was renamed Leningrad. At that time, it was decided to erect a **statue of Lenin**. On April 16, 1924, in the square of the Finland Station, which had been named Lenin Square, its foundation stone was laid in the form of a black granite boulder bearing the inscription "To Lenin". On the very same day a competition was announced for a project for the statue. After lengthy consideration, the project put forward by the sculptor Sergei Yevseyev and the architects Vladimir Shchuko and Vladimir Gelfreikh was selected as the most interesting. In May 1925 a model of the monument was completed. The statue was cast at the Leningrad Krasny Vyborzhets Plant. During the casting of the statue (4.35 m high), several blocks of greyish black granite for the pedestal (5.12 m high) were brought from the diabase deposit on the shores of Lake Onega. On November 7, 1926, the unveiling of the statue took place.

The statue of Lenin rises on a granite pedestal shaped like the round turret of an armoured car. The details of the monument are somewhat displaced, giving the viewer the impression of movement. On the bronze protrusion imitating the radiator of the vehicle, the words of Lenin's appeal are inscribed: "Long Live the Socialist Revolution!" Lenin is depicted uttering these words, his cap shoved into the pocket of his open coat, the thumb of his left hand is tucked in his waistcoat, and his right hand raised in an energetic forward movement.

The statue became the focal point of the district in front of the station. In 1927, the reconstruction of the territory adjacent to the station began: the goods station was moved to another site, the sheds and warehouses were demolished, a brick wall which stood a few metres from the monument and concealed it from the Neva was taken down. A wide new street was laid out on the river bank lined with trees and shrubs. This street was named Lenin Alley. Thus the Neva serves as a background for the statue (this is typical of many works of monumental sculpture in Leningrad).

When the Patriotic War of 1941–1945 began, the statue was protected with wooden boards held together by iron rings and topped with a wooden box of sand. This preserved the statue from the Nazi bombs and shells. During the war the Finland Station was the only one operating in the city. Through this station communications with the rest of the country were maintained along the Road of Life across Lake Ladoga. On February 7,

1943, after the ring of the enemy blockade was broken, the first train carrying foodstuffs arrived here.

After the war the square was reconstructed. According to the project of the architect Nikolai Baranov, Lenin's statue was moved to a new site, closer to the bank of the Neva (originally it stood approximately where the corner entrance to the Metro is situated today). The statue was placed on a green mound surrounded by gardens, descending to the Neva with an impressive granite staircase.

In the post-war years the building on the eastern side of the square was completed. On the site of little wooden houses modern buildings were erected, one of them the **House of Soviets of the Kalinin District**, which contains the district's administrative offices and a concert hall seating 800.

In 1955–1960, the new building of the Finland Station went up. Its huge central waiting-room is spanned by a vault 35 × 35 m and its clock-tower is crowned with a 30-metre spire of stainless steel. The façade of the building is divided up by 17 windows; above each of them is a sculptured panel depicting events in the revolutionary struggle of the people. During the construction work the part of the old station containing the exit through which Lenin passed (the western side of the station) was preserved.

Lenin went to the Finland Station many times. During his secret trips, when he crossed the Russia's border with Finland, he twice travelled with the steam-engine No. 293. In 1924, this steam-engine, along with all the other property of the Finland railway, was handed over by the Soviet government to the government of Finland. In 1957, the government of Finland presented the steam-engine No. 293 to the Soviet Union. This steam-engine stands in a specially constructed glass pavilion by the platform of the Finland Station.

Lenin Square at the Finland Railway Station

The armoured car from which Lenin made his speech in April 1917 was used in the October armed uprising; in 1939, after being overhauled, it was placed in front of the entrance to the Leningrad branch of the Central Lenin Museum (the Marble Palace). In 1972, the armoured car was removed to the vestibule of the museum to shelter it from the elements.

When you have taken a look at Lenin Square, walk along the Arsenal Embankment (Arsenalnaya Naberezhnaya) of the Neva to **Foundry Bridge** (Liteiny Most). At the back of the embankment named after the great Russian surgeon Nikolai Pirogov (1810–1881) rises the 17-storey **Hotel Leningrad**. Opposite the hotel, on a stone pedestal stands a model of the old 36-gun frigate *Kreiser*. Next to the frigate is a semicircular pool decorated with a bronze allegorical figure personifying the Neva.

Your path lies across Foundry Bridge (constructed in 1879) to the left bank of the Neva. For many years the bridge served the city without requiring any alterations. But with time it began to hinder navigation on the Neva. This became particularly noticeable when the Volga-Baltic Canal was built in 1964 and large-tonnage vessels began to sail along the Neva. In less than two years the bridge was completely reconstructed: it was widened from 23 m to 34 m; the width of the openings through which the ships sail was doubled, so that now even ocean-going vessels can pass through them. Only the carefully restored elaborate railings of the old bridge remain.

The railings of Foundry Bridge consist of individual units with repeated design: mermaids facing one another are holding an oval on which the coat of arms of St. Petersburg is depicted—a shield with a sceptre,

Taurida Palace

crowned with a two-headed eagle; on the shield two anchors lay across each other diagonally with their flukes upwards. One of these anchors (with two flukes and a cross-piece on its stock at the ring) is an anchor for sea-going vessels, while the other (without a stock but with four flukes) is for river-going vessels. This composition was called upon to show that St. Petersburg was a sea and a river port simultaneously, and the sceptre—that the city was the capital of the Russian Empire.

Foundry Bridge and neighbouring Shpalernaya Street (today Ulitsa Voinova) have gone down in the history of the October armed uprising of 1917. On the evening of October 24, from his last underground hide-out on Serdobolskaya Street, Lenin, accompanied by his bodyguard—the Bolshevik Finn Eino Rahja—headed for the Smolny, where the headquarters of the armed uprising was set up. They went part of the way by tram and then across Foundry Bridge and along Shpalernaya Street on foot. On the way they were twice stopped by patrols of the Provisional Government. But the Rahja's ingenuity and Lenin's composure helped them to reach the Smolny safely.

Shpalernaya Street, along which you continue your excursion, was renamed Voinov Street (Ulitsa Voinova) in 1918 in memory of Ivan Voinov, the Bolshevik who worked for the newspaper *Pravda*, and who was stabbed to death on July 6, 1917 by counter-revolutionary Cossacks.

Not far from Foundry Bridge, at No. 18, Voinov Street, is the **Mayakovsky Writers' Club**. This is the seat of the board of the Leningrad branch of the Union of Writers' of the RSFSR.

There is nothing remarkable about

the appearance of house No. 6 on the same street, the scene of many events in the history of Russian musical culture. In 1860–1870, the eminent Russian composers Tsezar Kui, Nikolai Rimsky-Korsakov and Modest Moussorgsky lived here.

To the west, the street is dominated by a building completely faced with marble. Today it houses the **All-Union Labour Protection Institute**. The institute, founded in 1927, carries out scientific research to ensure safe, healthy working conditions at enterprises.

The main part of Voinov Street runs eastwards from Foundry Bridge. In Petrine times the street was called First Row. It was built up only on what is now the left side, while the right side was lapped by the waters of the Neva before its banks were faced with granite. The opponents of Peter the Great's transformations mainly settled here in order to live further away from the restless, wilful monarch. Moreover, it was easier to flee St. Petersburg from here when necessary.

Several industrial enterprises were built here. Besides satisfying the needs of the army and the fleet, the city's industry was called upon to fulfil the requirements of the court. The tapestry factory which came into being in 1717 was to serve this purpose, and at the beginning of 1730 it was moved here, to the street which was later given the name of Shpalernaya (Tapestry), where it remained until 1858 when it was demolished.

The next sight on your excursion will be No. 34, Voinov Street, the **Leningrad State Archives of Literature and Art**. The archives of writers, composers, artists, architects, and journalists form its basis. The documents of theatres, libraries, publishing houses, radio and television companies, are also kept here.

Noteworthy on the opposite side of the street at No. 35a is a **former church**, built by Luigi Rusca in 1817–1818. It occupies a corner lot, and its main façade embellished with a six-column Ionic portico faces onto Voinov Street. The central premises of the building is shaped like a rotunda. The colonnade of 25 Ionic columns in artificial marble supports a cupola more than 18 m in diameter and decorated with lacunars. Today this building houses the **Leningrad branch of the Voluntary All-Russia Society for the Preservation of Monuments of History and Culture**. This organisation, devoted to the protection, restoration, or reconstruction of buildings of historical or cultural value, unites in its ranks almost 400,000 citizens of Leningrad. The scale of this work is enormous, for in Leningrad there are 2,165 monuments of history and culture protected by the state.

Further on, at No. 41–43, stand the former **barracks of the Cavalry Guards Regiment** (architect Luigi Rusca, 1803–1806).

The Cavalry Guards initially served as the emperor's body guards. However, the Cavalry Guards Regiment formed in 1800 was an ordinary household unit commanded by the emperor or the empress.

The façade of the barracks is decorated with a sturdy eight-column portico mounted on the arcade of the ground floor. In keeping with the building's purpose, the wings of the portico bear statues of Mars and Bellona, the god and goddess of war in ancient Roman mythology. On the corner of Voinov and Potyomkin (Potyomkinskaya) streets stands the huge green house—exhibition hall of the Leningrad firm "Flowers". Behind it, on the same side of Potyomkin Street, is one of the city's largest cinemas—the **triple-screen "Leningrad"**.

No. 47, Voinov Street is the site of one of Leningrad's most magnificent building—the **TAURIDA PALACE** (Tavrichesky Dvorets), which occupies an area of 65,700 sq m. The palace was erected in 1783–1789 on the

Hotel Leningrad

orders of Catherine the Great for her favourite, Count Grigory Potyomkin, who had been given the title of Prince of Taurida for his annexation of the Crimea (ancient Taurida) to Russia. The designer was the eminent Russian architect of the late 18th century, Ivan Starov.

The Taurida Palace is a splendid example of Classicism, the main trend in Russian architecture in the late 18th and early 19th centuries. The strict precise lines of the façades, the modest, restrained decoration, the use of elements of ancient architecture, and, in particular, columns supporting a pediment above a portico, such as the one you can see on the main façade of the palace, are typical of this style.

The luxurious interior décor of the Taurida Palace contrasts with its modest exterior. Beyond the main portico is an extensive elegant vestibule leading to the octagonal Dome Room with its monumental arches on marble columns, supporting a low drum crowned with a cupola. Splendid murals have been preserved here, ex-

ecuted in the grisaille style, a special type of decorative painting using only two colours and thereby creating the impression of a bas-relief. Further on is the Catherine Reception Hall, 75 m long, embellished with 36 columns of artificial marble and amazingly beautiful bronze chandeliers. This hall used to abut onto the huge winter garden, where exotic trees, rose and jasmin bushes grew under a glass roof and tropical birds fluttered amidst the greenery. In the centre of the garden there was a round colonnade containing a marble sculpture of Catherine the Great, the patroness of the owner of the palace. Prince Potyomkin of Taurida was fabulously rich. It is known that his hat was so heavily studded with diamonds that the prince could neither wear it nor hold it. Therefore, a special aide-de-camp carried this overweight headgear.

His contemporaries recall the ball given in the Taurida Palace on April 28, 1791, to commemorate the capture by the Russian troops of the Turkish fortress of Izmail. Three thousand guests, among them Catherine the Great, were present at the festivities. They were entertained by 300 singers and musicians and also by an unusual horn orchestra belonging to Potyomkin. Each of the 36 musicians making up the orchestra could produce but one single note on his wind instrument. Therefore, tremendous skill was required for the musician to play his note in the general melody at the right time.

During the ball the palace was lit by 140,000 multicoloured lamps and 20,000 candles. The fête cost the prince 200,000 roubles, the annual income from the quit-rent of 40,000 serfs.

The son of Catherine the Great, Paul I, who succeeded her on the Russian throne, avenged himself on Potyomkin for the latter's scornful attitude towards him ... by taking it out on the palace. On his orders this out-

Smolny Cathedral

standing work of architecture was turned into stables. The splendid parquetry was covered with manure and stalls were set up between the columns. After the death of Paul I the palace was restored, and Alexander I lived in it for a short time, as did other members of the royal family. In 1829, the heir to the Persian throne stayed here. Then for several decades the palace remained uninhabited. Later

on, in 1906, it was partially rebuilt for the State Duma, the Russian parliament. The winter garden was turned into a giant amphitheatre to be used as an assembly hall.

During the February revolution of 1917 the Taurida Palace became the centre of revolutionary events. On the evening of February 27, in one of the rooms in the left wing of the palace the Petrograd Soviet of Workers' and

Soldiers' Deputies representing the revolutionary democratic dictatorship of the proletariat and the peasantry began to operate. Members of the Provisional Committee, representatives of the landowners and the bourgeoisie, which later formed the Provisional Government, met in the opposite wing of the palace on the same evening. Thus, a dual system of power emerged in the country, the power of the Soviets which expressed the will of the workers and peasants, and the power of the bourgeoisie and the landowners in the form of the Provisional Government. This dual power continued until July 1917, when power throughout the country passed into the hands of the Provisional Government which set up a counter-revolutionary dictatorship.

After Lenin's return from ten years of emigration on April 4, 1917, he made a report at the Taurida Palace on the tasks facing the proletariat in the given revolution. In this report Lenin gave the exposition of the *April Theses* in which he marked out the path of transition from the bourgeois-democratic revolution to a socialist revolution.

After that, Lenin frequently spoke at the Taurida Palace. Here in March 1918 the 7th Congress of the Communist Party was held. The congress accepted Lenin's proposal that Soviet Russia should withdraw from the war with Kaiser's Germany, and conclude the Peace of Brest with its fettering conditions.

Quite a few other important events in the history of Russia are connected with the Taurida Palace. Today the Palace houses the Higher Party School. Party conferences and meetings of the Leningrad public are held there in an auditorium seating 1,057.

Not far from the Taurida Palace is the **tower of the main waterworks**, built of dark brick in 1863. Before that, the inhabitants of St. Petersburg had their water delivered to their homes

in buckets and barrels. The barrels were of different colours, indicating which little river or canal the water was taken from. When the waterworks was built, the length of the pipes of the St. Petersburg water supply system was 110 km. Today the total length of the Leningrad water supply pipes is more than 3,000 km. At this Leningrad's first waterworks powerful pumps draw water into the pipes from the Neva river, then it is filtered, chlorinated, and undergoes purification and then enters the block of clarifiers. Beyond the glass partitions, in an absolutely sterile room the water seeps through a many-metre-thick layer of gravel, quartz sand, and other filters. It takes eight or nine hours to purify the waters of the Neva and make them suitable for drinking. The procedure is the same at the other waterworks in the city. Everywhere the quality of water corresponds to the strict state standards of the USSR.

On the other side of the Taurida Palace, the verdant **Taurida Garden**, now a children's park, stretches over an area of 30 hectares.

On the southern edge of the Taurida Garden, on a street bearing the name of the great Russian writer and satyrist Mikhail Saltykov-Shchedrin (running parallel to Voinov Street) is a **museum in honour of the great Russian military leader Alexander Suvorov**, opened in 1904. The appearance of the building, the construction of which was funded by money collected in the form of subscription lists throughout all of Russia, is reminiscent of an ancient Russian fortress. The façade is decorated with huge mosaics depicting episodes from the life of the military leader—his departure on a campaign in 1799, and the Russian troops' crossing of the Alps.

The name of Alexander Suvorov (1729–1800) is inseparably linked with the heroic history of the Russian people. He played an outstanding part in the development of Russian and world military art.

Smolny

Throughout his long military service, he never once suffered defeat. Beginning as a corporal, Suvorov ended his service as a generalissimo, preserving, nonetheless, his soldier's modesty and simple way of life.

The museum's exposition will acquaint you with the main stages in the life and service of the military leader, his closest pupils and comrades-in-arms. Items taken from Suvorov's home, such as the old French clock, the massive amber pipe mouthpiece, and a number of books give you some idea of the life style of the future military leader. Some of Suvorov's personal belongings displayed at the museum, such as his desk, two plain wooden chairs, a copper kettle, and others, testify to Suvorov's modest lifestyle.

The exhibition also contains the medal struck in honour of the victories gained by the Russian army under Suvorov's command at Kinburn (1787), and Focsani (1783), at Rîmnic (1789), and near Izmail (1790), which made the Russian military leader world famous.

Now return to Voinov Street and continue your excursion. The small house at No. 9, Stavropol Street (Stavropolskaya Ulitsa), on the right side of Voinov Street, is one of the oldest buildings in the city. Erected in 1714, it belonged to the boyar Kikin, who organised a conspiracy against Peter the Great together with the tsar's son

Alexei. At that time, it was called the **Kikin Palace**. After the plot was uncovered and the owner of the house had been put to death, it housed the collections of the Kunstkammer, the first Russian natural science museum. The Kunstkammer was transferred to a building designed especially for it on Vasilyevsky Island and the Kikin Palace became the regimental hospital. Subsequently, the house was frequently rebuilt and retained almost nothing of its original appearance. During the Second World War the building was badly damaged by Nazi bombs and shells. Strange as it may seem, this disaster actually did more good than harm, for when the plaster crumbled traces of the original sculptural finish of the beginning of the 18th century were revealed on the stone brickwork. This made it possible to restore the Kikin Palace to its Petrine Baroque style after the later additions to the building had been demolished in 1953-1955. Thus the city acquired a new and extremely valuable architectural monument. Today the palace houses a children's music school and a consulting centre for music and art teachers.

In the garden on Voinov Street, on a four-sided pedestal rises a **monument to the revolutionary Felix Dzerzhinsky,** one of the leaders of the October armed uprising. The statue was unveiled in 1981. The sculptors Vladimir Gorevoi and Sergei Kubasov have captured in bronze his decisiveness and iron will.

You have come to the final stage of your excursion, the **ensemble of the Smolny Convent,** which is situated in Rastrelli Square (Ploshchad Rastrelli). The name Smolny comes from "Smolyanoi Dvor", meaning "tar yard". The tar yard was built on this site soon after the construction of St. Petersburg was begun. Here tar was prepared and stored for the ships built at the St. Petersburg shipyards. In 1723, the tar yard was moved to another district

in the city, and on its site Peter's daughter, the Tsarina Elizabeth, decided to establish a convent in 1744. In 1748, Bartolomeo Rastrelli, that outstanding master of Baroque, launched the construction of the cathedral. The framework of the cathedral was completed in 1764. Besides the cathedral, the architect built a quadrangle incorporating the cells, the refectory and other premises, creating a magnificently picturesque and imposing ensemble. The traditional motifs of Russian architecture and the innovatory methods of the secular architecture of the 18th century are embodied in Rastrelli's creations on an exceptionally large scale. Today the former Smolny Cathedral houses the **permanent exhibition Leningrad Today and Tomorrow**. The exhibits—the documents, photographs, examples of goods produced by Leningrad's enterprises— reveal the significance of the city as one of the largest industrial, scientific, and cultural centres in the country, a city of peace and friendship. The exposition gives one a graphic idea of the most important and pressing problems to be tackled in developing the city today, of the great contribution made by the people of Leningrad to the fulfilment of the resolutions of the Party and government aimed at further raising the country's economic and cultural level. One of the sections of the exhibition is devoted to the rise in the well-being of the people of Leningrad, the development of housing construction, the furnishing of the city with amenities and utilities and the fulfilling of the plan for its economic and social development.

One of the former convent buildings now houses the **Institute of the History of the Party of the Leningrad Regional Committee of the CPSU,** a branch of the Institute of Marxism-Leninism under the CPSU Central Committee. More than 4,000,000 documents of the Leningrad Party Organisation covering the entire period of its existence are kept in the Party archives of the institute. In the more than 60 years since its founding, the institute has published over 300 monographs, collections, and brochures, and has put out hundreds of articles on the history of the Communist Party.

The ensemble of the Smolny Convent was never finished. Rastrelli's project envisaged a structure with a 140-metre-high bell-tower, but the extravagance of Elizabeth (after her death only six roubles were left in the treasure while 16,000 dresses and gowns filled the Tsarina's wardrobes) had exhausted the state finances. The bell tower remained only in the plans.

When Catherine the Great acceded to the throne, she gave instructions that the Institute for Noble Young Ladies should be set up in the Smolny Convent, which had not been completed even at that time. The institute was the first state establishment of education in Russia for the daughters of the gentry. The building of the institute that was subsequently named **SMOLNY** was erected in classical style by the architect Giacomo Quarenghi in 1806–1808. It is situated to the south of the main Smolny Convent complex, on the bank of the Neva, at the back of an extensive square. The architect felt that the building should be greatly removed from the general "line" of buildings on the street, for the wide open space in front of the Smolny building improves the view of it.

The long façade (more than 200 m) is broken up by projecting side wings and a greatly emphasised central front. A portico of eight Ionic columns rises above the raised arcade of the entrance. A loggia beyond the columns and the flat pediment complete the design of the central part of the façade. The interior décor of the building is even more austere. Among its premises only the assembly hall stands out for its architecture. This huge hall which occupies the first and second floors of the south wing is embellished with an elegant colonnade. Your eye is sure to be caught by the austere stucco frieze and the originally stylised chandeliers in the hall.

In August 1917 the Institute for Noble Young Ladies was closed. The Smolny buildings were taken over by the Petrograd Soviet of Workers' and Soldiers' Deputies which had moved there from the Taurida Palace, and the Central Executive Committee (in 1917–1937 the supreme legislative managing and controlling organ of the republic, operating in the period between the All-Russia Congresses of Soviets), and later on, the Central and Petrograd Committees of the Bolshevik Party. The building also housed the Revolutionary Military Committee, which supervised the preparations for the armed uprising in October 1917.

Reports on the formation of Red Guard detachments, on political propaganda conducted in the regiments and word that the garrison's units had joined the Bolshevik side were received here. Armed workers stood on guard by the archway of the main entrance to the Smolny building. Bonfires blazed in the courtyard, which was cramped with lorries, carts, and cannons. Cannons also stood under the arches by the entrance. Next to it there were heaps of logs in case a barricade had to be built. In the gardens adjacent to the building on the Neva side the Red Guards had target practice.

On the evening of October 24, Lenin arrived at the Smolny and took direct control of the uprising. Messengers from the Military Revolutionary Committee were sent into the workers' districts and the barracks with the news that Lenin was at the Smolny leading the uprising.

On the morning of October 25 all the most important strategic objectives in the city were in the hands of the insurgents. The power of the counter-revolutionary Provisional Government was overthrown. On the same day at 10.40 p.m. the Second All-Russia Congress of Soviets of Workers' and Soldiers' Deputies convened in the Smolny assembly hall. Six hundred and forty-nine of its delegates represented 402 Soviets of Russia, the majority of them being members of the Bolshevik Party.

At 5 o'clock in the morning on October 26 the Congress approved the appeal written by Lenin *To the Workers, Soldiers and Peasants!* which proclaimed the victory of the socialist revolution.

The second sitting of the Congress began on October 26 at 9 o'clock in the evening. At this session Lenin's *Decree on Peace* and *Decree on Land* were adopted. The *Decree on Peace*, proclaiming that war was "the greatest crime against mankind", announced the complete rejection by the Soviet government of all the agreements by tsarist Russia aimed at annexation and proposed that all peoples at war and their governments should immediately begin negotiations on the conclusion of a universal, just and democratic peace. This document contained Lenin's idea on the possibility of the peaceful coexistence of states with different social systems.

The *Decree on Land* announced the immediate confiscation without compensation of all the landed estates, the abolition of private ownership of land and the establishment of public, or state ownership of land, and the transfer of the land to those who work it.

Then the Congress approved the first workers' and peasants' government in the world, the Soviet of People's Commissars headed by Lenin. The people of Russia thereby entrusted the government of their country to the Bolshevik Party.

Lenin lived at the Smolny for 124 days. The rooms in which he re-

sided and worked have been carefully kept as a memorial museum. After the Soviet government moved to Moscow on March 10–11, 1918, the Smolny remained the centre of the social and political life of Petrograd, and subsequently of Leningrad and the Leningrad Region. Today, it is the seat of the Leningrad Regional and City Committees of the Communist Party of the Soviet Union.

In the years after the Revolution, the look of the area around the Smolny changed somewhat. In 1923–1924, **propylaea**, colonnades forming the driveway to the Smolny were erected by the architects Vladimir Shchuko and Vladimir Gelfreikh. The architecture of the propylaea is impressive and austere: two five-column portico-type pavilions lining the straight alley leading up to the central façade of the Smolny. Above the Tuscan columns, the friezes on the propylaea bear the inscriptions: "The First Soviet of the Proletarian Dictatorship" and "The Workers of All Countries, Unite!" In 1967, for the jubilee of the Great October Socialist Revolution memorial plaques were mounted on the walls of the propylaea between the columns. They bear a list of the awards given to the Hero City of Leningrad and the Leningrad Region. Formerly paved with cobble stones, the square in front of the Smolny was made into a picturesque garden in the pre-war years. The paved alley lined with trees and shrubs leads from the propylaea past busts of Karl Marx and Friedrich Engels (sculptor Stepan Yevseyev), mounted in 1932, to the central portico in front of which a **statue of Lenin** was erected in 1927 (sculptor Vasily Kozlov, architects Vladimir Shchuko and Vladimir Gelfreikh).

There are several comparatively new buildings in the Smolny neighbourhood. The light-coloured corner building on the left side of Voinov Street and Rastrelli Square is the **House of Political Education of the**

Leningrad Regional and City Committees of the CPSU, built in 1973.

Opposite the propylaea stands an office block built in 1957–1958. Next to it, on the other side of Suvorov Avenue at the end of the 1970s the building of the **Executive Committee of the Leningrad Regional Soviet of People's Deputies** was constructed. This building is faced with light-coloured slabs of dolomite brought from the Estonian island of Saaremaa.

5

NEVSKY AVENUE—ARTS SQUARE—OSTROVSKY SQUARE—UPRISING SQUARE—ALEXANDER NEVSKY SQUARE

Estimated time of the excursion—3 hours. Nearest Metro station Nevsky Prospekt.

Tourist attractions: Exhibition of works for sale by Leningrad artists, the Stroganov Palace (18th century), the Kazansky Cathedral, the State Russian Museum (the former Mikhailovsky Palace), the State Museum of Ethnography of the Peoples of the USSR, the statue of Alexander Pushkin, the Yevropeiskaya Hotel, the Passazh Department Store, the Anichkov Palace, the Anichkov Bridge, the statue of Catherine the Great, the House of Friendship and Peace with Peoples of Foreign Countries, the Museum of the Arctic and the Antarctic, the Alexander Nevsky Monastery (18th century).

NEVSKY AVENUE (Nevsky Prospekt), Leningrad's main street, stretches for more than four kilometres from the Admiralty like a bowstring across the arc formed by the Neva within the city. This is Leningrad's busiest thoroughfare, with a history as old as the city itself.

As you already know from the brief history, long before the Northern War, the territory of today's Leningrad was part of the lands of Novgorod. The Great Novgorod Road

linked the Russian villages scattered about on the banks of the Neva with other lands of Novgorod. This road passed where the Ligovskaya Street, today Ligovsky Avenue (Ligovsky Prospekt) was later laid.

After the foundation of St. Petersburg in 1703 and the beginning of work on the Admiralty shipyard, trains of carts and sledges carrying iron, sail cloth, ropes, and oak, in short, all that was needed for the shipyard, passed along the Novgorod road. These vehicles had to approach the Admiralty by a round-about route along narrow paths that were not intended for heavy traffic, and therefore it was decided to link up the Admiralty shipyard directly with the Novgorod road. In a comparatively short period of time, a cutting was made through the sparse woodland from the Admiralty to the Novgorod road. This is how the "great perspective road" came into being. This name originates from the Latin word *perspicere*, which means to see right through, to see objects in the distance. In 1738 a decision was taken to rename the road the "Nevsky Perspective Road" and in 1783 it was shortened to Nevsky Prospekt (Nevsky Avenue).

By the mid-18th century this thoroughfare was already the city's main street, along which cathedrals, palaces and mansions, market rows and public buildings were being built. From the beginning of the 19th century rooming houses, hotels and later banks began to appear on Nevsky Avenue. In 1851 the building of the Moscow Station emphasised the part played by Nevsky Avenue as the most important thoroughfare in St. Petersburg.

The appearance of the avenue is extremely varied, for 18th-century houses alternate here with buildings of the 20th century. This is mainly explained by the fact that before the 19th century the River Fontanka formed the city's southern boundary; therefore, the groups of buildings on Nevsky Avenue between the Admiralty and the Fontanka were built considerably earlier than those between Anichkov Bridge and the Alexander Nevsky Monastery. The width of the avenue varies from 25 m (between the Admiralty and the River Moika) to 60 m (near the department store Gostiny Dvor).

As you admire the light-coloured buildings on the avenue, its festive appearance, its busy traffic, it is difficult to imagine how the street looked in the days of the blockade. The vague outlines of trolley-buses and cars frozen under the snowdrifts could be defined. Wooden shutters covered the windows of the empty shops. Among the few people on Nevsky Avenue would invariably be someone mustering the last of his strength to pull a child's sledge with the swathed corpse of one of his near and dear ones towards the cemetery...

In the post-war years improvements were made, the tramlines were removed, pedestrian underpasses and Metro stations were constructed, and lindens were planted in front of the Gostiny Dvor department store and on the streets adjacent to the avenue.

Today Nevsky Avenue is the cultural hub of Leningrad. There are numerous research centres, institutions of higher education, libraries, museums, theatres and cinemas, publishing houses and editorial offices of magazines on it and in the squares adjacent to it.

Your excursion along the avenue begins near the Admiralty. At the very beginning of Nevsky Avenue, at No. 1, is **Glavleningradstroi**, the main construction agency in Leningrad. The next building (No. 3) on Nevsky Avenue is associated with Lenin. Soon after his return from emigration, in April 1917, he spoke here at a meeting of Party functionaries on the content and methods of propaganda among soldiers.

In the years before the Revolution Nevsky Avenue was, to a certain extent, the financial centre of the Russian Empire. The section from the Admiralty to Anichkov Bridge was bristling with 28 banks, and banks and insurance offices were dotted about on Herzen and Gogol streets adjacent to the avenue as well. Not far from the corner on Nevsky Avenue and Gogol Street is house No. 9 (architect Marian Peretyatkovich, 1912) an imitation of the Palace of the Doges in Venice.

The granite revetment, the blocks of the arcades, the sculptural decorations on the façade of the building were brought by the banker Wawelberg from Sweden. Today it houses the Aeroflot booking office (next to it, in Kirpichny Lane, a bus service to the airport operates).

This is where Gogol Street branches off from Nevsky Avenue. In the corner house at No. 11/2 the outstanding biologist Nikolai Vavilov (1887–1943) lived from 1928 to 1940. The scientist is famed throughout the world for his work in the fields of gen-

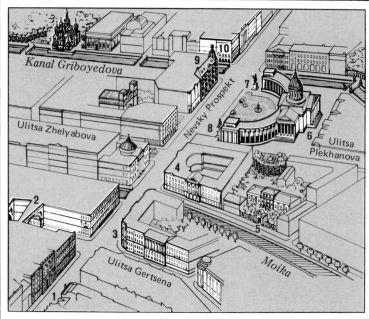

NEVSKY PROSPEKT (THE BEGINNING)

1. *Glavleningradstroi, the city air terminal*
2. *Archway of the General Staff Building*
3. *House No. 15 ("a house with columns")*
4. *Former palace of Count Stroganov*
5. *Herzen Teachers' Training Institute*
6. *Kazansky Cathedral, the Museum of the History of Religion and Atheism*
7. *Statue of the military leader Mikhail Kutuzov*
8. *Statue of the military leader Mikhail Barklai de Tolli*
9. *House of Books*
10. *Metro station Nevsky Prospekt*

etics, botany and selective plant-breeding. A memorial plaque on No. 13/8 Gogol Street tells you that the composer Pyotr Tchaikovsky lived here till his death on October 25, 1895. In this same building, in the restaurant Vienna (which is housed in the corner part of the basement), in July 1906, Lenin met with Party workers in connection with the uprising of soldiers and sailors in Sveaborg in that year.

The great Russian writer Nikolai Gogol (1809–1852) lived at No. 17 from 1833 to 1836. The unlit staircase from the courtyard leads up to the second floor and a flat consisting of two small rooms, and a tiny hall. The bedroom also served as a dining-room, and next to it there was a more spacious room with a divan by the wall and a large table by the window and a bureau, at which the writer used to work. Here he created *The Government Inspector*, *Taras Bulba* and the first chapters of *Dead Souls*.

Looking down Gogol Street from Nevsky Avenue you see the houses at No. 8 and No. 10 (1760s), which are embellished with moulded medallions, masks, vases, and friezes with images of gryphons. These are the oldest buildings on Nevsky Avenue. No. 8 houses the **exhibition of works on sale by Leningrad artists**. The comparatively new building at No. 14, erected in 1939 (a secondary school), has blended well with the previously formed ensemble in this part of the avenue.

From September 4, 1941 to January 22, 1944, the Nazis fired approximately 149,000 shells on Leningrad. With the help of aerial photography and sound ranging the Soviet command managed to establish that the enemy's heavy artillery were located in one of the villages to the south-east of the city. These data as well as careful observations confirmed that the northwestern side of the streets was the most dangerous. To cut down the number of casualties, street signs were put up on the northwestern sides of many Leningrad streets to warn people of the danger.

You can still see such a sign (white letters on a blue background) at No. 14. Beside it is a marble plaque telling that the old sign has been preserved in memory of the heroism and courage of the people of Leningrad during the 900-day siege.

To the left of No. 16 is a small section of Herzen Street (Ulitsa Gertsena), which ends at the arch of the General Staff. The architect Carlo Rossi built this section of the street along the Pulkovo meridian, and at noon on a sunny day you can check your watches by this street, for the façades of the houses cast no shade on the pavement.

On the opposite side of the avenue, the interesting white and yellow house at No. 15, decorated with two tiers of columns and pilasters (the people of Leningrad call it "the house with columns"), was built in the 1760s for the chief of the St. Petersburg police force. The famous architect Giacomo Quarenghi lived on the first floor of this house in 1800 when he first came to St. Petersburg. In 1858, the house became the property of the wealthy merchant family, the Yeliseyevs. The new owners rebuilt it, the oval windows on the main façade being made rectangular and the columns on the ground floor being replaced by pilasters. However, even after these alterations, the building still remained a valuable monument of early Russian classicism. Today it houses the **cinema Barricade**.

Beyond the bridge across the River Moika stands a building embellished with a graceful classical portico, the **former Dutch church** (No. 20) erected by the architect Paul Jaquot in 1837. Today it houses the Alexander Blok Library. On the opposite side of the avenue at No. 17 you will see the 18th-century **palace of Count Stroganov** (1753–1754), an outstanding work by the architect Bartolomeo Rastrelli. Moulded decoration covers most of the central part of the building. The arch over the gateway is embellished with double columns supporting the elaborate pediment on which the Stroganovs' coat of arms is depicted. On the coat of arms are two sables standing on hind legs and holding in their forepaws a shield divided into two parts: on the lower part fur is depicted; on the upper part, the head of a bear. Above the shield is a helmet and another bear's head. The coat of arms may be deciphered as follows: the bear is the master of the taiga, sable is the most prized fur. The fact

that they are depicted on the coat of arms speaks of the unlimited power of the Stroganovs in Siberia, where they owned vast lands, and of the countless riches of that region. The window casings on the first floor above the archway are distinguished by bas-reliefs of atlantes, other windows on this floor are framed with less luxurious decoration, each of them embellished with a lion mask and a medallion with a male profile.

The architectural appearance of the palace has been distorted somewhat with time owing to the fact that the windows of the ground floor have been made one third smaller. This was done because the level of Nevsky Avenue was raised and the stone embankment of the River Moika was constructed. At the end of the 18th century a number of interiors of the palace and the wings round the courtyard were subjected to alterations under the supervision of Andrei Voronikhin. Soon it will house the exposition

Kazansky Cathedral

of the department of Russian applied art of the State Russian Museum.

The complex of **buildings of the Herzen Teachers Training Institute** abuts onto the Stroganov Palace on the Moika Embankment and is one of the largest institutions in the country training secondary school teachers. Together, its 14 departments have a student body of more than 12,000. The main building of the institute was built in the 1760s with the participation of Alexander Kokorinov and Jean-

Baptiste Vallin de la Mothe. In front of the institute stands a statue of the outstanding Russian pedagogue Konstantin Ushinsky (1824-1870).

Almost next to the former Stroganov Palace on Nevsky Avenue stands the **House of Fashion**. Across from it extends a tree-lined street bearing the name of the outstanding Russian revolutionary Andrei Zhelyabov. This street bears a number of interesting sights. No. 25 is the **Chigorin Chess Club**, No. 21/23—the **Leningrad**

House of Trade, one of the largest department stores in the city. This building was constructed (architect Ernst Virrikh, 1907–1913) by using a large-size monolithic ferro-concrete frame resting on a ferro-concrete foundation sunk into the ground (to a depth of 3.5 m), the first time such a method was employed in Russia. At that time, St. Petersburg's architecture was experiencing a retrospective interest in Classicism. The decoration on the façade of the building is in the Empire style so popular at the beginning of the 19th century. The **shop Rapsodia** (No. 13), where music and musical literature can be bought and meetings with composers take place, will undoubtedly attract music lovers.

Statue of Mikhail Kutuzov

Back on Nevsky Avenue, next to the Stroganov Palace is one of the finest architectural monuments in Leningrad—the **Kazansky Cathedral**, designed and erected in 1801–1811 by the architect Andrei Voronikhin. The architect has created a magnificent edifice (height—71.6 m, length—72.5 m), with its main building facing onto Nevsky Avenue. The cathedral with its semicircular Corinthian colonnade (96 thirteen-metre-high columns) is the dominant feature in one of the most elegant squares of the city.

Huge bas-reliefs, approximately 15 metres long and almost two metres high, depicting Biblical subjects, grace the two butt-ends of the building facing onto Nevsky Avenue. The bas-relief above the left butt-end of the building was executed by the famous Russian sculptor Ivan Martos on the subject *Moses Parting the Waters*, the one above the right butt-end is a depiction of the *Brazen Serpent* by the sculptor Ivan Prokofyev.

In the niches of the northern portico (facing onto Nevsky Avenue) bronze sculptures have been mounted: Prince Vladimir (in the period of his rule in Kiev, in approximately 988, when Christianity was adopted in Russia)—sculptor Stepan Pimenov; John the Baptist—sculptor Ivan Martos; Alexander Nevsky—sculptor Stepan Pimenov; and St. Andrew—sculptor Vasily Demut-Malinovsky. The bronze doors of the northern portico, consisting of ten multifigured compositions taken from the Bible are particularly worthy of attention. This is an exact copy of the doors created in the mid-15th century by the Italian sculptor Lorenzo Giberti for the Florentine Baptistery. It took Giberti 27 years to create his work of art. Michelangelo said of these doors that they were splendid enough to serve as the gates of paradise. Gypsum models of the doors were preserved in St. Petersburg in the Academy of Arts and from them the founder Vasily Yekimov made the doors for the Kazansky Cathedral.

The cathedral's highly artistic interior decoration consisting of 56 monolithic red granite columns and a mosaic floor composed of multifarious Karelian marbles are bound to produce an unforgettable impression on you. The cathedral's interior is the work of Vladimir Borovikovsky, Orest Kiprensky and other outstanding Rus-

Bankovsky Bridge on the Griboyedov Canal

sian artists of the beginning of the 19th century.

In front of the main, western, entrance to the cathedral from Plekhanov Street (Ulitsa Plekhanova), is a small semi-circular square girded by a railing, designed by Andrei Voronikhin in 1811–1812. Its fine vertical posts and the middle part are decorated with rhombic insets. Together with the ornamental friezes they form two bands uniting the wide openwork wrought-iron sections into a single semi-circle 171 m in length. The square's old fountain, composed of large granite slabs and designed by the architect Thomas de Thomon, catches the eye. Constructed in 1809, the fountain originally stood at the side of the road to Tsarskoye Selo (now the town of Pushkin). It was brought to its present site in 1935.

After Russia's victory over Napoleon in 1812 the cathedral became a unique monument to Russian military glory. The standards taken as tro-

Nevsky Avenue in the evening. View of the former City Duma and Luigi Rusca's portico

phies and the keys from the fortresses captured by the Russian forces were displayed here. In the vault of the northern chapel by the wall (to the right of the entrance) lies the grave of Mikhail Kutuzov, the commander of the Russian forces, who died in 1813. He was buried on the spot where he prayed before he left to join his army in the field.

In 1837, when the 25th anniversary of the rout of Napoleon's troops in Russia was celebrated, **statues of Mikhail Kutuzov and Mikhail Barklai de Tolli** were erected in front of the cathedral. These statues were the work of the sculptor Boris Orlovsky and the architect Vasily Stasov.

Barklai de Tolli is depicted in a somewhat static pose, deep in thought, his right hand holding his cloak flowing from his shoulders and his lowered left hand gripping his field marshal's baton. Kutuzov is portrayed in a more dynamic pose with his drawn sword in his right hand and a field marshal's baton in his left, showing his troops the way to attack. Napoleon's standards with their broken staffs lie at the warriors' feet.

These statues are outstanding examples of realism in Russian monumental sculpture; they are authentic portraits reproducing expressions exactly.

On December 6, 1876, in the square in front of the cathedral a revolutionary demonstration, in which workers took part, was staged in Russia for the first time. During the demonstration a student of the Mining Institute, Georgi Plekhanov, subsequently one of the most prominent Russian Marxists, the first propagandist of Marxism in Russia, made an enthusiastic speech. As a consequence of this and other revolutionary gatherings, the tsarist government decided to lay out a public garden in this square so that such meetings could not recur near the cathedral. But this did not prevent other revolutionary rallies from being held here. Thus, on March 4, 1897, a large demonstration took place in this square at which the students of St. Petersburg protested against the arbitrariness of the prison authorities whose treatment of the revolutionary Maria Vetrova in the Peter and Paul Fortress drove her to suicide. Student unrest expressed itself here again in 1901.

On the day known as "Bloody Sunday"—January 9, 1905—workers who were marching to the Winter Palace where shot down in the square in front of the Kazansky Cathedral. In the days of the February revolution of 1917 the square became the constant site of revolutionary meetings and demonstrations protesting against the autocracy. These and other revolutionary events caused the square to be given the secret but honorary name of the Revolutionary Forum of St. Petersburg. Today the **Museum of** the History of Religion and Atheism, founded in 1932, is housed in Kazansky Cathedral.

The museum's collections consist of approximately 150,000 items, including paintings and sculptures, manuscripts and cult objects, Egyptian mummies, sarcophagi, the instruments of torture of the Holy Inquisition, and articles of decorative and applied art. Proceeding from a materialistic understanding of history and the basis of scientific data, the museum's exposition shows the place, role and function of religion and the church, the birth and development of free thinking and atheism in mankinds' historical development. The exhibition reveals the part played by religion in society as a form of ideology.

The exposition consists of the following sections: The Religion of Primitive Society; Religion and Free Thinking in the Ancient World; The Origins of Christianity; The Main Stages in the History of Atheism; Islam and Free Thinking of the Peoples of the East; Christian Sects in the USSR; Russian Orthodoxy and Atheism in the USSR. Here you can learn all about the history of individual religions.

Opposite the Kazansky Cathedral, on the corner of Nevsky Avenue and the Griboyedov Canal (Kanal Griboyedova) there rises a building faced with polished granite and crowned with a glass tower with a globe on the top (architect Pavel Syuzor, 1907). Before the Revolution this building belonged to the Singer Sewing-Machine Company. It was originally designed as an eleven-storey building, but, according to the decree of Nicholas I which was still in force at the time, all the buildings in the city had to be at least two metres lower than the Winter Palace, and so the Singer Company had to make their building six-storeys high with an attic. Today this building is known as the **House of Books** and is the home of many Leningrad publishing houses. On the ground and first floors you can visit the largest book shop in the city.

Now cross the Griboyedov Canal by **Kazansky Bridge**, built by Illarion

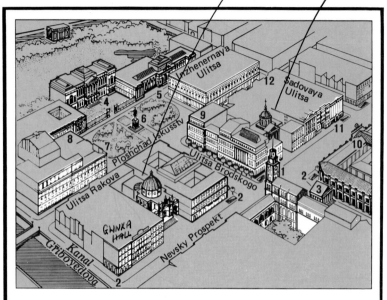

NEVSKY PROSPEKT—PLOSHCHAD ISKUSSTV

1. *Former fire observation tower*
2. *Metro station* Nevsky Prospekt
3. *Portico. The theatre box-office for foreign tourists*
4. *Former Mikhailovsky Palace, the State Russian Museum*
5. *State Museum of Ethnography of the Peoples of the USSR*
6. *Statue of Alexander Pushkin*
7. *Flat-museum of the artist Isaac Brodsky*
8. *State Academic Maly Opera House*
9. *Leningrad Philharmonia*
10. *Gostiny Dvor department store*
11. *Passazh department store*
12. *Komissarzhevskaya Drama Theatre*

Kutuzov, the father of the great military leader (the width of the bridge is five and a half times greater than its length) and continue your excursion along Nevsky Avenue. From the Griboyedov Canal embankment on your left you will see a church (architect Alfred Parland, 1883–1907) erected on the site where Alexander II was assassinated by members of the revolutionary terrorist organisation *Narodnaya Volya* (People's Will) on March 1, 1881. The revolutionaries believed that a popular uprising would flare up immediately after the assassination of the tyrant. But they were mistaken,

Statue of Alexander Pushkin near the Russian Museum

for there were no organised forces in the country capable of making the people rise to struggle against the autocracy. The leaders of the People's Will were put to death. Regardless of individual heroism, self-sacrifice, and devotion to the idea of Russia's transformation through revolution, the terrorist tactics of the members of the People's Will were wrong and counter-productive. At its Second Congress back in 1903, the Party of Bolsheviks rejected terrorism as a means of political struggle.

On the other side of Nevsky Avenue, along the Griboyedov Canal (behind the Kazansky Cathedral) you can see **Bankovsky** suspension **Bridge** decorated with figures of gryphons. In ancient Greece these mythical creatures were considered to be the guardians of gold, and, probably, for this reason they were mounted in front of the bank building erected by Giacomo Quarenghi in 1783–1790. Today this is the **Leningrad Voznesensky Finance and Economics Institute**.

The building opposite the House of Books on the other bank of the Gri-

boyedov Canal (No. 30) was erected in the second half of the 18th century. It is famed not for its architecture but, rather, for the fact that leading Russian musicians and great composers of Western Europe such as Hector Berlioz, Richard Wagner, Franz Liszt and Johann Strauss gave performances here. Since 1949 the **Lesser Hall of the Leningrad State Philharmonia**, a unique chamber music centre, is now housed here.

The ensemble of the former **Roman Catholic Church of St. Catherine**, designed by the architect Jean-Baptiste Vallin de la Mothe (1729–1800), stands on two neighbouring plots of land at No. 32 and 34. Inside the church the last **Polish King, Stanislaw Augustus Poniatowski**, lies buried. In 1795 he abdicated and lived to the end of his days in St. Petersburg. Here, to the right of the entrance lies buried the eminent French military leader, Marshal Moreau, who did not recognise the rule of Napoleon and emigrated from France. After Napoleon invaded Russia in 1812 Moreau obtained permission to fight in the Russian army. On August 15, 1813, in a battle near Dresden the marshal was wounded by a French cannon-ball and he died the following day. His ashes were interred with due ceremony in the cathedral on the main street of Russia's capital.

The corner house **with a pentagonal tower** on the opposite side of Nevsky Avenue (No. 29/31) was built in 1784 to the design of Giacomo Quarenghi. Before the Revolution this was the seat of the City Duma (the municipal council). The tower crowning the building was erected in 1804 (architect Giacomo Ferrari). It was originally used as a fire-observation tower, but then it was adapted in 1833–1854 for signalling by sight communications between St. Petersburg and the tsar's residences in the city's environs, as well as with Warsaw.

On the turret of the Winter Palace

facing the Admiralty (which has been preserved) a large rotating T-shaped frame was mounted; during night transmission lamps burned on its tips. Various positions of the frame corresponded to certain conventional signs. The latter were visually received by observers from other intermediate tower stations and transmitted further with the help of such mechanisms through transmission points mounted on watch towers.

The entrance to the Metro station *Nevsky Prospekt* is located at the foot of the tower. Next to it your attention will surely be drawn by a graceful **classical portico** (architect Luigi Rusca, 1802–1806). When the Metro station was being constructed, the portico was dismantled and later recreated according to the surviving sketches. The **box-office where foreign tourists can buy theatre tickets** may be found in this building.

The short Brodsky Street (Ulitsa Brodskogo), named in honour of the eminent Soviet artist Isaac Brodsky (1883–1939), runs off to the left of Nevsky Avenue. It joins the avenue with **ARTS SQUARE** (Ploshchad Iskusstv), an ensemble created by architect Carlo Rossi. In the houses lining the square are three museums and three theatres, including the well-known **State Russian Museum**, the **State Academic Maly Opera House**, and the **Leningrad State Philharmonia**.

The group of buildings in the square occupy a considerable area between the Griboyedov Canal, the River Moika, Garden Street (Sadovaya Ulitsa), and Nevsky Avenue. Development of this area began when St. Petersburg was first being constructed. The **Mikhailovsky Palace** was built for Mikhail, the brother of Nicholas I, by Carlo Rossi between 1819 and 1825.

Its main building is situated at the back of a forecourt formed by the administrative premises. The high railing separating the forecourt from the square is considered to be one of the best examples of wrought-iron work in Leningrad. It is dissected by three gates, the gate posts of which are decorated with military accoutrements. Under the arcade supporting the protruding central eight-column portico, ramps allowed carriages to drive right up to the palace's main entrance. A wide granite staircase decorated with

Nevsky Avenue and (right) **Gostiny Dvor** *Department Store*

bronze lions (copies of classical originals) leads up to the doors. On the sides of the portico, between the rounded windows of the first floor, Corinthian semi-columns rise in rhythmical order. As one of his contemporaries testifies, Rossi considered the palace he created for Mikhail to be reminiscent of the Louvre. The main building of the palace, which served as Mikhail's residence, was built up like the side buildings in two floors but was twice as high.

A park was laid out at the back of the palace. There, near the Moika, Carlo Rossi built a **graceful pavilion** from which a granite terrace with a wrought-iron railing and staircases leads down to the river.

Sculptures were widely used in embellishing the Mikhailovsky Palace and its interiors. The original decoration of the vestibule, the main staircase, and the White Hall, which has survived to our day, are among the best examples of interiors in the style of Russian Classicism. In the 1890s the palace was re-designed as the **State Russian Museum**, which was opened to the public in 1898. Just like the State Tretyakov Gallery in Mos-

cow, it is a veritable treasure-house of Russian art. A visit to the Russian Museum is given as a separate excursion (No. 9).

The Mikhailovsky Palace has become the compositional centre of the new architectural ensemble. On the eastern side of the palace Rossi laid out the Garden Street to the Field of Mars. Further on, he built a new street parallel to Nevsky Avenue which came to be called Engineers' Street (Inzhenernaya Ulitsa). The part of Engineers' Street that lies to the east of the palace was built up with domestic buildings. At the beginning of the 20th century they were demolished and in 1902–1911 the **Ethnography Museum** was erected on this site.

At the State Museum of Ethnography of the Peoples of the USSR you can learn of the customs and traditions of the peoples living in the Soviet Union, their culture, the radical changes in the life of these peoples as a result of Lenin's nationalities policy. This is the country's main ethnography museum. Founded in 1901 as a department of the Russian Museum, it became an independent museum in 1934.

The museum's unique collections consist of 450,000 exhibits, including valuable

NEVSKY PROSPEKT—OSTROVSKY SQUARE

1. *Metro station* Gostiny Dvor
2. *Saltykov-Shchedrin Public Library*
3. *Statue of Catherine the Great*
4. *Pushkin Academic Drama Theatre*
5. *Architect Rossi Street*
6. *Leningrad State Theatre Museum, Lunacharsky Theatrical Library*
7. *Vaganova School of Choreography*
8. *Carlo Rossi Pavilions*
9. *Anichkov Palace, Palace of Young Pioneers*
10. *Anichkov Bridge*
11. *Grocer's* (Gastronom) *No. 1*
12. *House of Friendship and Peace with Peoples of Foreign Countries*

carpets, national costumes, weapons, embroidery, leather goods, bone and wooden artifacts, and domestic utensils. Here you can see works of folk art: lace from Vologda, painted objects by the artists of Palekh and Khokhloma, Ukrainian and Byelorussian embroidery, jewellery from the Baltic republics and from Azerbaijan, Tajik paintings on wood, woodwork inlaid with bone and mother-of-pearl by Georgian craftsmen, Turkmen carpets, dolls, pottery, and ceramics ...

In 1957, a **statue of Pushkin** was erected in the centre of the public garden in Arts Square. The poet is depicted reciting poetry, his hand is outstretched in a free gesture and his head is proudly thrown back. The graceful, four-metre-high statue reveals to us the inspired image of the poet. The author of the monument, sculptor Mikhail Anikushin, wrote about his creation: "Pushkin was a bright personality; he was simple in his actions and clear in his thoughts. Therefore I tried to get rid of all the details that might hide that clear image of our great poet ... I wanted the statue—Pushkin's figure—to radiate joy and warmth." The sculptor was awarded the Lenin Prize for this work.

Standard façades for the buildings in Arts Square and on what is now Brodsky Street were designed by Rossi. Each owner of a plot of land had the right to build a house of his own choice, but only on the condition that the façade overlooking the street or the square conform to Rossi's standard project. In keeping with the project, the different architects created a remarkable architectural ensemble.

The famous Soviet artist Isaac Brodsky lived on the western side of Arts Square at No. 3, flat l, from 1924 to 1939. Today this flat, where he painted most of his famous works, is a **memorial museum** housing approximately 200 paintings and works of graphic art by Brodsky, his personal effects and furnishings.

One of the main attractions of the museum is the collection of works by great Russian artists at the turn of the 20th century put together by Brodsky himself. These are mainly landscapes, portraits, small compositions, sketches by Ilya Repin, Vasily Surikov, Arkhip Kuindji, Valentin Serov, Boris Kustodiyev, Mikhail Nesterov, and others.

A memorial plaque hangs at No. 5, where the well-known Soviet sculptor Vasily Kozlov, the author of the statue of Lenin at the Smolny, spent the last twelve years of his life (1929 to 1940).

At the corner house (No. 1), the **State Academic Maly Opera House** is situated. Erected in 1830–1833 by the architect Alexander Bryullov, its façade was designed in complete conformity with Rossi's standard project. The Opera House has the rather mod-

est appearance of an urban residence.

Before the Revolution the French court troupe used to give performances to the small audiences of aristocrats at the Mikhailovsky Theatre, as it was called at the time. Founded in 1918, the Maly Opera House became a major centre of Soviet musical culture.

Along the other side of Arts Square, the corner building looking out onto Brodsky Street is occupied by the **Leningrad Philharmonia**, which was named after the composer Dmitry Shostakovich in 1976. The building housing the Philharmonia was erected by the architect Paul Jacquot in 1834–1839 (the façades were designed by Carlo Rossi) for the Noblemen's Assembly. The hall of the Assembly was frequently used for concerts owing to its excellent acoustics. The eminent composer Anton Rubinstein gave performances here, and Pyotr Tchaikovsky conducted the orchestra playing his Sixth (Pathetique) Symphony.

After the Great October Socialist Revolution the hall was given over to Leningrad Philharmonia, which was set up in 1921. The Academic Philharmonic Orchestra was headed by the late Yevgeny Mravinsky, an outstanding conductor, since 1938. In the concert hall of the Philharmonia eminent Soviet and foreign musicians, singers, and conductors gave their performances.

An outstanding event in the history of the Philharmonia was registered on the night of August 9, 1942, when in spite of the trying days of the blockade, the orchestra of Leningrad's radio, conducted by Karl Eliasberg, played the Seventh Symphony of Dmitry Shostakovich. The composer began writing this symphony in the besieged city. At the time, he was a member of the air defence unit, quartered in the conservatoire in Theatre Square. Frequently, the letters "VT"

Anichkov Palace

were outlined in the margins of his score, a sign never known before in the history of music. These letters stand for *vozdushnaya trevoga*, which is the Russian for air raid. This mark made, the composer would go up to the roof of the conservatoire building to put out the enemy incendiary bombs. The symphony begun in July 1941 was completed by December of that year. It was first performed in March 1942 in Kuibyshev and then in Moscow. Soon the symphony was performed in London and New York.

In the depositories of the Saltykov-Shchedrin Public Library a poster has been preserved announcing to Leningraders that the symphony was to be played on August 9, 1942. The text read over Leningrad radio before the concert has also been preserved. "Comrades," said the announcer, "today an important event in the cultural life of our city will take place. In a few minutes you will hear the Seventh Symphony by Dmitry Shostakovich, our outstanding fellow townsman, performed in Leningrad for the first time. He has written this remarkable work in our city in the days of the Patriotic War, while the enemy has been

trying to break through into Leningrad, while the Nazi villains have been showering our city with bombs and shells, when the Germans have been shouting all over Europe that the days of Leningrad were numbered. Shostakovich has written this symphony calling for struggle and conforming our belief in victory ... Listen, the concert is on the air now ..."

All the radio stations in the Soviet Union transmitted the symphony, and the radio waves from blockaded Leningrad were received in many countries throughout the world.

Opposite the Philharmonia stands the **Hotel Yevropeiskaya**, one of the most luxurious hotels in Leningrad.

Now take a last look at Arts Square and return to Nevsky Avenue for the rest of your excursion. You will pass a unique building occupying a whole block on the right side at the widest part of the avenue. This two-storey building with a continuous line of arcades is the **Gostiny Dvor** department store (architect Jean-Baptiste Vallin de la Mothe, 1761–1785). In old Russia merchants visiting the city used to put up at the *gostiniye dvory*, or guest houses, which also served for business. The building looks out onto four streets; its perimeter is more than a kilometre, and the façade on Nevsky Avenue is 230 m long.

During the blockade of Leningrad the Gostiny Dvor was seriously damaged by bombs and fires. Now, while preserving its external appearance, it has been replanned inside to house 300 small shops under a single roof, and is now the largest department store in the city. More than 300,000 shoppers bustle through the store every day.

When the building was reconstructed, and the present shopping premises replaced the small shops, the teams of workers and builders discovered eight large, extraordinarily heavy bricks under the floor. When examined closely, these bricks turned out to be of pure, high quality gold with a total weight of 128 kg. There was apparently a jeweller's shop in these premises before the Revolution, and the owner had evidently decided to hide his gold by making it into ingots looking like bricks.

Opposite the Gostiny Dvor there is one of the largest department stores in the city, the **Passazh** (meaning "passage" or "arcade"). Its entrances are both on Nevsky Avenue and in Rakov Street (Ulitsa Rakova). In a single day 250,000–270,000 shoppers visit this department store selling goods for women. Right down in the middle of the long gallery is the **Komissarzhevskaya Drama Theatre**. Here in 1904–1906 the company headed by the outstanding Russian actress Vera Komissarzhevskaya staged plays that reflected the mood of the progressive Russian intelligentsia. In the interpretation of this theatre the plays of Russian playwrights sounded like a sharp protest against the reactionary political order of tsarist Russia. During the first revolution in Russia in 1905–1907 performances of Gorky's plays frequently turned into political manifestations. The modern Komissarzhevskaya Theatre is comparatively new,

Pushkin Drama Theatre

appearing during the blockade, at the end of 1942. This theatre's repertoire includes primarily Soviet plays.

As you walk further down Nevsky Avenue you will cross Garden Street (Sadovaya Ulitsa) and pass the building of the Saltykov-Shchedrin Public Library (we shall talk about this library later on) and come out in **OSTROVSKY SQUARE** (Ploshchad Ostrovskogo), one of the city's most interesting ensembles.

The area occupied by this square and the districts adjacent to it began to take shape soon after Nevsky Avenue was laid out. At that time, the boundary of St. Petersburg ran along the River Fontanka. The building team headed by Lieutenant-Colonel Mikhail Anichkov, who built the first bridge across the river, was quartered here. To this day the bridge retains the name of Mikhail Anichkov.

In 1750, on the bank of the Fontanka, a palace for Count Alexei Razumovsky was built by the architects Mikhail Zemtsov and Grigory Dmitriyev. The palace came to be known as the **Anichkov Palace** (owing to the nearby bridge). The front of the palace looks out over the Fontanka and the plain

Saltykov-Shchedrin Public Library RUSSIAN NATIONAL LIBRARY.

side (northern) wall of the building faces onto Nevsky Avenue, which was at that time a small, unimportant street.

Since 1937 the palace has housed the **Palace of Young Pioneers.** The old premises of the palace have been restored and reconstructed, so that the children now have at their disposal more than 300 rooms and halls, accommodating hundreds of interest groups and clubs. Ten thousand young Leningraders belong to the

technology, tourism, arts and crafts, sports, natural science, booklovers', young sailors' and young geologists', chess, and other clubs, and make use of the laboratories.

In the 18th century a large garden abutted onto the western façade of the Anichkov Palace. In 1828, the building of the present **Pushkin Academic Drama Theatre,** designed by Carlo Rossi, was erected on the site of this garden. The theatre's main fa-

Reading-room in the library

çade is decorated with a six-column loggia raised on a high basement storey. The entire building is girded by a frieze of theatrical masks and garlands, and its front is crowned with the chariot of Apollo, the patron of the muses (sculptor Stepan Pimenov). Images of the muses grace the main façade.

Since its foundation, the theatre (in 1832–1917 it was called the Alexandrinsky Theatre after Alexandra, the wife of Nicholas I) has played an outstanding part in the country's public life, propagandising progressive Russian drama. Many outstanding actors have appeared on its stage. The theatre's present repertoire contains plays by Russian, Soviet, and foreign playwrights.

The eastern side of Ostrovsky Square, framed by a shady garden, is surrounded by beautiful wrought-iron railings. Adjacent are two garden pavilions. These pavilions and the railings were designed by Carlo Rossi in 1817–1818. Statues of Russian warriors sculptured by Vasily Demut-Malinovsky are mounted between their columns.

On the opposite side of this square

stands the **Saltykov-Shchedrin Public Library**. The library's first building (architect Yegor Sokolov, 1796–1801) is situated on the corner of Nevsky Avenue and Garden Street. In 1828–1832, Rossi built an extension onto it overlooking Ostrovsky Square. The walls of the new building are decorated with bas-reliefs and sculptures of scholars, orators, philosophers, and writers of ancient times.

A statue of Minerva, the goddess of wisdom, the patroness of the sciences, crowns the building. The helmet of the goddess is embellished with a tiny sculpture of the sphinx, the smallest sphinx in Leningrad. The sculptures on the façade of the public library testify, as it were, to the tremendous wealth of human knowledge and wisdom stored within its walls.

The Leningrad Public Library, opened in 1814, is one of the largest in the world. A memorial plaque on the building reminds you that Lenin was a constant visitor to the library between 1893 and 1895. During these visits Lenin secretly met with his comrades from the revolutionary underground movement, most often frequenting the room which is today marked by a memorial plaque and named after him.

In the year the library was opened its one and only reading room could seat just forty-six people. At that time, its depositories held 238,000 volumes (among them only eight were in Russian or Church Slavonic). By 1917 the library's stocks had reached 3,000,000 volumes.

In the years of Soviet rule the stocks have grown almost eightfold and now total more than 25,500,000 items. Approximately 2,000,000 people visit the library in the course of a year. The library lends out some 10,000,000 copies of books. Here you will find literature in 89 languages of the peoples of the USSR, in all European languages, and also in 156 languages of Africa and the

Anichkov Bridge

Orient. This is the second largest library in the country after the Lenin State Library in Moscow.

Books are exchanged with more than 2,600 organisations from 112 different countries. Every year the library's collections are supplemented by some 800,000–900,000 books, maps, journals, and newspapers. The stock of Russian books is the most complete collection of printed editions in Russian from the beginning of book-printing in Russia. Of special interest are the early-printed books and the collection *Free Russian Printing*, which includes revolutionary works published abroad or underground in Russia before 1917.

The stocks of foreign books are vast and include works in almost all languages on a wide range of subjects. The library has collections of West-European publications printed before 1500; a collection entitled *Rossica*, which incorporates works on Russia in foreign languages; translations of works by Russian writers, and books published in foreign languages in Russia.

In the manuscripts section there is an extremely large collection of old Slavonic and Russian hand-written books and manuscripts, among them the *Ostromirovo Gospel* (11th century), 15th-century chronicles, papers and autographs of Peter the Great and Alexander Suvorov, and also the only copy in the world of *Chasovnik* (Breviary) published by the first printer in Russia, Ivan Fyodorov, in 1565 on the orders of Ivan the Terrible. This is the second Russian dated printed book after the *Apostle*.

Among the rare books is the personal library of Voltaire. Another unique acquisition is a collection of Krylov's fables printed in 1865, the smallest book in the world. The size of a postage stamp, it has approximately 500 characters on each of its 104 pages, and the microscopic print is so clear that the text can be read with the naked eye.

In the stocks of literature of the peoples of the Orient there are books, journals, and newspapers in more than 20 languages, including works dating back to the 3rd century B. C. A xylographic publication of the famous Chinese Tusu Tsi Ch'en encyclopaedia (more than 1,300 volumes) as well as the encyclopaedia of the Tsin dynasty (more than 1,000 volumes) are kept here. An extremely rare edition on the history of the Taiping uprising (the peasant war in China in 1851–1864), and Sanskrit editions on the history of Hindu philosophy and social topical themes can also be found here.

In the manuscripts section, of considerable interest are the extant parts of the archives of the Bastille, the police dossier of Voltaire, the letters of Erasmus of Rotterdam, Leibniz, Rousseau, Diderot, the autographs of Rossini, Mirabeau, Robespierre, Napoleon, Byron, Béranger, Heine, and other valuable materials. Quite recently three manuscripts were discovered here—the philosophical compositions of Immanuel Kant. They were deciphered with the help of West German scientists affiliated with the Kant archives in Marburg.

Before the library, in the small garden in Ostrovsky Square, stands a **statue of Catherine the Great** (author of the project Mikhail Mikeshin, sculptors Matvei Chizhov and Alexander Opekushin, designer of the pedestal and superviser of the work David Grimm, 1873). The empress is depicted in an ermine robe, holding a sceptre, and surrounded by her associates at the foot of the high granite pedestal. On the front side of the monument is Catherine's favourite, the political and military personage, count Grigory Potyomkin of Taurida stepping on a Turkish turban. Beside him stands Generalissimo Alexander Suvorov. On the other side of Potyomkin is Field Marshal Pyotr Rumyantsev-Zadunaisky, and behind him, holding an open book, Yekaterina Dashkova, the Director of the Russian Academy of Sciences. Then comes the poet Gavriil Derzhavin, the Admiral Vasily Chichagov, and other eminent figures in Russia at the end of the 18th century.

A certain conventionality in the composition of the monument is evident, for the statue of Catherine the Great (4.35 m) is almost twice as high as the other figures and the stance of the empress is theatrical and pompous. Nevertheless, the monument is of artistic value owing to the realistic interpretation of the personages, each of whom is sculptured with portrait likeness.

Behind the Pushkin Drama Theatre extend two buildings of the same type, the walls of which, like those of the theatre, are painted yellow and decorated with white columns. They form the Architect Rossi Street (Ulitsa Zodchego Rossi), the width of which

Sculptural group on Anichkov Bridge

is the same as the height of the buildings, namely 22 m. Furthermore, the length of each building exceeds its height exactly tenfold.

This street was laid out in 1828–1834 as part of the present Ostrovsky Square ensemble. Initially, the ground floors, which looked like an open arcade, were intended to house shops. However, the merchants of the main shopping arcade (Gostiny Dvor) nearby were afraid of competition and succeeded in having the arcade bricked up.

In the butt-end of the building facing the theatre and forming the right side of the street is the **Leningrad State Museum of Drama and Music** (No. 6a, Ostrovsky Square). Its approximately 400,000 exhibits tell the history of the Russian drama and musical theatre from its very outset to the present day. Visitors to the museum may also listen to recordings of arias, scenes, and monologues performed by great Russian stage artistes.

Here you will also find the **Luna-charsky Theatrical Library**, the oldest and largest theatrical book depository in the USSR housing more than 350,000 Russian and foreign plays, sketches of costumes and sets, letters, and memoirs. In the card index on the history of Russian drama and musical theatre a vast collection of materials is kept, dating from 1800 to the present day.

This building also houses the **Vaganova School of Choreography** founded in 1738 as classes training dancers for the court theatres. Later, it became a school which played an outstanding part in the creation of Russian ballet. Anna Pavlova, Mikhail Fokin, George Balanchin, Vakhtang Chabukiani, Galina Ulanova, and many other famous masters of Russian and Soviet ballet studied here. Agrippina Vaganova, after whom the school is named, an outstanding ballerina and choreographer, taught here from 1921 to 1951.

Now that you have seen the sights of Ostrovsky Square, return to Nevsky Avenue.

On the right side of the avenue at No. 52 stands the **State Puppet Theatre**, the first professional puppet theatre in the USSR, founded in 1918. Besides Soviet plays, its repertoire includes works by Czech, Hungarian, American, and other foreign playwrights.

The **Leningrad Academic Comedy Theatre**, founded in 1929, is located on the corner of Nevsky Avenue and Little Garden Street (Malaya Sadovaya Ulitsa) at No. 56. For a number of years the outstanding Soviet director and stage designer Nikolai Akimov worked here. The ground floor of the theatre houses one of the city's largest grocer's shops.

Next to the Comedy Theatre at No. 58 is the **Leningrad House of Scientific and Technological Propaganda**, the centre for disseminating the latest achievements of science and technology. On display here are samples of the finest goods manufactured by Leningrad's industry.

Just a few minutes walk from here you come to **Anichkov Bridge** already mentioned in connection with the ensemble in Ostrovsky Square. Today's bridge (54 m long, 37 m wide) was built in 1839–1841 (engineer Andrei Gotman, architect Alexander Bryullov). Formerly, a narrow drawbridge with granite towers stood on the site.

The bridge is famous for its **equestrian statues**, sculptured by Pyotr Klodt. One of them depicts a young man leading a horse; the other—a youth attempting to control a mettlesome horse. Each of the two equestrian statues was cast twice, to make one for each of the four corners of the bridge. However, the sculptor's design was not carried out completely. Before the sculptures were mounted on the bridge, Nicholas I ordered that two of the statues be sent to Berlin as a present to the Prussian king. These sculptures were erected there in front of the Grand Palace and were so highly valued that Klodt was elected a member of the Academy of Arts of Berlin and then of Paris and Rome. In place of the bronze groups sent to Berlin, plaster moulds, painted to look like the remaining bronze groups, were erected. In the autumn of 1843 these were replaced by metal sculptures, though not for long ...

In 1846 Nicholas I again ordered that two of Klodt's groups be taken down from the Anichkov Bridge and sent abroad, this time as a gift to the King of Naples. The bronze horses and youths were erected in Naples in the garden of the San Carlo Theatre, and, till 1850, plaster sculptures replaced them in St. Petersburg. It was suggested that Klodt should cast a copy of his two sculptures in bronze again. But the sculptor decided that one of the capital's central bridges deserved to have something better than

Gate of the Institute of the Arctic and the Antarctic

identical pairs of sculptures, and so his suggestion of preparing two new sculptures was accepted. In 1850 they were mounted on the pedestals of the Anichkov Bridge. The third group depicts a youth kneeling and winding the bridle round his hand trying to restrain the horse as it rushes forward. The fourth group captures the moment when the young man has been thrown down under the hooves of the fiery stallion as it rears.

Near Anichkov Bridge at No. 21 on River Fontanka Embankment (Naberezhnaya Reki Fontanki) is the **House of Friendship and Peace with the Peoples of Foreign Countries**. The Leningrad Branch of the Union of Soviet Societies for Friendship and Cultural Relations with Foreign Countries operates here. This large-scale public organisation acquaints the people of Leningrad with life in other countries and, likewise, tells people abroad about the achievements of Leningrad in science and culture. The Leningrad

Stanislavsky Centre for Workers in the Arts

branch of the Society for Friendship and Cultural Relations has 20 local branches and unites in its ranks members from more than 500 factories, offices, and other establishments. In Leningrad there are branches of the societies for friendship with the socialist countries, as well as branches of the following societies: USSR—Great Britain, USSR—France, USSR—Italy, USSR—Norway, USSR—Sweden, USSR—Finland, and USSR—Japan, the society of Soviet-Indian contacts and the sections of the societies USSR—Denmark and USSR—FRG.

This is also the seat of the **Leningrad Peace Committee**. Here a book in a red cover contains comments in almost all the languages of the world, expressions of admiration at the courage of Leningrad, words professing belief in the fraternity of mankind. The President of the World Peace Council, Romesh Chandra, said that the word Leningrad means the same in all languages: revolution, peace, unsurpassed courage, and friendship with all peoples on Earth.

This same building also houses the Leningrad regional section of the So-

viet Peace Fund. Means from this fund go to aid peoples struggling to eliminate the threat of war and imperialism, fighting for freedom, independence and social progress. Hundreds of thousands of Leningraders, honouring the traditions of international solidarity, make a weighty contribution to the fight for peace.

On the opposite side of the Fontanka, the old mansion at No. 34 houses the **Institute of the Arctic and the Antarctic**, the largest scientific research centre of its kind in the world.

On a granite pedestal by the institute stands the bust of the great Norwegian explorer, Roald Amundsen. This bust is the work of the Norwegian sculptor Karl Paulsen and was presented to the Soviet Union by the government of Norway as a sign of recognition of Soviet achievements in the exploration of the Arctic and the Antarctic.

The building of the institute is a remarkable monument of mid-18th-century Russian architecture. In 1712, Peter the Great presented this plot of land to Field Marshal Boris Sheremetev. The present building was erected in 1750–1755 by two outstanding ar-

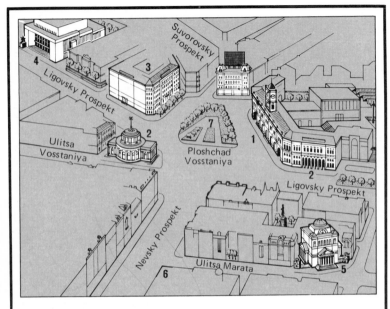

NEVSKY PROSPEKT—PLOSHCHAD VOSSTANIYA

1. *Moscow Railway Station*
2. *Metro station* Ploshchad Vosstaniya
3. Oktyabrskaya *Hotel*
4. *Grand Concert Hall* Oktyabrsky
5. *Museum of the Arctic and the Antarctic*
6. *Metro station* Mayakovskaya
7. *Obelisk to the Hero-City of Leningrad*

chitects, Fyodor Argunov and Savva Chevakinsky. The general outlines of the edifice are mainly in keeping with the traditions of the comparatively modest architecture of the early part of the 18th century. However, the Corinthian pilasters, the elaborate window surrounds, and the sculptural ornamentation on the facades testify to the fact that in the second half of the 18th century Baroque was becoming more prevalent in Russian architecture.

In the mid-19th century the mansion was occupied by the Field Marshal's descendant, one of the richest men in Russia, Nikolai Sheremetev. The composer Mikhail Glinka used to visit here. When the artist Orest Kiprensky was living at this house, Alexander Pushkin sat for him to have his portrait painted.

Now you have digressed from your main excursion route somewhat and must return to Nevsky Avenue. It should be mentioned that the remaining part of the Avenue up to Uprising Square (Ploshchad Vosstaniya) was built up largely at the end of the 19th century and does not include unique monuments like the ones you have seen in the first part of your route.

Uprising Square and the Moscow Railway Station

However, No. 41, built in the middle of the last century by the architect Andrei Stakenschneider for Prince Beloselsky-Belozersky is worthy of note. Its façades, which overlook Nevsky Avenue and the embankment of the River Fontanka, bear a compositional and decorative appointment typical of the 18th century. The palace interior stands out for its artistic integrity. Among other worthwhile buildings is that at No. 68/40, which was connected with the activity of Lenin in 1905. Moreover, in 1842–1846 the great Russian critic and revolutionary-democrat Vissarion Belinsky lived in a flat here, where he was frequently visited by Ivan Goncharov, Fyodor Dostoyevsky, and other writers of the 19th century. The writer Ivan Turgenev lived in this house in 1851.

The neighbouring building, No. 70, houses the Leningrad organisation of the Union of Journalists of the USSR. In the 19th century it belonged to General Sukhozanet, a hero of the war against Napoleon. The building was erected in the 1820s by architect Domenico Quadri. Its façade is classical in design. The wrought-iron railing on the balcony is distinctive. The vestibule is decorated with columns faced with artificial marble, the hall finished with a moulded frieze consisting of military accoutrements, and many decorative plafonds.

Not far away, at No. 86, you will see the **Stanislavsky Centre for Workers in the Arts**. In the 1830s this old building was rebuilt by the architect Gaspare Fossati. Before the Revolution it was one of the many palaces of Prince Yusupov. The building is effective and imposing owing to the high colonnade mounted on the projecting part of the ground floor. The upper part of the side wings is not interrupted by window apertures and is embellished with luxurious bas-reliefs of tastefully arranged military accoutrements.

On Marat Street (Ulitsa Marata), which runs off to the right from Nevsky Avenue, the first Russian revolutionary aristocrat Alexander Radishchev (1749–1802) lived at No. 14 from 1776 to 1790. Here he wrote his book *A Journey from St. Petersburg to Moscow* denouncing the autocracy and serfdom, for which the author was deprived of his aristocratic title and banished to Siberia.

A little further on, at No. 24a, there

is the only **Museum of the Arctic and the Antarctic** in the world, founded in 1937. At the museum you can learn about the nature and the history of the exploration of the Arctic and the Antarctic, about the progress made in building an economy and providing cultural facilities inside the Arctic Circle in the Soviet Union. The museum's collection contains approximately 20,000 exhibits, including maps, photographs and models of ships, exploration routes and the personal effects of famous polar explorers, equipment, apparatuses and instruments used by Soviet scientists in the Arctic and the Antarctic.

Your walk along Nevsky Avenue is coming to an end. Here you will arrive at **UPRISING SQUARE** (Ploshchad Vosstaniya), which is quite rightly considered to be the gates of Leningrad, for every day 75 long-distance trains and 105 suburban trains leave the platforms of the Moscow Station there. To the left, on the corner of the square closest to you (at the intersection of Nevsky and Ligovsky avenues), is the **pavilion of the Metro station**, and in the centre of the square is a garden from which a splendid view of Nevsky Avenue and the Admiralty opens out.

The origins of Uprising Square are linked with the city's early history. This was the site of the intersection of Bolshaya Perspektivnaya Doroga (Great Perspective Road, as Nevsky Avenue was called before 1738) and the road to Novgorod, now Ligovsky Avenue, where a huge patch of waste ground formed, now covered by Uprising Square. At the beginning of the 19th century, on the edge of this waste ground (where the pavilion of the Metro station now stands) the Church of the Sign was erected, giving the square its first name—the Square of the Sign (Znamenskaya Ploshchad). But the square remained just as desolate as before and was still on the remote outskirts of the city.

Church of the Annunciation of the former Alexander Nevsky Monastery (Laura)

In 1851, when trains began to run between St. Petersburg and Moscow, the Moscow Railway Station was built in the Square of the Sign by the architect Konstantin Ton. A hundred years later, the station premises were rebuilt by the architect Vladimir Kuznetsov and were adapted to the needs of the rapidly growing flow of passengers. The station's façade overlooking the square has preserved its original appearance.

In the mid-19th century a **hotel** (now the **Oktyabrskaya**) was built opposite the station. In 1961, the hotel was reconstructed and next to the old building new blocks mushroomed to form a vast complex stretching along Ligovsky Avenue.

The former Square of the Sign witnessed important historical events which played a decisive part in the life of the country. In February 1917, the square was the site of frequent meetings. The Bolshevik speakers were calling to overthrow the tsar, to free the revolutionaries who were languishing in prison and to put an end to the highly unpopular imperialist war. On February 25, a mounted police force rushed at those present at the meeting. The soldiers and Cossacks brought into the square took the side of the workers and began to defend them. One of the Cossacks killed the district superintendent of the police force with his sabre. The troops started to go over to the side of the people.

On February 26 (March 11), 1917, a demonstration in the Square of the Sign, which was trying to make its way from the outskirts of the city into the centre, was fired upon by the police. Forty people were killed and dozens were wounded. Strikes and mass protests flared up into an uprising. On February 27, the tsar was overthrown in Russia. To commemorate these events in the Square of the Sign, it was renamed Uprising Square.

At the centre of Uprising Square towers an obelisk "To the Hero-City of Leningrad". The authors of the monument, Alexander Alymov and Veniamin Pinchuk, succeeded in making it equally impressive from all angles of vision. It seems to be situated on the point of intersection of three axes of the square: Nevsky Avenue, the Hotel Oktyabrskaya, and the Moscow Station.

The obelisk, crowned with the Gold Star of the hero-city, has a total height of 33 m (the height of the star is about 2 m). Its pentagonal base is decorated with high reliefs devoted to the theme of Leningrad's defence during the Great Patriotic War of 1941–1945.

The unveiling of the obelisk took place on May 9, 1985—the forty-year anniversary of Victory in the Great Patriotic War.

Not far from Uprising Square is Alexander Nevsky Square (Ploshchad Alexandra Nevskogo), the final point of your excursion along Nevsky Avenue. On your way there, take a look to your right, down Poltava Street (Poltavskaya Ulitsa). Here you will see a most unusual architectural ensemble:

a high fortress wall with battlements in the form of "swallows' tails", reminiscent of the Moscow Kremlin, and a mighty tower with gun-slots and the same type of battlements. This structure was not intended for fortification, but for decoration. It was erected in 1914 by the architect Stepan Krichinsky as a type of screen in front of the railway stock-yard.

Continuing along Nevsky Avenue, take note of No. 139. Here two outstanding contributors to the arts spent their childhood years: composer Vasily Solovyov-Sedoi (author of widely renowned song *Moscow Nights*) and actor Alexander Borisov. Both of them were friends of Yevgeni Nikolayev, son of General Alexander Nikolayev, a hero of the Russo-Japanese war of 1904–1905, who lived on the first floor of this building. After the Revolution General Nikolayev joined the people and became a Red Army commander. During the civil war he was taken prisoner, refused to renounce his convictions, and was publicly hanged by the White Guards.

Once at **ALEXANDER NEVSKY SQUARE** you will see the former **Alexander Nevsky Monastery** (or **laura**, denoting the highest rank of monastery). In Russia before the Revolution there were only four such *lauras* including the Alexander Nevsky Monastery which was raised to this rank in 1797. It was named after the great warrior, the Prince of Novgorod, Alexander Nevsky (1220–1263), on the occasion of his canonisation.

The main entrance to the monastery is embellished by a graceful **gate church** (architect Ivan Starov, 1783–1785), and beyond it there are several graveyards. To the left of the main entrance lies the 18th-century **Lazarevskoye Cemetery**, the oldest in the city. It came into being soon after the foundation of the monastery in 1716 when Natalya Alexeyevna, the sister of Peter the Great, was buried here. Many eminent figures in Russian culture, such as the scholar Mikhail Lomonosov and the architects Andrei Voronikhin, Andreyan Zakharov, and Carlo Rossi, lie at rest here.

To the right of the main entrance you will see the **Tikhvinskoye Cemetery**. Here on the gravestones you will find the names of the composers Mikhail Glinka, Pyotr Tchaikovsky, Modest Moussorgsky, Nikolai Rimsky-Korsakov, the writer Fyodor Dostoyevsky, the artist Alexander Ivanov, the architect Vasily Stasov, the sculptor Pyotr Klodt and other prominent figures in science and the arts.

The architects Domenico Trezzini and Ivan Starov assisted in building the monastery. Its oldest part is the tower to the left of the main gate (constructed in 1722). In this two-storey building there are two churches: the upper church erected in honour of Alexander Nevsky, and the lower one, the Church of the Annunciation. Among the stone slabs of the Church of the Annunciation a marble gravestone is immured bearing the inscription (believed to have been at the request of the Generalissimo himself): "Here lies Suvorov". Many other burial places in this church have gravestones sculptured by Ivan Martos, Fyodor Gordeyev, and other outstanding Russian masters.

This building houses the **Museum of Urban Sculpture**, which embraces all monumental sculptures adorning the city. They are repesented at the museum as models, many of which were created by the authors themselves. You can see the original models for the equestrian groups on the Anichkov Bridge, showing the creative effort of their sculptor, Pyotr Klodt. The collection in the Soviet section of the museum comprises a large number of models made by the sculptors themselves. In the centre of the hall stands a model of the well-known statue of Lenin at the Finland Station.

Especially noteworthy in the monastery complex is the **Cathedral of the Trinity** (Ivan Starov, 1778–1790), one of the finest examples of Russian classicism, and the **Metropolitan's residence** (Mikhail Rastorguyev, 1756–1759), an outstanding work of Russian Baroque. Beyond the Cathedral of the Trinity is yet another cemetery bearing the graves of veteran Bolsheviks and revolutionaries.

The Hotel Moscow, one of Leningrad's largest, is the focal point of Alexander Nevsky Square.

The **Alexander Nevsky Bridge**, the longest bridge in Leningrad (906 m), completed in 1965, spans the Neva from the walls of the Alexander Nevsky Monastery. The system for raising the bridge is an original one. With the help of a hydraulic drive the span of the drawbridge can be raised in two minutes, opening the way to large-tonnage vessels. This bridge links Nevsky Avenue with the formerly remote outskirts of the city, the district of Malaya Okhta, which is today a district of intensive housing construction.

6

STRIKE AVENUE—STRIKE SQUARE—KIROV SQUARE—KOMSOMOL SQUARE

Estimated time needed to get to know the sights on this excursion is 2 hours. Nearest Metro station—Narvskaya.

Tourist attractions: the Narva Gate (19th century), the Gorky Community Centre, the statue of Sergei Kirov, the January 9th Children's Park, the Kirov Factory industrial amalgamation, the monument to the Heroic Komsomol, the former estate of Alexandrino, and the Lenin Southern Esplanade Park.

On your previous excursions you have mainly walked around the central districts of the city. Excursions 6 and 7 will take you by bus as well as on foot, for example, down Strike Avenue and Moscow Avenue, where you will see how the outskirts of Leningrad have been built up in Soviet times.

From its very inception, St. Petersburg has been linked with Moscow, Narva, and other towns in Russia by highways. At each entrance into the city there was a gate guarded by soldiers who checked the documents of those leaving and arriving, and levied a toll for the right to enter the city. Some of the southern districts of Leningrad have taken their names from these guard-posts, for example, the Narva Gate district.

The road that led from the city to Peterhof (now Petrodvorets) and Oranienbaum (now Lomonosov), the so-called Peterhof Road, laid the foundation for the present Strike Avenue. This was once a favourite spot for the rich aristocrats who built their suburban mansions and estates here. But as capitalism developed in Russia the noblemen's estates had to give way to factories. Thus, the Neva, Moscow, and Narva Gate districts became workers' districts on the outskirts of the city, although they were not formally within the city limits.

Today the Kirov district of Leningrad, or the former Narva Gate district, famed for its revolutionary traditions, has enterprises where steel is smelted, the modern machines are created, ships are built and repaired, fabrics are manufactured and building materials are produced. The Leningrad Merchant Seaport is located here; sailors from many different countries are well acquainted with it. Every year more than 4,000 vessels dock here.

New modern housing estates have spread far beyond the bounds of the

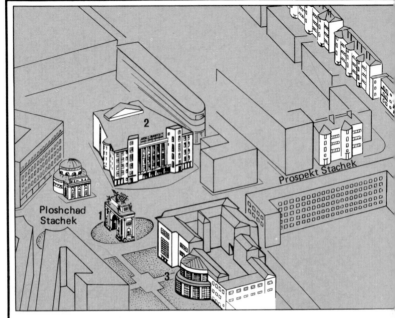

PLOSHCHAD STACHEK—
PROSPEKT STACHEK—
KIROVSKAYA PLOSHCHAD

1. Narva Gate
2. Gorky Community Centre
3. Kirov department store and
   a food-take-away

old Narva Gate district. In the years of Soviet power the area of housing in this district has increased dozens of times over. The Metro and other forms of modern transport link the district with the centre of the city.

STRIKE AVENUE (Prospekt Stachek), 8,471 m long, was given its present name in honour of the revolutionary struggle of the workers of the Narva Gate district. **STRIKE SQUARE** (Ploshchad Stachek), from which our excursion begins, is one of the places associated with "Bloody Sunday", January 9 (22), 1905, the day the tsarist government opened fire on a peaceful procession of St. Petersburg workers.

Naturally, the square retains almost nothing of its former appearance: with the exception of the Narva Gate everything here is new. At the foot of the gateway arch a garden has been laid out and the square is lined by new blocks of flats, a department store, one of the largest shops in Leningrad, a dining complex, and beyond it the stadium of the Kirov Factory industrial amalgamation. On the other side, next to the pavilion of the *Narvskaya* **Metro station** stands the Gorky Community Centre. You can get from the department store to the Metro station by the pedestrian underpass.

The main architectural and histori-

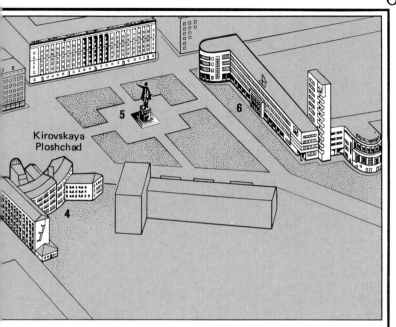

4. *Tenth Anniversary of the
   October Revolution School*
5. *Statue of Sergei Kirov*

6. *District Soviet of People's
   Deputies*

cal sight in the square, the **Narva Triumphal Gate** erected to mark Russia's
victory in the Patriotic War of 1812 is
one of the many monuments in Leningrad commemorating the glory of
Russian arms. The gate, designed by
Giacomo Quarenghi, was originally
constructed of wood. Alexander I
generously remunerated the architect
for his work by awarding him an order and bestowing upon him the title
of honorary citizen of Russia, the latter of which was very much appreciated by Quarenghi.

In 1811, when Napoleon's army and the
Italian forces were preparing for their campaign against Russia, the viceroy of Italy ordered all Italians working in Russia to return to their homeland, including the
architect Giacomo Quarenghi. But Quarenghi, who considered Russia to be his true
homeland, refused to return to Italy and
was therefore deprived of Italian citizen-
ship and condemned to death in absentia.
So the architect lived and worked in St. Petersburg to the end of his days.

Returning to Russia after their victory over Napoleon's armies, the soldiers marched triumphantly through
the wide archway of Quarenghi's
gate. In the 1820s the architect Vasily
Stasov designed a new gate of stone
and metal to replace the weather-
beaten wooden one, largely preserving Quarenghi's composition. The
site for this gate was selected on the

Strike Square

Peterhof Road (today Strike Avenue).

In 1834, a single-span stone archway was completed. It was faced with sheets of copper and decorated with columns, and in its composition imitated the ancient Roman triumphal arches. The gate was considerably more attractive than Quarenghi's. Besides the chariot of Victory, which formerly crowned the arch, Stasov decorated his structure with allegorical figures of Glory, inscriptions recording the guards regiments that had become famous in the war, and the sites of great battles. Once he had worked out his project, Stasov suggested erecting statues of Mikhail Kutuzov and Mikhail Barklay de Tolli between the columns on the piers of the archway, but subsequently he rejected this idea. Instead of sculptures of the military leaders he introduced into the arch's ornamentation figures of ancient Russian warriors holding out laurel wreathes. In the post-war years this valuable monument, which was damaged by Nazi bombs and shells, was carefully restored.

In the near future Stasov's idea of creating a museum commemorating the victory over Napoleon inside the top part of the arch will be realised. The exposition will concentrate on the military glory of the Russian people in the Patriotic War of 1812.

In 1927, on the tenth anniversary of the Great October Socialist Revolution, the **Gorky Community Centre** (architects Alexander Gegello, David Krichevsky, and Vladimir Railyan), one of 200 community centres in Leningrad, celebrated its grand opening in Strike Square. More than 50 amateur art groups involving approximately 2,500 people operate there. Art groups from the community centre are well known in Leningrad, for instance, the people's amateur theatrical society, the people's ballet theatre, the symphony orchestra, the vocal ensembles, and the orchestra of Russian folk instruments. The participants in the community centre's amateur art activities go on tours abroad, for instance, to the GDR, Hungary, Finland, Norway, and Japan. Some 1,400 children and teenagers attend the centre's science and arts circles and clubs.

The community centre's auditorium seating 1,900 is impressively spacious and brightly decorated. The semicir-

Narva Triumphal Gate

cular boxes descending in tiers to the stage and the semicircular balconies rhythmically divide up the auditorium's side walls.

To the right of the Gorky Community Centre, on the side of a block of flats you will be attracted by a **panel**, approximately 200 sq m in area, dedicated to the revolutionary traditions of the old Narva Gate district. A worker carrying a red banner is depicted in the centre of it. The panel is executed in the sgraffito—a decorative technique in which the outer thin layer of

plaster is scratched away, thereby revealing the inner layer, which differs in colour from the outer one. Sgraffito was widespread in Italy in the 15th–17th centuries.

In Strike Square an avenue of the same name begins. Lined with reconstructed factories, new boulevards, gardens, Metro stations, and new buildings, it is joined by Tractor Street (Traktornaya Ulitsa) at the beginning of its right side. It was here that large-scale housing construction began in Leningrad in 1925–1927 on a site

Maxim Gorky Community Centre

where little cottages were chaotically scattered. This street was given its name to commemorate the mass production of the first tractors at the Krasny Putilovets Factory (now the main enterprise of the Kirov Factory industrial amalgamation). The street, 320 m long, is formed by a complex consisting of 15 three- and four-storey blocks of flats joined up by arches and semi-arches.

On the righthand side of the Avenue take note of the **Tenth Anniversary of the October Revolution School** (No. 5), which was completed in 1927 to mark the tenth anniversary of the Great October Socialist Revolution. This is one of hundreds of new schools built in Leningrad in Soviet times. The school's design is rather interesting—it is shaped like a hammer and sickle, the symbol of the union of workers and peasants. The school is equipped with laboratories, studies, workshops, and an astronomical observation tower.

In Leningrad's State History Museum there is an exercise book bearing the inscription: "Book of Special Visitors to the Tenth Anniversary of the October Revolution School". Its pages are filled with dozens of messages in Russian, English, Spanish, German, and other languages. Among them are enthusiastic comments on the school by Maxim Gorky, Henri Barbusse, Anatoli Lunacharsky, and many others.

In the south the avenue widens out, forming **KIROV SQUARE** (Kirovskaya Ploshchad). A **Statue of Sergei Kirov** (sculptor Nikolai Tomsky, architect Noi Trotsky, 1938) stands in the centre of the square. In this monumental sculpture, which is exceptionally expressive in its silhouette and dynamic quality, the sculptor has managed to capture the unbending will of the courageous Bolshevik who headed the Leningrad Party organisation in 1926–1934 (the overall height of the monument 15.5 m, figure of Kirov— 7.7 m). A bronze model of the monument was on show before the Soviet pavilion at the World Exhibition in Paris in 1937, where the sculptor was awarded a silver medal.

In the years before the Revolution the site of the present Kirov Square was a huge rubbish dump lined with the dilapidated wooden cottages of the village of Tentelevka. In the pre-war years the square had already changed beyond recognition. Today on the southern side of the square stands a building of original design— the district Soviet of People's Deputies (architect Noi Trotsky, 1934). The main part of the building, a horizontal block with three panels of glass, contrasts sharply with the vertical part, which is 50 metres high.

To the south of the district Soviet, the **9th of January Children's Park** covers an area of 12 hectares. The park is named after that unforgettable morning of January 9th, 1905, when workers of the Narva Gate district gathered here on what was then a patch of waste ground to make their way to the Winter Palace, carrying icons and portraits of the tsar. The procession was halted at the Narva

Statue of Sergei Kirov

Gate and in Palace Square when troops opened fire on them.

The park is encircled by a graceful wrought-iron railing. In 1901, this railing, which had received the highest award at the World Exhibition in Paris, was mounted on the high base round the garden of the Winter Palace. But it concealed a considerable part of the palace's façade, thereby spoiling the ensemble in Palace Square. Therefore in 1919 the railing was dismantled and relocated. In 1924, it was put up in the Children's Park, one of the first public

gardens to be laid out in the workers' districts of Leningrad.

For the most part, the residential districts with their modern, multi-storey housing complexes on Strike Avenue to the south of Kirov Square were erected in the post-war period. However, you can still find interesting old monuments here. In 1783, on Peterhof Road, as Strike Avenue was called at that time, milestones designed by the architect Antonio Rinaldi were set up. One of the remaining milestones, or rather verst-stones, stand to the right of the intersection of Strike Avenue and Trefolev Street marking the distance—six versts—from the post office (1 verst—1.06 km).

Also noteworthy is the **Horseshoe-Shaped House** at No. 45, which belonged to Princess Yekaterina Dashkova in the 18th century. The princess took an active part in the coup d'état at the palace in 1762 which put Catherine the Great on the throne. The empress generously rewarded her associates: Dashkova was presented with an estate by the road to Peterhof (architect believed to be Giacomo Quarenghi). In 1975, the restoration of this residence was completed and it is now the **Wedding Palace**.

Beyond the viaduct across Strike Avenue, carrying a branch railway line linking the merchant port with the city stations, an enormous area is taken up by one of the largest enterprises in the Soviet Union, the **Kirov Factory industrial amalgamation**.

The workers of the factory are famous for their skill and revolutionary and battle traditions. Lenin first visited the factory in December 1894 (at that time it was called the Putilov Works); then in May 1917 he addressed a meeting of many thousands of workers here. Lenin went to the factory a third time at the end of October 1917 when he asked the workers to speed up the production of the armoured train that was to support the operations against counter-revolutionary detachments attacking Petrograd. The workers of the Putilov Works carried out Lenin's orders honourably.

In December 1917, the factory was nationalised. In 1924, the mass production of tractors began here for the first time in the USSR. In the post-war five-year-plan periods the factory has supplied the country with tractors, motors for combine harvesters, turbines, motor vehicles, cranes, and other machines and mechanisms. During the siege of Leningrad, when enemy bombs and shells were raining down on the city and the front line was three or four kilometres away, the workers of the factory were producing fighting vehicles.

In the post-war years the factory has been rebuilt and reconstructed. Today this enterprise is a unique factory and laboratory of technological progress, equipping many branches of the economy with sophisticated machinery.

Opposite the factory buildings stands the **Community Centre** built in 1967 and named after the revolutionary and factory workers' leader, Ivan Gaz. This centre, with its huge library, cinema, lecture halls, and rooms for the centre's clubs and amateur art activities, is extremely popular among the workers of the factory and their families. A **Bronze Bust of Ivan Gaz** has been erected in front of the community centre.

The Strike Avenue district to the south of the Kirov Factory, known as Avtovo, is a huge construction site. To the south of the Gaz Community Centre, at the intersection of Strike Avenue and Krasnoputilovskaya Street, lies the circular **KOMSOMOL SQUARE** (Komsomolskaya Ploshchad) adorned by an ensemble created in 1955–1960. A circular garden has been laid out in the middle of the square. If you walk down the street to the right of the square, you will approach the small square in front of the

factory gates where a pink granite obelisk rises. In 1891, the workers' first May Day celebrations in the history of Russia were held here. At that time, there was a glade on this spot amidst birch and aspen trees. From all corners of St. Petersburg progressive workers came here on the first Sunday in May 1891 to mark this international workers' festival. Although the first May Day was kept a strict secret, thousands of workers learned about it.

But now let us return to Komsomol Square. To the south, to your left stands the **monument to the Heroic Komsomol** (sculptor Vladimir Gordon and others). The central figure in the composition is a young man in the military uniform of the early Soviet period. The authors have created a generalised image of this young Soviet youth — purposeful, energetic, full of *joie de vivre*, eternally devoted to the people and the ideals of communism. This spot was chosen for the monument because it was precisely here, in a former workers' district, that the first revolutionary youth organisations in Russia were set up. The monument was unveiled on the 50th anniversary of the Komsomol in October 1968. In the base of the monument a capsule containing a letter to the Komsomol of the year 2018 was immured.

Beyond the old **Krasnenky Cemetery** your attention will be drawn by a **building of unusual design** on the left. This is Bus Station No. 5. Inside, the buses can move easily, because the huge 96-metre-long roof is not supported by pylons. This method of roofing buildings with assembled concrete arches is being used for the first time in Soviet and foreign practice.

In front of the station, on the spot where the Leningraders welcomed the victorious Soviet soldiers, a garden has been laid out near the ferroconcrete pill-box, which has been preserved since the war. The **Victor**

Tank, a heavy KV-85 tank, one of the mighty fighting vehicles that participated in the battles at Leningrad, was mounted on a granite pedestal here in 1951 at the suggestion of the Kirov Factory workers and one of the designers of the KV-85, Jozef Kotin. The KV-85 tanks were famed for their excellent performance during the Second World War. Back in 1941 Hitler's commanding officers forbade their Panzer forces to enter into combat with them, and all operations against them were left to German artillery and air force. In order to deal with the Soviet tanks better, the Nazis began to manufacture Panther and Tiger tanks. The Soviet answer to this was the invention of new heavy tanks under Kotin's supervision, the most powerful ever used in the Second World War. In 1952, on the grounds of the Kirov Factory that produced these fighting machines, a heavy tank of this type was placed as a monument.

On the left side of the avenue your attention will also be caught by a yellow building with two towers (No. 158), erected in 1761 and rebuilt at the end of the 18th century by the architect Ivan Starov. Today this building, which was restored after the war, serves as a second community centre for the workers of the Kirov Factory. Here a large library, a cinema and a concert hall, reading rooms, and ballrooms are accessible to visitors. It also has premises for amateur art activities.

Not far away, there is yet another 18th-century building, reminiscent of the Taurida Palace. This is the **former estate of Alexandrino**, which belonged to Count Ivan Chernyshev. During the war it was reduced to ruins. In the post-war years this monument of architecture has been restored to its original appearance.

Near Alexandrino, Strike Avenue forks; the road to the left leads to Narva and then to the capital of Soviet Estonia, Tallinn, while the road to the right goes to Petrodvorets, approximately 17 km away. The common grave on this spot is one of the numerous resting places of the defenders of Leningrad. For hundreds of years this spot has been called "the halt", for troops used to stop here for a rest on the way from Peterhof to St. Petersburg, and courtiers often rested here on their journeys between the capital and Peterhof.

On your right, on the shore of the Gulf of Finland, lies the **Lenin Southern Esplanade Park**, the first part of which was opened in 1970 to mark Lenin's birth centenary. The festivities culminated in immuring in the base of an obelisk a metal capsule containing a letter from the founders of the park to future generations.

The obelisk is the architectural focal point of the park. It is original in its composition, which consists of a gigantic hammer and sickle. On the right of the obelisk stands a monumental granite stele bearing the inscription: "To Lenin. 1870-1970." A large rectangular pool with fountains graces the park here. From the central square an alley leads to the park's main clearing, the central part of which is embellished with the carpet of a green parterre, 300 m long and more than 30 m wide. The parterre is lined with firs and trimmed lindens. The central clearing divides the park into two parts—western and eastern. In spring the western side of the garden is particularly attractive when the lilac is in bloom. In the eastern part your attention will be drawn by the fairyland fortress in the children's playground.

7

MOSCOW AVENUE—PEACE SQUARE—MOSCOW GATE SQUARE—MOSCOW SQUARE—VICTORY SQUARE

***Estimated time needed to see the sights on this excursion—3 hours. Nearest Metro station—**Ploshchad Mira.*

Tourist attractions: The former guardhouse (19th century), the Palace of Furs, the Moscow Triumphal Gate (19th century), the Kirov Elektrosila factory, the Moscow Victory Park, the Chesma Palace (18th century), the Statue of Lenin, the Monument to the Heroes of the Defence of Leningrad, the Pulkovo Observatory.

The southern part of the city is transected by **MOSCOW AVENUE** (Moskovsky Prospekt), a thoroughfare as straight as an arrow. Over a large stretch the widest (approximately 60 m) street in Leningrad, Moscow Avenue was built precisely along the Pulkovo meridian, which is slightly to the east of Greenwich at 30°19.6′.

After Tsarskoye Selo, the residence of the Russian monarchs, came into being in the 18th century, a road called Tsarskoye Selo Avenue was built for communication with St. Petersburg. At the end of the Russo-Turkish War of 1877–1878, owing to the extremely important operations conducted on the Balkan Peninsula, the avenue was renamed Transbalkan

Avenue. It was given its present name in 1956.

Your excursion begins at the northernmost point of Moscow Avenue, **PEACE SQUARE** (Ploshchad Mira), former Hay (Sennaya) Square, which came into being in the 1730s. Before the Revolution the square and the narrow muddy lanes adjacent to it were known as the gloomiest part of St. Petersburg. Fyodor Dostoyevsky provides a graphic description of life in this district in his novel *Crime and Punishment.*

The Revolution did away with the St. Petersburg slums. The square was paved, and lined with lindens. Impressive tall buildings replaced the demolished houses. One of the older buildings still standing here is the **former guardhouse** (Vikenty Beretti, 1818–1820) which was intended for lodging military patrol. Not only fined officers, but also administratively indicted civilians served their sentences here. Thus, in March of 1874 Fyodor Dostoyevsky was held here (in the cell whose windows face east) for having published a forbidden article in the journal *Grazhdanin* (Citizen), of which he was editor.

As you walk from Peace Square along Moscow Avenue to the south you will see on your right one of the oldest institutions of higher education in the country, founded in 1809, the **Academician Obraztsov Institute of Rail-Transport Engineers** (No. 9). The River Fontanka, which intersects the avenue, was the city's southern boundary in the 18th century. Be sure to take a look at the marble and granite pillar with a sundial standing on the river's bank. This is one of the few remaining verst-posts on the avenue; it was erected in 1774 by the architect Antonio Rinaldi. The figures on post mark the distance in versts from the post office to Tsarskoye Selo (now the town of Pushkin)—22 versts, and to Moscow—673 versts.

On the other bank of the Fontanka, on the tower at No. 19 is the largest and most exact clock in the city. This building houses the **All-Union Institute of Metrology**, named for its founder, Dmitry Mendeleyev. In the past this institution was known as the Central Chamber of Weights and Measures. In many ways, thanks to the management of Mendeleyev, the chamber was turned from an exhibition of weights and measures into a centre developing and manufacturing sophisticated apparatuses for measuring lengths, masses, time, temperature, pressure, magnetic current, light, and other physical values.

The scientist worked here from 1893 and lived in this house from 1897 till he died on January 20 (February 2), 1907. In 1931, a **statue of the scientist** (sculptor Ilya Gintsburg) was erected in the garden of the institute on the site of a summer-house where Mendeleyev liked to rest. On the wall of the next house you will see a huge Mendeleyev's table of the periodical system of elements. Beside it are the scientist's famous words: "Science begins when you begin to measure."

Across the street is the **Technology Institute**, founded in 1828, and housed in a monumental building. Here, during the first Russian bourgeois-democratic revolution of 1905–1907, Lenin gave a report, and in 1905 the first St. Petersburg Soviet of Workers' Deputies met here; the memorial plaques on the façade state that outstanding Russian revolutionaries and scientists studied and worked here.

A **statue of Georgi Plekhanov** (1856–1918), the eminent theoretician and one of the first propagandists of Marxism in Russia (sculptor Ilya Gintsburg, 1925), has been erected in front of the building.

The two-storey residence here at No. 33, Moscow Avenue is connected with the name of Plekhanov. This house, built in 1800, was the seat of the **Free Economics Society**, the first scientific, agricultural and economics society in Russia which was established in 1765. Today it accommodates a **branch of the State Public Library** where the literary heritage, the huge library and some of the personal effects of Georgi Plekhanov are kept. One of the rooms has been made into an exact replica of his study in Geneva (from January 1880 to February 1917 Plekhanov was forced to live in emigration). Almost all the furniture, the engravings and books are authentic, brought to the Soviet Union by Plekhanov's wife, the first curator of this museum, and sent by his daughters from France.

Beyond the bridge across the Obvodnoi Canal begins a district of mainly new buildings. To the south of the canal the avenue becomes wider. Take a look at the corner building beyond the bridge (No. 65), the **former slaughter house**, built in 1821–1825 by the architect Joseph Charlemagne in the style of Russian classicism. The building is remarkable for its proportions. The central building is designed as a cube, the lower part of which is rusticated and cut by three high archways. The strict smoothness of the walls is broken only by moulded panels decorated with cornucopias.

On the opposite side of the avenue stands the **Palace of Furs** (No. 98). Its dredth fur auction, held in 1985, drew more than 300 representatives of foreign firms.

Behind the Palace of Furs you will see the former **Novodevichy** (New Maiden) **Convent** (architect Nikolai Yefimov). Beyond the convent is **MOSCOW GATE SQUARE** (Ploshchad

MOSKOVSKY PROSPEKT—
PLOSHCHAD MIRA—
MOSKOVSKIYE VOROTA—
PLOSHCHAD POBEDY

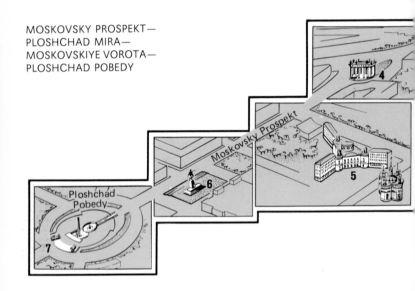

ground, first, and second floors house the exhibition halls, and the huge refrigerated storerooms, where the furs are kept, are down in the basement. The international fur auctions held here three times a year are attended by representatives of firms from many countries. Leningrad's first international fur auction was held in 1931. In 1932 35 foreign businessmen participated in the sale. And the one hundred Moskovskiye Vorota) with the **Moscow Triumphal Gate** rising in its centre. It was erected in 1834–1838 by the architect Vasily Stasov to commemorate the Russian victory in the Russo-Turkish War of 1828–1829. At that time, the Moscow Gate was the largest prefabricated cast-iron structure in the world. Following the design of the architect, the sculptor Boris Orlovsky decorated the gate with

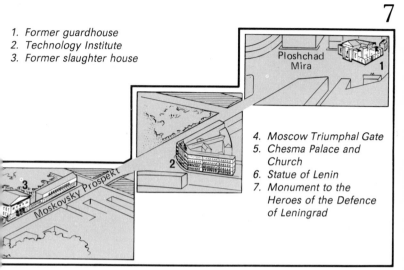

1. Former guardhouse
2. Technology Institute
3. Former slaughter house

Ploshchad Mira

4. Moscow Triumphal Gate
5. Chesma Palace and Church
6. Statue of Lenin
7. Monument to the Heroes of the Defence of Leningrad

Moskovsky Prospekt

depictions of military trophies and the winged genii, Plenty, Glory, and Victory. In 1941, the iron blocks of the gate were used as anti-tank obstacles on the southern reaches to Leningrad. In 1958–1960, the gates were restored, after the missing parts were cast at the Kirov Factory.

Not far from the Moscow Gate, on both sides of the avenue, there stand the buildings of one of the largest enterprises in the country, the **Kirov Elektrosila factory**. In 1911, the electrical engineering workshops of the Siemens-Schukkert firm were built here to assemble small electrical machines and apparatuses. After the Revolution the first plan for the development of the republic's economy, based on the plan for the electrification of Russia (GOELRO) and worked out on the initiative of Lenin, envisaged the establishment of a huge network of electric power stations.

These power stations needed equipment and so the workshops were turned into a high-capacity industrial enterprise during the pre-war five-year plans.

The generators for many of the country's hydroelectric power stations have been manufactured at Elektrosila. During the siege of Leningrad the factory's production was aimed at serving the needs of defence. In spite of the frequent bombings and artillery shellings (on November 7, 1943 alone, more than 200 large high-explosive and 400 fragmentation and incendiary bombs hit the factory grounds), the Elektrosila workers continued to supply the front with the equipment it needed.

In the last few decades, the capacity of the Elektrosila turbogenerators has increased a thousand times over. Elektrosila generators produce nearly two-thirds of the country's total elec-

Moscow Triumphal Gate

tric power. The factory has its own research institute, and dozens of other research institutes across the country are helping it carry out the "Intensification-90" programme.

To the south of Elektrosila, beyond the granite viaduct across the avenue, lies the **Moscow Victory Park** (Moskovsky Park Pobedy) with its shady walks and beautiful flowerbeds.

In the autumn of 1945 the people of Leningrad decided to commemorate the victory in the Second World War by laying out a magnificent park. Regular and landscape styles have been combined in its planning. The main walks in the park are perfectly straight, while the little paths adjacent to them are planned freely, in the form of curving lines. The park is decorated with bronze busts of militarymen, natives of Leningrad, who have twice been awarded the title of Hero of the Soviet Union, and also busts of those twice awarded the title of Hero of Socialist Labour: the eminent statesman Alexei Kosygin, the foremost lathe operator Alexei Chuyev, Academician Alexander Vinogradov, the world-famous ballerina Galina Ulanova and the cosmonaut Georgi Grechko. Statues of Heroes of the Soviet Union, the courageous partisan Zoya Kosmodemyanskaya and the soldier Alexander Matrosov, who blocked with his chest an enemy firing embrasure during a battle, stand on the walks running from the fountain. On the edge of one of the ponds in the park stands a monument to the French patriot, Raymonda Dien, who lay down on a railway track on February 23, 1950 to stop a train carrying tanks intended for fighting against the patriots in Vietnam.

The Grand Fountain is included in the composition of the Moscow Victory Park's main entrance. In the size of its basin (25 m in diameter) and the height of its central jet (12 m), the fountain is considered to be the biggest in Leningrad.

In the depths of the park beyond its eastern boundary rises the **Lenin**

Moscow Victory Park. Avenue of Heroes

Sports and Concert Complex, which was completed in 1980 and is the second largest indoor stadium in Europe, seating 25,000 spectators. The address of the complex is No. 8, Gagarin Avenue (Prospekt Gagarina), but this magnificent building of sparkling glass is clearly visible from the western edge of the Victory Park. Competitions in 15 different sports can be held in the stadium, including football and hockey matches, track-and-field events. It is also the venue of conferences, meetings, congresses, festivals, concerts, ice-ballets and film-showings.

The internal planning of the arena is asymmetrical, allowing for one large stand of seats and three small ones. When necessary, the premises can be transformed. For football matches, for example, the arena, which is the size of a real football pitch, is covered with a green carpet, and the four stands can seat 25,000 spectators. During speed skating competitions the side stands dis-

appear and the butt-ends of the rounded walls are opened into an ice-track 333.3 m long and 12 m wide. During ice-hockey matches the stands can be dismantled and moved to form other stands around the field.

While competitions are in progress in the stadium, 640,000 cu m of fresh air are pumped in every hour (warm air in winter, and cool air in summer).

However, let us now return to our main excursion route on Moscow Avenue. In the square (across the avenue) between the new blocks of flats and the ten-storey Rossiya Hotel a **statue of the outstanding Russian writer and revolutionary democrat Nikolai Chernyshevsky** (1828–1889) was erected in 1947 by the sculptor Vsevolod Lishev.

To the south, on the left side of Moscow Avenue, construction is underway of a new premises for the Saltykov-Shchedrin Public Library (see Excursion No. 5). The library's stock is estimated to increase to

40,000,000 volumes by the end of the century. The complex on Moscow Avenue is being built as an integral whole: a nine-storey central structure for the storage of up to 20,000,000 volumes, surrounded by three-, five-storey buildings full of reading rooms and offices. The library's 16 reading rooms will be able to accommodate up to 2,000 people at once. The book storage rooms will contain all literature published in the USSR since 1975, as well as that of other countries obtained on an exchange basis.

Farther along, on your left, you will see the highly interesting **Chesma Palace and Church** built in the 1770s by the architect Yuri Felten. The palace was built as a place where Catherine the Great could stop for a rest on her way from St. Petersburg to her country residences.

The palace acquired its name in 1780 in commemoration of the victory of the Russian fleet over the Turkish fleet at Chesma Bay in the Aegean Sea in 1770. In 1768, the Osman Empire declared war on Russia with the intent of seizing Transcaucasia, the Northern Caucasus and the Ukraine. The battle of Chesma was one of the most outstanding and heroic achievements in the Russo-Turkish war of 1768–1774.

The graceful **Chesma Church** (architect Yuri Felten, 1777–1780), one of the rare pseudo-Gothic structures in Leningrad, was built near the palace. Today you will find the church at No. 12, Gastello Street (Ulitsa Gastello). Here in 1977 an exposition devoted to the victory at Chesma Bay was opened, where documents, maps, models of men-of-war, 18th-century naval instruments, the Russian and Turkish flags, weapons, medals, and portraits of outstanding Russian naval commanders are on display.

By the church there is a small military cemetery, in which veterans of the Russian army who had ended

Statue of Lenin in Moscow Square

their days in a home for invalids at the Chesma Palace are buried. During the Second World War fighters who died defending Leningrad were buried here.

Slightly to the south of the Chesma ensemble sprawls **MOSCOW SQUARE** (Moskovskaya Ploshchad). Its eastern side is lined by one of the largest edifices in Leningrad, the **House of Soviets**, an office block approximately 50 m high and 220 m long

House of Soviets

(architect Noi Trotsky et al., 1936–1941). This building is decorated with sculpture, huge columns and a portal of polished granite. The central part of the façade is emphasised by two tower-like projections. It is embellished with the emblem of the Russian Federation (11 by 11 m in size, sculptor Igor Krestovsky) and a frieze 103 m long (sculptor Nikolai Tomsky).

A focal point in the square is the **statue of Lenin**, which was unveiled in April 1970 to commemorate the birth centenary of the leader of the Soviet people (sculptor Mikhail Anikushin, architect Valentin Kamensky). The sixteen-metre-high monument portrays Lenin making one of his speeches. In the words of the sculptor, he wished to express the "concentration of will and energy, the embodiment of humaneness, unwavering conviction and inexhaustible striving for a great goal". On the side of the pedestal the laconic inscription reads: "To Lenin on his centenary. April 1970."

Some 200 m to the south, you will find yourself in **VICTORY SQUARE** (Ploshchad Pobedy), the centre of which is graced by a magnificent **monument devoted to the heroes of the defence of Leningrad during the Second World War** (by Lenin Prize winners Mikhail Anikushin, Sergei Speransky, and Valentin Kamensky). The Soviet people donated more than 2,000,000 roubles to the construction of this memorial. Hundreds of thousands of Leningraders and visitors to the city helped to build it, working from morning till late at night without respite. There was something surprisingly exalted about this effort; and though the volunteers who joined in it were of different generations, they were united by a common goal. On May 9, 1975, on the thirtieth anniversary of the victory of the Soviet people over Nazi Germany, the monument was unveiled.

The monument faces the south, where the fiercest battles for Leningrad were fought. The centre of the composition consists of a 48-metre-high granite obelisk with the inscription 1941–1945 in gold. The foot of the monument is embellished with seven-metre-high sculptural group called "The Victors" (a Worker and a Soldier), symbolising the inseparable ties between the army and the people. On either side of the main staircase, groups of bronze sculptures stand on granite pedestals. On the left side are "Sailors", "The People's Avengers" (Partisans), and "The Builders of the Defences"; on the right side are "Soldiers", "Founders", and "People's Volunteers". These four-metre-high sculptural compositions show you the heroes of the besieged Leningrad. The obelisk standing inside a broken ring is of profound symbolic significance, reflecting, as it does, the idea of breaking through the enemy blockade. The inscription on the outside of the ring reads: "For your feat, Leningrad". The inside of the ring is faced with copper sheets on which sculptural depictions of awards presented to the city are surrounded by banners. The texts from the awards made to Leningrad are inscribed in bronze letters here.

The granite steps descend to the memorial hall housed under the monument where the feats of the city's defenders are recorded in bronze and mosaics, and are reflected in mementoes of the war. The tragic and noble melodies of the song *Holy War* and Shostakovich's Seventh Symphony alternate with the rhythmic beating of the metronome which ticks away on the radio as it did when the besieged city was struggling to stay alive. But life went on in the city, as can be seen from the calendar of each of the 900 days of the blockade. The chronicle of Leningrad's feat is recorded on the pages of the Bronze Memorial Book erected on a granite pedestal in the centre of the memorial.

On the western side of Victory Square stands the nine-storey building of the **Pulkovskaya Hotel**, erected for Intourist by the Finnish firm Polar. In accordance with the traditions of Finnish builders, a capsule containing issues of the Soviet newspapers *Pravda* and *Leningradskaya Pravda*, and the Finnish newspapers *Uusi Suomi* and *Kansan Uutiset*, coins, and a text which states that "the construction of the hotel was executed in the interests of strengthening friendship, mutual assistance and co-operation between the Finnish and Soviet peoples" was immured in its foundations on May 27, 1980. Not far from here stands an additional building of the hotel, built in 1986.

As you continue your excursion along Moscow Avenue you will see before you the **PULKOVO HEIGHTS**. On Pulkovo Hill be sure to note the curious structure (on your right)—a **pavilion** open on all four sides. At its centre, between the columns, stands the grey polished granite basin of a fountain. Four stone sphinxes "guard" the fountain. These sculptures gave this structure, built in 1809 by the architect Thomas de Thomon, the rather unusual name of the Four Witches.

When you reach the Pulkovo Heights (75 m above sea level), you turn left (the road to Pulkovo Airport leads off to the right); the road going up into the hills will take you to the cemetery of the defenders of the city during the war. On the hillside the **"Old Man"** (Starik) **pavilion** constructed by the architect Andrei Voronikhin in 1809, has been preserved. At that time, Pulkovo Hill was a sort of park, occupying the area from the summit to the foot of the main hill in the Pulkovo Heights.

On the right rises the **Pulkovo Observatory**, which has been the country's main astronomical centre for 150 years already (since 1839). In September 1941, the observatory was in the foremost lines of the defence of

Chesma Church

Sculptural groups of the Monument to the Heroes of the Defence of Leningrad

Leningrad and was badly damaged by bombs and artillery shells. Restoration work began immediately after the war, and in May 1954 the observatory started operating again.

The Pulkovo astronomers have at their disposal the latest equipment for space research, such as radio-locators, special radio telescopes, and electronic and television equipment.

The observatory's scientists have developed the world's first programme-controlled telescope: the electronic and coding control machine scans the heavens with the telescope and orients it in the necessary direction according to a previously fed program.

The Pulkovo Heights have been the site of some of history's fiercest bat-

Victory Square

tles for Leningrad: during the Civil War they became the insurmountable barrier in the path of the counter-revolutionary forces; during the Second World War they were again witness to the heroism of the city's defenders. Never in the history of the city of Lenin has this strategic barrier been taken by enemy forces.

8

THE HERMITAGE

Housed in the former Winter Palace on the Neva's embankments in the very heart of Leningrad is the Hermitage, the Soviet Union's largest museum (see Excursion No. 3).

The Hermitage, as its name suggests, is a place of seclusion. It is the name that Russia's Empress Catherine the Great bestowed on the part of her palace where she kept unique art treasures. Historians consider this museum to have been founded in the year of 1764, when a collection of 225 paintings purchased in Berlin was first deposited in the Winter Palace. A mere ten years later, in 1774, the collection already boasted 2,080 paintings, as well as drawings, cameos, sculptures and diverse objects of virtu. All these treasures were stored in rooms to which only the empress and her court had access. Catherine wrote of her possessions in the Hermitage that "all this is only for the mice and myself to admire!"

The October Revolution of 1917 gave the public at large access to this treasure-house of art and culture. Today the Hermitage's collections comprise more than 2,790,000 items, including paintings, sculptures, graphics, various objects of applied art, coins, medals and diverse insignia, arms and armour, archeological artifacts and other treasures from all over the world dating from hoary antiquity to the present.

Perhaps only the British Museum and the Louvre can rival the Hermitage in scale and importance. The Soviet Union's largest ancient Greek, Roman and Oriental collections, as well as unique examples of applied art, are kept at the Hermitage. Over 3,000,000 people visit the Hermitage annually.

"This is a giant among the world's museums," said the well-known French ballet master, Helen Treilen, "in which one inadvertently forgets that outside it is the end of the 20th century. The works of the great masters captivate our every feeling, thought, and desire."

A complete picture of its outstanding collections can be gained only after many visits to the Hermitage. Unfortunately, the foreign tourist does not usually have enough time for more than one visit. So this guide will indicate and describe only the most interesting items. Please note that since the exhibits are changed from time to time, the references to room numbers may not always be correct.

Hermitage

The Grand Staircase will take you up to the exhibition rooms. But first a few words about the Grand Staircase itself. Originally built by Bartolomeo Rastrelli, it was badly damaged during the fire of 1837. Though architect Vasily Stasov made some alterations during the restoration work, the staircase remains astoundingly magnificent with its gilded wall mouldings, dazzling white marble statues, and an enormous plafond depicting the Greek Gods on Olympus.

From the upper landing proceed through the **Field Marshals' Hall**, which has retained this name from earlier times when it was a gallery of portraits of Russia's field marshals, and along the corridor hung with tapestries, to the **Pavilion Hall**, designed in 1856 by the architect Andrei Stakenschneider. The Pavilion Hall is part of the **Small Hermitage** built next door to the Winter Palace by Jean Baptiste Vallin de la Mothe between 1764 and 1767. The interior design incorporates elements of Moresque, Renaissance, and Classical architecture. The graceful columns of white marble support an elegant gallery. The sunlight is reflected through its fenestration onto 28 crystal chandeliers. Note the murmuring sound of the water dripping from the four Fountains of Tears, about which the following legend is told:

One day the Crimea's cruel Khan Girei summoned his stonemason Omer and said:
"Make the stones weep to carry my name through the ages!"
However, the craftsman devoted his talent to extol not the harsh potentate but the women whose youth and beauty had faded behind the latticed windows of the Khan's closely guarded harem.
As the Koran forbids the representation of the human figure, Omer resorted to allegory. He hewed a niche into a slab of marble to indicate the depth of suffering felt by the women of the harem and carved a flower at the top and petal-shaped cups. The water trickles out of the flower into these cups like tears on tender cheeks. At the foot of the fountain, the artist carved a snail, which holds back the water in the basin for a brief while. This symbolic representation of doubt in the power of the Khan intimates that it is not everlasting and will flow away like water.

These fountains are actually exact replicas of the Fountain of Bakhchisarai in the Crimea designed in 1764 by

One of the rooms in the Hermitage

the Persian master Omer.

The mosaic floor, laid between 1847 and 1851, is an imitation, with certain modifications, of the mosaics unearthed in 1780 during the excavations of Emperor Titus' (79–81 A.D.) baths in Rome.

A somewhat curious exhibit, the **Peacock Clock** is sure to catch the eye. It is designed in the shape of a large peacock perched on a tall oak-tree stump with two spreading branches. This stump stands on a round base. A cage with little bells and an owl of oxidized silver are suspended from one of the branches by a cord; below the cage there is a squirrel nibbling a nut. On the other side, the peacock is flanked by a small stump with a life-size cockerel on it. In the foreground are representations of mushrooms, leaves, acorns, and even a pumpkin; a closer look will disclose snails and lizards and two squirrels in the branches. There is a small aperture with two rows of numerals, Roman and Arabic, in the cap of the largest mushroom, and above it sits a barely discernible grasshopper.

The clock was made in London by the famous English watchmaker and jeweller, James Cox, and was purchased from him as a gift for Empress Catherine the Great by Prince Grigory Potyomkin, her favourite.

When the clock is wound up, all the figures move on the hour; first the owl turns its head, rolls its eyes and stamps its foot. Meanwhile the cage revolves and the little bells in it tinkle melodiously. When the tinkling ceases, the peacock spreads its tail feathers, turns to display its plumage, and gracefully bows its head. Finally the cockerel springs into action, arching its neck, opening its beak, and crowing.

The dial with its two rotating discs can be seen in the large mushroom cap. The Roman numerals indicate the hours, the Arabic, the minutes, while the jumping grasshopper ticks off the seconds. When fully wound, the mechanism, which is in good working order, keeps the clock running for a fortnight.

From the Pavilion Room make your way to the Councillors' Staircase (once used by the members of the State Council, Russia's highest law-making body between 1810 and 1917, when they arrived at the Winter Palace for sessions presided over by the tsar), then go down to the ground floor, pass through the Hall of Twenty Columns with its mosaic floor consisting of several hundred thousand tesserae and a collection of Italian vases and enter Room No. 128 to see the gigantic **Kolyvan vase**.

This marvellous vase was made of Altai jasper by Russian stone-cutters. It weighs 19 tons and is more than 2.5 metres high. Its oval mouth is some five metres long and over three metres wide. It took two whole years to cut this single slab of jasper from the rock, a thousand men to haul it to the Kolyvan lapidary factory, and another twelve years to produce the finished article.

From Room No. 128 pass through Room No. 106 to Room No. 107 where the **Antiquities Department** displays its collections. One of the notable Roman sculptures here is the **bust of Emperor Philip the Arabian** (3rd cent. A.D.) whose features, close-cropped hair, deeply furrowed forehead and bushy brows speak of the brooding, imperious nature of this "soldier-emperor".

In Room No. 109 note the statue of the goddess of love and beauty known as the **Venus of Taurida** (3rd cent. B.C.), since it stood in the Taurida Palace of Prince Potyomkin for many years. The statue's anonymous sculptor embodied the aesthetic ideals of his time in this work. The well-proportioned, softly modelled nude figure, the flowing silhouette and serene, restrained posture—all serve to emphasise the chastity of the

Leonardo da Vinci. Madonna Litta

Rembrandt. Portrait of an Old Man in Red

Rubens. Coronation of Maria Medici

sculptor's concept of female beauty. The statue was unearthed near Rome in 1718 and was subsequently acquired by Peter the Great in exchange for the holy relics of St. Brigitta.

We suggest you begin your acquaintance with the **culture and art of Ancient Greece** by examining the collection of vases on display in Room No. 111. Deserving of note is the magnificent wine vessel **The Swallow's Arrival** in Case No. 12, attributed to Euphronius (6th cent. B.C.). The scene on the vessel depicts a man, a youth, and a boy who welcome with joy the first swallow of spring. Inscribed above the heads of each are their comments in ancient Greek: "Look, a swallow!" says the man. "A swallow, indeed, I swear by Heracles!" the youth exclaims. "Spring is here at last!" the boy rejoices.

Room No. 115 contains the ancient Greek **figured vessels** unearthed in 1869 on the Taman Peninsula (Krasnodar Territory, RSFSR) during excavations of the Greek town of Phanagoria. Two of the vessels are remarkable for their exquisite workmanship: one representing the golden-haired Aphrodite, emerging from a half-open seashell and the other, a marvellous sphinx-shaped vessel. Unlike the Egyptians, the Greeks depicted the sphinx with wings, a lion's body and a woman's head. The Phanagorian Sphinx (by an anonymous craftsman, 5th cent. B.C.) has pensive blue eyes, cheeks lightly tinged with pink, lips of scarlet, curly tresses, and a body of delicate whiteness. This mythological creature radiates an enchanting and enigmatic loveliness.

In Room No. 120 pause to have a look at one of the Hermitage's most

Hall of Roman sculpture

celebrated gems, the famous **Gonzaga Cameo** executed in Alexandria in the 3rd century B.C. The cameo is carved on a three-layered oval piece of sardonyx, making for an exquisite play of colour; it bears two profiles in relief of the Egyptian ruler Ptolemy II Philadelphus and his wife Arsinoë. The composition emphasises the indissoluble link between the king and queen.

In the 16th century, the cameo was in the possession of the Gonzagas, the dukes of Mantua—hence the name. Early in the 17th century, Rubens saw it and declared that it was "the most beautiful in all of Europe". The cameo found its way to Prague, from whence it was taken to Stockholm and thence to Rome. Later, after the occupation of Italy by Napoleon, it was brought to France. In 1812 Josephine, Napoleon's wife, presented the cameo to the Russian Tsar Alexander I as a token of gratitude for the concern shown the ex-empress.

Return to the first floor via the Councillors' Staircase, turn right and enter Room No. 207, where the **display of 13th–18th-century Italian art** begins. Note the two da Vincis exhibited in Room No. 214. The first is the **Madonna with a Flower** or the Benois Madonna, as it was once called after its former owner—an excellent example of the great Italian master's early work. Leonardo portrays the touching image of a young woman observing her child's awakening consciousness with affectionate delight. The streams of light bring out the form and warmth of the human body. The other masterpiece is the **Madonna Litta**, so called after Duke Litta, who once owned this gem; this work, too, stresses maternal love as the supreme human value.

Turn into Room No. 229 to admire the work of Raphael Santi. His **Madonna Conestabile** was painted when the artist was but 16 or 17 years old. Depicted against the background of lush green meadows, a limpid lake and azure sky is the serene melancholic figure of the Virgin with the Christ Child in her arms. It is believed that the gilded frame with its relief-carved decoration of gryphons was designed by the master himself. This room boasts another Raphael, **The Holy Family**, otherwise known as the Madonna with the Beardless Joseph. Raphael's somewhat idealised presentation of his characters is devoid of the typically expansive Italian temperament; it is rather pensive and serene.

Further on, in Room No. 230, you will find the Soviet Union's sole work by the great Renaissance sculptor, artist, architect and poet, Michelangelo Buonarroti, notably his **Crouching Boy**, which was originally intended for the tomb of the Medici, the rulers of Florence. The figure is exceedingly expressive; though the head is bowed and the face hardly visible, the taut muscles of the body produce a striking impression of the great inner strength that enables one to withstand pain.

Titian, the head of the Venetian school of painting, is represented in Rooms No. 219 and 221 by eight canvases, one of which is the **Mary Magdalene**. The artist does not conform to the traditional New Testament image of the repentant sinner who retired to the desert, but rather, portrays a lovely Venetian woman with a luxurious head of golden hair, sensual lips and tear-filled eyes, overwhelmed by a fervent passion further enhanced by the turbulent landscape in the background.

In a later piece, despite the crisis that occurred within the Renaissance movement, Titian continued to demonstrate his love of man, a feature especially evident in his **Saint Sebastian**, depicting the Christian saint pierced by Roman arrows. Though death is imminent, the spirit embodied in the character that Titian portrays is indomitable. The master used not only a brush but at times even his fingers to execute this work.

The display of **Spanish art of the 15th-early 19th centuries** mounted in Rooms No. 239 and 240 features a rich collection of works by El Greco, Ribera, Zurbaran, Velazquez, Murillo and Goya.

Proceed through Room No. 243 with its collection of West-European arms and armour to Room No. 245 where **17th-century Flemish art** is exhibited. During this period, as the result of the Netherlands revolution of the 16th century, Flanders rapidly advanced both economically and culturally, and its commercial ties grew and flourished. Thus 17th-century art is optimistic, extolling the beauty, richness and abundance of the world.

One of the greatest artists of the period was Anthony Van Dyck, a brilliant exponent of portraiture. Thus in his **Self-Portrait** the sensitive hands and languishing eyes speak of the master's artistic temperament.

The inner world of man is superbly revealed in another piece—the **Male Portrait**, in which Van Dyck accentuates intellect and the eternal struggle between good and evil. Though only one man is portrayed, the painting gives the distinct impression that to the left of him is someone else to whom he must prove the correctness of his convictions.

Room No. 247 has works by the man who was possibly the greatest master of his time, Peter Paul Rubens. His **The Union of Earth and Water** is an allegory reminding the Flemings that their country's outlet to the sea is essential for its prosperity. Portrayed are Cybele, the goddess of the Earth, carrying the horn of plenty—the symbol of fertility and wealth—and Neptune, the sea god holding his traditional trident. In this picture, as in most of his works, Rubens extols wealth and abundance along with the

joy of living.

One of Rubens's world-famous canvases, the **Portrait of a Chambermaid**, is indicative of the artist's wide range of abilities. The personage depicted is apparently a somewhat idealised representation of the artist's daughter Clara, who died in 1623, two years before the picture was painted. The contrast between the rigid posture, calm bearing and sombre garb and the maiden's tender youth imparts a subtle note of lyricism.

Room No. 261 exhibits **Dutch art of the 15th and early 17th centuries**. Beginning with Room No. 249 is a display of **17th-century Dutch art**. The Hermitage prides itself on its extensive collection of Rembrandts. Room No. 254 contains 25 paintings by this great master, among them his celebrated **Danaë**.

According to Greek mythology, the oracle predicted that King Acrisius would die by the hand of his grandson. To save himself, the king confined his one and only daughter Danaë in a tower. Zeus, who fell in love with her, visited her in the form of a golden rain. As a result, she bore a son, Perseus, who slew Acrisius and thus fulfilled the oracle's prediction.

Rembrandt has depicted Danaë in excited anticipation of Zeus arrival. She reaches out for the golden beams of light which impart a limpid warmth to her nude form.

One of Rembrandt's finest works is **The Return of the Prodigal Son**, a picture amazing for its inspired colouring. Illumined in the darkness are but the face of the father, gone blind from years of waiting, his enfeebled arms, and the kneeling figure of the prodigal son. The work's basic motif of the tragic lot of a man who has squandered his life is coupled with readiness to extend a helping hand to a person in dire need.

French art of the 15th–20th centuries is found in first-floor Rooms No. 272–297 and second-floor

Vincent van Gogh. Ladies from Arles

Rooms No. 314-332 and 343-350. In Room No. 276 the visitor finds one of Luis Le Nain's best known works **The Dairywoman's Family**. Through want and grim austerity, the sense of dignity expressed on the peasants' faces reflects the note of courage that permeates the composition as a whole.

The emergence of a new trend—Classicism—in French art is associated with the work of Nicolas Poussin. This trend asserted civic responsibility and the triumph of reason. One of his best works, **Tancrede and Herminie**, is on display in Room No. 279; the **Landscape with Polyphemus**, is a reflection of the artist's dream of a harmonious and rationally ordered world. The Cyclope Polyphemus towers above a hillside, almost blending into it, bewitching the river nymphs by playing on his pipe.

Antoine Watteau, the son of a common roof-maker, rose to fame as one of the greatest of French painters; as opposed to the abstract, static personages of academic traditions, he represented live, flesh-and-blood, non-stereotyped people, such as, for instance, **A Capricious Woman**, in Room No. 284.

Room No. 287 features Jean Antoine Houdon's famous **statue of Voltaire**, an expressive representation of the great French philosopher and writer, highlighting his daring mind and love of life striving to overcome the weakness of old age.

The 1870s in French art were marked by the appearance of the Impressionist movement, whose representatives rose up against the conservatism of traditional bourgeois salon painting. The French Impressionists are well represented in Rooms No. 319-320 and the adjoining rooms.

Room No. 315 features works by the great French sculptor Auguste Rodin. Rooms No. 343–345 are filled with a collection of 37 paintings by Henri Matisse. Works by Pablo Picasso are on display in Rooms No. 346 and 347, while Room No. 350 presents a collection of landscapes by Albert Marquet, one of the greatest modern French painters.

Now go back down to the first floor. You can reach Rooms No. 298–302 with their exhibition of **English Art of the 17th–19th centuries** via Room No. 288. Here you will see some fine paintings by the two great English artists, Joshua Reynolds and Thomas Gainsborough, as well as the celebrated Green Frog service.

Some first-floor rooms exhibit collections from the **Department of the History of Russian Culture**. Note the splendid **vase** in Room No. 173 carved in 1798 of walrus tusk by the Arkhangelsk master Nikolai Vereshchagin. In 1803 this precious object was dispatched as a gift to the Emperor of Japan, but was never presented to him because of Japan's refusal to establish contacts with Europe.

A most curious exhibit on display in Room No. 169 is a **clock** the shape and size of a goose egg, assembled in 1769 by the self-taught mechanic Ivan Kulibin and presented to Empress Catherine the Great. This amusing timepiece not only indicates the hour but also plays strains of music on each quarter-hour, while at noon it performs the theme from a cantata the inventor composed in honour of the Empress. At each hour little doors open in a small aperture at the side to disclose miniature figures, cast in gold and silver, enacting the scene of the Resurrection of Christ.

Room No. 162 features mosaics executed in the workshop of Mikhail Lomonosov, the great Russian scholar and artist. Here is also a portrait of Peter the Great by Lomonosov himself.

Continue on to the **Malachite Room** (No. 189) with its windows opening out onto the Neva River embankment. It is so named because its columns, pilasters and mantel-pieces are faced with malachite which combines most pleasingly with the gilded mouldings of the ceiling and doors, the white walls and the maroon silk upholstery. The numerous malachite objects such as vases and caskets on display here are wrought of stone and copper and faced with the lovely green mineral. Note the small cabinet known as the **Tropical Forest**, decorated with palm leaves, plumage, and flower petals made of minute pieces of malachite of various shades and hues which have been painstakingly assembled.

The neighbouring Room No. 190 contains the silver **tomb of the great 13th-century Russian warrior Alexander Nevsky** made at the St. Petersburg Mint in 1750–1753 from almost one and a half tons of silver. The sarcophagus is embellished with episodes in relief from the life of Alexander Nevsky and is crowned by a pyramid adorned with the prince's monogram and portrait.

Before leaving the Hermitage, we suggest you stop by the **Throne Room of Peter the Great**, right behind the Field Marshals' Hall. Its ceiling has gilded decorations, and on its walls are two paintings of the battles of Lesnaya in 1708 and Poltava in 1709, the turning points of the Northern War against Sweden. At the far end above a throne of gilded silver and seasoned oak made by the English master Nicholas Clausen in 1731, hangs a formal portrait of Peter the Great and Glory painted by the Venetian artist Jacopo Amigoni in the 1730s.

Passing through the neighbouring **Armorial Room**, which was intended for gala receptions, we reach Room No. 197, the **Military Gallery**, a

8

splendid monument of Russia's military glory, built to commemorate the victory over Napoleon. Its 322 portraits of eminent Russian generals were painted in the 1820s by the English painter George Dawe and the Russian artists Alexander Polyakov and Wilhelm Golike.

Your final stop in the Hermitage is the neighbouring **St. George's Room** (No. 198), which occupies a floor space of 800 square metres or close to 9,000 sq. feet. Running around three of its walls is a gallery supported by rows of 48 slender twinned marble columns. On the end wall, over the place where the throne once stood is a large relief of St. George slaying the dragon with his spear. The magnificent parquet floor, composed of 16 different varieties of wood, repeats the pattern of the ceiling, enhancing the balance and harmony of the decoration.

Where the imperial throne once stood is an enormous **mosaic map of the USSR** (27 sq. m) composed of 45,000 tesserae of semi-precious stones. Green and brown jasper designates plains and mountains respectively. The rivers, seas, and oceans are of lapis lazuli. Cities and towns are represented by 450 silver stars while Moscow is singled out by a ruby star surmounted by a hammer and sickle of diamonds. "Leningrad" is written in letters of alexandrite, a semi-precious stone that changes from red to green depending on the light that falls on it.

9

THE RUSSIAN MUSEUM

Our excursion along Nevsky Avenue has already given you an idea of what the Russian Museum looks like from the outside. Its 130-odd rooms contain a veritable treasure-house of Russian art—more than 300,000 works dating from the 11th century to the present. The collections are housed in the former Mikhailovsky Palace and in what are known as the Rossi Wing and the Benois Building. The latter was built between 1912 and 1916 according to a design by Leonty Benois.

As the Russian Museum, like the Hermitage, periodically mounts new displays, the information we furnish on pieces and location may not be entirely accurate.

Begin your excursion on the first floor of the former Mikhailovsky Palace, where in Rooms No. 1–4 works of **old Russian art** are on display. The first exhibit is the 12th-century icon of the **Angel with the Golden Hair** by an anonymous master. The image is enchanting for its lyricism and gentleness. As the technique and style are close to those of the Byzantine icon-painting tradition,

it is believed that this piece was executed by a Greek icon-painter working in Russia.

In the same room is the famous 14th-century icon of **Saints Boris and Gleb**, the younger sons of Prince Vladimir of Kiev murdered by their elder brother Svyatopolk, who was called the Accursed for that reason. They were canonised by the Russian Orthodox Church in 1071. Regarded as one of the most elegant and refined of the early Russian icons, some art historians attribute it to the Vladimir-Suzdalian school of icon-painting, while others believe it to be one of the few extant examples of the early Moscow School.

Exhibited in Room No. 3 are works by the great mediaeval Russian icon-painter Andrei Rublyov, who worked roughly between 1370 and 1430. There are only a few icons known beyond doubt to have been executed by Rublyov himself. One is the **Apostle Paul**, a surviving fragment of the stupendously impressive iconostasis of the Cathedral of the Assumption in Vladimir. The figure is well-proportioned and subtly delineated, while the expression of the holy man is pensive. The colour scheme was devised specially for the icon to be seen from a distance. Like other works by Rublyov it is highly poetical and humane.

Conspicuous among the icons of the 15th to 17th centuries displayed in Room No. 4 are works by Dionysius and Simon Ushakov both of whom demonstrate an elegance of line. Dionysius and his school portrayed personages imbued with an ethereal light, full of gentle motion and poetry.

Collected in Rooms No. 5-14 are **paintings and sculptures of the 18th century**. A supreme achievement of 18th-century Russian portraiture is **The Field Hetman** (Marshal) by Peter the Great's court painter Ivan Nikitin (circa 1688-1741). This is an authentic psychological characterisation couched in an image of austere simplicity. Beside it hangs **Self-Portrait with Wife** by Andrei Matveyev (1701-1739), an eminent Russian painter of the early 18th century. The artist's concentration on the psychological aspect of his subjects is praiseworthy.

Room No. 6 contains pieces representative of mid-18th-century Russian art, a period when secular art flourished. Among them are the mosaic portraits produced in the workshop of the great Russian scholar, artist and poet, Mikhail Lomonosov (1711-1765). Some were done by Lomonosov himself, including **a portrait of Empress Elizabeth, daughter of Peter the Great**; it is wondrously picturesque, and its colours are lovely. In the same hall are portraits by Alexei Antropov (1716-1795), distinguished by their concrete, straightforward characterisation, a major feature of the emerging realistic trend in Russian art of that century.

In Room No. 7 stands a **statue of Tsarina Anna Ioannovna with a Moorish Boy**, sculpted by Carlo Bartolomeo Rastrelli (1675-1744); the artist emphasised the arrogance and unpleasant temper of this cruel ruler, as he depicts her during a court ceremony.

Fyodor Rokotov (1735/6-1808), an eminent Russian portraitist, is exhibited in Room No. 8. The fine characterisations and exquisite colour schemes make his **portraits of Santi, The Surovtsev Couple** and **The Unknown Man in a Red Uniform** outstanding examples of 18th-century Russian art. **Vladimir and Rogneda** by Anton Losenko (1737-1773), on display in Room No. 9, initiated the trend of painting events from Russian history. In this work, the artist sought to denounce the criminal abuse of power. Thus, spurned by Princess Rogneda of Polotsk, Prince Vladimir of Novgorod invaded her city, sacked it, killed Rogneda's father and brothers, and forced her to become his wife. For this painting Losenko was awarded the title of Fellow of the Academy of Art and granted a professorship.

In Rooms No. 9 and 10 stand busts sculpted by Fedot Shubin (1740-1805), a great realist master. One of his finest pieces is the **head of Mikhail Lomonosov**, demonstrating his esteem for the Russian scholar. Shubin's **bust of Emperor Paul I** is interesting as well. This is a vivid, almost satirical characterisation daringly revealing the unbalanced nature of the uncomely autocratic ruler. In another bust, that of Paul's mother, Catherine the Great, he portrayed the tsarina as a law-giver.

Of interest in Room No. 10 are

Russian Museum

the works of Dmitri Levitsky (1735–1822), whom Catherine the Great commissioned to paint a series of portraits of the young students of the Smolny Institute for Noble Young Ladies. The best in this series is the **Portrait of Khovanskaya and Khrushcheva**, in which the two girls act out a pastoral scene with Khrushcheva, garbed in male attire, courting Khovanskaya, dressed as a shepherdess.

Several works by the eminent sculptor Mikhail Kozlovsky (1753–1802), an exponent of early Classicism, are shown in Room No. 11. His work reflects the progressive ideals of the Russian enlighteners of the second half of the 18th century who advocated patriotism and a sense of civic duty. Note the architectural design of this room, known as the Room of White Columns. All its original decor has remained intact, including furniture, torchères, parquetry, and paintings on the walls and ceiling, all according to designs Carlo Rossi created especially for this reception-room.

Exhibited in Room No. 12 are several magnificent, highly realistic portraits by Vladimir Borovikovsky (1757–1825). Borovikovsky was a major adherent of sentimentalism, a new trend in Russian art, which extolled man's affinity with nature and praised unaffected human emotions. These ideals are manifest in such canvases as **Catherine the Great on a Walk**, the **Portrait of Arsenyeva** and the **Portrait of Borovsky**. This room also contains pieces by Russian sculptors of the late 18th century and first half of the 19th century, conspicuous among which are tombstones and busts by Ivan Martos (1754–1835).

Russian art of the first half of the 19th century is represented in Rooms No. 14–17, where the work of Vasily Demut-Malinovsky (1779–1846), the first Russian sculptor to pay tribute to the common man, is of special interest. Thus, his **Russian Scaevola** expresses the self-sacrifice and heroism of Russia's patriots in the Patriotic War of 1812 against the forces of Napoleon.

Legend has it that Caius Mucius, a young Roman patrician, stole into the Etruscan enemy camp to kill their king. He was captured but demonstrated his contempt for torture and death by thrusting his right hand into red-hot coals and holding it there without flinching. Astounded by the young Roman's courage, the Etruscan king set him free and abandoned the siege of Rome. Caius Mucius thus acquired the name of Scaevola, the left-handed.

Demut-Malinovsky's sculpture (in Room No. 14) portrays an episode from the War of 1812. Napoleon ordered that every foreigner drafted into his troops have the letter "N" branded on the hand. This was done to a Russian peasant captured by the French. When he learned what this brand meant, the peasant grabbed an ax and chopped off the hand with the mark of Bonaparte.

Of special interest in Room No. 15 is **The Last Day of Pompeii** by Karl Bryullov (1799–1852), depicting the destruction of this ancient city by the eruption of Mount Vesuvius in 79 A.D. In working on this piece between 1830 and 1833, the artist faithfully adhered to the account of eye-witness Pliny the Younger, a Roman historian. The artist emphasised that even in the face of the blind, uncontrollable whim of the elements, man can preserve his dignity.

Room No. 15 likewise contains canvases by Ivan Aivazovsky (1817–1900), the greatest of Russia's

One of the Museum's rooms

Napoleon, when national self-awareness grew and revolutionary ideals emerged among the Russian aristocracy. Representative of these new-found ideals is the **portrait of Yevgraf Davydov**, whose inspired face and unconstrained posture, along with the contrasting colours, denote a brave soldier prepared to fight for his country.

Now descend to the ground floor to have a look at painting and sculpture of the first half of the 19th century in Rooms No. 18-24. In Room No. 19 there are several paintings by Alexei Venetsianov (1780-1847), one of the founders of genre painting in Russia. This realist master depicted the common peasant with affection and respect; indeed, prior to his emergence as a figure in Russian art, peasants were hardly portrayed at all. His characterisations are individualised and authentic. Thus, in his works **The Boy Tying His Bast Shoe, The Threshing Floor, Peasant Children in a Field**, and **The Sleeping Shepherd Boy** strikingly manifest are the democratic aspirations of 19th-century Russian art. Although the artist tended to idealise the Russian countryside with its age-old traditions, he unquestionably had broken fresh ground, thus influencing the further development of Russian art.

In Room No. 20, we find works by Venetsianov's pupils. The works of serf artist Grigori Soroka (1823-1864) are of interest. Lyricism and unaffected naturalness abound in his landscapes. His best known work is unquestionably **The Anglers**.

Dominating Room No. 21 is **The Apparition of Christ Before the People** by Alexander Ivanov (1806-1858), based on the evangelical story of the coming of the Messiah. The artist has

19th-century seascape painters. The finest is his celebrated **Ninth Wave** illustrating the grandeur of the human spirit in grappling with the elements. The subject was suggested by the old sailor's superstition that in storms and gales at sea the ninth wave is the most fearful and fatal. In this picture we see a handful of men clinging to the mast of a sunken ship in a gallant attempt to save themselves. The rays of the rising sun, penetrating the clouds, illuminate the waves towering above them.

No one can remain indifferent to the astoundingly picturesque, highly optimistic landscapes of Silvestr Shchedrin (1791-1830) displayed in Room No. 16. These are mainly views of Italy, which the artist adored; he depicts quiet bays and harbours and seaside towns beneath sunny azure skies.

Room No. 17 contains a magnificent gallery of portraits by Orest Kiprensky (1782-1836), who won repute with his depictions of personages from the 1812 Patriotic War against

White Room

depicted John the Baptist pointing out the approaching Christ to the people as the long-awaited saviour, the incarnation of justice and good. Though religious in content, the painting had an ethical and philosophical significance on the eve of the abolition of serfdom. Ivanov spent nearly 25 years creating this masterpiece, producing some 600 sketches in the process. Some of the sketches on display are valuable in their own right as they shed light on the artist's compositional technique. However, the painting on exhibit is the preliminary version closest to the original at the Tretyakov Art Gallery in Moscow.

Room No. 24 features works by Pavel Fedotov (1815-1852) the initiator of the critical trend in Russian painting. Considering it his paramount task to portray the mores of contemporary society, he lashed out at the greed, hypocrisy, and intellectual paucity of officialdom, the merchant class and the petty aristocracy. Exhibited is one of his best known works, **A Marriage of Convenience**. An impoverished major seeks to better himself by a profitable match. We see a matchmaker in the sitting-room of a wealthy merchant family, while the prospective bridegroom waits jauntily in the doorway.

Rooms No. 25-74 exhibit **Russian art of the second half of the 19th century**.

By the 1860s, social genre painting, expressing the artist's critical attitude to his environment, had reached maturity. The most prominent representative of this trend was Vasily Perov (1833-1882) whose works, exhibited in Room No. 25, strikingly mirror the democratic ideals of the time. While sharply censuring the negative aspects of Russian reality, he shows a deep sympathy for the common folk and their grievous lot. He is especially ruthless in his indictment of the clergy. Thus in **A Monastic Repast**, the subjects depicted are the incarnation of avarice and vicious hypocrisy. We see a corpulent self-contented prior, a young monk hurrying a servant to open another bottle of wine, a wealthy lady, a high-ranking official invited by the fawning clerics to partake of their "humble repast" and a beggar woman with her children futilely pleading for a few crumbs. However, in his later works Perov paid less attention to social comment and concentrated on such themes as the one depicted in **Hunters Resting**.

In their treatment of historical subjects, Russian artists of the second half of the 19th century, faithful to democratic principles, sought to understand the events and authentically depict the atmosphere and people of the period. A place of prominence in realistic historical painting is held by Nikolai Ghé (1831-1894). The episode depicted in his **Peter the Great Interrogating Tsarevich Alexei at Peterhof**, in Room No. 26, took place in 1718. Alexei, son of Peter the Great, was involved in a conspiracy against his father, but when the plot was uncovered he fled abroad. The emperor enticed his heir back, had him tried and ordered that he be sentenced to death. The artist has taken the scene of the interrogation in Monplaisir for his subject. The emperor casts a reproachful glance full of angry contempt at Alexei, who cannot conceal his obstinate but impotent rage. In this painting the author has sought to reflect the struggle between progress and reaction in early 18th-century Russia.

The paintings of Ivan Kramskoy

Icon of The Glorification

Karl Bryullov. Italian Noon

Ilya Repin. The Volga Boatmen

(1837–1887), ideological leader of the democratic trend in Russian art, are displayed in Room No. 27. In 1863, Kramskoy and a group of students in their final year at the Academy of Arts refused to produce graduation pieces on the required theme from Scandinavian mythology, claiming it was too far removed from reality. They walked out in protest and in St. Petersburg in 1870, with Kramskoy as the driving spirit, set up Russia's first association of progressive artists known as the *Tovarishchestvo peredvizhnykh vystavok* (the Association of Itinerant Exhibitions), which is why they came to be known as the *Peredvizhniki*, the Itinerants. Strikingly reflected in their work is censure of injustice coupled with affirmation of and support for the liberation movement and similar social causes. Kramskoy's portraits feature progressive figures in Russian art, science and letters such as the sculptor Antokolsky, the philosopher Solovyov, and the astronomer Struve, to mention but a few.

In Room No. 31 pause to admire the splendid landscapes of Fyodor Vasilyev (1850–1873), including a **View of the Volga with Barks**, the romantic mood of which is filled with freshness, and **The Thaw**, which conveys the sad lot of the impoverished Russian villages lost amidst the snowy expanses. The acme of the collection of paintings by Ivan Shishkin (1832–1898), an eminent 19th-century landscape painter, is **Ship-Timber Grove** in Room No. 32. This work is a forceful manifestation of the artist's perception of the world. Indeed, despite the concrete and realistic reproduction of the natural surroundings in this piece, Shishkin has created an image immediately recognisable to all who have ever been in Russia's woodlands.

Rooms No. 33–35 primarily exhibit genre paintings by the *Peredvizhniki* artists, including Firs Zhuravlyov (1836–1901), Vasily Maximov (1844–1911), Grigory Myasoyedov (1834–1911) and Vladimir Makovsky (1846–1920).

Rooms No. 36 and 37 acquaint you with the works of Vasily Vereshchagin (1842–1904). A brave naval officer who participated in many engagements, he detested war, tirelessly denouncing its cruelty and inhumanity. Particularly appealing are the series of pictures extolling the heroism of the Russian soldiers in the Balkans during the Russo-Turkish war of 1877–1878. Also worthy of note are **Entrance to a Mosque**, **Portrait of a Japanese Priest**, and **The Nikko Shrine**, inspired by the artist's extensive travels to Japan, India and Tibet.

The loveliness of Russian scenery, the radiance of moonlit nights and sunlit mountain peaks, is conveyed by Arkhip Kuindji (1842–1910), whose landscapes are displayed in Rooms No. 38 and 39. The mastery of **A Moonlit Night on the Dnieper**, which reproduces the greenish silvery sheen of the wide river in the evening, is truly a delight. When the piece was first exhibited in St. Petersburg in 1880, many viewers demanded to see the other side of the canvas, suspecting that it was artificially lit from behind. Many were sure that the artist had some special secret, and to this day, its arresting beauty invariably causes the museum-goers to pause before it in admiration and wonder.

Proceed now through an inner passageway to the first floor of the Benois Building, which houses an exhibition of **Russian art of the second half of the 19th century**. Shown in Room No. 46 is the work of the remarkable painter Vasily Polenov (1844–1927), who treated not only landscapes and genre scenes but also historical subjects. Noteworthy is his **Christ and the Adulteress**, a New Testament subject. When the Hebrew priests asked Christ what to do with the adulteress, who by tradition should have been stoned, he said: "Let he who is without sin among you, cast the first stone." To research the subject matter for this picture, Polenov travelled to Palestine, Syria and Egypt. The ancient temple depicted on the canvas actually exists. But the basic motif is the secular understanding of Christ as the poor wanderer whose wisdom and mercy are contrasted to the vicious hypocrisy of the priests, inciting the mob to stone the woman.

Rooms No. 47–50 are filled with works by Ilya Repin (1844–1930), the great Russian realist painter, whose vibrant canvases are a skilful portrayal of Russian society of the second half of the 19th century from a democratic point of view. His paintings are striking reflections of the Russian people's struggle for emancipation, their strength, inner richness and beauty, and patriotic aspirations.

Exhibited in Room No. 47 is the final version of his splendid **The Volga Boatmen**. The artist intended his depiction of the incredibly hard and bitter lot of the barge-haulers as a scathing indictment of the Russian people's harsh bondage under autocracy. The barge-haulers stumble along the bank of the Volga in scorching sun. The spiritual richness of the team leader's prototype aroused the artist's admiration. Behind him is a man bowed over, his face filled with hatred for the misery of his bitter lot. In the middle is a young man in a pink shirt whose untanned face—evidently he is a new member of the barge-hauler's team—is screwed up with pain; this youth is the symbol of protest against the trampling of human dignity.

On view in the next room is Repin's

well-known historical painting, **The Zaporozhye Cossacks Composing a Letter to the Turkish Sultan**, which took the artist more than twelve years to complete. The event depicted occurred in 1675 when the Zaporozhye Cossacks wrote a contemptuous, sarcastically worded reply to the Turkish Sultan Muhammad IV's ultimatum that they denounce their independence and enter his service. The artist has furnished psychologically profound characterisations at a moment of comic relief—the ataman wears a broad grin on his face and the scarlet coated Cossack is in the grips of a side-splitting belly-laugh. The colour scheme conveys the vividness of Zaporozhye Cossacks' life and imparts a note of optimism. The works by Ilya Repin rank among the supreme achievements of Russian and world art.

Towards the close of the 19th century, Russian artists showed a growing interest in Russian folklore. This is most clearly manifested by Victor Vasnetsov (1843-1926), whose canvases are displayed in Room No. 51. One of his many paintings, based on a subject borrowed from Russian fairytales, is his **Knight at the Crossroads**. The hero has paused by a stone, the inscription upon which reads: "Further passage barred to man, beast, or fowl." The ominous landscape with crows hovering over a marsh and the mortal remains of fallen warriors instills a sense of anxiety. But despite the sinister inscription, the dauntless knight will clearly choose the most dangerous road in his struggle against the forces of evil.

The next rooms, No. 52 and 53, are devoted to the celebrated historical painter, Vasily Surikov (1848-1916). Most of his works are on display at the Tretyakov Art Gallery in Moscow. However, the Russian Museum has his **Conquest of Siberia by Yermak**, depicting a decisive moment in Russia's late-16th-century thrust eastward into Siberia, when Yermak's Cossack bands defeat the forces of the Tartar Khan Kuchum. As the painter himself put it, the essence of the event is the "clash of two worlds". In his **Suvorov Crossing the Alps** and **The Taking of the Snow Fortress**, Surikov has portrayed the courage and spiritual strength of the Russian people. His monumental **Stepan Razin** depicts the legendary hero and leader of a 17th-century peasant revolt in Russia.

The work of leading Russian landscape painter Isaac Levitan (1860-1900) is displayed in Room No. 54. Continuing the traditions of the realistic school of landscapists, his art reached another milestone in Russian painting. His **Golden Autumn** is typical of his works as a whole. His fellow-artist Mikhail Nesterov aptly defined the gist of his approach to nature when he said: "Levitan has revealed the enormous beauty concealed in every Russian landscape, its soul and loveliness!"

An exhibition of **art of the late 19th and early 20th centuries**, encompassing the relatively brief period from the 1890s to the October Revolution of 1917, is mounted on the first floor of the Benois Building. Though brief in years, this singularly eventful stage comprises a whole chapter in Russian art history. The cultural complexities of the time are reflected in the plethora of styles, artistic associations, groupings and artistic credos.

One painter whose work was prominent in the artistic development of this period as a whole was Valentin

Simon Ushakov. Icon of The Trinity

Serov (1865-1911). The most outstanding of his portraits in Rooms No. 56 and 57 is the **Portrait of Countess Orlova** with its striking element of social characterisation. Her arrogant manner, gaze and sumptuous garb mark her as an aristocratic lady of fashion in St. Petersburg's high society. In assessing his creative efforts, the poet Valery Bryusov remarked: "Serov's portraits almost always pass judgement on his contemporaries. As a collection, they will preserve for posterity the whole joyless truth about the men and women of our time."

Displayed in Room No. 58 are the paintings of Mikhail Vrubel (1856-1910), an artist of singular talent who showed an enormous interest in folklore. The image of the Demon acquired especial prominence in the artist's pictures with the passage of time. This figure came to represent solitude and anguish. Initially Vrubel's **Demon** was associated with his illustrations for Lermontov's poem of the same name; however, in his large canvases, the image acquired an independent significance, mirroring the dramatic social conflicts of the time.

In 1898, several St. Petersburg artists set up an association which they called *Mir Iskusstva* (The World of Art). In their manifesto they called for a high level of professional skill and stylistic perfection. Works by *Mir Iskusstva* artists such as Alexander Benois, Yevgeni Lanseray, Lev Bakst, Konstantin Somov, Victor Borisov-Musatov, and their follower, the outstanding stage designer Alexander Golovin (1863-1930), are on view in Room No. 60.

Of interest in Room No. 61 are the stage sets and landscapes by Konstantin Korovin (1861-1939). Besides his landscapes, remarkable for their freshness of vision, immediacy of perception, and daring colour schemes, Korovin's well-known **Portrait of Fyodor Chaliapin** is also exhibited. The painting depicts the famous singer sitting by a window which opens out onto a garden.

Portraiture also features prominently in the works of Boris Kustodiyev (1878-1927) (Room No. 82). His genre scenes are well known, especially his **Shrovetide**, depicting a festive episode in Russian provincial life in the colourful manner of the traditional *lubok* prints. Likewise of interest is his **Merchant Wife's Tea** which, despite a certain simplification of form, is marked by decorativeness and precise draughtsmanship. In it Kustodiyev ridicules the carefree, mindless life of a young lady of that social class.

A place of prominence in pre-revolutionary art is likewise held by Kuzma Petrov-Vodkin (1878-1939), whose paintings are shown in Room No. 92. Known as a theoretician of art, he was also a skilful draughtsman and painter. The salient features of his style were already manifest in such an early piece as **Boys at Play**. The theme of motherhood held an important place in his works, as is illustrated by his picture **Mother**.

Finally, in the groundfloor Rooms No. 102-120 of the Benois Building we come to the exhibit of **Soviet art**. We do not list room numbers for this section as displays in this department change frequently, and there are often new acquisitions.

The emergence and development of Soviet art is associated with the changes that occurred after the 1917 October Revolution. A new kind of culture and art came into being. New subjects appeared and fresh characterisations became prominent. The artist's attitude to society underwent fundamental changes as he now found himself directly involved in the state's efforts to produce a new type of harmoniously developed person with higher intellectual and spiritual requirements. Throughout its history, the substance of and trend in Soviet art have been determined by the principles of Marxist aesthetics, which presuppose a civic approach on the part of the artist, active participation in social and cultural advancement, dedication to humanitarian ideals and fidelity to realism.

The exhibit acquaints the visitor with trends and tendencies in socialist realist art and with the works of current leading Soviet artists.

Thus, if we take Kuzma Petrov-Vodkin, mentioned earlier, we see that in the years following the 1917 October Revolution he began to address himself to subject matter relevant to the revolutionary changes taking place. In his **Death of a Commissar** he asserts the need for a sense of civic responsibility. The mortally wounded commissar's strength is waning, but his eyes are turned toward the receding column of Red Army men. Time seems to stand still as the glorious feats of revolutionary valour are reflected in the eyes of the dying man. Another masterpiece by this painter is his famous **1919. On the Alert.** As White Guard armies advance on revolutionary Petrograd and factory whistles call the working class to arms, a working-class family in its shabbily furnished room seems to be caught up in a moment of apprehensive anticipation.

In the magnificent landscapes of Martiros Saryan (1880–1972), the breathtaking scenery of the artist's native Armenia suggests a specific compositional approach. The portraits, landscapes, and other works of Pyotr Konchalovsky (1876–1956) occupy a place of honour, as do the excellent still-lifes of Ilya Mashkov (1881–1944), and **The Vow of the Siberian Guerrillas** by Sergei Gerasimov (1885–1964).

Sculpture occupies a prominent place in this department. Here stands a scaled-down bronze copy of the celebrated **Factory Worker and Collective-Farm Woman** by Vera Mukhina (1889–1953). Cast of stainless steel for the Soviet Pavilion at the Paris World Fair of 1937, it now rises before the entrance to the USSR Exhibition of Economic Achievements in Moscow. The model displayed here illustrates how the proportions of the two figures were made to conform to the pavilion's architectural style. The broad stance of the figures was in keeping with the horizontal expanse of the pavilion and the raised hands emphasised its vertical thrust.

The finest effort of sculptor Alexander Matveyev (1878–1960), who lauded courage and civic duty, is the bronze group **October**, composed of three figures: a factory worker, a peasant and a Red Army soldier, symbolising the triumph of the October Revolution. A replica of the sculpture stands before the October Concert Hall near Nevsky Avenue.

The strong influence of the revolutionary poster with its heavily stressed silhouette is evident in the work of the well known painter Alexander Deineka (1899–1969). The unexpected angle, deliberate displacement of perspective, and a certain graphic quality of his artistic idiom are evident in his

Defence of Sevastopol, an excellent reflection of the infinite courage demonstrated by the Soviet sailors in mortal combat against the Nazis.

The best of Alexander Samokhvalov's (1894–1971) many portraits of his contemporaries is his **Girl in a Striped Jersey**. When his neighbour, the young schoolteacher Zhenya Adamova posed for the artist in 1932, neither imagined that the painting would be exhibited in places as far flung as Paris and Istanbul, nor that it would be reproduced in Rome and Bucharest, nor that it would eventually be called the Soviet Gioconda. The artist has furnished the image of a young Soviet woman in the very bloom of health, cheerful, aware of her intellect, and full of vigour. The explicit and impressive composition and muted colour scheme emphasise the painting's artistic merit.

Arkady Plastov's paintings are dedicated to Soviet rural life. Gely Kor-zhev's triptych **Communists**, like his other works, is imbued with a grand sense of civic duty and social responsibility. The finest works of Mikhail Nesterov, Nikolai Roerich, Pavel Korin, Ivan Shadr and Yevgeni Vuchetich are also presented in this section.

The final section is devoted to folk and applied art. The ground floor of the Benois Building exhibits block-printed fabrics, Tula toys, Russian lace, carved elements of 19th-century Volga peasant log cabins, hand-painted Palekh lacquered boxes, Khokhloma painted woodenware, etc. On display in Rooms No. 49–53 in the Rossi Wing is **old Russian applied art of the 11th-17th centuries** and in Rooms No. 54–65 **applied art from the 18th to the early 20th centuries**. The exhibition of Soviet applied art is displayed in Rooms No. 36–38, on the ground floor of the former Mikhailovsky Palace.

10

PISKARYOVSKOYE MEMORIAL CEMETERY

A drive to Avenue of the Unsubdued (Prospekt Nepokoryonnykh) will take you to the Piskaryovskoye Memorial Cemetery.

The very name of this avenue reflects the heroic feats of the defenders of Leningrad—its population and the soldiers of the Leningrad Front who countered the Nazi hordes with courage and fortitude.

You have already learned from the historical chapter in this book how events developed on the Leningrad sector of the front at the onset of the war.

The enemy launched his first massed air raid against the city on September 8, 1941. On that same day the Nazi troops effected a complete blockade of Leningrad. The German High Command expected to strangle the city in the grip of hunger. During the siege over 640,000 people starved to death, and more than 16,000 Leningraders were killed in the air raids and during shelling. At first the dead were buried in various cemeteries, but after February 15, 1942, only in communal graves near the village of Piskaryovka on the northern outskirts of the city.

Dmitry Pavlov, one of the leaders in the Leningrad defence, wrote: "The cemeteries and their approaches were piled with frozen, snow-covered corpses. Nobody had the strength to dig the frozen ground. The local air defence groups resorted to blasting great pits in the ground and into such spacious graves they lowered dozens, at times even hundreds, of bodies without knowing their names.

"Let the dead forgive the living, for at that desperate time they were unable to fulfil their duty to the end, even though the deceased were worthy of far better burial rites in tribute to their honest working lives."

Approximately 470,000 of those who perished between 1941 and 1943 lie buried in communal graves at the Piskaryovskoye Memorial Cemetery.

Along the Avenue of the Unsubdued you approach the solemn ensemble created on a 26-hectare tract of land by the architects Yevgeni Levinson and Alexander Vasilyev. This necropolis is fenced in by hundreds of metres of metal railing, the rods of which part over regular intervals to make places for urns draped in mourning cloths. Side by side with these symbols of sorrow one sees the delicate outlines of a sprouting sprig—a symbol of life triumphant.

The entrance to the memorial field is flanked by two pavilions, their walls faced with dolomite. The severe geometric forms of the pavilions, their massive square columns, bring to mind ancient propylaea. Inscriptions scrolled on their friezes (words by the poet Mikhail Dudin) glorify the heroism of those who lie buried here:

To you our valorous defenders.
Unfading your memory in grate-
ful Leningrad will live.
Its lives to you posterity owes.
The glory immortal of heroes shall in
posterity's glory be multiplied.
To you, in the great war the victims of
siege.
Eternal your feat in the hearts of
posterity lives.
To you noble heroes glory immortal.
Your own lives align with the lives of
the fallen.

Inside the pavilions is a museum exposition dedicated to the siege of Leningrad. Here you can see a schematic map of the city's defences and read statements made by volunteers as they were departing to fight the Nazis. On display here is one of the most tragic documents of the war, the diary of Tanya Savicheva, a Leningrad schoolgirl. On its pages are entries, scrawled in a childish hand, noting the deaths of the members of Tanya's family. (Tanya herself was evacuated from Leningrad in critical condition; however, the weakened child could not overcome what she had gone through and died far away from Leningrad on July I, 1944).

The exposition displays many documents and photographs showing the heroic work of the drivers on the Road of Life laid over the ice of Lake Ladoga. From November 22, 1941 to April 24, 1942 (152 days) 1,004 motor vehicles, many of them carrying passengers and supplies, were lost under the ice when it was broken by Nazi bombs and shells.

Behind the pavilions is a spacious terrace, rising above the cemetery. In its centre, in a frame of polished black stone, burns the Eternal Flame kindled on May 9, 1960, the day the Piskaryovskoye Memorial Cemetery was opened. A ceremonial cortege escorted a torch lighted by the Eternal Flame on the Field of Mars near the graves of the fighters for the Revolution.

To the left of the Eternal Flame is a granite-paved pool. The mosaic at its bottom depicts a torch with an oak branch and red ribbons entwined around it.

From the terrace granite steps lead down to the central alley of the cemetery. An endless line of granite tombstones, covering the communal graves, extends along this alley. The tombstones are engraved with oak leaves and the dates of burial: 1941, 1942, 1943 ... A crossed hammer and sickle or a five-pointed star are engraved over the dates, depending on who was buried in this grave—civilians or soldiers who fell in the battles for Leningrad.

The main parterre of the cemetery, 300 m long and 75 m wide, is enclosed by a green wall of trees. In the depth of the parterre stands a stele, 150 m long and 4 m high. Its central part bears columns of blank verse written by the poetess Olga Berggolts. They begin with the following lines:

Here lie the people of Leningrad,
Here are its citizens—men, women,
and children,
With them the Red Army soldiers
Who gave up their lives
Defending you, Leningrad,
Cradle of the Revolution.
Their noble names we cannot here list
So many beneath the eternal
protection of granite here lie,
But you who to these stones hearken
should know

Piskaryovskoye Memorial Cemetery. General view

No one is forgotten, nothing is
forgotten ...

This text, sounding both as a requiem and a hymn, ends with the words:

... So to your immortal life
Let in this sad and solemn field
The grateful people eternally their
banners dip,
O Motherland and hero-city
Leningrad.

The granite of the stele is covered with reliefs depicting soldiers and civilians—the defenders of Leningrad. The stele is flanked by reliefs of dipped banners, on its buttends wreaths and overturned torches, symbolising extinguished lives, are carved. By the wreaths kneel a Woman, a Worker, a Soldier and a Sailor, personifying the entire Soviet people mourning the fallen.

The compositional centre of the Memorial is a six-metre-high bronze

Statue of the Motherland

statue of a woman symbolising the Motherland (sculptors Vera Isayeva and Robert Taurit). She holds a garland of oak and laurel leaves which she is placing on the graves of the nameless heroes.

The austere and majestically restrained aspect of the memorial ensemble, the dark and sombre hues of the bronze and granite reflect the depth of the people's grief. Here, in this solemn field, where the very air seems to be filled with grief, nobody is left unmoved. The impact of sorrow does not obscure the exploit of the Leningraders. Every person who comes here probably feels his obligation to the hundreds of thousands of heroes lying in the communal graves. Their lives and their deaths are a bequest to us, the living, to fight for peace and happiness for all people, to prevent any repetition of a tragedy like that of Leningrad.

11

THE LENINGRAD METRO

The question of building an underground road in St. Petersburg arose back at the beginning of the 19th century. A resident of the city, a self-taught man by the name of Torgovanov, submitted a bold project to Alexander I—that of a tunnel to be dug from the centre of the city to Vasilyevsky Island. The Russian ruler rejected the project and ordered the inventor to sign a pledge "not to engage in hare-brained schemes in the future, but to exercise his efforts in matters appropriate to his estate". Other, more developed projects were subsequently forwarded, but they, too, received no recognition.

Many arguments were advanced against the construction of an underground road. The "city fathers" stated that the excavation works would "violate the amenities and respectability of the city"; the landlords affirmed that underground traffic would undermine the foundations of the buildings; the merchants feared that "the open excavations would interfere with normal trade"; but the most violent adversaries of the novelty were the clergy, who insisted that "the underground passages running near church buildings would detract from their dignity". Thus all the projects for the construction of an underground passage in St. Petersburg, and later in Petrograd, remained on paper.

Revolution, civil war, the hardships of the restorative period put off the idea of building a Metro in Leningrad for many years. However, the city grew, its boundaries expanded, and the need for a new, cheaper and faster type of transportation was imperative. In January 1941 a decision was taken to build a Metro in Leningrad. However, the war foiled all plans. Work was slowed down on June 24, 1941, and soon stopped altogether. It was renewed in the early 1950s, when the city had repaired its war damages.

On November 15, 1955, the first line of the Metro was opened—from Avtovo to Uprising Square; its length was 10.8 km. This date is the "birthday" of the Leningrad Metro.

The laying of underground lines in such a city as Leningrad is fraught with many difficulties. The builders had to break through ancient Cambrian claystone series formed almost 600,000,000 years ago. Not infrequently they encountered gigantic boulders, five and more metres in diameter. The work was also complicated by the Neva—the river had to be crossed three times.

The construction of the Leningrad Metro generated numerous innovations. Among them, for instance, are the single-spanned vaults of the deep-lying stations Ploshchad Muzhestva, Polytekhnicheskaya, and others. The absence of supporting columns makes for freer movement of passengers on the platform.

The Leningrad Metro is highly economical. All its stations are situated higher than the tunnels, as if on little hills. As they leave the stations, the trains go down an incline (power economy), and they arrive on an up-grade slope (less power or compressed air spent on braking).

For the first time in the world subway construction stations without boarding platforms were built in Leningrad. The central hall has a series of niches with closed doors that separate it from the tunnel. The doors of the niches open only when the train has come to a full stop and its doors are in line with the niche doors—just as in a lift. The system was therefore named a "horizontal lift".

The platformless type of station has definite advantages: the possibility of contact between passengers in the hall and the moving train is excluded; 36 per cent less excavation work is needed; the diameter of the tunnel remains the same throughout its entire length; and their most important merit is that they have preconditioned the automatisation of underground traffic. The trains stop automatically at precisely established places without manual operation. Automatic devices slow down the movement of the train much more smoothly and accurately than drivers do.

At the beginning of 1986 the total length of the Leningrad Metro lines was over 83 km, more than 44 stations functioned, and the average operational speed of the trains was 40.1 km/hr (the average speed of Leningrad streetcars is 16.9, of trolley-buses 16.3, of buses 19.8 km/hr). During rush-hours the interval between trains in the Metro is 1.5 minutes.

When the stream of passengers thins out the longest interval between trains is 5 minutes. Two and a half million passengers use the Leningrad Metro every day.

Currently four Metro lines operate in Leningrad: the Kirovsko-Vyborgskaya, the Moskovsko-Petrogradskaya, the Nevsko-Vasileostrovskaya and Pravoberezhnaya lines.

We invite you to tour the underground arteries of the city and witness for yourself their beauty and efficiency. As you view the Leningrad Metro you will probably note a diversity in architectural styles, ranging from the majestic, or even somewhat pompous decorativeness, to modest utility. There is nothing unusual in this—the architectural designs of the stations reflect the time when they were built.

The Kirovsko-Vyborgskaya Line

We suggest you begin your tour of this line at its southern terminal **Prospekt Veteranov** (Veteran's Avenue). The pillars of the underground hall of this station are faced with black labradorite, the floor is flagged with grey granite slabs that have black insets framed with brass strips. The pillars are also decorated with metal insets. In contrast to the subdued colouring of the floor and pillars, the walls are faced with bright, golden "gazgan" marble.

Leninsky Prospekt (Lenin Avenue). One should note the columns of the underground hall: faced with red granite, they widen towards the top. They are very effective against the background of the unpolished white marble walls. *Leninsky Prospekt* and *Prospekt Veteranov* are not deep stations and therefore have no escalators.

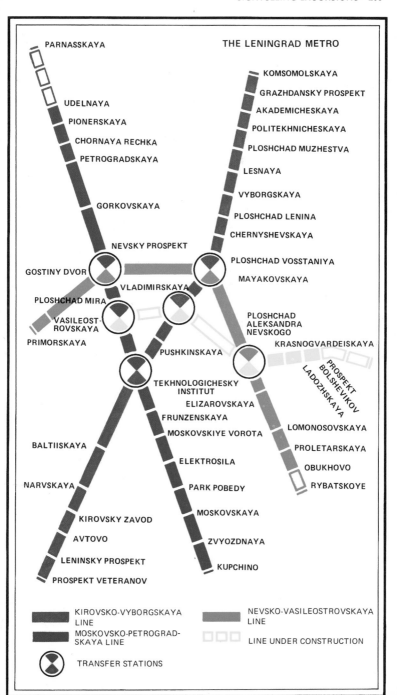

PARNASSKAYA

THE LENINGRAD METRO

KOMSOMOLSKAYA
GRAZHDANSKY PROSPEKT
AKADEMICHESKAYA
POLITEKHNICHESKAYA
PLOSHCHAD MUZHESTVA
UDELNAYA
PIONERSKAYA
CHORNAYA RECHKA
PETROGRADSKAYA
LESNAYA
VYBORGSKAYA
PLOSHCHAD LENINA
CHERNYSHEVSKAYA
GORKOVSKAYA

NEVSKY PROSPEKT
PLOSHCHAD VOSSTANIYA
GOSTINY DVOR
MAYAKOVSKAYA
VLADIMIRSKAYA
PLOSHCHAD MIRA
PLOSHCHAD
VASILEOST-
ALEKSANDRA
ROVSKAYA
NEVSKOGO
PRIMORSKAYA
KRASNOGVARDEISKAYA
PUSHKINSKAYA
PROSPEKT BOLSHEVIKOV
LADOZHSKAYA
TEKHNOLOGICHESKY
INSTITUT
ELIZAROVSKAYA
FRUNZENSKAYA
LOMONOSOVSKAYA
MOSKOVSKIYE VOROTA
PROLETARSKAYA
BALTIISKAYA
ELEKTROSILA
OBUKHOVO
NARVSKAYA
PARK POBEDY
RYBATSKOYE
MOSKOVSKAYA
KIROVSKY ZAVOD
ZVYOZDNAYA
AVTOVO
LENINSKY PROSPEKT
KUPCHINO
PROSPEKT VETERANOV

KIROVSKO-VYBORGSKAYA
LINE
NEVSKO-VASILEOSTROVSKAYA
LINE
MOSKOVSKO-PETROGRAD-
SKAYA LINE
LINE UNDER CONSTRUCTION

TRANSFER STATIONS

Avtovo. The surface vestibule of this station is on Strike Avenue (Prospekt Stachek), not far from where the front line passed during the siege of Leningrad. This circumstance determined the décor both of the station and of its surface pavilion. An inscription on the base of the latter's dome reads: "Glory eternal to the valorous defenders of Leningrad who withstood the enemy attacks on the hero-city!"

Passengers descend to the station by a wide, gently descending semicircular staircase. The gratings, chandeliers, and lamps are decorated with laurel branches, gilded swords and other emblems of military valour. The shallowness of this station made it possible to build a flat roof over the underground hall. The roof is supported by 46 pillars aligned in two rows. Particularly noteworthy are 16 columns faced with patterned pressed glass. This material, used as a decoration for the first time, is just as strong as marble. A golden strip of anodised aluminium winds around the columns in a spiral holding, as it were, the glass slabs on which five-pointed stars, banners, and laurel wreaths are depicted.

The architects and engineers had to overcome many difficulties to achieve the desired optical effect. For despite the embossed ornamentation the concrete shaft of the columns was clearly visible through the transparent, scintillating glass; this, naturally, had not been planned by the authors of the design. Finally, with the aid of optical researchers, a solution was found: facets on the inner surface of the glass slabs were cut at an angle of 80°. As a result the light reflected by the facets, does not reach the concrete shafts. In this manner, all the columns seem to be glass monoliths.

The end of the hall is decorated with a mosaic of a young mother holding her child—a symbol of peace.

Kirovsky Zavod (Kirov Factory). This station was named in honour of one of the largest enterprises in Leningrad. The architectural décor of the interior is devoted to the theme of industrialisation. The walls of the underground hall are faced with veined light-grey Caucasian marble. Over the two rows of columns supporting the vaulted ceiling run silvery high-reliefs with representations of symbols of the basic branches of industry: oil extraction, coal mining, iron and steel, and power production.

The soft, diffused light streaming from square plafonds produces the illusion of an open sky in this underground hall. Each of these lowered plafonds is a lattice made of organic glass, behind which luminescent lamps are mounted. Louvers have been used here for the first time in world practice.

Narvskaya. The revolutionary past and the labour exploits of the workers of the Narva Gate area (now Kirov District) are the themes reflected in the décor of this station. The high arches forming the entrances to the vestibule are decorated with an ornament depicting banners, shields, oak and laurel branches—symbols of courage and glory. The main decoration of the vestibule at the top of the escalator is an enormous sculptured panel depicting workers, peasants, scientists, students. In the central part of the panel is a sculpture of Lenin making a speech from atop an armoured car.

The underground hall is faced with ivory-hued marble from the Urals. The 48 pylons supporting the vaulted roof are decorated with sculptured groups of workers, miners, metallurgists, teachers, sailors. The lighting system is quite original: waves of light seem to ripple over the ceiling as they flow out from the moulded torches on the friezes, the crystal arcs fuse into a continuous sparkling vault that is reflected in the polished granite floor.

Baltiiskaya (not far from the Baltiisky Railway Station). The vestibule of this station is decorated with bas-relief portraits of outstanding Russian naval commanders of the 18th and 19th centuries: Fyodor Ushakov, Mikhail Lazarev, Vladimir Kornilov, Pavel Nakhimov and Stepan Makarov. The vault of the underground hall is supported by two rows of columns faced with sea-green marble from the Urals. This hall has neither chandeliers nor torches; the sources of light (1,200 electric bulbs) are concealed by the cornices. The greyish-blue marble of the walls, the vaults, reminiscent of swelling sails, the absence of any decorative details produce the impression of the open sea. The end wall is covered with a mosaic, *The Volley from the Aurora*, laid out with large slabs of marble and coloured stone.

Tekhnologichesky Institut (the Technological Institute). The decoration of this station is devoted to Russian and Soviet science. The underground hall, its walls faced with white marble contrasting with the black floor, is light and spacious. Marble arches in the centre lead into a smaller hall from which a stairway leads to transfer lines; the arcade is decorated with 24 bas-relief portraits of Mikhail Lomonosov, Alexander Popov, Kliment Timiryazev, Ivan Pavlov, Ivan Michurin and other outstanding figures in Russian and Soviet science; the portraits alternate with laurel and palm wreaths. At the centre of the hall are bronze medallions depicting bas-reliefs of Karl Marx and Lenin.

Pushkinskaya. This station is next to the Vitebsk railway terminal which services the town of Pushkin (formerly Tsarskoye Selo, where the poet spent his boyhood). The underground hall is faced with snow-white marble, the floor is laid out with polished slabs of dark-red Ukrainian granite. The vaulted ceilings are decorated with moulded wreaths. A double row of tall bronze lamps with crystal bowls leads up to a sculpture of Pushkin (sculptor Mikhail Anikushin) standing against the background of a lyrical landscape in the park at Tsarskoye Selo.

Vladimirskaya. The design of this station is simple and austere. The white marble walls are decorated with anodised metal. The central hall is somewhat shorter than the platforms: for the station was not planned for large numbers of passengers. The lofty vestibule at the top of the escalator is decorated with a mosaic panel depicting Plenty.

Ploshchad Vosstaniya (Uprising Square). The theme of the socialist revolution is reflected in the décor of this station. It is remarkable for its gleaming light, ornamented white arches, and bronze medallions depicting the major phases in preparing and carrying out the October armed uprising: Lenin's speech from an armoured car in front of the Finland Railway Station, Lenin's stay in Razliv, from where he directed the preparations for the uprising, the volley fired from the cruiser *Aurora*, the storming of the Winter Palace, the proclaiming of Soviet power and other important events of 1917.

The pylons supporting the vaulted ceiling of the hall are faced with red marble, the floor is of polished granite slabs. Notwithstanding the great depth of this station, the air in it is pure and fresh, as it is in all other Leningrad Metro stations; they are heated in the winter and air-conditioned in the summer.

Ploshchad Vosstaniya is the last station on the Leningrad Metro's first section, which was commissioned in 1955. In the summer of 1958, trains began to run through a new section connecting *Ploshchad Vosstaniya* and *Ploshchad Lenina.*

Polytekhnicheskaya *Metro Station*

Chernyshevskaya. This station is somewhat smaller than the others. Its underground hall is austere in appearance. Decorative silvery ventilation grids match well the grey marble of the walls. The slabs have been arranged so that the veins of the marble form an intricate pattern.

Ploshchad Lenina (Lenin Square). This station is built into the left wing of the Finland Railway Station. The surface vestibule is decorated with a monumental mosaic panel, "Lenin, Leader of the Revolution". The colour scheme in the underground hall is based on the contrast between red and white. Here, too, as in the *Chernyshevskaya* station there is no complicated decorative ornamentation.

Vyborgskaya and **Lesnaya**. These stations are part of the section that was subsequently extended further north; they were opened to passengers in the 1970s. Both stations (similar in their construction plans)—are of the column type. At the *Vyborgskaya* station the columns and walls are faced with pinkish-beige travertine (calc tufa), a porous stone used for the first time in Metro construction. The columns of the *Lesnaya* (Forest) station are faced with white Estonian marble, "koelga", while the walls are faced with green ceramic tiles. The end wall of this station is covered by a decorative composition entitled "The Sun"

Ploshchad Muzhestva and **Polytekhnicheskaya**. These stations, like the two preceding ones, are similar to each other in construction—single-spanned with a central platform between the tracks. The artistic conception of the *Ploshchad Muzhestva* (Square of Courage) station is imbued with the idea of the heroism and staunchness of the Leningraders in the years of the Great Patriotic War (1941–1945). The architecture of the underground hall is solemnly austere: a grey granite platform and dark marble walls softly illuminated by fixtures in the form of inverted pyramids.

The décor of the *Polytekhnicheskaya* station is pleasingly quiet. The side and end walls of the station are

Underground vestibule of **Elektrosila** *Metro Station*

faced with travertine. The colour of this stone matches the copper sheen of the metal finishing details. Console light fixtures with incandescent lamps are arranged along the walls. Bright bands of light illuminate the letters forming the name of the station.

Akademicheskaya (Academic). This station is situated at the intersection of the two major thoroughfares of the Vyborg District: Science Avenue (Prospekt Nauki) and Civilian Avenue (Grazhdansky Prospekt). The dominant architectural feature in the underground hall is an arcade. The stainless steel décor on the columns and arches harmonises with the white marble walls.

Grazhdansky Prospekt (Civilian Avenue) and **Komsomolskaya**. These last two stations on the northern section of the Kirovsko-Vyborgskaya line were completed in 1978. The pylons and walls of the underground hall of *Grazhdansky Prospekt* station are faced with greyish-beige marble. The state emblem of the Soviet Union is depicted on the butt-end wall.

The *Komsomolskaya* station is combined with the railway station Devyatkino. The gigantic roof (166 × 43.5 m) is held up by widely spaced supports.

The Moskovsko-Petrogradskaya Line

The majority of the stations on this line are located along Moscow Avenue. Your excursion on this line begins at **Kupchino**, a station in the southern part of the city, where some half a million people live. There is no underground hall here; the entrance hall is connected by underpasses with the Kupchino railway station platforms and with a large open square next to the railway tracks on the east.

Zvyozdnaya (Stellar). The design of this station is dedicated to outer space exploration. The walls of the underground hall, faced with light-hued marble, are slightly inclined inward. Its lighting cornice is made up of convex sheets of aluminium. Silvery aluminium lattices, decorated with stars, gleam softly on its end wall. In the entrance hall there is a sculptural composition dedicated to the first cosmonaut, Yuri Gagarin. The round vestibule at the top of the escalator is roofed with a snow-white dome with a decorative ring at its base faced with golden smalt.

Moskovskaya. This station has no surface vestibule or platforms. The entrance hall is entered through passages running under Moskovsky Avenue. The design of the underground hall is restrained and laconic.

Park Pobedy (Victory Park). This is the first station in world subway construction practice to be equipped with a "horizontal lift", that is, it has no boarding platforms. A row of recessed doors along the walls of the underground hall form a unique rhythmic line. Each doorway is decorated with rounded strips of ribbed metal. Patterned glass cornices along the walls conceal lamps that emit a soft, diffused light. Decorative arches are set in the butt-end walls; the arches seem to lift the roof, creating an impression of considerable height.

Elektrosila. This station takes its name from the large machine plant located nearby on Moscow Avenue. The end wall of the hall is decorated with a ceramic panel reflecting in stylised and somewhat conventional form the theme "Electrification of the USSR".

The grey-blue marble of the pylons, the small hall and long tunnels with their wide passenger platforms resemble the *Chernyshevskaya* station you have already seen. The architects of this station stressed the industrial motif in its décor: the lines of the rectangular openings between the underground hall and the platforms resemble slits in machine casings, and in the upper parts of these openings

light fixtures in the form of pulleys are mounted.

Moskovskiye Vorota (Moscow Gate). The pylons of the underground hall are faced with beautiful red and white marble and inclined, their sides decorated with shining strips of polished aluminium. The overall impression is that a line of military banners held aloft by silvery flag-staffs is extended along a hall flooded with bright light. At the butt-end wall there is a composition consisting of military accessories—copy of one of the compositions on the memorial to Russian military glory at the Moscow Gate.

Frunzenskaya. Marble pylons widening towards the bottom are a notable feature of the passenger hall. The walls are faced with white polished marble, the floor is laid out in grey and black granite. The end wall is decorated with a bas-relief portrait of Mikhail Frunze, a leading Soviet military commander, surrounded by his comrades-in-arms, against a background of unfurled flags. The bas-relief is made of aluminium and red smalt.

Tekhnologichesky Institut-2 (a transfer station). This station is distinguished for its graceful simplicity. The floors are laid out with slabs of polished grey and black granite, the walls are faced with white marble, a soft light emitted by luminescent lamps flows from the ceilings. The décor of the station reflects the theme "Science Serves Communism". This idea is presented in inscriptions mounted in superimposed letters on the pylons. The inscribed texts convey the outstanding achievements of Soviet science and technology, among them the launching of the first artificial earth satellite, the building of the atomic-powered ice-breaker *Lenin*, the space flight of Yuri Gagarin, and so forth.

You have visited the stations of the second section of the Leningrad Metro, the section extending from *Tekhnologichesky Institut-2* to *Park Pobedy* that went into operation in 1961. It must be pointed out that these stations were built at a time when methods of standard design and construction were being actively introduced into Soviet architectural practice. Standard structures thus appeared in the Metro, too. Among them are the surface pavilions of the stations *Frunzenskaya, Elektrosila*, and *Park Pobedy*, all built according to a single design. Each of these structures is a squat pavilion topped by a low dome. These standard buildings differ significantly from the earlier stations in the simplicity and rationalism of their architecture.

In 1963 a number of new stations were opened — *Ploshchad Mira, Nevsky Prospekt, Gorkovskaya*, and *Petrogradskaya* — in the section running from the Technological Institute to Lev Tolstoy Square on the Petrograd Side. We shall dwell on them below.

Ploshchad Mira (Peace Square). The interior of the surface vestibule of this station is faced with bluish-grey slabs, its outside walls are covered with reddish granite. Marble-coated columns support the roof of the spacious hall. The façade of the pavilion is decorated with a 20-metre stained-glass panel with aluminium lattices.

The floors of the underground hall are laid out with slabs of dark-grey granite, the walls of the platforms and the pylons are faced with tiny (2 × 2 cm) glazed tiles. The pylons are topped with decorative grids. Light shed by luminescent lamps is diffused through frosted glass and the golden-hued grids, thus creating the impression of a luminous ceiling.

Nevsky Prospekt (Nevsky Avenue). The staircases, designed to accommo-

date a large stream of passengers, lead from the street level down to a wide, spacious vestibule. The architectural décor of the station was designed to utilise, as fully as possible, every metre of space. The configurations of the pylons and vaulted ceilings of the underground hall reiterate the form of tubing rings — structural elements of the station. The lower parts of the pylons are covered with horizontal ribbing of polished aluminium. The walls of the train tunnels are faced with red-lined glass tiles.

Gorkovskaya. The plinth of the circular vestibule is covered with Ukrainian granite, while its walls are faced with grey Estonian stone. The stained-glass panels are framed with black tiles, and golden-hued tiles decorate the summer café that adjoins the station. Light, warm colours dominate in the underground hall, its pylons are covered with dolomite ("Estonian marble") from the island of Saaremaa. The modest architectural décor of the hall includes motifs from Maxim Gorky's works.

Petrogradskaya. The rectangular entrance hall of this station adjoins a round vestibule at the top of the escalator. Wide use was made of glass, aluminium and dolomite in the finishing work of the vestibule. The underground hall has no boarding platforms; the passengers board the trains directly from a middle hall separated from the track tunnels by automatically operating doors. The walls of this hall are faced with light-coloured ceramic semi-cylinders, and an illuminated band of anodised grids runs along the base of the vaulted ceiling. The light sources are concealed by the grids. The floor of the hall is laid out with granite. A grid covers the end wall, serving as a background for a golden-hued panel featuring the profiles of a young man and woman.

This line has been extended to include three new stations: *Chornaya Rechka, Pionerskaya*, and *Udelnaya*.

The Nevsko-Vasileostrovskaya Line

The construction of this line was commenced in 1964. The first section, with the stations *Vasileostrovskaya, Gostiny Dvor* and *Mayakovskaya*, was opened in 1967, marking the 50th anniversary of the October Revolution. A second section went into operation in 1970: the stations *Yelizarovskaya* and *Lomonosovskaya. Primorskaya*, the terminal station, was opened in 1979. Finally, in 1981, the *Proletarskaya* and *Obukhovo* stations were opened to passengers.

Your tour of the third line of the Leningrad Metro begins at **Primorskaya** (Maritime). This station is located in the northwestern part of Vasilyevsky Island (Vasilyevsky Ostrov). Long ago this was right on the outskirts of the city. Now rows of high-rise buildings (including the Pribaltiiskaya Hotel) occupy the former wastelands, and tree-lined boulevards have been laid out. The surface vestibule of the station stands in the centre of a residential area, on the bank of the river Smolenka. Presumably, this vestibule will eventually be built into the new administration building of the Leningrad Metro.

The décor of the underground hall features rectangular greyish-green marble columns, a grey and black granite striped mosaic floor, and greyish-white marble wall facings. The entire design reminds you of the proximity of the sea. The piers between the columns are decorated with high reliefs of ships of the Russian and Soviet naval fleets whose glorious history began in the city on the Neva.

Vasileostrovskaya. The above-ground glazed pavilion of this station was erected on a high platform. Insets of a darker colour stand out from the white marble walls of the vestibule at the top of the escalator, and a cornice containing light fixtures is mounted on its upper part. The walls of the underground hall are faced with marble, the floor is laid out with a combination of granite and aluminium.

Gostiny Dvor. This station has two exits on the surface but no surface pavilions. Both exits are built into 18th-century architectural monuments— the Gostiny Dvor (an arcade housing rows of shops) and the former Engelgardt mansion. The main entrance is under the arcade of the Gostiny Dvor. Behind the low, old arcade the vestibule of the station looks particularly spacious. Its walls are faced with light-coloured "koelga" marble, and light fixtures are built into the plicated ceiling. Over the four escalators (this is one of the most crowded stations) an enormous (6 × 20 m) stained-glass panel depicting the events of July 1917 is mounted. Here, at the walls of the Gostiny Dvor, on the order of the Provisional Government, a peaceful demonstration of workers, soldiers, and sailors marching under the slogan "All power to the Soviets!" was shot down. The white walls and silvery cornices contrast picturesquely with the dark doors of anodised aluminium in deeply recessed niches and with the dark-grey granite floors.

Mayakovskaya. This station, too, has no surface pavilion. Its exit is built into a large building at the corner of Nevsky Avenue and Marat Street. The architectural design of the underground hall is quite original, featuring neither arcades nor pylons. The walls are faced with small plates of deep-red smalt. Bevelled protuberances jutting from the doorways stress the dynamic rhythm of the interior. The butt-end wall carries portraits of the poet Vladimir Mayakovsky, after whom the station is named. The portraits are done in a graphic manner—a white marble inlay on red granite. The figure of the poet (in hammered copper) stands in the above-ground vestibule.

Ploshchad Alexandra Nevskogo (Alexander Nevsky Square). The vestibule of this station, incorporated into the building of the Moskva Hotel, is finished in diverse materials: dolomite, marble, wood, and ceramic tiles. The station is named after Alexander Nevsky, a Russian prince who distinguished himself in the 14th century in battles against foreign invaders. There are no traditional cornices or vaulted ceilings in the hall; its far end carries a decorative copper panel entitled *Alexander Nevsky*.

Yelizarovskaya. The station is named after an outstanding revolutionary figure, Mark Yelizarov. The underground hall is decorated with a bas-relief, *Uprising of the Proletariat*, mounted on an ornamental grating at the end of the hall.

Lomonosovskaya. Its location near the Lomonosov Porcelain Works influenced both the choice of the name and the décor of this station: the shades of colour and rounded architectural forms of the underground hall are reminiscent of delicate porcelain. The construction of the ceiling in the entrance hall is noteworthy: a massive console plate is supported by powerful props clearly visible from the street through a glass enclosure. The circular vestibule at the top of the escalator is decorated with wooden panels and anodised metal.

Proletarskaya (Proletarian). The surface vestibule of this station is in the centre of a former working-class suburb. The lower tier of the pavilion is faced with granite, its walls, both outside and inside, are covered with Estonian dolomite. The circular vestibule leading to the escalator is completely enclosed in glass. The architectural décor of the underground hall is dedicated to the theme "The working class is the leading force in Soviet society." Marble-faced white columns are crowned with a frieze moulded in the form of an unfurled red banner. The butt-end wall of the station carries a bronze composition, *Hammer and Sickle*, the symbol of the union of workers and peasants.

Obukhovo. The façades of the octagonal surface pavilion of this station are covered with polished marble and decorated with stained-glass panels. In the underground hall lamps stand along the platform at 12-metre intervals. The architecture of the station includes motifs reflecting the revolutionary traditions of this part of the city (the former Neva Gate) and the events of 1901 known as the Obukhovo defence (a strike of the Obukhovo factory workers). This theme is also treated in the bas-relief mounted on the butt-end wall of the underground hall.

Pravoberezhnaya (Right Bank) Line

The line is so named because it follows the right bank of the Neva to one of the city's newer districts. This seven-kilometre line with four stations was put into operation on the eve of 1986. This section was under construction for nearly four years. The line, which passes beneath the Neva, carries up to 30,000 passengers during rush hour.

Ploshchad Alexandra Nevskogo-2 (Alexander Nevsky Square-2). The station's second vestibule, like its first, is located on this square, though on the opposite side, at the end of Nevsky Avenue. The floor of the escalator vestibule is laid with Karelian granite, while the walls are faced with white marble and decorated with large stained-glass windows. The main vestibule is structured with columns and designed to accommodate eight-car trains. The white-marble gallery is somewhat reminiscent of ancient Russian architecture, which is quite appropriate for a station named after the legendary military leader of Old Russia. The station interior has yet another original motif: the walls are covered with overlaid golden petals looking like ancient Russian chain mail. The butt-end of the transfer hall bears a bas-relief panel depicting Russian warriors on horses.

Krasnogvardeiskaya (Red Guard). This station does not have an outside pavilion; its entrance hall is located underground, beneath the square and can be reached from the street via twelve access tunnels. The walls of the escalator hall are faced with red-coloured marble. Opposite the escalator is a light fixture made of hammered copper. Each individual lamp is cut at a sharp angle at the top, in the form of a five-pointed star through which the light rays pass. The main vestibule is illuminated by seven such lamps in a circular design, occupying almost the entire area of the ceiling. Inside the circle are compositions of stamped copper. The side walls are faced with a strip of pink marble.

Ladozhskaya (Ladoga). The outside pavilion stands on the square of what will soon be a new railway station. The façade of the pavilion is faced with dolomite and granite. A glass-encased lamp towers over the roof. The

architectural composition of this station is devoted to one of the most heroic pages in the history of the siege of Leningrad—the legendary Road of Life that crossed Lake Ladoga. The portals above the entrance to the escalator tunnel, as well as those at its foot, are faced with grey-blue marble (the colour of the lake's waters). The main underground vestibule is faced with the same grey-blue marble and decorated with a frieze of polished granite bearing the name of the station. Along either side of the platform stand two rows of milestones—or rather, white marble standard lamps designed as such—bearing memorial dates. The floor is laid with grey granite slabs framed with strips of black labradorite.

Prospekt Bolshevikov (Avenue of the Bolsheviks). This station's circular above-ground vestibule is located in a future park area. The second storey of the pavilion is finished with an anodized alloy, while the façade is faced with dolomite—a light-coloured stone from the Estonian island of Saaremaa. The high-ceiling of the entrance hall has a ribbed construction, which creates the effect of a soaring cupola. The underground vestibule has no columns, but is covered by three vaults, at the junctions of which are powerful lamps. The contrast between the granite base of the side walls and the open white vaults adds to the laconism of this station's interior.

By the time this book comes off the press new stations will have appeared on the lines of the Leningrad Metro. Therefore, we apologize ahead of time if you do not find descriptions here of all the stations of the Leningrad Metro operating when this book is published.

THE ENVIRONS OF LENINGRAD

Petrodvorets
Pushkin
Pavlovsk
Razliv
Repino

To the Reader

In all likelihood you have had an opportunity to observe the bustle of Leningrad and have admired its straight thoroughfares, spacious squares, granite embankments, magnificent palaces, numerous monuments, bridges and churches. But your impression of this beautiful city on the Neva will not be complete until you have seen the charming estates nearby: Petrodvorets (formerly Peterhof), Pushkin (formerly Tsarskoye Selo), and Pavlovsk. Here you will find palaces, fountains, and parks designed by world-famous architects and built by anonymous Russian craftsmen more than 250 years ago.

Below we shall acquaint you with the artistic treasures of Leningrad's suburbs and introduce you to the Karelian Isthmus, a favourite holiday spot for many Leningraders, and to Razliv, where Lenin took refuge from the Provisional Government in July and August of 1917.

During the last war, which, as you might know, is called the Great Patriotic War in this country, Petrodvorets, Pushkin, Pavlovsk and Repino were occupied by Nazi forces, who ruthlessly destroyed everything they could not plunder. The looted and gutted palaces, the ruined parks and fountains are only part of the vile deeds perpetrated by Hitler's soldiers. The commission set up to ascertain the extent of the damage inflicted established that it amounted to a staggering total of 20,000 million roubles. You will surely see the multitude of documentary photographs there of the ruined architectural monuments near Leningrad right after the Nazis were driven out. Even a cursory comparison with their present brilliance will be sufficient to ascertain the stupendous amount of restoration work done.

It is no exaggeration to claim that the restoration work done on these palaces and parks ruined by the Nazis is as stupendous a feat as their original construction.

In 1986 a Leningrad team of restorers was awarded the Lenin Prize for their restoration of the palace and park ensembles of Leningrad's suburbs. The laureates include artist and restorer Alexei Kochuyev, architect Alexander Kedrinsky, art specialist Anatoly Kuchumov, gilding master Pyotr Ushakov, and artists and restorers Nadezhda Ode and Yakov Kazakov. Several of them contributed their efforts to the search for the various masterpieces stolen by the invaders. Anatoly Kuchumov, for example, took part in evacuating valuable museum pieces to Novosibirsk. However, before the war had even ended, he was assigned the task of finding stolen works of art. Kuchumov and his colleagues followed the vanguard units of the Soviet Army into each city as it was liberated from the fascists. They found stolen furniture, paintings, books, porcelain, and sculptures. Dozens of paintings by outstanding masters were returned to Leningrad's museums thanks to their efforts.

In the 1980's the palace and park ensembles of Petrodvorets, Pushkin, and Pavlovsk were made into state palace and park museum-reserves of great artistic value.

And now, we shall wind up this short introduction and invite you to have a look at the fountains of Petrodvorets, the broad, tree-lined paths of the Pushkin Park, the salons of the Pavlovsk Palace, and to derive hours of pleasure from the priceless handwork of the masters of the past, known and unknown.

We suggest going out by bus or car. It is roughly a half hour ride to Petrodvorets, Pushkin, or Pavlovsk and about an hour ride to Razliv and Penaty on the Karelian Isthmus.

PETRODVORETS

The history of Petrodvorets, one of the most exciting places in the environs of Leningrad, which until 1944 was called Peterhof ("Peter's Court" in German), goes back to the early 18th century, when it was built to commemorate Russia's victories in its effort to acquire an outlet to the Baltic Sea, a "window on Europe". In fact the leitmotif of virtually all its fountains is Russia's naval might.

In May 1703, Peter the Great started the building of St. Petersburg along the broadest section of the Neva's estuary. Further out, to guard the approaches from the Baltic, the fortress of Kronstadt was erected on the Island of Kotlin in the Gulf of Finland. The emperor, who supervised this work personally, often visited the island, and a small cottage was hastily put up on the Gulf's southern shore so he would have a place to rest.

While the Northern War was still being fought, the tsar paid little heed to ornamentation, but after the victory at Poltava in 1709 and the naval victories at Gangut and Grangam in 1714 and 1720 respectively, he decided to build a sumptuous town near his new

capital to demonstrate his empire's power and wealth.

However, before the envisaged gardens and parks could be laid out on the marshy clay along the southern shores of the Gulf of Finland, an extensive drainage system had to be installed and soil and fertilizer brought by barge to replace the layers of clay removed. Tens of thousands of maples, lindens, chestnuts, fruit trees, and shrubs, as well as fine statues and paintings, costly fabrics, building materials and equipment for fountains, were brought here from all over Russia and from abroad. And though the newly planted trees and shrubs were frequently swept away by storms and floods, every effort was made to repair the damage.

After the end of the Northern War, Peter the Great began to work seriously on the development of Peterhof, personally drawing up plans and providing not just general directions but detailed instructions as to what should be done.

Among the eminent Russian and foreign architects and sculptors who made major contributions to the pro-

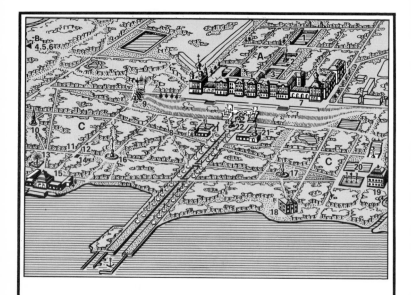

PARKS OF PETRODVORETS

A. **Upper Park 1.** Mezheumny Fountain **2.** Neptune Fountain **3.** Oak Fountain
B. **Alexandria Park 4.** Court Chapel **5.** Cottage **6.** Farm Pavilion
C. **Lower Park 7.** Grand Palace **8.** Triton Fountain **9.** Chess Hill and Roman fountains
10. Pyramid Fountain **11.** Umbrella Fountain **12.** Little Oak Fountain **13.** Sun Fountain
14. Bird cages **15.** Monplaisir Palace **16.** Adam Fountain **17.** Eve Fountain **18.** Hermitage
Pavilion **19.** Marly Palace **20.** Golden Hill Cascade **21.** Cup Fountain **22.** Grand Cascade
and Samson Rending the Jaws of the Lion Apart

ject were Johann Friedrich Braunstein, Mikhail Zemtsov, Bartolomeo Rastrelli, Niccolo Michetti and Mikhail Kozlovsky.

The waterworks for the system of fountains was built in 1721 and 1722 under the direction of Vasily Tuvolkov, Russia's first hydraulics engineer. The intricate system of pipes and ducts of this masterpiece of 18th-century fountain construction stretches for nearly 22 km. There are no pumping stations at all; the water flows downhill by force of gravity

Grand Cascade

while the fountains operate according to the principle of communicating vessels.

Construction and improvement of the fountains and waterworks system continued into the mid-19th century. Now there are a total of 144 fountains and four cascades. In both artistry and engineering the fountains of Petrodvorets are truly unique.

After the Great October Socialist Revolution of 1917, Peterhof, with its fountains, statues and palaces, was placed under state protection and nationalised. On May 18, 1918, the Grand Palace saw its first excursion of ordinary Soviet citizens. Today the parks and gardens of Petrodvorets are a favourite recreation spot for Leningraders.

Nazi Germany attacked the Soviet Union on June 22, 1941. As Hitler's troops approached Leningrad, a massive effort was undertaken to evacuate Peterhof's treasures. The museum's staff, fearlessly defying the shelling and bombing, hastily packed all they could of the collections. All in all 7,363 objects d'art and 49 statues from the Grand Cascade and from the gardens of the Monplaisir Palace were evacuated. Unfortunately, due to the lack of time, the shortage of transportation, and insufficient manpower, not all the treasures could be evacuated or safely stored away. So when the Nazis burst into Peterhof on September 23, 1941, 34,214 museum exhibits including paintings, statues, vases and the like, as well as 11,700 priceless volumes from the palace libraries, remained behind. Still standing were such imposing bronze groups from the Grand Cas-

Marine Canal

Wing Beneath the Coat of Arms (Grand Palace)

cade as *Samson*, the *Neva*, the *Volkhov*, and the *Tritons*, and several statues from the Upper Park.

For almost 900 days the Nazis occupied Peterhof, looting and destroying whatever they could in blind hatred for the Soviet people and Russian culture.

Finally, when on January 19, 1944, Soviet troops liberated Peterhof, they came face to face with a true nightmare.

The beautiful palaces lay in ruins. The lovely parks were pitted with trenches and dug-outs. The Nazis had cut down some 14,000 centuries-old trees, destroyed the fountains, wrecked the waterworks, and carted off statues, bas-reliefs, vases, mascarons, and even bronze door handles.

Just a couple of months later, on March 29 of that year, the government issued an edict slating priorities concerning the restoration of Leningrad and its environs. However, before this program could be initiated, it was necessary to clear the town of mines. Sappers from the Baltic fleet defused more than 20,000 mines and 100,000 shells in Petrodvorets alone. Working alongside them were the Petrodvorets specialists who, like archaeologists, carefully sifted the earth and rubble to locate any fragments of architectural or sculptural décor that might have survived. In the summer of 1944 and the spring of the following year, thousands of volunteers from Leningrad went out to Petrodvorets on Sundays to help. Their valiant efforts allowed the Lower Park to be opened on June 17, 1945, while on August 25, 1946, after almost five years, the fountains again began to play. Addressing a meeting in honour of the event held near the Grand Cascade, Academician Joseph Orbeli said: "Even during the darkest hours of the war, we all believed the day would come when the beautiful fountains of Petrodvorets would play once more and their bronze statues would gleam in the sun." And now the silvery jets of the Petrodvorets fountains are turned on daily at 11.00 a.m. from May through October.

Now that you have learned something about the history of Petrodvorets, we invite you to visit the parks and palaces, and see the fountains of this world-famous beauty spot.

The square where you leave your bus or car terminates in a balustrade on its northern side. Beyond this a green slope descends steeply to a small plain stretching right to the shoreline of the Gulf of Finland. This is a part of the Lower Park which in all occupies an area of more than 102 hectares. However, before going to see its sights, we suggest you walk along until you reach the middle of the façade of the Grand Palace. You will now find yourself standing on a marble terrace facing the sea, and from here you will have a magnificent view of the **GRAND CASCADE** with its 17 statues adorning its waterfalls, 29 bas-reliefs, 142 jets and 64 fountains.

Though the Grand Cascade was built in the first quarter of the 18th century, it assumed its present appearance only in the mid-19th century. Two streams of water spurt out of masks representing Neptune. On their way down, they are replenished by the jets of the fountains on the Cascade's staircase and the *Basket* Fountain. Rippling down the steps, flanked by gilded bas-reliefs, the water comes to oval terraces where the statues of an old man with an oar in his left hand and a young woman stand. These two beautiful and finely sculptured figures personify the Volkhov and Neva rivers.

Further on, the water tumbles out of the mouths of dolphins into a pool, in the centre of which a **sculpture of Samson rending the jaws of the lion apart** towers on a massive pedestal of ashlar. Though the beast has dug its claws into the giant's thigh in a frenzy, Samson has rent its jaws, and from this yawning cavity a 20-metre jet of water spurts into the air. The fountain was erected to commemorate the Battle of Poltava which was fought on St. Samson's Day, June 27, 1709 and marked the turning-point in the Northern War.

On their retreat from Peterhof, the Nazis carted away the Samson, the most interesting of all the statues embellishing the Grand Cascade. It was decided that a new one should be cast, but unexpected difficulties arose. It appeared that though the statue had been photographed thousands of times, no exact measurements had ever been taken. This Herculean labour was undertaken by sculptor Vladimir Simonov who carried out a great deal of research to reproduce the famous figure. On September 14, 1947, Samson once again took his place at the centre of the Cascade.

It has been said that the fountains of the Grand Cascade are a symphony in water, glorifying the triumph of Russian arms. Indeed, nearly all the elements are geared to this central theme. Thus at Samson's feet water spurts from the mouths of the eight dolphins symbolising a calm sea. They form a circle around Samson's feet, like a wreath for the hero. The four streams spurting out to the cardinal points of the compass from the jaws of the four lions' heads recessed in the pedestal symbolise the worldwide glory rendered to Samson for his victory. Also in his honour are the fountains shaped as Tritons blowing conch shells in the upper grotto by the balustrade. They start to work in the morning only after the column of water spewing from the lion's jaws reaches 20 metres, its maximum height.

On the central terrace of the Grand Cascade is the **Basket Fountain** whose 28 jets of water form a basket inside of which 11 vertical jets resemble a bouquet of flowers. In the allegorical language of the 18th century, a basket of fruit or flowers signified wealth and plenty.

Nearly all the statues along the Grand Cascade have an allegorical significance. Thus, on one of the lower terraces **two gladiators** stand face to face, each holding an extinguished torch and a serpent to symbolise victory and the defeated enemy.

Perseus, of whom there is also a statue in the Grand Cascade, accomplished many heroic exploits, including slaying the Gorgon Medusa who could petrify any living creature with her glance. The golden statue of this Greek hero is a symbolic representation of Peter the Great.

The focal point of the Petrodvorets water gardens, the Grand Cascade is organically connected with the Grand Palace, the ensemble's main building.

The **GRAND PALACE** was built from 1714 to 1724 by Johann Friedrich Braunstein, Jean-Baptiste Leblond and Niccolo Michetti. Later, numerous alterations and modifications were introduced. The eminent Russian architect Mikhail Zemtsov was involved in the work carried out during the 1730s, while the world-famous architect Bartolomeo Rastrelli supervised the construction between the mid-1740s and the mid-1750s, the crucial chapter in the building of the palace.

Preserving the original divisions of a central section and wings connected by galleries, he added side-wings extending southwards towards the Upper Park. At the western and eastern ends of the palace he took down the modest wings terminating the galleries, and built in their stead the *Wing Beneath the Coat of Arms* at the western and the *Church Wing* at the eastern end. He successfully blended medieval Russian architectural elements with characteristic Baroque forms.

After Rastrelli, architects Jean-Baptiste Vallin de la Mothe added the *Chinese Rooms*, and Yuri Felten—the *Dining-Room*, the *Chesma Room*, the *Throne Room*, the *Partridge Drawing-Room*, and others. Between 1845 and 1850, further alterations in the interior design of the palace were made by court architect Andrei Stakenschneider.

In the **Exhibition Room** you will find various documents tracing the history of the palace's construction. There is information on the nationalisation of the royal estate of Peterhof after the 1917 Revolution, when it was turned into one of the most interesting museums in the world. Further exhibits tell of the destruction wrought by the occupying Nazi troops and the painstaking efforts made in post-war years to restore the building and its lavish interiors.

Ascend the **Oak Staircase** (architect Alexander Leblond) to the **Oak Study of Peter the Great**. As the name suggests, the chief embellishment here is the carved oak wainscoting executed by the French sculptor Nicolas Pineau and his associates in 1718-1720. A variety of themes, such as military and naval paraphernalia, musical instruments, and bas-relief portraits of Peter the Great and his wife Catherine are presented.

Upper Park

In 1941, only eight panels, the sup-raporte and the oak doors were evacuated. Most of the oak wainscotting was destroyed. Restoration was extremely time-consuming, with restorers spending up to 18 months to carve a single oak panel. However, today it is virtually impossible to distinguish the panels produced by Soviet masters from those by early 18th-century master-carvers. If you take a closer look, you will see that some of the panels are of a lighter hue—the sole indication that they are of more recent vintage.

Standards glorifying the victory of the Russian arms in the Northern War and a desk clock made in Augsburg, Bavaria, in the early 18th century that is believed to have belonged to Peter the Great are also on view here.

Next to the Oak Study is the **Royal Bedchamber** which was reproduced entirely on the basis of indirect data, as neither drawings, plans, nor pre-war photographs remained. The restorers had only the drawings architect

Yuri Felten made for the Grand Palace, which were preserved in the archives of the Petrodvorets Museum. It appeared that this room was linked by a corridor with a similarly appointed room in the women's quarters of the palace, evidently conceived as the tsar's bedchamber. In the late 18th century, Paul I ordered architect Vincenzo Brenna to design a special stand for this room on which the crown could be mounted, and ever since, this room has also been known as the *Crown Room*.

The focal point of the bedchamber is an alcove in which stands a carved gilded 18th-century bed. The walls are draped with late 17th-century hand-painted Chinese silk. The plafond, which was taken from the Hermitage, features a scene from the myth of Venus and Adonis.

Knowing that her lover Adonis will be slain by the jealous god Mars, Venus implores him not to set out for the hunt. However, he ignores her pleas and is gored to death in the forest by a wild boar. Touched by Venus' grief, the gods transform Adonis into an anemone.

Other pieces of interest are an 18th-century English clock, Chinese porcelain, and an 18th-century chest of drawers of German make.

Now you will enter a room the interior decoration of which is typical of Russian palaces of the first quarter of the 18th century. On display here are paintings from the collection of the Marly Palace in the Lower Park. The room contains early 18th-century delftware and a closet made in Hamburg at about the same time. The portraits of Peter the Great, his wife Catherine I, and his favourite, Prince Alexander Menshikov, were all painted during their lifetime. Several measuring instruments stand on the chest of drawers. The bookshelves hold a number of early 18th-century editions. The zigzag parquet was designed by Bartolomeo Rastrelli.

The gilded carving, plafonds and exquisite parquet in the next room are characteristic of Rastrelli's work. Among the items exhibited here are a suite of mid-18th-century Dutch furniture, a chest of drawers, a bronze clock from France and a chandelier made by Russian craftsmen.

The next room shows the influence of Classicism, which began to replace the Baroque trend in Russia in the second half of the 18th century. To reflect the ideas of their time, adherents of this style addressed themselves to the art of ancient Greece and Rome, and depicted their contemporaries as mythological heroes.

The classical trend is also seen in the works of applied art exhibited here, those of both Russian and West European origin. They date back to the second half of the 18th century.

Be sure to have a look at the vases by British potter Josiah Wedgewood, who invented a special kind of stoneware which enabled him to create vessels of different tints with figures and embellishments in relief after the ancient Greek style. Subsequently he turned to the production of porcelain.

A French clock, a small English oval table, and the portraits of the Empress Catherine the Great and her husband Peter III that hang on the walls also date back to the second half of the 18th century.

In the following room, there is a display of mid-19th-century Russian applied art. On view in a late-19th-century cabinet of French workmanship is the *Coral Service*, a most artful imitation of coral, made at a Russian pottery works. The bronzes and furniture are also of Russian make.

The next room you enter is known as the **Guards'** or **Crimson Room**. The name derives from its having served as the room for the officers who guarded the private quarters of the Empress. Of interest is a suite of 18th-century English furniture designed by the famous master Thomas Chippendale. Characteristic of his style is a functional expediency of form and comfort, combined with elegant line and elaborate embellishment. Also on view here are several chairs made in Russia in the Chippendale style; only experts can tell the Russian copies from the originals.

Now we come to the **Standards Room**, which is a characteristic example of 18th-19th-century palace interior design. There are various explanations as regards its name; some claim that regimental standards of the guardsmen billeted in Peterhof during the summer were stored here, others suggest that the name stems from the yellow fabric that once covered the walls and was of the same colour as the Imperial Standard. On view here are several formal portraits, including one of Peter the Great with Minerva and others of his daughter Elizabeth, the Empress Catherine the Great and the Empress Anna Ioannovna.

Worthy of attention among the works of applied art displayed is a 19th-century French clock with beautifully sculpted figures depicting the parting of Hector and Andromache (a scene from Homer's *Iliad*). Two early-19th-century candelabra and an Empire chandelier, both of French make, as well as carved gilded furniture are on display in this room.

The next room is traditionally known as the **Empress's Study**, a designation emphasised by furnishings and décor alike. There are a late-18th-century desk and a bureau, and early-19th-century candelabra, all of French make, an Indian sandalwood casket which belonged to Catherine the Great, and Sèvres and Meissen porcelain. The walls are hung with portraits of the Empress Elizabeth, Catherine the Great, Tsar Alexander I as a young man, King Stanislaw Poniatowski of Poland, and other royal heads. The gilded armchairs and a settee were produced in the second half of the 18th century by the famous French cabinet-maker Georges Jacob.

In the **Dressing-Room**, note the silver toilet service consisting of a looking glass and two candlesticks, believed to have been presented by King Louis XV of France to the Russian Empress Elizabeth, and also an early-19th-century Russian porcelain toilet service. The chests of drawers were made in Germany in the 1760s and 1770s. The portraits of the Empress Elizabeth, Catherine the Great, and Emperor Paul I were made during their lifetime.

The Dressing-Room adjoins the **Lounge**, which likewise served as one of the state bedchambers. The walls here are covered in patterned Chinese silk that is more than three hundred years old. Most of it was destroyed during the last war except for a portion on the western wall which was restored. Otherwise, lengths of silk executed in identical technique and of the same pattern from the stores of the Grand Palace were used. Wherever there was not enough material, the restorers devised new compositions in faithful accord with the original technique, each of which demonstrates a high degree of authenticity. The parquet is composed of oak, palm and birch. The silk upholstery of the large ottoman and its cushion covers are the work of Russian serf craftsmen.

The walls of the **Partridge Drawing-Room** are covered with silk ornamented with partridges—hence the name. The original silk was manufactured in Lyons, France, in the 18th century after a design by, and under the supervision of Philippe de Lassalle. Later it was replaced by Russian silk made at a Moscow mill in the early 19th century. During the war the fabric was destroyed by fire. Luckily, the restorers chanced upon a 23-metre length of this silk, which was used for the western wall. The northern and eastern walls are covered in silk woven in modern times on hand looms at the Moscow Institute of Silk Research. The finest weavers could produce no more than six to ten square centimetres of this amazing cloth in a day.

The interior decoration of this room

is typical of 18th-century Russian palaces. On display here are a Russian girandole produced in the 1780s, an English chiffonier believed to have been made in the 1760s by the firm of John Cobb, a French chest of drawers, some mid-18th-century Meissen porcelain and a French timepiece made at the turn of the 19th century.

The adjoining room is known as the **Eastern Chinese Study**, so called because it lies east of the centrally positioned Portrait Gallery. From records for 1728 we know that the walls were covered in white Chinese satin. The room had Chinese lacquered screens and furniture likewise upholstered in white Chinese satin. The walls are presently finished in crimson silk with a raised pattern of baskets of flowers. The plafond on the ceiling depicts exotic birds, butterflies and beetles. All the painting, carving and gilding was done by Soviet restoration workers.

The **Portrait Gallery** which comes next is the central hall of the palace and one of the most sumptuously appointed of all the premises as regards interior decoration. The walls are completely covered with 368 female portraits done by Pietro Rotari and his pupils. This collection was acquired from the painter's widow by the Empress Catherine the Great who ordered that they be hung in the palace. They miraculously escaped the ravages of war and were placed back after the room was restored. Artistically they are not particularly outstanding, but as they comprise a collection of documents depicting the costumes of the period, the room was also known as the Study of Fashion and Grace. The young women depicted are of interest chiefly for their Turkish, Hungarian and other costumes.

Passing through the **Western Chi-**nese Study we come to the **White Dining-Room**, one of the state rooms, which is ornamented in the early classical style with dazzling white mouldings representing the trophies of hunting and angling, garlands of flowers and fruit, cupids and musical instruments. The magnificent gilded crystal chandeliers of an amethyst hue are Russian work. Fortunately, they escaped the ravages of war by being evacuated. Also on display is a state dining-table laid with 30 place settings. The 196-piece porcelain dinner service was produced at an English pottery in the 1760s specially for Catherine the Great. As the English Queen Charlotte appreciated its cream colour it came to be known as Queen Charlotte's Service.

After the White Dining-Room, you pass through the **Audientz**, or **Ladies-in-Waiting Hall** to enter the spacious **Throne Room**, which was intended for gala receptions and official ceremonies. The throne, made by Russian craftsmen, is the original and belonged to Peter the Great. Above it hangs a portrait of Catherine the Great on horseback, painted in 1762. Besides an abundance of portraits of members of the Romanov dynasty there are 12 bronze chandeliers and bronze sconces of Russian make produced in the 1780s.

The décor of the next **Chesma Room** is dedicated to the naval engagement that occurred between the Russian squadron and Turkish fleet in June 1770 in the Bay of Chesma in the Aegean Sea. The battle culminated in a spectacular victory for the Russians. In general, the décor, consisting for the most part of paintings by the German artist Philippe Hackert, glorifies Russia's victory over Turkey in the war of 1768–1774.

Throne Room

The paintings illustrating the Chesma engagement were commissioned in 1771. However, upon examining the preliminary sketches, Count Alexei Orlov, who had commanded the Russian squadron, criticised one which depicted a ship exploding in flames. The artist explaned that he had never actually witnessed such an event, so Orlov decided to show Hackert what a real explosion looked like. The St. Barbara, a 60-cannon Russian frigate, was chosen for the demonstration. With the blessing of the Russian Empress and the Duke of Tuscany, the frigate, which rode at anchor seven miles offshore from Livorno with several other Russian ships under Orlov's command, was filled with barrels of gunpowder and blown up. Goethe observed that this was the most costly model any artist had ever used.

The mahogany furniture in this room was made by Russian craftsmen in the first third of the 19th century. The marble busts of Catherine the Great and her favourite, Grigory Orlov, were sculpted in Carrare in the second half of the 18th century.

In 1985 the restoration of the palace's main staircase, with its great pictorial plafond, statues and vases, rich gilded décor, palm-wood steps, and elegant figured railing, was completed. At the centre of the plafond, occupying an area of 36 sq m, is Aurora, the Roman goddess of Dawn, in a gilded carriage. At hand is Genius with a torch, chasing away the Night. The abundance of colour and light create the effect of the coming of Spring.

The opening of the main entrance will make it possible to alter the excursion route. Visitors will now start with the state rooms—the Chesma Room, the Throne Room, and others—and finish with the living quarters.

The Grand Palace is actually the focal point of the whole of Peterhof since, rising above the bluff which descends toward the Lower Park, it acts as a link between the Lower and Upper parks.

Now walk through the **UPPER PARK**, which occupies an area of 15 hectares between Red (Krasny) Avenue and the southern façade of the Grand Palace. It is best to start your walk from the open-work wrought-iron gates and the 10-metre-high pylons embellished with Corinthian columns which stand at the southern end of the park.

The first fountain you encounter is known as the **Mezheumny**. The name, which in old Russian parlance meant "uncertain" or "six of one, half dozen of another" is most likely due to the several modifications the fountain has undergone. At present, it consists of a round pool and a dragon with wings outspread in the centre surrounded by four dolphins.

Next comes the **Neptune Fountain**, the focal point of the Upper Park. It is embellished with a three-tiered group of sculptures reminiscent of a fountain of the same name that stands before the Rathaus in the GDR's capital of Berlin. This is not surprising, as the fountain was imported from Nuremberg. To mark the end of the Thirty Years War of 1618-1648, the Town Council of Nuremberg decided to put up a large fountain in the market place. The entire affair, consisting of 27 figures and other decorative elements, was executed between 1650 and 1658. However, when the fountain was almost finished, it was discovered that there was not enough water in the local streams and rivers to make it work, and so the fountain had to be dismantled and placed in storage. Much later, in 1782, when Prince Paul, the heir to the Russian throne, visited Nuremberg during his travels through Europe, it was offered to him for the sum of 30,000 roubles. The bargain was sealed, and in 1799 the Nuremberg Neptune fountain was erected in the Upper Park at Peterhof. Subsequently, in 1896, the Russian authorities allowed German sculptors to take moulds of it, and in 1902, a replica was finally put up in Nuremberg. During the war, the Nazis stole the fountain. However, Soviet troops tracked it down in Germany and in 1956 it was reinstalled in the Upper Park once again.

The **Oak Fountain** in the vicinity is named after a fountain shaped like an oak which stood there in the 18th century. Today, nothing is left of the original piece.

At the centre of the circular granite-faced pool stands a marble sculpture of a putto donning a tragic mask. Dolphines on the points of the star spurt out jets of water.

Now you will come to the **Square Ponds** right by the walls of the Grand Palace, marking the end of your walk around the Upper Park. They are not actually square, but rather, 54 × 45 m apiece.

At the centre of the western pond stands the marble statue *Italy's Venus* (a 19th century copy of the original by Italian sculptor Antonio Canova), while the eastern is decorated with the marble statue *Apollo*, a copy of the original executed in classical times.

If you go through the gates of the Upper Park in the northeastern corner, you will come out on to a small square from which a straight road leads to the **ALEXANDRIA PARK**, which is worth a visit if you have time to spare.

At the entrance is the **Court Chapel**, built between 1831 and 1833 after designs by the Berlin architect Karl Friedrich Schinkel, Adam Menelaws, and Ludwig Charlemagne. Built in Gothic style, the chapel has tapered corner towers with wrought-iron decorations. Mounted on brackets around the chapel's outer perimeter are the figures of 43 saints sculpted by Vasily Demut-Malinovsky. This building is the Alexandria Park's most valuable architectural monument.

Standing on the crest of a hill in the park's eastern part is another curious building known as the **Cottage**. Actually a palace, it was built in 1829 by Adam Menelaws, an Englishman by birth, who had found a second homeland in Russia. Many gifted Russian master-carvers, plasterers, parquet-layers and other craftsmen executed his designs for the interior décor. In 1842, a marble terrace, designed by the court architect, Andrei Stakenschneider, was built to adjoin the eastern façade of the Cottage.

The occupying Nazi forces inflicted vast damage on the Cottage, destroying the furniture and interior décor and ruining the façades. Restoration work was completed only in 1979.

Outwardly the Cottage resembles the country houses of English gentry. It was built in the Gothic style, characterised by the application of authentic Gothic architectural elements without regard for their designation or structural function. The façade is embellished with tracery lancet arcadings, balconies, high pediments and a representation of the coat of arms of Alexandria—a shield and an unsheathed sword thrust through a wreath of white roses.

For the most part the exhibits on display in the Cottage, which is now a museum, are authentic and date back to the times when the palace was a royal residence. When the war broke out in 1941, its staff succeeded in evacuating 1,981 of the total 2,500 museum pieces.

The main entrance to this building is on the southern side, through an impressive porch topped by a lancet arcading. Embedded in the wall above the door is a stone from the former Turkish fortress of Varna captured by Russian troops during the Russo-Turkish war of 1828–1829. On one side of the stone is the following Russian inscription in gold ligature: "This stone is from Varna. September 29, 1829."

The excursion begins with the **Study of the Tsarina Alexandra Fyodorovna** (wife of Nicholas I). The painted design on the stove resembles the tracery of a Gothic window. The stucco on the ceiling in the shape of heavily embellished Gothic rosettes is the work of plasterer Mikhail Sokolov. Its bay window is glazed with tinted glass in imitation of the stained-glass windows of medieval castles. The clock, furniture, candlesticks and other pieces are decorated with Gothic ornamental motifs. The windows and doors are embellished with garlands of flowers and fruits—the work of Russian master-carver Vasily Zakharov.

On view here are items from the porcelain factories of St. Petersburg and Berlin. Also of interest are the portraits, including Alexander Bryullov's water-colour study of Tsarina Alexandra Fyodorovna in the Cottage's Drawing-Room. The bronze candlesticks executed in Gothic style by 19th-century Russian craftsmen, a timepiece in the form of a Gothic chapel by the same craftsmen, bronze incense burners and a mid-19th-century French chandelier complete the décor.

You now come to the **Grand Drawing-Room**, the main room on the ground floor. The décor is not particularly sumptuous. The designers have evidently sought to impart a degree of cosy intimacy. The magnificent wood-carving on the windows and doors, also by Vasily Zakharov, and the exquisite marble columns embellished with floral motifs executed by sculptor Paolo Triscorni are sure to attract attention. Despite the endeavour to impart a certain intimacy to the room's overall design, Gothic motifs are manifest in the furniture, in the design of the 19th-century Russian carpet, which duplicates the design on the ceiling, and in the porcelain clock, a copy of the façade of the Rouen Cathedral, made in the 1830s by Pyotr and Vasily Vakhrameyev and Nikolai Yakovlev, the master-potters from St. Petersburg Porcelain Factory.

The **Library** next to it is a typical example of pseudo-Gothic interior decoration with its bookcases, German screens with representations of knights and ladies in medieval garb, the timepieces imitating the Gothic façades of medieval churches, or the ivory and mother-of-pearl model of the castle built on Pfauen Island near Potsdam in 1795–1797.

The **Grand Reception Hall** has an interesting display of works by Russian painters of the second quarter of the 19th century, among them Orest Kiprensky and Silvestr Shchedrin. The furniture was built by Russian cabinet makers in the 1840s. Also of interest are a silver chandelier from France designed in the late 1820s, as well as crystal and porcelain of Russian workmanship.

The **Dining-Room**, too, displays some superb pieces of Russian glass and porcelain of the middle of the 19th century. The most outstanding among them is the **Personal Service**. Commissioned in the early 1830s specially for the Cottage, it originally consisted of 314 porcelain and 353 crystal pieces, each bearing the coat of arms of Alexandria. Additions were still being made to the service at the beginning of the 20th century.

From the Dining-Room you enter the **Small Reception Hall** whose furniture of rosewood with gilt bronze and porcelain insets was made by Russian craftsmen in the mid-19th century but in an 18th-century style. The 19th-century porcelain figurines exhibited here are genuine Meissen, created after 18th-century models.

Go up the staircase to the first floor. The rooms here are more modestly decorated than those downstairs. The first rooms you come to were for the sons of Nicholas I. As they were fanatics for parade-ground drill, it is not surprising that these rooms are hung with charts illustrating parades, military exercises and Russian uniforms. **The Classroom of the Heir Apparent**, the future tsar Alexander II, is also filled with picture albums of army uniforms. As a matter of fact, even the walls of the **Valet's Room**, which served as wardrobe, are covered with drawings of military accoutrements.

Similarly "militarised" is the **Dressing-Room**, in which one finds Gothic-style furniture of ashwood designed by the well-known cabinet maker Heinrich Gambs. The prints and lithographs here depict various episodes of the Russo-Turkish War of 1828–1829. The Russian victory culminated in the signing of a peace Treaty in Adreanopolis which ensured freedom of navigation in the straits of Bosporus and Dardanelles for Russian and foreign merchant vessels, and which also granted autonomy to Moldavia, the Rumanian province of Walachia, and Serbia, and gave Greece independent statehood.

The next room is the **Study of Nicholas I**. It is starkly and austerely fur-

Samson Fountain

nished, very much in accord with the tastes of this harsh despot. Of interest here are some 17th-century Dutch landscapes and a collection of miniature portraits.

Originally the small painted illustrations of medieval manuscripts were called miniatures; subsequently, in the 16th century, small water-colour portraits were also termed miniatures. In the mid-18th century, the term was extended to cover gouache paintings on ivory, and ever since, small works of art, including portraits, have been referred to as miniatures.

Well known 18th- and 19th-century Russian and foreign masters are represented by the works hung near the mantelpiece and in the spaces between the windows.

Next door is the **Room of Maria Nikolayevna** (daughter of Nicholas I), also in Gothic style. However, the mid-19th-century furniture is of a style introduced by André-Charles Boulle, the celebrated ebonist at the court of Louis XIV, who gave his name to a style of furniture notable for its ormolu and marquetry of ivory, tortoiseshell and mother-of-pearl. The Sèvres and Meissen porcelain is quite lovely, as is the timepiece made by the Russian watchmaker Ivan Yurin in 1860 which showed the time in 66 provincial seats of Russia and in Russian America, the name by which Alaska was known until 1867.

Regrettably, not all the rooms in the Cottage have retained their original décor. Thus, the next room, the **Study of Maria Fyodorovna**, wife of Emperor Alexander III, has an interior decoration of a far later period, namely, the 1890s, and is characteristic of the Art Nouveau style. The walls are covered in fabric embellished with a floral design. The furniture is simple and comfortable. Also characteristic of Art Nouveau is the late 19th-cen-

tury French coloured glassware on the shelves, and the porcelain from the royal factory in Copenhagen. There are late 19th-century porcelain vases of Russian make.

The last room on the first floor is the modestly decorated **Room of Alexandra Nikolayevna** (daughter of Nicholas I) which was designed in the late 1820s by architect Adam Menelaws. This is, incidentally, the only room of any of the daughters of Nicholas I that has remained intact. It was closed after Alexandra Nikolayevna died in childbirth. Russian mahogany furniture of the 1830s and 1840s and bronze, glass and porcelain virtu of the second quarter of the 19th century of Russian, French and German make can be seen here. Of particular interest is the *Doll's Service* from the St. Petersburg porcelain factory and the Meissen porcelain.

Proceed up to the second floor and enter the **Naval Study of Nicholas I.** Arrayed on the desk are a spy-glass, a megaphone horn, a theodolite, a compass, and other instruments. Through the spy-glass the tsar used to watch the naval exercises conducted off Kronstadt. The walls are covered with engravings, paintings and lithographs illustrating the defence of Sevastopol during the Crimean War of 1853–1856. On the right, by the wall, is a model of the monument unveiled to Russian Admiral and Antarctic explorer, Mikhail Lazarev.

The Cottage—a museum of Russian and West European art of the second quarter of the 19th century—is the only extant monument in Leningrad's environs which illustrates the emergence of the Romantic trend in Russian art of that period.

Now proceed to the **LOWER PARK**. To do so, walk back from the Alexandria Park to the square outside the eastern wing of the Grand Palace and descend to the Lower Park by the ramp. To your left will be an elegant one-storey building topped by a garret and balustrade. This is the **Conservatory** designed and built in 1722–1725 by Johann Friedrich Braunstein and Mikhail Zemtsov to protect the delicate plants from the sea breezes. It was heavily damaged by the occupying Nazi forces and was rebuilt in 1954 according to an extant early 18th-century drawing.

In the middle of the garden in front of the Conservatory is the **Triton Fountain**, depicting Triton grappling with a sea monster. Overcoming excruciating pain, Neptune's son has wrenched the monster's jaws apart. A jet of water shoots up to a height of eight metres from the monster's mouth. The frightened tortoises at the foot of the pedestal seem to be scuttling away in all directions. Like other fountains at Petrodvorets, the Triton Fountain is of allegorical significance, commemorating the Russian naval victory at Hängo Peninsula in July 1714, during the Northern War.

The entire sculptural group was originally cast of lead in 1726 after a model by Carlo Rastrelli. Some 150 years later, it was replaced by an electroplated copy made in Berlin. The Nazis stole the sculpture and destroyed the works. After the war, Soviet sculptor Alexander Gurzhyi produced a model on the basis of an extant 18th-century drawing and in 1956 the entire group was cast in bronze.

Located south of the Conservatory is one of the most fascinating cascades in Petrodvorets: it is known as the **Chess Hill** or the **Cascade of Dragons**. In front of a grotto on the upper terrace crouch three bronze dragons spurting water from their mouths. Mounted on stone pedestals flanking the cascade are marble figures of mythological personages executed by Italian sculptors in the 18th century. Looking upwards to the left is the following arrangement of figures: first comes a *Priestess*, next *Olympia*, symbol of the city where the temple of the Olympian Zeus stood, and where the original Olympic Games were held, then *Jupiter*, the supreme deity in ancient Roman mythology who is identified with the Greek Zeus, *Flora*, the goddess of flowers, and *Neptune*, the Roman sea god who is identified with the Greek Poseidon. On the right side of the cascade stand figures of *Pluto*, god of the underworld, again *Flora*, *Vulcan*, god of fire and patron of blacksmiths, who is identified with the Greek Haephestus, *Adonis*, beloved of Venus, goddess of love and beauty, and finally *Ceres*, goddess of the harvest and fertility, who is identified with the Greek Demeter.

In the broad space at the foot of this cascade are the two **Roman fountains** designed in 1739 by architect Karl Blank in collaboration with Ivan Davydov. They are so named as they originally resembled the fountains standing in front of St. Peter's in Rome. They were completely rebuilt in 1799.

From this square, several avenues fan out. We advise you to take the path running north-east to reach the nearby **Pyramid Fountain**, whose 505 jets of water rise up to different heights in seven tiers to form a pyramid. Falling into a rectangular basin, the water overflows in four cascades that run down into a channel around the fountain's perimeter. The fountain was designed by Mikhail Zemtsov and

Niccolo Michetti, who was given detailed instructions by Peter the Great as to what this pyramid should look like.

This fountain was also destroyed by the Nazis during the war; they dynamited the ducts, shattered the marble balustrade, vases and spillway steps, and stole the bronze slab. Restoration of this complex structure was begun in 1946 and completed in 1953.

Return to the Roman fountains and continue toward the seashore. Halfway to the sea is a **statue of Peter the Great** by the eminent Russian sculptor Mark Antokolsky erected in 1884. The original was taken by the Nazis during the war, but fortunately a model of it was found in one of Leningrad's museums and the monument was recast in bronze.

To the right of the monument is a rectangular pond in the midst of which is an islet of porous tuff with an amusing sculptural composition mounted on it. It consists of a column topped by two golden discs placed edgewise, and surrounded by 16 gilded dolphins. As the column slowly rotates, 72 jets of water burst out of the discs to produce the impression of the sun's rays. Construction was begun in 1721, and subsequently, the afore-mentioned architect Yuri Felten made improvements and modifications, which led to its present shape and gave it the name by which it is now known—the **Sun Fountain**.

Erected in 1721–1722 in the vicinity of the Sun Fountain were **two bird cages** for peacocks and songbirds. The one on the eastern side was rebuilt time and again, but the other, on the western side, is almost unchanged and represents a unique specimen of early 18th-century park architecture.

Located at this point are several surprise or trick-fountains, namely the **Umbrella**, the **Little Oak** and the **Little Spruces**. Though built after Peter's death, they are similar to those whose designs he dictated, like the one in the shape of an ordinary-looking wooden or wrought-iron garden bench near the palace of Monplaisir ahead of you. The moment an unsuspecting visitor would sit down on such a bench, streams of water would spurt out from all sides, causing the visitor to flee in embarrassment to the amusement of the ladies and gentlemen strolling along the nearby paths. Such trick-fountains were not Peter the Great's idea as the Hermitage in Leningrad has an old Brussels tapestry with an amusing scene by such a fountain.

The Umbrella Fountain was built at the close of the 18th century. It consists of an umbrella-like canopy with a circular seat underneath. The festooned decoration along its rim conceals 164 pipes from which jets of water spurt the moment anyone sits down on the seat.

The nearby **Little Oak Fountain** looks just like all the other oak trees in the park. However, be on the alert, as this seemingly innocuous tree may suddenly be transformed into a plethora of showers, as will the treacherous "tulips" at its foot. Having escaped the unexpected showers, visitors usually plunk themselves down on the nearby wooden benches, only to be drenched once again by the 41 jets coming from the back of each of these benches.

During the war, the Little Oak Fountain was destroyed by the Nazis. In 1951, restorers discovered a small twig of lead with two copper leaves. With this and the available sketches,

Psyche Fountain in the garden of the Monplaisir Palace

this curious 18th-century fountain was rebuilt.

Proceeding southward from the Little Oak Fountain, you reach **three spruces of various heigths**. They have branches of pipe onto which needles of tinplate have been artfully soldered. You may think these trees are real, but beware, as they are really trick-fountains that start to play unexpectedly, to the great amusement of onlookers. The Nazis destroyed them during the war, and their restoration was extremely difficult, as there were no drawings or even any detailed descriptions. Yet, here they are delighting visitors once again.

Now return to the statue of Peter the Great and proceed toward the shore, where Peter the Great's favourite haunt, **MONPLAISIR PALACE**, stands.

Behind the statue, which is to the south of this building, is a square garden bordered by low buildings on three sides. This is the palace's main entrance. In the middle is the **Wheatsheaf Fountain**, which consists of 25 jets of water brought together to produce the impression of a sheaf of wheat heavy with grain. The other four fountains in this small garden are known as the **Bells**. Bursting out of slits beneath the round pedestals of four gilded statues (*Psyche*, the *Apollino*, the *Faun with a Kid*, and *Bacchus with a Satyr*) the jets of water are transformed into limpid bells. The entire composition was designed by Peter the Great himself. The pedestals are not all identical in form; two are decorative vases, two are columns.

As to the buildings flanking the garden on three sides, take note of the main building on the seafront—a 67–metre–long structure of brick pointed with lime, as was the fashion in Holland in the 18th century. Its central section is topped by a four-tiered hipped roof fenestrated with oval dormer windows and embellished with a carved wooden vase. This is the focal point of the palace which bears the name of Monplaisir.

It is believed that German architect and sculptor Andreas Schlüter, who also helped design Peter the Great's Summer Palace in St. Petersburg, contributed to the planning. However, the emperor himself was responsible for the overall architectural concept of Monplaisir. Though it took from 1714 to 1723 to build this palace, it is rather small and very cosy. The emperor was especially fond of it. Even after the two-storey High Chambers had been put up, as the nucleus of the Grand Palace, Peter the Great preferred to stay here whenever he came to Peterhof. It was here that he received foreign guests and held parties and family celebrations.

During the Nuremberg trials of

the chief German war criminals, Academician Joseph Orbeli, the then curator of the Hermitage, described the vast damage the Nazis had inflicted on Monplaisir. It was converted into an army barracks, and everything that could be burned, including the priceless wooden wainscotting, was consumed in the army stoves the pipes of which were let out through crudely pierced holes in the priceless moulding of the ceilings. It took a large team of specialists, vast efforts, and creative research in addition to enormous financial outlays before the Monplaisir Palace could be reopened to the public in 1961.

We suggest you begin your excursion in the **eastern wing**, one of the two light glass pavilions that adjoin the central section of the palace on the western and eastern ends. Dominating the interior decoration are four curtain walls of glass and a tall tent-shaped ceiling. The walls are hung with paintings mounted in black lacquered frames. Possibly the most interesting of them is the picture above the door in the western wall by the French painter Jacques Courtois. It is entrancing by virtue of the dynamic sense of motion of the equestrians, conveyed in the sharp contrast with the tranquil tenor of the landscape in the background. The other genre scenes, episodes from ancient myths and seascapes were executed by Dutch painters of the 17th century and comprise the nucleus of Peter the Great's collection of paintings at Monplaisir. This was the first art gallery in Russia.

Through a tall glass door enter the **Eastern Gallery** with its long arcading of 16 large glazed doors running down the left-hand side. The doors have a filling of small panes of irides-

cent, wavy glass known as "moon glass", which could not be produced in large pieces. These panes were completely destroyed during the war, and the present glass, which is outwardly identical to the few extant old specimens, was made with the help of specialists from the Leningrad Technological Institute.

The right-hand wall is wainscotted in carved oak and hung with 21 paintings by Dutch and Flemish masters. The more curious of the paintings are two completely naturalistic pieces. One is *Engraving with a Male Portrait* depicting a meticulously drawn board with an engraving of an old man pinned to it. The torn edge, the spider on the board and the other details produce the illusion of reality. The same aim is evident in the anonymously painted *Still-Life with Medals and Timepiece*, whose insignia and antique cameo create the optical illusion of actually being arrayed in front of the viewer.

In the middle of the plafond embellishing the ceiling is an allegorical picture of Summer, while the rest of its surface is covered by an attractive decoration in pink and sky-blue.

Go through the oak doors into the **Lacquered Study**, the first of the rooms in the palace's central section; here one inadvertantly feels as though he has stepped into a fairy-tale room.

All 94 elegantly painted panels were produced by Russian icon-painters under the supervision of the Dutch artist, Hendrick van Bronkhorst. Having made a thorough study of the technique of Chinese lacquer painting, they spent some 18 months painting these miniatures on linden panels. However, as they could not bring themselves to abandon the traditions of Russian art, they

Lacquered Study in the Monplaisir Palace

imparted a characteristic national flavour to a subject quite typical of Chinese painting. In this manner, the magic bird traditional in Chinese art came to resemble the Russian Firebird of fairy-tale fame while the exotic Chinese plants resemble the modest wild flowers so popular with Russian artists.

Besides the lacquered panels, there are gilded wooden wall brackets that are also adorned with lacquer designs and a plafond with an allegorical representation of Autumn.

Likewise, the pattern on the parquet, designed by Peter the Great himself, is noteworthy. The rest of the interior décor was worked out by the architect Johann Braunstein and executed by master-carvers and cabinet-makers from Moscow.

During the war, the Lacquered Study, which for 220 years delighted visitors with its exquisite décor, was completely destroyed. The priceless panels were used as firewood or made into pillbox walls. After the enemy was driven from Peterhof, the museum staff chanced upon three panels in one such pillbox; they are currently located between the windows on the southern wall. Proceeding from these extant specimens, the artists of Palekh recreated the amazing and delightful work of their forerunners which had been so barbarously destroyed.

Now enter the **State Hall**. The overall interior design and decoration is identical with that of the galleries. Thus, pictures are mounted in oak wainscotting, while a magnificent plafond and richly sculptured frieze adorn the ceiling. The paintings on the exuberantly moulded corners of the ceiling symbolise the four elements; thus on the northern side, which faces the sea, we have Neptune, representing Water; on the eastern side, Flora, the goddess of fertility, for Earth; on the southern side, Vulcan, the god of the fire, for Fire; and on the western side, the goddess Juno, for Air. The corner joints are decorated with allegorical figures of the four seasons: old men donning furs represent Winter; maidens, garlanded with flowers, Spring, women holding ears of corn, Summer, and young men wreathed with wine leaves, Autumn.

In the middle of the hall is a drop-leaf table of German make upon which stands a crystal cup with a volume of one and a quarter litres; in the times of Peter the Great, it was known as the Great Eagle Cup. Conspicuous among its lavishly engraved ornamentation is the emperor's monogram and the two-headed eagle, the emblem of the Russian Empire. Filled to the brim with wine, the cup would be offered as a penalty or forfeit and had to be drunk in one gulp. Beside the cup are two copper candlesticks of Russian make.

The walls are hung with 22 paintings by Dutch and Flemish masters, among which three pieces by Adam Silo, an artist famed for his accurate representation of ships with all their rigging, should be pointed out. It is said that Peter the Great would check the knowledge of naval academy graduates against these pictures as regards rigging, sails, and so forth.

During the reign of Peter the Great, this hall was used for the gale receptions of the diplomatic corps and for balls. The broad glazed doors open out onto a gallery extending along the palace's northern side and leading to the small garden on the southern side through which you entered Monplaisir.

The adjoining room, the **Kitchen**, was only decorated to resemble one. The sumptuous meals served to guests at the numerous banquets held at Monplaisir were actually cooked elsewhere. The walls are faced with tiles painted with Dutch landscapes, sailing vessels, cottages, drawbridges and windmills. Nazi vandals smashed the tiling, and after the war Soviet restoration workers had to master the secrets of Dutch tile-making to reproduce the palace's original appearance. The ceramic decorations in this interesting room were also restored.

The Kitchen's floor is done in stone tiles; the room features a large hearth with more Dutch tiles and a stone sink into which water is piped from a special tank in the attic. On the oaken shelves is 18th-century painted delftware, polychrome Chinese porcelain plates of the early 18th century, and British pewter dishes bearing the trade marks of London firms and with a rose, which since 1671 has indicated that the item so marked was intended exclusively for export.

Next door is the **Pantry**, where table services and linen were stored. Today the room contains a collection of Russian glassware from Petrine times, including decanters bearing the emperor's monogram and several peculiar Chinese teapots made of brown stoneware of unknown origin. How they came to be in Monplaisir is still something of a mystery; some claim they were a gift to Peter the Great from the Emperor of China, others that they were imported to Europe by a Dutch trading company.

Adjoining the central hall on the western side is the **Naval Study of Peter the Great**, the oak wainscotting is inlaid with tile inserts depicting 13 types of early-18th-century warships. The original furnishings are no longer extant, so after the war this room was refurnished with more or less similar items of no small interest, like the elegantly ornamented metal casket from Tula that belonged to Peter the Great, the bureau between the windows with its tortoise-shell and ebony decoration, and the small elaborate table at the opposite wall which was in another Peterhof palace before the war. Some say that the Emperor himself helped make it. The chair by the table bears the Emperor's monogram.

Of all the rooms in the Monplaisir Palace, the Naval Study suffered most at the hands of the Nazis. When Peterhof was liberated, its northwestern corner was completely gone and nothing was left of the interior décor. The tiled inlay by the door is one of the few things that survived in this room.

The doors in the Naval Study's southern wall lead into the **Bedroom**.

The four-poster bed under a low canopy is a replica, as the original is in Peter the Great's Cottage Museum in the Estonian capital of Tallinn. However, the patchwork quilt belonged to the Emperor and is said to have been made by his wife, Empress Catherine. The sculptured mantle of the fireplace is quite fine. Depicted here are military regalia and the insignia of Russia's highest military order, that of St. Andrew, instituted by Peter the Great. By the fireplace is an English walnut bureau. On it are a wooden travelling mug, three nested glasses, and a salt-cellar made and painted by craftsmen from Arkhangel. Also on view here are some of the Emperor's personal effects, including a Chinese dressing-gown and a night cap. Opposite the fireplace is a curiously ornamented washstand made in the 17th century by Spanish craftsmen from Pamplona, while on the corner cabinet near the window stands the emperor's ornate jug and wash-basin and a towel dating back to his reign.

Turn now into the **Secretary's Room**, where an officer on duty charged with carrying out the Emperor's orders was stationed. The decorative tiling with Dutch landscapes is similar to that in the Kitchen. There are 24 paintings, all of which were evacuated during the war and have now been mounted in black frames and suspended on red ribbons in place of cords in exactly the same fashion as in the Emperor's day.

Of greatest interest are two seascapes by Adrian van der Salm (both executed on wood in grisaille). One is of the roadsteads and coast of Amsterdam, and the other of the North Russian port of Arkhangel. A *Coastal Town*, a lyrical seascape with ships outlined against the buildings of a city in the background, hangs above the door leading into the Bedroom.

During the war the Nazis destroyed the furniture, the oak wainscotting, and the parquet. A big hole was made in the sculpture of the magnificent fireplace to let an iron stove pipe through.

Now enter the **Western Gallery**, the plafond of which also features the Four Seasons. Enclosed in the central medallion is a representation of the flower goddess Flora personifying Spring; in the eastern quarter is a representation of a young man holding a tambourine set against the background of the rising sun as the symbol of Morning; while in the western quarter of the plafond by the entrance is the figure of the same man against the background of the setting sun. On the northern wall are two seascapes by Adam Silo and Willem van der Velde the Elder and two works by Franz van der Horn presenting a panorama of the canal in the Dutch town of Saardam (now Zandam) of which Peter the Great was especially fond. In 1697, he lived in Saardam incognito in the home of a common blacksmith while working at the local shipyards.

A small genre piece called *A Friendly Conversation* hangs on the eastern wall. It is believed that one of the two young men depicted is Peter the Great himself. Nearby is another genre piece entitled *Breakfasting by a Keg*, and again it is believed that one of the characters represents the Emperor.

We leave the Monplaisir Palace through the west wing with its German chairs of carved walnut, some of which bear the maker's trade mark and the date of manufacture, 1713, under the seat. The walls are hung with paintings by Dutch and Flemish masters.

Almost adjacent to the western wing is the Catherine Wing built at the end of the 1740s and used for balls and masquerades. The palace interiors were redesigned by Giacomo Quarenghi in the 1780s and were again subject to remodelling at the beginning of the 19th century. Be sure to note the Guryevsky Service on display in the Yellow Room. Comprising several thousand pieces, this is one of the largest and finest services in Europe. It was made at the St. Petersburg china factory at the beginning of the 19th century.

The eastern side of the gardens of the Monplaisir Palace ends in the **Baths Wing**, which was erected in 1748 and rebuilt in 1865–1866. Adjoining this structure is the **Assembly Hall** built after a design by Bartolomeo Rastrelli. Its interior décor includes tapestries woven in St. Petersburg in the 1730s. Next door to the **Baths Wing** is the small Chinese Garden with the **Shell Fountain** laid out in the second half of the 19th century. Again, like many other structures of the Monplaisir ensemble, both the garden and fountain were destroyed by the Nazis and had to be restored after the war.

Running along the edge of the palace's northern façade is a white stone terrace with a bronze statue of Neptune cast by an anonymous Russian craftsman in 1716. However, it was not here in the times of Peter the Great, having been acquired from another museum in 1932.

Walk west along the seafront terrace to reach one of the most fascinating of Peterhof's fountains, the **Adam Fountain**, built in 1721. Peter the Great commissioned the marble statue from Venetian sculptor Giovanni Bonatti in 1718. The fountain's design is well integrated with the entire layout of this section of the Lower Park. Its 16 jets spurt from the foot of the statue into an octagonal pool from which eight pathways radiate out to other structures in the park. In 1941, when Nazi forces were approaching Leningrad, the statue of Adam was buried. After the war, it was dug up, and following some restoration, it was reinstalled again in 1946.

Continue walking west, cross the canal through which the water from the Grand Cascade flows out to the Gulf of Finland, and you will come to the **Eve Fountain**. Its white marble statue, like that of the Adam Fountain, is by the Venetian sculptor Giovanni Bonatti. The actual fountains were designed by two different architects, the first by Nicolo Michetti, and the second, several years later in 1726, by Russian architect Timofei Usov. In the early months ot the war, the statue of Eve was also buried in the grounds of the Lower Park. However, the Nazis built a pillbox right over the spot, and the statue was heavily damaged, requiring much effort to restore it. Both fountains started to work again in 1948.

Now turn north-west towards the **Hermitage Pavilion**. As you already know, a *hermitage* is a place of retreat, and such pavilions were common on the royal country estates. The pavilion is placed in the western quarter of the Lower Park symmetrically to Monplaisir in the eastern quarter. This two-storey structure is only 11 m high. Though the decoration is rather modest, it is elegant, with wrought-iron railings on the first-floor balconies and pilasters with plain Corinthian capitals along the façade.

Golden Hill Cascade and the Marly Palace

The pavilion was designed by Johann Friedrich Braunstein, with the participation of Peter the Great himself. The ground-floor kitchen and first-floor fireplace were built according to his instructions. He also invented a table and chair that could be mechanically hoisted from the ground to the first floor and advised that the first floor walls be covered with pictures. However, construction was completed only in the summer of 1725, after the Emperor's death.

There was good reason for calling it a Hermitage, as it stands by the very edge of the Gulf of Finland, away from the park's main walks. It was surrounded by a water-filled moat, and the only way in was across a drawbridge. Once inside, banqueting guests were hidden from prying eyes.

Located on the ground floor was the vestibule, the kitchen and the servants' quarters, while the whole of the first floor was taken up by one huge room, in the middle of which stood a dinner table set for 14. A special system of pulleys was devised to raise the central part of the table from the ground floor after it was set. All that the guests had to do to order dishes and wines was to place a note in the middle of the table and ring a little bell. The central part of the table together with the note would descend and a little later, rise again with the dishes and wine requested.

Now the ground and first floors are connected by a flight of oaken stairs, which did not exist in the days of Peter the Great as guests were hoisted upstairs in a pulley-raised chair. However, when on June 10, 1797, Emperor Paul I sought to ascend in this fashion, a cable snapped and the infuriated monarch found himself stranded between the two floors. In a fit of rage, he ordered the chair to be chucked out and the hoisting arrangement destroyed and had built the flight of stairs that remains to this day.

The first-floor banqueting room is rather large, occupying a total floor space of 80 sq. m. Its windows and balcony doors offer a magnificent view of the sea and the Lower Park. The walls of the room are covered with pictures—124 works by Dutch, Flemish, French, Italian and German masters of the 17th and 18th centuries—separated by thin strips of gilded wood. One painting by an unknown Russian artist is a copy of the picture of the Battle of Poltava (June 1709) done by Peter the Great's favourite painter Ivan Nikitin.

The Hermitage Pavilion was hard hit during the war, with but a pile of rubble left of the hoisting machinery and an oval first-floor table. The building was reopened only in 1952. Today the ground-floor and the **Pantry** contain a permanent exhibition relating to the building's history, while the **Kitchen** houses a display of 18th-century crockery and kitchen utensils. The restored oval first-floor table bears a display of mid-18th-century Dutch faience and Russain glassware.

West of the Hermitage Pavilion is the **Marly Palace** complex built between 1719 and 1723 by Johann Friedrich Braunstein. It was so named by Peter the Great after his visit to the hunting lodge of the French kings at Marly le Rois, demolished at the close of the 18th century. This is an unpretentious two-storey building with a mansard roof whose western and eastern façades are embellished by balconies with elaborate wrought-iron railings bearing the monogram of Peter the Great. Of the original interior decoration a collection of pictures purchased for Peter the Great, a slate-topped table the Emperor himself helped make, and a number of other objects remain.

In early 1944, the retreating Nazis blew up the palace. Its restoration was completed only in 1982 and today it houses a museum with 15 rooms containing valuable collections of paintings and minor arts of the first half of the 18th century, including some elegant furniture of Russian and West-European make, faience, ivory, glassware, and no small number of Peter the Great's personal effects.

In front of the Marly Palace's main (eastern) façade is a **rectangular pond**, which in the times of Peter the Great was stocked with exotic fish. On the western side of the palace is a **semi-circular pond**, whose four sectors converge on a small platform from which it is believed that Catherine the Great fed her goldfish.

The Marly fountain complex lies south of the aforementioned rectangular pond. Like the Chess Hill complex in the Lower Park's eastern half, the **Golden Hill Cascade** is the focal point of the western half. Built in 1721–1723 after a design by Peter the Great and the architect Niccolo Michetti, it was remodelled and given its present appearance in 1732, when Mikhail Zemtsov lifted the level of its sections higher and sheathed its risers in gilded copper; thus the cascade gained its present name, Golden Hill. The effect is indeed of a wall of gold bathed in a shower of falling water.

The cascade terminates in a marble wall topped by statues of Neptune, flanked by Triton blowing his horn on the left and Bacchus on the right. Attached to low pedestals are three gilt mascarons of fantastic sea creatures designed by Mikhail Zemtsov. Along the cascade's inclined walls stand statues of mythological heroes: Minerva, followed respectively by Vulcan, Venus, the Faun, Flora and Neptune on the western side, and Flora, Mercury, Venus, Apollo, Andromeda, and a Nymph on the eastern side. The entire design was intended to extol Russia's prowess in the fields of war, commerce, science and navigation.

The two powerful fountains below, conceived and designed by Peter the Great, are known as the **Menazherny Fountains**—from the French word *ménager*—"to save". There is good reason for this name as water is used quite thriftily in these fountains. It appears that the jets of water, which are some 30 cm across, are actually hollow due to a system of wedges which have been inserted into the fountain in such a manner as to leave a gap of but half a centimetre around their inner perimeter.

Located between these fountains and the southern bank of the rectangular pond are four curious fountains called the **Triton Bells** after the kneeling figures of Triton-boys, who, placed in small pools of a fanciful shape, hold aloft cups upon which bells rest. The jets of water stream down over the sides of these bells into the cups, and thence into the basins to immerse the figures in a cloud of spray.

Having seen the more interesting sights in the western half of the Lower Park, we suggest you return to the bank of the channel linking the Grand Cascade with the Gulf of Finland. Earlier you had a chance to admire the Grand Cascade from above, and gain a striking impression of the golden statues glittering against the background of the verdure of the Lower Park and the blue of the sea; now you will see the same golden statues against the backdrop of the Grand Palace through the sparkle of innumerable jets of water, which, along with the fountains flanking the channel, produce a truly breathtaking sight.

As you approach the pool, in the centre of which towers the mighty figure of Samson, have a look at the **colonnades**. Built by Andrei Voronikhin in 1803 and partially remodelled by Andrei Stakenschneider in the 1850s, they screen off the quiet green pathways of the Lower Park from the bustling crowds around Samson. Contrived of white and grey marble and pink granite and embellished with effigies of lions, they enrich the overall impression of symmetrical harmony that is so characteristic of Petrodvorets.

In front of these colonnades are two round fountains, each of whose basins are composed of 40 well-fitted pieces of marble. There are two semicircular marble benches in the corners of the flowerbeds which were designed in the 1850s by Andrei Stakenschneider. Behind them are **marble fountains** with gilded statues of a **Nymph**, on the western side, and a **Danaide**, on the eastern side.

The nymphs were female deities whom the Greeks believed to inhabit rivers, springs, fountains, etc. while the Danaides were the 50 daughters of Danaus, who for slaying their much-hated husbands, the fifty sons of King Aegyptus, were punished by the gods and compelled perpetually to fill a bottomless cask with water in Hades. This myth comes to mind as you catch sight of the bronze figure of the Danaide holding a jug from which the water streams endlessly, as if indeed into a bottomless cask. Evacu-

ated early in the war, the two statues escaped destruction.

Now you have completed your walk around the Lower Park, and with it your excursion to Petrodvorets. However, before you go, we would like to remind you that Petrodvorets is more than a collection of marvellous fountains, magnificent palaces and lush-green parks. It is also a town whose clock-and-watch factory, built in 1950, has earned worldwide renown with its assorted timepieces ranging from watches for deepsea divers and Arctic explorers with a 24-hour dial to watches with braille dials for the blind and extremely accurate quartz watches.

Petrodvorets is likewise a centre of science and culture. Currently under construction on a territory of more than 300 hectares is the new Leningrad University complex which boasts not only labs and auditoriums but also hostels, gyms, and catering, shopping and consumer service establishments. Amidst the woodlands, more complexes are being built for other establishments of higher education which will eventually move to more spacious premises outside Leningrad proper.

Petrodvorets is also a marvellous holiday resort with several health and holiday centres, one of which is the Petrodvorets Sanatorium (famous for its mineral springs), which celebrated its sixtieth anniversary in 1988.

Yet the museums and parks naturally occupy a prominent place in the life of the town. On November 26, 1973, in honour of the singular contribution made by its population to the restoration of the complex of palaces and parks, and on the occasion of the 250th anniversary of the complex, the town of Petrodvorets was awarded the Order of the Badge of Honour.

PUSHKIN

Your tour of the town begins at the Egyptian Gate, a sort of entrance to the town of Pushkin. Built in 1829–1830, these towers were designed by Adam Menelaws. In his project he evidently used motifs from the temple at Karnak that was built by the Egyptians in the 2nd century B. C. The gates consist of two pylons completely covered with bas-reliefs depicting scenes from life in Ancient Egypt.

To the left of the Egyptian Gates stands a **statue of the great Russian poet Alexander Pushkin** (sculptor Leopold Bernstam). During the occupation the statue was used as a shooting target. One hundred and fifty wounds were inflicted on the great poet's statue by the Third Reich *kulturträger*.

As you drive along the streets of the town you will see on your left a large residential area with multi-storey apartment houses, but you will bear right, towards the centre of the palace-and-park zone; passing several blocks, we arrive at the **Catherine Palace**.

The land on which the town of Pushkin stands once belonged to the Novgorod boyar republic and was subsequently incorporated in the centralised Russian State. In 1617 these lands were seized by Sweden.

At the beginning of the Northern War the troops of Peter the Great took back the lands along the Neva and on the southern shore of the Gulf of Finland; the territory where the town of Pushkin stands today was also liberated then. At that time there was nothing here but a small country estate: a wooden house, a shed, barns, and a garden divided into four parts by two intersecting lanes. Peter the Great presented this estate to his favourite, Prince Alexander Menshikov. However, the tsar, angry at the prince for some reason, soon took back his gift and some time later presented it to his wife, the future Empress Catherine I.

In the years 1718–1724 the new mistress of the estate ordered the architect Johann Friedrich Braunstein to build, in place of the old wooden house, a two-storey "stone mansion". Changes were also made on the adjacent territory. Jacob Roosen, a skilful gardener, laid out a beautiful terraced garden on the gentle slopes of a low hillock. The higher part of this parkland was called the Upper Garden, and the farther tract—the Lower Garden. The part of the garden adjoining the building on the west was called

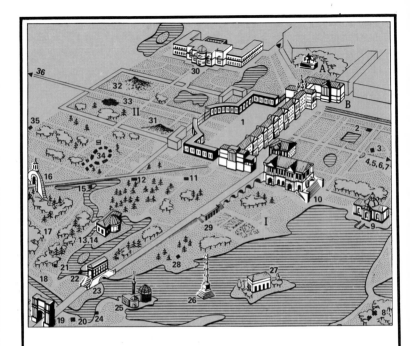

PARKS OF PUSHKIN

I. Catherine Park II. Alexander Park A. Statue of Alexander Pushkin B. Lyceum
I. Catherine Park 1. Catherine Palace **2.** Upper Bath **3.** Lower Bath **4.** Fish Canal
5. Hermitage **6.** Hermitage Cuisine **7.** Marine Column **8.** Admiralty **9.** Grotto **10.** Cameron Gallery, Agate Rooms **11.** Kagul Column **12.** Evening Hall **13.** Concert Hall
14. Ruined Kitchen **15.** Chinese Summer House **16.** Grande Caprice **17.** Rose Field
18. Vittolovsky Canal **19.** Gatchina Gates **20.** Ruined Tower **21.** Little Grotto **22.** Tower
Bridge **23.** Marble Bridge **24.** Pyramid Summer House **25.** Turkish Baths **26.** Chesma
Column **27.** Hall on the Island **28.** Milkmaid Fountain **29.** Granite Terrace
II. Alexander Park 30. Alexander Palace **31.** Mushroom **32.** Parnas Hill **33.** Chinese
Theatre **34.** Chinese Village **35.** Chapel **36.** Arsenal

the Menagerie; elk, hares, and wild boar were kept there for the tsar's hunt.

The building was completed in August 1724. Hundreds of guests assembled to celebrate this event at a festive dinner. Since then the former estate was known as the Tsar's Village (Tsarskoye Selo).

It should be noted that fate was not kind to the Catherine Palace. Every successive monarch held that it was obligatory for him to either tear down or build something here.

The diary kept by the future Empress Catherine the Great (at that time the wife of the crown prince) contains the following entry: "Tomorrow they

Catherine Palace (general view)

tear down what has been built today. This house was levelled to the ground and built up again six times ..."

In 1752, the services of Bartolomeo Rastrelli were enlisted for the reconstruction of the palace. What did the famous architect find in Tsarskoye Selo? First Johann Friedrich Braunstein had built the two-storey stone mansion (1724), in 1744 Alexei Kvasov had put up two side-wings, connecting them to the main building by one-storey galleries. Three years later the architect Savva Chevakinsky added two more buildings to the sides of this structure—the chapel and the so-called "hall"—also joined to the central part by galleries. Thus, the palace continued to expand, with no heed paid to an integral composition.

Rastrelli decided to integrate all the separate parts of the building into a single whole. With this in mind he replaced the galleries with three-storey structures, while in the place of the former "hall" he built a stately stair-

case. The palace thus became much taller, and its main façades, decorated by the architect with columns, statues, and mouldings, extended for over 300 metres.

According to contemporaries, Rastrelli surpassed himself in this work. His inventiveness was truly amazing. He succeeded in building this majestic line of façades, avoiding uniformity, never slipping into monotony, composing a beautifully flowing melody (there are no other words for it) in stone ... In the precise rhythms, in the elegant Baroque proportions Rastrelli alternates the powerful line of columns with wide window openings, and the building seems almost weightless without losing any of its impressive stateliness.

The outer appearance of the palace was amazingly luxurious. The gilded decorations glittered effectively against the blue background of the building. It was said that when Empress Elizabeth arrived at Tsarskoye

Selo with her court and foreign ambassadors to view Rastrelli's work, everybody was astounded by the marvellous beauty of the building and loudly expressed their delight. Only the French ambassador uttered not a single word. In response to Elizabeth's question concerning his silence the Frenchman courteously replied that he did not see the most important thing—the case for this gem ...

Arriving at the palace, guests would first take in the dazzling splendour of the main façade. Then, entering the palace, they ascended its magnificent staircase and a stately suite of rooms opened before them.

In the reign of Catherine the Great (1762-1796) the Grand Palace underwent substantial alterations. The gilt on the ornaments and sculptures (which at that time were made of wood) proved to be short-lived. At the order of the empress the mouldings were painted (not gilded) and the wooden statues with the peeling gilt were removed. The formerly one-storey side wings were built up higher, new entrances were added. The palace took on its general present-day appearance.

In Russian art and architecture the second half of the 18th century was marked by the affirmation of the traditions of Classicism. It was namely in this style that a galaxy of famous architects worked in Tsarskoye Selo in 1760-1790, among them Charles Cameron, Giacomo Quarenghi, Yuri Felten, Antonio Rinaldi, and others. That was the time when the priceless gems of Tsarskoye Selo—the Alexander (Alexandrovsky) Palace, the Cameron Gallery, the Concert Hall, the Upper Bath and the Lower Bath pavilions, and also the building that was later to house the Lyceum were erected.

In the first half of the 19th century the territory of the former Menagerie was replanned to become a landscape part of the Alexander Park. Here, in the 1820s, the architect Adam Menelaws erected several buildings in the Gothic style that stressed the romantic nature of this part of the Alexander Park.

In the late 19th and early 20th centuries no further building or landscaping was done in Tsarskoye Selo.

However, construction of the town itself proceeded at a fairly lively pace. In 1808, a general construction plan had been drawn up; it envisaged the expansion of Tsarskoye Selo to almost double its area.

The new streets and boulevards of the town were laid out in chessboard order on the basis of that precise plan.

Many technical innovations that were introduced throughout Russia are associated with Tsarskoye Selo. The first railway line in Russia, built in 1834, ran between Tsarskoye Selo and Pavlovsk, another royal residence; three years later Tsarskoye Selo was connected by rail to St. Petersburg, then the capital of the Russian Empire.

Running water and sewerage appeared in Tsarskoye Selo in 1887. An electric power plant was commissioned almost at the same time, so that Tsarskoye Selo became the first "electrified" town in Europe.

Tsarskoye Selo was visited on more than one occasion by Lenin. In the years 1891, 1893 and 1894 Lenin used to visit the family of a close friend of his, a participant in the revolutionary movement, Alexander Shukht, who lived in Tsarskoye Selo. The house no longer exists. In 1895, at No. 11, present-day May Day Street (Pervomaiskaya Ulitsa), Lenin conducted a conference of the members of the St. Petersburg social-democratic group (this house also no longer exists). In May 1900, Lenin spent about two hours in the park of Tsarskoye Selo, hiding from police sleuths.

After the victory of the Great October Socialist Revolution the treasures of Tsarskoye Selo became the property of the people. The palaces were turned into museums, the parks into favourite recreation spots. The mansions of Tsarskoye Selo, formerly the property of the nobility, were turned over to medical institutions and child-care organisations. Most probably this was why in 1918 the town was renamed "Detskoye Selo" — Children's Village. The railway station has retained this name to this day, while the town itself was renamed in honour of the great Russian poet Alexander Pushkin in 1937 on the centenary of his death.

During World War II the town of Pushkin was occupied by the Nazis. Priceless treasures went up in flames, many works of art were destroyed or stolen; the invaders felled time-honoured trees in the parks, blew up unique pavilions, and destroyed wonderful sculptural compositions.

The town of Pushkin was liberated on January 24, 1944. Restoration work was immediately commenced. By the beginning of the 1950s many architectural and art monuments had been restored. However, the damage caused by the Nazis was so great that restoration of its palaces and parks is still being conducted.

Time heals wounds, but it doesn't erase memory. Today only photographs of marble fragments blackened by the fires of war show just how extensive the damage was. However, these only serve to enhance the achievements of those who have restored these architectural creations to their original beauty for all to admire.

You should begin your excursion to the museums and parks of Pushkin with the **small garden** by the Lyceum. Of course, you have already noticed the statue of Alexander Pushkin that stands here. It is one of the finest statues of the great Russian poet. This work of the sculptor Robert Bach was paid for from funds collected by public subscription. Its foundation stone was laid in 1899, when the hundredth anniversary of the poet's birth was celebrated, and it was unveiled in 1900. The poet is depicted as a youth, in his Lyceum uniform, sitting, lost in thought, on a park bench.

Close by the monument is an old church, built in 1734-1747. This is the oldest surviving structure in the town. Near the church stand the four-storey building of the **LYCEUM**, an educational institution intended for children from "distinguished families".

In the years 1789-1791, the architect Ilya Neyelov built a separate four-storey structure next to the northeastern part of the Catherine Palace. Modest in architectural design, it presented a contrast to the splendour of the palace. Originally the building was meant for the grandchildren of Catherine the Great. When the grandchildren grew up, one of them, Emperor Alexander I, gave the building over to the Lyceum that was founded in 1810. It was reconstructed under the direction of architect Vasily Stasov, and on October 19, 1811 the Lyceum was opened.

On the ground floor were the service quarters and the apartments of the tutors; on the first floor, the dining-room, the infirmary and dispensary, a small conference-hall, and the office; on the second floor, the classrooms and Grand Assembly Hall, the physics laboratory, and a room containing newspapers and periodicals; the bedrooms were on the top floor, the library was located in an archway.

The first enrolment at the Lyceum listed thirty boys, their ages ranging from 11 to 14. One of them was Alexander Pushkin. In its early years (1811-1817) the Tsarskoye Selo Lyceum was full of enthusiasm for the new Russian and French literature, the product of the Age of Enlightenment. This enthusiasm brought many of the Lyceum's pupils together in a literary society, which set the atmosphere for the whole school. The heart and soul of this society was the young Pushkin, whose poetry even then voiced ideas condemning Russian autocracy and serfdom.

Ascending the main staircase (which is lighted by bracket fixtures in the form of the oil-lamps used here at the beginning of the previous century) we reach the second and third floors where the rooms are kept just as they were in the Lyceum of Pushkin's time.

On the second floor is an **Entrance Hall**, its windows facing the Lyceum's garden. From this hall a door leads to the **Newspaper Room**, where the students read newspapers and journals. The Lyceum subscribed to eight foreign and seven Russian papers and journals. During the Patriotic War of 1812 the boys spent much of their time here.

Through an arched doorway you pass into the **Grand Assembly Hall**—the most spacious room in the Lyceum. The walls are painted to look like pink marble. The décor is enhanced by murals on the end wall and mirrors in the piers. Here on January 8 (20), 1815, an examination was held at which the young Pushkin, in the presence of the outstanding Russian poet Gavriil Derzhavin, read his famous poem *Memories in Tsarskoye Selo*. Here, too, on June 9, 1817, the graduation ceremonies were held for the students who had completed the Lyceum course.

From the Grand Hall you go on to the rooms where the pupils did their homework. Further are the **classrooms**, furnished exactly as in the time of Pushkin. The physics laboratory with contemporary instruments and the music-room with an old-fashioned clavichord are also on this floor.

The third floor has also been restored to the appearance it had in Pushkin's time. On both sides of a long corridor are the dormitories of

Statue of Alexander Pushkin

the pupils, divided by partitions that do not quite reach the ceiling.

A black plate on one of the dormitories reads: "No. 14. Alexander Pushkin." It contains a narrow bed, a chest of drawers, a wash-stand, and a small bureau. On the bureau are arranged a candlestick, candle-snuffers, an inkwell, a sand-box used as a paperweight, and paper.

It seems as though the young poet has just left his room for a minute.

When the town of Pushkin was liberated from the enemy on January 24, 1944, there was not a single habitable house in it. The Lyceum together with the Catherine Palace lay in charred ruins. The first window to be glazed in the town was the window of Pushkin's room in the Lyceum.

The exposition of yet another museum connected with the poet's name, the **ALL-UNION PUSHKIN MUSEUM**, is housed in the northern wing of the Catherine Palace. (In 1989, due to the repairs of its premises the museum's exposition was moved to a new place.) All told, there are more than 60,000 storage units in this museum.

The display in the **first four rooms**

is devoted to the poet's childhood. Here we see his family tree, the coat of arms of the Pushkins, data on Pushkin's enrolment in the Lyceum, on the enthusiasm the Lyceum pupils shared with the entire country when, in 1812, the Patriotic War was launched against Napoleon's armies who had attacked Russia. On display in showcases are the yellowed pages of the manuscripts of Pushkin's first verses, the standard of the Moscow Infantry Regiment that fought near the village of Borodino (August 26, 1812) in a battle that marked the turning-point in favour of Russia in this war. Some years later, on December 14, 1825, this same standard was borne to Senate Square in St. Petersburg by the officers and men who rebelled against the tsar.

Rooms No. 5–9 are dedicated to the St. Petersburg of 1817–1820. The documents displayed in these rooms describe the theatrical life of the St. Petersburg of Pushkin's time, the activities of the members of secret revolutionary societies united by anti-feudal ideals, by a strong wish to democratise Russia. Pushkin closely associated with some of the leaders of these secret societies, though he did not belong to any of them; the revolutionaries protected the poet, not wishing to subject him to the dangers connected with the struggle against autocracy and serfdom.

Although not a member of any secret society, Pushkin expressed the aspirations of a whole generation of revolutionary-minded nobility. In May 1820, he was banished from the capital to the south of Russia on the pretext of an official business transfer. The documents in the exposition speak of this exile, of Pushkin's wanderings in the Crimea and the Caucasus. His poems and letters tell how stirred he was by the victories and defeats of the Greeks who rose in 1820 against Turkish rule, by the struggle of the Spaniards and Italians for democratic rights and liberties.

Lyceum

Rooms No. 10–13 reflect the period of the disfavoured poet's exile at his home estate in the village of Mikhailovskoye. These halls display furniture and various articles from Pushkin's time. Quite interesting materials are devoted to Pushkin's work on the tragedy *Boris Godunov*, one of the great works in world dramaturgy.

Rooms No. 14–18 contain exhibits relating to the uprising in St. Petersburg on December 14, 1825 of revolutionaries from the nobility (the Decembrists) against autocracy and serfdom, and to Pushkin's brilliant novel in verse, *Eugene Onegin*, that is rightfully called an encyclopedia of Russian life of his time.

That the poet sympathised with the cause of the revolutionaries is reflected in the memorial relics, in his manuscripts (one of them features a drawing, in the poet's hand, of a gallows with five Decembrists hanging on it; the caption reads: "It could have been me ...").

The displays in **Rooms No. 19–27** are devoted to the final years of the poet's life (1830–1837), years marked by the flourishing of his talent. The exposition opens with materials relating to his famous Autumn at Boldino. The poet was forced to stay at his estate at the village of Boldino from September 3 to November 30, 1830 due to a severe cholera epidemic. Pushkin languished in enforced quarantine, separated from his fiancée Natalya Goncharova. During this semi-incarceration the poet wrote profusely and avidly: within those three months he produced about forty works.

When you come into **Room No. 22**, note a very original display—Nashchokin's Little House. In Moscow Pushkin had a close friend, Pavel Nashchokin, famous for his eccentricity and wit. Pushkin was a frequent guest in his home. Nashchokin ordered a precise copy (in miniature) to be made of his Moscow house, with all it contained—furniture, utensils, decorations. In a letter to his wife, written March 4, 1836, the poet speaks of this wonder: "Nashchokin's little house had been brought to perfection; it lacks only miniature people ..."

Several rooms of Nashchokin's Little House are on display. On the left is the dining-room, with its table laid for 10 persons. In a corner at the back of the room is the "butler's pantry". On the right is the drawing-room, in it stands a chess-table with tiny chessman carved of ivory, a card-table with a pack of cards, a miniature grand piano on which, as Pushkin wrote to his wife, "a spider might well play". In the right foreground is the entrance hall with its cheval glass; on its shelf lie a top hat and a cocked hat. In the right background one sees into a room that, most probably, depicts the one in which Pushkin stayed when he visited Nashchokin.

Regrettably, not all the miniature appurtenances have been preserved, but over 300 objects displayed here give a visual idea of a typical Moscow interior in Pushkin's time.

Room No. 24 displays materials reflecting the work of the poet on the

Park Gates

history of the peasant war waged under the leadership of Yemelyan Pugachov in 1773–1775. Pushkin visited many of the places where the events of this revolt unfolded and recorded the recollections of eyewitnesses; he writes with great warmth of Pugachov, the people's champion, the leader of the oppressed peasantry.

The museum's exposition is constantly expanding. Not long ago a silver spoon bearing the monogram of one of Pushkin's friends from the Lyceum, Wilhelm Küchelbecker, was found in Siberia during the construction of the Baikal-Amur Railway. Küchelbecker was sentenced to hard labour in Siberia for his participation in the Decembrist uprising of December 14, 1825. The museum has also added to its collection two rings that belonged to Ivan Pushchin, Pushkin's closest friend, as well as personal effects of the Decembrist poet, Kondraty Ryleyev, and other valuable items.

The name of Alexander Pushkin and his works are highly esteemed in the Soviet Union. During the years of Soviet power his works have been published more than 2,400 times in

90 languages of the peoples of the USSR, in a total edition of over 157 million copies. Hence the wide popularity the museum has attained during its relatively short lifetime (it was opened in the Catherine Palace in 1967).

We now go on to the **CATHERINE (YEKATERININSKY) PALACE**—the centre of the architectural composition of the entire landscape and palace complex.

Your tour begins with the wide Main Staircase, designed by architect Ippolito Monighetti in 1861. The staircase occupies all the space between the west and east façades of the palace. White marble steps, decorative plates and vases of Japanese and Chinese porcelain—all this stresses the stately nature of this interior. The ceiling is decorated with paintings by Italian artists of the 17th and 18th centuries.

The exposition begins at the south wing of the palace. The first premises as you go along is the **Cavaliers' Dining-Room**, designed by Bartolomeo Rastrelli. This chamber was severely damaged during the occupation and was restored in the postwar years. The mirrored walls seem to create multiple reproductions of the gilded statues, ornamentation, and exotic sea-shells. In a corner of the room is a built-in decorative tiled stove, adorned with niches and columns, a characteristic feature of Rastrelli's interiors. The gilded armchairs of the Dining-Room were also designed by Rastrelli. The carved table by the window is laid with the *Hunter's Service* made in 1760 at the St. Petersburg porcelain factory.

From the Cavaliers' Room high arched doors lead into the **Grand Hall** of the palace (it was also called the Throne Room), a splendid specimen of the Baroque style. The hall is most impressive for its carved and gilded moulding and the pictorial plafond *The Triumph of Russia*, an allegory

glorifying Russia's victories, the blossoming of science and the arts. Rastrelli's genius is vividly manifested in the ornamentation of this hall (860 sq m).

You pass through several chambers that have as yet not been restored to their former splendour and are used merely for temporary expositions.

In the first display room you will notice a drawing of the first Tsarskoye Selo palace that was built by Johann Friedrich Braunstein for Catherine I. Here, too, is a wooden model of the palace built by the architect Alexei Kvasov in 1744. Its purpose was to give the then sovereign Empress Elizabeth a visual idea of the future building so that she could sanction its construction (however, this did not preclude subsequent radical alterations). What the Catherine Palace looked like before the war may be judged by the enlarged plan shown here of the first floor of the palace; photographs of the beautiful chambers destroyed by the Nazis are mounted on this plan.

The second display room demonstrates the tragedy of the Catherine Palace and the parks during the German occupation of the town of Pushkin. As soon as the war began many artistic treasures were evacuated. The Nazi troops broke into the town on September 17, 1941. They turned the Catherine Palace into a soldiers' barracks, destroyed or stole everything that was left in the museum rooms.

The Soviet troops who liberated Pushkin saw, instead of the former splendid palace, only charred ruins. Photographs expose the vandalism of the fascists: as they retreated they set 11 bombs in the palace, a 1,000 kg each. Fortunately, the bombs were found in time and defused by Soviet troops.

The expositions of the third, fourth, fifth, and sixth rooms show how, through the efforts of scientists, artists, and restoration workers the masterpieces of Russian culture lost during the war are being resurrected. Materials on the history of the Amber Room are also presented here.

Its décor, created by the architect Andreas Schlüter and the master-carvers Gottfried Tusso and Ernst Schacht, first belonged to King Friedrich Wilhelm I of Prussia. In 1716, following the conclusion of an alliance treaty with Russia, the Prussian king presented the amber panels to Peter the Great as a diplomatic gift. The amber panels were delivered to St. Petersburg, and from here 76 strong guardsmen carried—literally carried—the valuable load to Tsarskoye Selo in six days. In 1755, Rastrelli mounted the panels in the Amber Room. There were not enough panels to complete the décor, therefore the architect used mirror insets, while for the upper part of the walls he employed an excellent imitation amber.

The precious amber panels were looted by the Nazis and have not been found to this day.

Having viewed these display rooms, continue on to the **Picture Gallery**. Of the 130 canvases that hung here before the war, 114 (the most valuable) were evacuated and thus preserved. One of the most handsome rooms in the palace, it takes up the entire width of the building. The chief decoration of the room are paintings by Dutch, Flemish, French, and Italian masters of the 17th and early 18th centuries. A considerable number of them were acquired by the artist Georgy Groot in Prague in 1745.

Besides the genre paintings presented here, there are two interesting battle-pieces by the French artist Pierre Denis Martin devoted to the Northern War: *The Battle at the Village of Lesnaya* (1708) and *The Battle of Poltava* (1709). The paintings, which were commissioned by Peter the Great, are arranged in a manner simi-

Main entrance of the Catherine Palace

lar to that prevalent in the Portrait Gallery at Petrodvorets.

The exposition in the seventh room predominantly features works of applied art, created for the Catherine Palace in commemoration of the Russian victory in the Russo-Turkish War of 1768–1774. Objects of particular interest are a large carpet of Russian make with an allegorical representation of the Russian victory and decorative vases with lids in the form of the helmet worn by Minerva, the patron deity of war, and medallions with a map of the Mediterranean Sea. These vases were commissioned for the Russian court at a porcelain factory in Berlin.

We should like to draw your attention to a sculptural composition in marble: General-Field Marshal Pyotr Rumyantsev reports to Catherine the Great on the victory of the Russian troops in the Russo-Turkish War at the Kagul (July 21, 1770). This victory opened the way for the Russians beyond the Danube. The sculptor was Paolo Triscorni.

Works of art of Turkish origin are also displayed here. Among them is a table inlaid with mother-of-pearl, a gift to Catherine the Great from the Turkish Sultan when peace was signed between the two countries, and beautifully ornamented Turkish trophy arms.

The exposition of the eighth room is devoted to the 1780s, an important stage in the history of Tsarskoye Selo when Charles Cameron—an outstanding master of Russian classicism—created a number of splendid interiors in the palace. The beauty of one of them—the stately Lyons Hall—is indirectly evidenced by fragments of the inlaid parquetry shown in this room. The floor of the Lyons Hall was composed of rare sorts of wood (rosewood, palm, amaranth tree and others) and decorated with mother-of-pearl inlays. Stolen by the fascists and taken away to Ger-

many, the parquet panels were found near Berlin in 1947 and returned to the town of Pushkin.

The exhibits in the ninth and tenth rooms are devoted to the works by the outstanding Russian architect Vasily Stasov in Tsarskoye Selo. Notably, he designed the interior decoration for the private rooms of Emperor Alexander I.

The next room on the tour is **Alexander I's State Study**. It contains a splendid marble fireplace ornamented with Ionic columns. Scenes from the myth about Cupid and Psyche are painted on the vaulted ceiling. Several authentic objects preserved from the beginning of the 19th century are on display in their original places: an openwork bronze chandelier made in St. Petersburg in the first quarter of the 19th century; a vase manufactured at the St. Petersburg porcelain works in 1818, depicting the entrance of Alexander I into St. Denis, a suburb of Paris, on March 14, 1814; a clock, candelabra and knick-knacks on the table fashioned of malachite and bronze. The other objects (a desk covered with a green baize cloth and walnut furniture) were created anew in the postwar years on the basis of archive data and an old water-colour of the State Study. This room is adjoined by the Vaulted Communicating Room and the Oval Anteroom.

The eleventh room displays photographs of the vandalism of the fascist invaders, who destroyed many art treasures of the Catherine Palace.

Next you come to one of the most interesting works of Charles Cameron—the **Green Dining-Room**. The interior moulded decorations of this room, executed by the Russian architect Ivan Martos, is dominated by classical motifs.

The purpose of the next room follows from its appellation—the **Butler's Room**. The interior decoration is considerably more modest than that of the Green Dining-Room. The par-

Grand Pond (view from Cameron Gallery)

quet floor is superb, a composition of circles and polygons. The pilasters, painted to resemble marble, stress the classical style of the interior. The card-tables you see here were made at the end of the 18th century.

Further you pass into the **Blue Room**, one of the most sumptuous rooms of the palace, designed by Charles Cameron. The architect made wide use of carvings, mouldings, gilt, mirrors, decorative silks, marble and inlaid wood, achieving a marvel-lous effect. Today the entire appear-ance of this room is as close as possi-ble to that of the interior created by Cameron. Many of the details are au-thentic. The floor-lamps of blue glass with crystal and biscuit figures, for in-stance, were made in St. Petersburg at the end of the 18th century. The carved gilded armchairs and the bronze fire-irons also date back to that time. But the silk with the blue flowers print was manufactured in the post-war years at the Moscow Krasnaya Roza textile mill (with the aid of surviving samples of the original fabric); Cameron's original drawings were used to recreate the plafond.

In the **Carved** and **Picture Studies**, carving, painting and moulding are artistically blended. These rooms were restored in the post-war years to their original appearance, as designed by the architect Vasily Stasov.

The next room is the **Bedchamber**. Its colour scheme ranges from palegreen to light blue. Numerous elegant faience colonettes are arranged along the walls of the room, or grouped toward its centre to form an open alcove. Delicate painting covers the doors, and on the walls are moulded medallions with allegoric figures executed by Ivan Martos, an eminent Russian sculptor. Particularly noteworthy in the furnishings of this room are a forged steel table and a gilded fire screen, the work of Russian craftsmen from the town of Tula. A small inlaid wooden table was made by workers from Okhta (a suburb of St. Petersburg).

Continuing your tour of the palace rooms you enter the **Chinese Blue Room**. It is so called because for 150 years its walls were covered with blue Chinese silk on which bright Chinese landscapes and genre scenes were drawn in India ink. This silk was looted by the Nazis. After the war the silk was remade and repainted on the basis of fragments that had been preserved. By a fragment of the door and photographs the restoration workers reconstructed the designs painted on the doors. Charles Cameron's marble fireplace was painstakingly reassembled. The restorers had but a few pieces of it, found among the charred ruins of the palace.

Most of the furniture in this room was made at the end of the 18th century. The décor was supplemented with a painting of Empress Elizabeth in her youth, represented as Flora, the goddess of flowers (by Johann Groot)

and a picture, *View of the Imatra Waterfall* (gouache), by Silvestr Shchedrin.

Through the **Gallery Anteroom** you enter the gallery of the palace chapel. The anteroom walls are covered with silk, designed with figures of pheasants and swans. This fabric was made by Russian serf-weavers on hand looms in the late 18th century. The light and rich shade of the silk lends the simple room a festive air.

The gallery of the palace chapel is a kind of balcony. In the 18th century it was used as a pew occupied by the members of the royal family during service. Originally the decoration of the gallery was created by Bartolomeo Rastrelli. After the fire of 1820 it was renovated by Vasily Stasov.

By narrow stone steps you descend into the main part of the chapel. It suffered severely during the occupation; the Nazis stole 96 icons, the beautifully painted plafond, and many of the architectural details.

Finally, the last room on your excursion round the palace is the **Chapel Vestibule**, a singular front hall leading into the main part of the chapel. Designed by the architect Vasily Stasov, it was built in 1843 in place of former living quarters. Stasov, a past master of the classic style in architecture, in this case changed his artistic manner and designed the Chapel Vestibule in conformity with the décor of the chapel proper that was designed by Bartolomeo Rastrelli in Baroque style. To match the décor of the chapel Stasov created an interior with carved doors, delicately voluted plafonds and wall panels, and columns with gilded capitals. This hall is impressively sumptuous with its abundance of light and the harmonious combination of white and gold.

Your excursion through yet another museum of the town of Pushkin has come to an end. We suggest that you now take a stroll in the park. An interesting feature of the Catherine Park is

Cameron Gallery

that it consists of two parts, each with its own style. Long ago a definite classification was established for various styles of parks.

The *French* (architectural) *Park* is distinguished for the clear, geometric planning of its wide, straight walks. Its pavilions and statues are visible from afar, the trees and shrubs are clipped, forming decorative hedges. The *English Park*, which is basically landscaped, is an attempt at imitating nature. It has no architecture at all; there are no geometrically planned walks, no clipped green clumps of shrubs and trees. The *Italian Park* reproduces the hilly gardens of Italy.

All these varieties of landscape planning and gardening are reflected in the Catherine Park.

And now we invite you to the **Catherine Park**. From the centre of the façade of the Catherine Palace walk in a southeastern direction. This "regular" part of the park was laid out in the French tradition. On the left you see a light-toned pavilion called the **Upper Bath**. It was built by the architect Ilya Neyelov in 1777–1779 as a bathhouse for the royal family. The exterior of the pavilion is fairly modest, but its in-

terior décor was at one time very ornate. Besides all the bathrooms there was also a lounge with decorative murals. The interior designs of the Upper Bath were based on the murals in the rooms of the Golden House of Emperor Nero, discovered during excavations in Rome.

After the expulsion of the Nazis from Pushkin nothing but the shell of the Upper Bath remained—the roof and murals had been destroyed. Today the pavilion has been practically returned to its original appearance. The plafond and two panels above the doors depict scenes from the myth of Phaëthon, son of Helios the Sun god.

To prove his divine origin to a son of Zeus, Phaëthon begged his father to be allowed to drive the chariot of the Sun round the Earth for one day. Unable to control the horses, the youth brought the chariot dangerously close to the Earth and scorched it; therefore Zeus, in order to save the people struck Phaëthon down with a thunderbolt.

An amusing story is associated with the Upper Bath pavilion. The Austrian Emperor Joseph II, travelling *incognito*, lived in this pavilion for some time in 1780. The secret of the Austrian monarch was soon discovered, but no one let on that they even suspected his true identity. The distinguished traveller made it a rule to put up only at inns. Catherine the Great, aware of this whim of the emperor, ordered the bathrooms to be closed in the pavilion, and new furniture to be installed quickly—furniture that would give the place the appearance of a modest hostelry. The part of the landlord was played by the head gardener of the park. The trick was successful. Joseph II was very pleased with the "inn" he lodged at during his stay in Tsarskoye Selo ...

The alley you walk along is adorned with marble statues of gods and goddesses, created by Italian sculptors at the beginning of the 18th century: an Amazon, holding a shield with an eagle fighting a lion depicted on it, a symbol of the victory of Russia over Sweden in the Northern War; Hercules—an allegorical image of Peter the Great; Galatea astride a dolphin and others.

Not far from the Upper Bath is the **Lower Bath**. It used to be called the Cavaliers' Bath House, since it was used as a bathhouse for the courtiers. The Lower Bath has a more elaborate layout than the Upper: its central circular hall is surrounded by six circular and four rectangular booths. The interior decoration of the place has not been preserved.

At the far end of the alley you see, among the trees, a building, the colours of which echo those of the Catherine Palace. This is the **Hermitage**, one of the most interesting buildings in the town of Pushkin. On the way to the Hermitage you cross the **Fish Canal**, constructed in the early years of the existence of Tsarskoye Selo; it was intended for breeding fish for the table of Catherine I.

A remarkable creation of Russian architecture, the Hermitage was built in 1744-1756 by the architects Mikhail Zemtsov, Alexei Kvasov, Savva Che-

vakinsky and Bartolomeo Rastrelli. The blue of the walls of this pavilion harmonises with the whiteness of its 64 columns. The façade is decorated with wreaths, masks, and shells.

During the reign of Elizabeth, the daughter of Peter the Great, the aspect of the Hermitage and the adjacent grounds were even more attractive. The building was surrounded by a water-filled canal or moat with drawbridges; the ground between the moat and the walls of the pavilion was laid out with white and blue marble in a chequered pattern; and an elegant balustrade separated them from the stone-faced bank of the moat. The balustrade was decorated with gilded carved figures. The roof of the Hermitage, too, was distinguished for its splendour. Painted white and green, it had a balustrade on which gilded figures of carved wood also stood.

Inside the Hermitage there was a large hall with four corner galleries; at the end of each was a small room. The first storey of the pavilion, where guests were received, was particularly luxurious. Its large hall was for dinner parties and merry-making without servants. Stairs were non-existent—the guests were lifted in special chairs. From the basement five laid tables could be lifted by special mechanisms—and, what is more, slates were mounted into them for the guests to write their orders to the servants below. The daintiest dishes were served: "nightingales' tongues", "lips of young elk", and the like. When the guests wished to dance, the tables were lowered and parquet flooring was moved into place. The banquet hall turned into a ballroom.

Today the Hermitage is much less pretentious. At the close of the 18th century, on the orders of Catherine the Great, the moat surrounding the building was filled in with earth, the white and blue marble slabs between the moat and the Hermitage were taken up, many of the statues

Agate Room

mounted on the façade and the roof of the pavilion were removed. Irreparable damage was inflicted on the Hermitage during the fascist occupation.

Turning right, you cross the Fish Canal, along the edge of a pond you reach the **Grotto** pavilion. Designed by Bartolomeo Rastrelli, it was built in the years 1753–1757. At first the interior of the Grotto was decorated with colourful sea shells: 210,000 large shells and 17.5 poods (286 kilograms

or 630 lbs) of small shells were used. The multi-coloured decoration in combination with tufa rock created the illusion of a fairyland cave. The roof was edged with an elegant stone balustrade.

But tastes changed with the times, and Catherine the Great decided that the interior of the Grotto should be remodelled in keeping with the principles of strict Classicism. The balustrade was pulled down, the shells removed and the architect Antonio

Rinaldi drew up a new design: the interior of the Grotto acquired the Classical style moulding that has survived to the present day. Still, the sumptuous exterior decoration does give us an idea of the plan conceived by the first architect of the Grotto, Bartolomeo Rastrelli.

In the latter part of the 18th century, during the reign of Catherine the Great, the Grotto became a storehouse for works of classic art, among them statues and moulded copies. Of works of a later period, there was the famous statue of Voltaire sitting in an armchair, the work of the sculptor Jean Antoine Houdon.

During the reign of Paul I the Grotto was stripped and everything inside it removed. Many unique works of art disappeared completely. For example, the statue of Voltaire was for a long time thought to be lost, but more than half a century later it was discovered in the cellars of the Taurida Palace. Today this statue is on display in the Hermitage in Leningrad.

In the late 19th century a stone jetty was built in front of the Grotto and two bronze statues were put up there—*The Dying Gaul* and *The Gladiator*. The wrought-iron grids of the Grotto are a splendid specimen of Russian workmanship.

Several dozen metres from the Grotto you can see another, no less beautiful, structure of the park—the **Cameron Gallery**. It was built by Charles Cameron on the site of a pavilion that had originally been intended for playing ball. Between the columns of the Gallery the architect placed bronze busts, mostly copies of classic originals. On the staircase he put statues of Flora and of Hercules Farnese (the original, created by the 4th-century B. C. sculptor Lysippus, had not been preserved, but an early Roman copy of it was owned by the aristocratic Italian family of Farnese, hence the appellation of the statue). The models for these statues were copied in 1786 by the Russian sculptor Fyodor Gordeyev, and they were cast in bronze by Vasily Mozhalov, a famous master of artistic casting.

During the occupation of Pushkin the fascists stole both statues—Hercules and Flora. They were found in the German town of Halle in the yard of a copper-smeltery among the scrap-metal being prepared for smelting. In 1947 the statues were returned to Pushkin, where they were renovated and put back on their pedestals on the stairs of the Cameron Gallery.

In the architecture of the Catherine Palace ensemble the Cameron Gallery occupies a special place. As it adjoins the parkside façade of the palace, it becomes, as it were, the continuation of this façade. The vast Catherine Park is capable, it might seem, of engulfing in its wide vistas any architectural creation; however, the elegant and relatively small Gallery is placed so that it dominates the whole park, its green sea of foliage, systems of ponds, canals, bridges, monuments, and numerous pavilions. Let us now ascend the grand staircase and have a look at the sculptured portraits of ancient philosophers, orators, political figures and generals.

After viewing the Gallery you pass into the so-called **Hanging Gardens** laid out on a platform supported by thick stone pillars. The platform is paved with sheets of lead that are covered with a layer of soil thick enough to maintain the growth of flowers, shrubs, and even trees.

From the Hanging Gardens you descend by a ramp to the park and then walk toward the **Granite Terrace** (located on a high elevation, it overlooks the surrounding landscape). This spot affords a splendid view of the area of the Grand Pond. This part of the Catherine Park is laid out in the English landscape style.

The pink and grey Granite Terrace was built in 1808–1810 by the architect Luigi Rusca. Fifty years later it

Marble Bridge

was decorated with statues of the Venus de Medice, Apoxyomenus, Diana, and a Faun with a Kid (copies of classic originals). A copy of the Apollo Belvedere stands in the centre of the small square in front of the terrace.

From the Granite Terrace you go down to the **Grand Pond** and come out on the **Granite Quay**. In the middle of the pond, on a small artificial island, shaped like a truncated pyramid, stands the tall **Chesma Column** erected in commemoration of the vic-

tory of the Russian fleet over the Turkish in the Russo-Turkish War. Twenty-five metres high, this multicoloured marble and granite column was built in 1771–1778 by the architect Antonio Rinaldi. It is crowned by a bronze eagle (the symbol of Russia) crushing a Turkish crescent moon (sculptor Ivan Schwartz). The column's body was decorated with rostra, a bronze memorial plaque, and three bas-reliefs depicting naval battles—in the Chios Strait, the Chesma

Bay, and near Militene. During the war the bas-reliefs disappeared. It was assumed that the Nazis had taken them and melted them down. They had tried to destroy the column as well by tying a rope to it and attempting to pull it down. However, the rope broke and the column remained standing. In the 1950s the column underwent some restoration work, though the bas-reliefs were considered lost. But the bas-reliefs had not disappeared altogether. Restorers scoured the bottom of the pond around the column and found remnants of the bas-reliefs, which had fallen in the water when the Nazis took the bronze ornaments off the Chesma Column. These remnants, together with materials kept at the Military and Naval Museum (in particular, a collection of drawings of military vessels of all countries and time periods) made it possible to reproduce the bronze bas-reliefs.

From the Granite Quay you walk several steps along the edge of the pond and turn right, into a path running parallel to the pond. In the centre of a picturesque little square you see one of the finest decorations of the Catherine Park, the **Milkmaid Fountain**, immortalised in a poem by Alexander Pushkin. On a cliff, in a mournful pose, sits a maiden holding a fragment of a broken jug that lies at her feet. From the broken mouth of the jug a stream from the only spring in the park flows into a tiny basin that had been hollowed out of the granite. The fountain was created in 1816 by the sculptor Pavel Sokolov. The prototype for the sad milkmaid was the heroine of a fable by Jean de La Fontaine, *The Milkmaid or the Jug of Milk*.

Having admired the Milkmaid, return to the path skirting the pond and continue on your way through the park. Ahead of you, in the south-west corner of the pond, you see the blue and white **Marble Bridge** spanning the channel connecting the Grand

Pond and a group of smaller ponds and channels.

This bridge was built by the architect Vasily Neyelov in 1770–1776. The blue and white marble gallery of the bridge is simple and perfect. It is decorated with Ionic columns and an elegant balustrade. Neyelov first built a wooden model of the bridge that was taken apart and sent to the Urals, to Yekaterinburg (now the city of Sverdlovsk). There the elements of the future bridge were made of marble and then conveyed to Tsarskoye Selo where they were assembled. For 200 years people have been admiring this beautiful creation.

Your visit to the Catherine Park has now come to an end. There is another landscape and palace complex in the town of Pushkin we advise you to see: the Alexander (Alexandrovsky) Park adjoining the Catherine Park on the north.

This part of the town was likewise greatly damaged by the Nazis. Of the structures still standing, the most interesting one and the chief attraction is the **Alexander Palace**. Built by the architect Giacomo Quarenghi in 1792–1796, it was commissioned by Catherine the Great for her favourite grandson, the future Emperor Alexander I. This building is near the street along which you arrived at the Lyceum.

While the Catherine Palace reflects the prevalence of Baroque in Russian architecture in the middle of the 18th century, the Alexander Palace is a beautiful example of the Classicism that prevailed in Russian architecture at the close of the 18th century. The palace building has neither vivid colours nor moulded decorations. The principal colours are yellow and white. A snow-white Corinthian colonnade connects the side-wings. At the end of the 1830s **two bronze statues**, representing youths playing Russian games, were placed in front of the central part of the colonnade (sculptors Nikolai Pimenov and Alexander Loganovsky).

The Alexander Palace interiors were designed by Giacomo Quarenghi. These decorations, however, no longer exist: at the order of the last Emperor of Russia, Nicholas II, they were changed practically in all the palace rooms. During the German occupation the palace was severely damaged. Today the façade has been restored to its original appearance.

And so this is the end of your excursion to the parks and museums of Pushkin, one of the finest and most charming of Leningrad's environs. You have viewed the splendid works of world-famed architects and sculptors, have enjoyed the beauty of the shady gardens and parks of Pushkin. In our next chapter we shall offer you an excursion to yet another enchanting spot within no more than a few minutes' drive from Pushkin—the town of Pavlovsk.

PAVLOVSK

Pavlovsk and Pushkin are only four kilometres apart. We therefore advise tourists to combine the two excursions.

After Peterhof and then Tsarskoye Selo were created, a search was begun for suitable places for the royal hunt near the new residence of the Russian monarchs. The area of today's Pavlovsk was chosen, since it abounded in elk and other game. The first structures to go up in this locality were two small wooden hunting lodges that were humorously called "Krik" and "Krak".

In 1777 Catherine the Great gave this land, as a gift, to her son Paul (the future Emperor of Russia Paul I). Building was commenced with the active participation of Charles Cameron. Parks and gardens were laid out, and a palace, pavilions and summer houses were built by serfs living in the nearby villages and by crews of sailors quartered in Tsarskoye Selo.

In the 1790s Pavlovsk became the official summer residence of Paul I, no longer the heir to the throne but the Emperor of Russia. Cameron, the favourite architect of Catherine the Great, as well as many others of her retinue, was dismissed by Paul I. He was replaced by Vincenzo Brenna, an Italian architect. Brenna expanded the Grand Palace and reconstructed the summer houses and pavilions in the park.

A characteristic feature of Brenna's style is the combination of Classicism with elements of romanticism. He made the Grand Palace more ostentatious in appearance, built the Stone Staircase leading down to the Slavyanka River and landscaped the Big Circles (one of the areas of the park). Streets were laid out and houses were built near the park.

During the first quarter of the 19th century Andrei Voronikhin, a brilliant Russian architect, participated in the construction of Pavlovsk. The Grand Palace, damaged by fire in 1803, was restored under his supervision; he also designed the bridges spanning the narrow Slavyanka River. Charles Cameron, invited back after the death of Paul I, also embellished Pavlovsk. He built a number of structures, including the Three Graces pavilion, that is situated south of the Grand Palace. Carlo Rossi, famed for his magnificent architectural ensembles in St. Petersburg, also worked in Pavlovsk. True, in Pavlovsk Rossi designed mainly railings, decorative vases, summer houses, and wrought-iron gates.

By the middle of the 19th century Pavlovsk had become one of the most beautiful estates not only in Russia, but in Europe as well. Thus it remained until 1941, when Nazi Germany attacked the Soviet Union.

During the early months of the war the majority of the Pavlovsk Palace treasures were taken out or hidden. Over 12,000 museum exhibits were evacuated. A large number of the museum pieces—interior decoration objects from the Grand Palace, statues and other art treasures—were buried in the ground or bricked up in the walls of the palace cellars. This work was carried out by the staff of the museum under enemy fire. So, despite the fact that the invaders set fire to the palace as the Soviet troops launched their offensive in January of 1944, the hidden collections remained intact. The palace itself, however, deprived of its dome, roof, and floors lay in ruins.

The scope of reconstruction work in Pavlovsk was truly great. The Nazis despoiled the park—they felled tens of thousands of trees, destroyed handsome pavilions, bridges, and other structures.

Photographs of the ruins of the Grand Palace, an outstanding architectural monument, were presented as accusatory documents at the Nuremberg trial of the chief German war criminals. The enormous damage inflicted on world culture by the Nazis was noted by the London Congress of Architects. It was stressed that mankind had become poorer by the loss of such monuments as Pavlovsk.

The restoration workers performed truly amazing labour feats in order to return to their original appearance the masterpieces of applied art, architecture, and landscaping seemingly lost forever. Over 40,000 fragments of the moulded decorations were collected and thus it became possible to restore the fine moulded décor of the palace; gardeners planted over 60,000 new trees in the parks in place of those that were felled and maimed by the fascists.

It would seem that the losses were irreparable. People who visited the environs of Leningrad soon after the end of the siege were of the opinion that all that had been destroyed would remain as majestic ruins reminding posterity of the genius of the architects and the vandalism of the fascists.

The restoration of the Pavlovsk Palace may truly be looked upon as a resurrection from death. Restoration work is still going on in the Pavlovsk Park today.

Now, when you have learned something of the history of Pavlovsk, we invite you to view the chambers of its palace and take a walk in the park. The **Pavlovsk Park** spreads over an area of more than 600 hectares. One of the largest parks in the world, it combines areas of regular and landscape planning, conditioned, to a certain extent, by the terrain—the meandering Slavyanka River and the undulating hills and valleys. To see the whole park in one day is quite difficult. Therefore your itinerary includes only places of interest in the vicinity of the Grand Palace, the compositional centre of the Pavlovsk Park.

The **GRAND PALACE**, with its combination of monumentalism and lightness, is an impressive structure. The flat dome crowning the building is supported by 64 white columns. The ground floor, where the living quarters were located, is quite noteworthy. It was built as a monumental socle on which the first and second floors rest. From the north-west side (from the Slavyanka River) the Grand Palace looks like a sumptuous country residence, while from the south-east (on the side of the main entrance) the horseshoe-shaped building lacks the

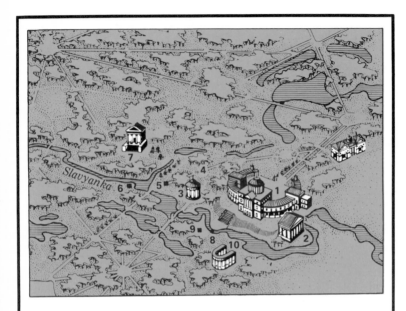

PARKS OF PAVLOVSK

1. *Grand Palace*
2. *Pavilion of the Three Graces*
3. *Temple of Friendship*
4. *Twelve Paths*
5. *Monument to My Parents*
6. *Pil-Tower*
7. *Mausoleum of Paul I*
8. *Centaur Bridge*
9. *Cold Bath*
10. *Apollo Colonnade*

simplicity and privacy characteristic of country palaces: it is an imposing structure, the official residence of the Emperor Paul I.

In 1872, a monument to Paul I, sculpted by Ivan Vitali, was erected before the palace. His head in an enormous three-cornered hat thrown back, his legs planted wide apart in sturdy Hessian boots, the emperor appears to be attending a review of his grenadiers.

We suggest you begin your excursion with the first floor, distinguished for its opulent interiors. You pass through the Lesser Hall on the ground floor and find yourself in the **Egyptian Vestibule**. Originally it was decorated

Grand Palace

by Charles Cameron in association with the Russian sculptor Ivan Prokofyev. The décor of this chamber was destroyed by fire in 1803. The sculptural decoration of the vestibule, imbued with the motif of ancient Egyptian art, was restored from sketches made by Andrei Voronikhin. Twelve statues symbolise the months of the year. The first is January, the statue standing at the right of the arch leading to the staircase.

You ascend to the first floor by a staircase with elegant wrought-iron banisters and enter the **Main Vestibule**, created in the 1790s. Charles Cameron, Vincenzo Brenna, and Andrei Voronikhin successively took part in its planning and decoration. The vestibule is richly decorated with mouldings depicting primarily arms and armour. The panel by the staircase displays Russian military standards, Turkish turbans and bunchuks (staffs topped with either a ball or sultana of horsehair)—attributes of Tur-

kish military commanders. These motifs recall Russia's victories in the Russo-Turkish War (second half of the 18th century).

Adjoining the Main Vestibule is the **Italian Hall**. Charles Cameron is credited with the design and in part with the architectural and artistic finish of this room. After Pavlovsk was liberated from the Nazis the restoration of the palace was commenced in this room. The hall is in the centre of the palace; natural light streams in through apertures in the dome, creating an impression of airy lightness. Vincenzo Brenna participated in the creation of this central state hall (1789). The fire of 1803 damaged the hall and Andrei Voronikhin designed some new décor, notably, the sculptured eagles on the cornice and the caryatides supporting the cornice at the base of the dome.

The walls of the hall are faced with pink artificial marble and decorated with classical bas-reliefs. The patterned stone floor and the streams of light pouring from above are reminiscent of the sumptuous chambers of the palaces of Ancient Rome—hence its appellation.

The hall is circular and divided vertically into three parts. This division is stressed by the horizontal gilded moulded cornices. The gallery and cupola stress the ceremonial nature of the Italian Hall. The gallery is adorned with a wooden (white and gilt) balustrade. Sculptural portraits are placed above the arches, while its niches carry compositions such as *The Roman Wedding*, and *The Three Graces*. Authentic Roman sculptures of the 1st and 2nd centuries A. D. are also presented here: *Venus with a Dove, Faun Playing a Flute, The Dancing Satyr, Eros Stringing His Bow*. Some of the sculptures were purchased from an English collector by Catherine the Great. It should be noted that the collection of classic sculptures in the Pavlovsk Palace is second in the Soviet Union only to that of the Hermitage in Leningrad.

As you leave the Italian Hall look at the magnificent chandelier of Russian make that is suspended on a long rod from the dome. Its bronze and ruby-coloured glass are supplemented by crystal "ostrich feathers".

From the Italian Hall you return to the Main Vestibule, go through it, turn left, and enter the comparatively modestly furnished **Valet's Room**, where the excursion through the northern suite of chambers starts. During royal receptions a duty officer would sit in this room, ready at all times lest the Emperor should summon him.

Next comes the **Dressing-Room**, a rectangular room with rounded corners designed by Cameron. The walls are decorated with exquisite mouldings and murals, executed to the project of Vincenzo Brenna. Their soft tones blend handsomely with the moulded tracery of the low relief. By the window you see an ancient Ro-

man sculpture entitled *The Faun and the Panther* (2nd century A. D.).

From the Dressing-Room you proceed to the modestly finished **Communicating Room**. The carved gilded furniture set was made in 1825 to Carlo Rossi's design. Note paintings hanging in this room—landscapes of the Pavlovsk Park as it was at the end of the 18th century.

The next adjoining room is the **Library**, a large, slightly curved hall added to the palace by Carlo Rossi in 1824. Before the war the bookcases standing here held over 20,000 volumes; collections of engravings, draughts, and drawings were kept in table-drawers and showcases. Many of the books and art objects from the collections were saved, but the beautiful décor and furniture of the Library were destroyed during the occupation of Pavlovsk. At present restoration work is under way in the Library, following which the hall will be open to visitors.

Paul I's Lesser Study. The most valuable part of this room is its unique décor. A portrait of Peter the Great hangs on the wall. Particularly interesting items are a desk made in the 18th century by a French craftsman, an antique grandfather clock decorated with masonic signs and, in front of the fireplace, a mahogany screen that is inlaid with ivory and copies of classical cameos. The superb chandelier is the work of a French master.

The next room is **Paul I's Library**. Faced with artificial white marble, its walls are hung with carpets decorated with scenes from La Fontaine's fables. Woven in Paris, these carpets were presented to Paul in 1782 (at that time still the heir to the throne) by the French king, Louis XVI.

A large mahogany writing table, trimmed with bronze, stands in the centre of the room. The table is supported by 12 carved ivory legs. On it stands a tall model of the porticoed Temple of Vesta, the goddess of the

Centaur Bridge

Paul I's Library

hearth in Roman mythology. Beautiful candelabra grace the table, as does a carved amber and ivory writing-set. All these objects were created in St. Petersburg by Russian craftsmen. The low bookcases along the walls also serve as pedestals for marble sculptures, among which the work of the sculptor Mikhail Kozlovsky, *Sleeping Cupid and the Club of Hercules*, is most noteworthy.

From the Library you pass on into the **Carpet Room**. Its walls are deco-rated with tapestries covered with scenes from Cervantes' *Don Quixote*. Like the carpets in the preceding room, these tapestries were a gift to Paul I from Louis XVI.

The furniture in this chamber is also quite interesting: a mahogany and ivory writing table, a set of carved gilded furniture decorated with Lyons embroidery (made in 1784 by the famous Parisian cabinet-maker Georges Jacob); fine marble statues, amber and ivory ornaments, and porcelain vases from Japan and France...

At last you come to the final room in this suite—the **Hall of War**. For a time after Paul I's ascent to the throne, this chamber was used as the lesser throne room. The white artificial marble facing the walls, the gilded mouldings, the depictions of ancient Roman weapons and armour on the walls—all this imparts a reserved stateliness to this not-so-large hall. Arched openings in the ceiling—lunettes—are decorated with bas-reliefs devoted to themes of the Trojan War, busts of Roman emperors stand in niches. One niche is occupied by a stove crowned with an eagle sitting on flaming cannonballs.

Through a door in the left-side wall you enter into one of the central rooms of the Pavlovsk Palace—the **Greek Hall**. Its layout resembles that of a Greek patio, but the graceful greenish columns, so effective against a background of white marble walls, also make it look like the interior of a temple in Ancient Greece. Copies of Greek and Roman statues stand in niches. The beams over the columns and the ceiling of the hall are decorated with fine moulding. Two elegant six-sided lanterns of gilded bronze and marble lamps hanging on long chains between the columns complement the decorations of the hall.

The magnificent vases, clocks and candelabra standing on the marble mantels and console tables are quite noteworthy. The beautifully embroidered window draperies were made in Paris in 1782. True, by the middle of the 19th century they were in such a dilapidated condition that they were taken down and stored away for over a hundred years. In the post-war years the creation of the French weavers was resurrected by Soviet specialists. Now the fine draperies once more occupy their place in one of the handsomest halls of the Pavlovsk Palace.

Today the Greek Hall is used as a small concert hall in which recitals are often rendered for lovers of old classical music.

The next room you enter is called the **Hall of Peace**. Octagonally shaped, it has four opulently decorated niches. In its architectural plan the Hall of Peace is very much like the Hall of War. However, here there are no military attributes, their place is taken by allegories of peaceful life—agricultural implements, baskets of flowers and fruit, grapevines, musical instruments... Instead of the ferocious eagle crowning the stove in the Hall of War, here, in the Hall of Peace, Juno's peacock tops the decorative stove (Juno is the Roman goddess of marriage and women). Bows and quivers full of arrows do appear in the ornamentation of the gilded doors, but in this case they are not weapons but symbols of love striving for peace.

In the Hall of Peace there is a tripod-vase of crystal and red-gold glass exceptional for its fine proportions. It was made in 1811 at the St. Petersburg glassworks to the design of Andrei Voronikhin, and it is one of the most beautiful works of applied art in the Pavlovsk Palace.

The windows of the Hall of War, the Greek Hall and the Hall of Peace afford a superb view of the Slavyanka. From the western window of the Hall of Peace you see the enchanting panorama of a waterfall cascading from the Apollo Colonnade down its stony course to the Slavyanka.

The next room is the **Library of the Empress Maria Fyodorovna**. On the wall hangs a tapestry from the Don Quixote series. Created in 1780, it depicts an episode in which the knight seeks the advice of the "enchanted head". White bookcases arranged along the walls of the room serve as consoles for marble sculptures (18th-century copies of classic originals); only one of the sculptures, *Muse by*

Picture Gallery

the Rock (near the window), is an authentic original created in Rome in the 2nd century A. D.

By a rounded wall at the back of the room stands a bronze-inlaid mahogany desk made in 1784 in the workshop of David Röntgen. Behind the desk stands a wide armchair decorated with horns of plenty—their openings served as flower-vases. The upholstery of the chair is elegantly embroidered. The magnificent 18th-century mosaic parquetry was made of twelve varieties of wood (amaranth, mahogany, rosewood, palm, and others) brought from India, Ceylon and other lands. A crystal chandelier of Russian craftsmanship suspended from the ceiling by gilded bronze chains completes the interior décor.

This room is adjoined by the small **Boudoir** (architects Vincenzo Brenna and Andrei Voronikhin). Its principal feature is a white marble fireplace with a mirrored niche trimmed with gilded bronze and porphyry. Two monolithic porphyry columns from Rome are mounted on tall marble pedestals. The columns are topped with gilded bronze capitals on which rests a wide pediment with gilded mouldings.

Eighteenth-century marble pilasters made in Rome, covered with paintings on motifs from the Loggia of Raphael in the Vatican, harmonise with the classical forms of the fireplace. Ancient Roman bas-reliefs (the 2nd century A. D.) and marble medallions (Italian, 18th century) with portraits of Alexander the Great and his mother, Olympia, are placed between the pilasters.

Noteworthy amid the furniture of the Boudoir is a table made in 1789 in St. Petersburg. The palace as it was before additions and landscapes from the Pavlovsk Park are depicted on its porcelain top. The elegant upright piano standing by the left wall was made in London in 1774. Many famous musicians visiting Pavlovsk per-

Apollo Colonnade

formed on it. The lamp of bronze and green glass hanging on long chains was designed by Andrei Voronikhin specially for this room.

Next you enter the **State Bedchamber**. It must be pointed out that the room was actually never used as a bedchamber, having been included in the state suite of rooms only in deference to court traditions, emphasising, as it were, the high position of the owners of the palace and the opulence of the décor. The walls of the chamber are covered with silk on which a pattern of flowers, fruit and musical instruments is painted. The magnificent gilded canopied bed is decorated with delicate carvings. This bed, as well as the couch and armchairs in the room, were made to the order of Paul I by the famous Parisian cabinet-maker Georges Jacob.

In a glass showcase on a special table you see the 64-piece Sèvres toilet set that was commissioned by the French Queen Marie-Antoinette and presented to Paul I's wife when she visited France in 1782. The articles in this set are embossed with chased gold and enamel inlays imitating precious stones. The small three-legged tables of gilded bronze, blue lapis lazuli and marble standing in the Bedchamber are approximate copies of ancient originals found in the ruins of Pompeii.

The next chamber is the **Empress Maria Fyodorovna's Dressing-Room**, designed by Vincenzo Brenna in 1797. The surface of its walls, which are faced with artificial white marble, is divided into numerous decorative panels covered with elaborate mouldings by the outstanding Russian sculptor Ivan Prokofyev. The geometric pattern combines well with the rich floral design and scenes from Roman and Greek mythology.

A particularly interesting feature in this room is the "steel set". It includes a dressing table, small vases, candlesticks, a footstool and a chair. Several thousand parts, forged and faceted to give them a "steel diamond" finish, were assembled to make this unique set in 1788 by Semyon Samarin, a worker of the Tula armoury.

The suite ends with a small chamber; the **Room for the Ladies-in-Waiting**, where these ladies used to wait for the Empress to come out of her private chambers. The gilded carved suite in this room was made by Russian craftsmen at the close of the 18th century. Its silk upholstery was produced by serf weavers at the Lazarev Brothers manufactory near Moscow. One of the palace's finest statues, *The Vestal Offering Sacrifice*, stands in a niche in the wall. (The statue is the work of the French sculptor Louis Simon Boizot.)

In ancient Rome the priestesses of Vesta, the goddess of the domestic hearth, were called vestal virgins. They were responsible for keeping alive the sacred fire in the temple of their goddess. At their consecration they took a vow of celibacy, violation of which was punished by death.

Another interesting article in this room is a bronze clock standing on a mahogany writing desk. The clock represents a scene from an opera by the French composer Pierre Alexandre Monsigny, *Le Deserteur*, that was very popular in its time at court. The music box that serves as the base of the clock plays tunes from this opera every hour. The clock stood still for 150 years, until skillful restorers brought it back to life.

You have now seen all the state chambers of the main building. To reach the west wing of the palace you will have to pass through three communicating rooms.

The **First Communicating Room** features a marble fireplace with a mirror in a gilded frame above its mantel; on the mantelpiece stand decorative porcelain vases made in the late 18th century at German porcelain works (in Berlin and Ludwigsburg). The **Second Communicating Room** is faced with pink artificial marble. The niches carry cobalt-blue porcelain vases adorned with tiny gilded figures of child-satyrs and wreaths of ivy (the work of Russian craftsmen). An expressive 18th-century marble sculpture depicts a scene from an ancient Greek myth: the infant Ganymede being carried off by an eagle.

From this room you proceed into the **Picture Gallery**. Among the masterpieces displayed here is a sketch made by Peter Paul Rubens for his *Pietà*, and also paintings by Angelica Kauffmann, Jean Baptiste Greuze and Hubert Robert (the last three were specially commissioned by the royal family).

The Picture Gallery collection can claim no system in genres or schools, its haphazard nature was conditioned by the tastes of the palace's owners. In addition to the works already mentioned there are also genre scenes and landscapes painted by Dutch artists. On consoles in the piers stand vases made from minerals in a variety of colours by Russian craftsmen of the 18th and early 19th centuries.

From the Picture Gallery you enter a small and elegantly decorated room—the **Third Communicating Room**. Its walls are faced with pink marble and decorated by panels with delicately painted glass inlays. When Pavlovsk was being restored in the post-war years Soviet artists brilliantly recreated the plafond which was originally the work of Pietro Gonsago.

The **Throne Hall** is the largest (400 sq m) and most stately chamber of the Pavlovsk Palace. Built in 1798, it was designed for official receptions and ceremonies. It is square in shape, but its corners are rounded off by deep niches into which handsomely decorated stoves were built. The white marble walls of the hall contrast with its polished mahogany doors and opulent gilded candelabra. The stateliness of this room is stressed by its arched doorways supported by caryatides.

The plafond was created by Soviet masters using the original sketches made by Pietro Gonsago. This gifted decorator could not realise his plan during his lifetime. Only 150 years later, during the restoration of the hall, did the artist's dream become a reality. The painting of the plafond represents a colonnade against the background of the sky, creating the illusion of still greater height and spaciousness. The beauty of the room is accented by the carved gilded furniture, its silk upholstery covered with rich Russian embroidery, and by the large, bronze-inlaid crystal lanterns.

At first this room was called the Grand Hall, but soon after it was built Paul I's throne was placed in it, thus giving it its new name—the Throne Hall. In 1814 a grand reception was held here for the officers of the Guards regiments who had returned home after the victory over Napoleon. The throne was removed from the room for the reception and was never returned. The "banquet tables", all set for a sumptuous meal, give one an idea of the luxurious manner in which state dinners were served at the royal court.

Note the *Gold Dinner Service,* made specially for the Pavlovsk Palace at the St. Petersburg porcelain factory. The service consisted of 606 items. The vases, decorated with sculptured groups devoted to mythological subjects, are also quite notable. They were made of gilded porcelain at the same factory as the dinner service. Enormous porcelain vases made at Sèvres in the late 18th century complete the furnishing of the hall.

Adjacent to the south-west wall of the Throne Hall are two chambers used as service rooms. The northern is the **Orchestral Chamber.** Here the musicians of the court orchestra that played at royal dinner receptions and

balls sat near a mirror-paneled door leading into the room. South of the Orchestral Chamber is the **Buffet,** from which the servants brought out the dishes to the table. Here in glass showcases you can see samples of the dinner and tea sets intended for state receptions and for everyday use of the inhabitants of the Pavlovsk Palace. Note the original bronze chandelier hanging in the Buffet. The crystal lily-of-the-valley bouquet adorning this chandelier was made by Russian craftsmen in the 18th century.

The Orchestral Chamber leads into the rectangular **Knights' Hall,** intended for ceremonial receptions of the Knights of Malta. The Knights' Hall is decorated with mouldings and bas-reliefs depicting Bacchic dances, ceremonial processions and sacrifices. The moulded décor of the walls gradually merges with the ornamental painting on the plafond—the painting imitates the moulding. The hall contains a collection of classical sculptures dating back to the 2nd–3rd centuries A. D. A hall of this kind was an obligatory feature of many 18th-century Russian palaces, for this was a period of great enthusiasm for the art of ancient Greece and Rome. Most noteworthy among the sculptures in this hall are the *Nympth and a Seashell, Boy with a Bird,* and *Roman Wearing a Toga* (this statue was damaged in a fire in 1944).

Through a door at the end of the Knights' Hall you go into the **Room of the Horse-Guardsmen,** once the headquarters of the Palace Guard, a duty detail of officers from the Horse-Guardsmen's regiment. On the left is a door into the **Hall,** beyond which is a service staircase. An exposition devoted to the restoration of Pavlovsk after the Great Patriotic War of 1941-1945 is on display in both rooms.

With this your excursion through the halls of the first floor comes to an end. To see the semi-official ground-floor rooms, where the royal owners of the palace usually lived and spent their time, you must return to the Ladies-in-Waiting Room and descend to the ground floor by a service staircase.

The tour of the ground floor chambers begins with the **Ballroom**. Its pink and light blue décor impart a certain cosiness to the room. This impression is enhanced by the delicate gilded mouldings, the graceful sprigs and the Greek vases. On the walls hang paintings by Hubert Robert, a famous 18th-century French artist, very fashionable in his day, who painted mainly classical ruins. The owners of Pavlovsk commissioned Robert to execute twelve paintings; four of them (1784) are on display in the Ballroom.

On the left and on the right of the Ballroom are the **Old Drawing-Room** and the **Billiard Room**. The first is noteworthy for its large tapestries presented to Paul I in 1782 by Louis XVI. The tapestry on which a leopard is attacking a zebra symbolises Asia; another one, depicting youths carrying an Abyssinian chieftain, is an allegory of Africa. Retaining the original brightness of their wonderful colours, these tapestries are of high artistic value.

In the Billiard Room the artistically fashioned card-tables created by late-18th-century Russian craftsmen are a point of interest. Here, too, stands a unique musical instrument, a clavichord with an organ. Commissioned by Catherine the Great, it was made in St. Petersburg in 1783. Originally it stood in the Taurida Palace, which was a gift from the Empress to her favourite, Prince Potyomkin. As you have probably noticed, there are no billiards in this room, despite its name. In the middle of the 19th century the billiard table was taken away to Strelna (another royal residence near St. Petersburg), and was never returned to Pavlovsk.

On the left of the Billiard Room is the **Dining Hall**, the largest of the ground-floor palace chambers. Its décor is austerely formal. The white pilasters stand out effectively against the pistachio-green of the walls, around which runs an elegantly moulded frieze with figures of cupids, lions, vases, and floral ornamentation.

In this room the royal family and particularly close members of their retinue dined. On display here is the dinner service for special occasions, created at the Royal porcelain factory in 1827. Take note of the fruit bowls, adorned with heroes from classical mythology—Mars, Venus, Ulysses, and others. The soup bowls and other dishes of various shapes bear the coat of arms of the Russian Empire—the two-headed eagle. This accounts for the service's appellation—the Coat of Arms service.

To the left of the Dining Hall is the **Corner Room**. It was reconstructed after the war from extant fragments and from the original drawings made by Carlo Rossi, the author of its décor. The walls of the room are faced with artificial marble of a violet-lilac tone and are beautifully ornamented. The plafond, covered with paintings of classical masks, harmonises with the walls. The festive nature of the room is emphasised by the amber-coloured doors of Karelian birch. The exquisitely shaped and finished greenish amphora standing by the window was created by lapidaries in the Altai.

The next room in the suite of domestic chambers on the ground floor is **Paul I's New Study** (called so in distinction from the Old Study). It was designed by Giacomo Quarenghi and built under his supervision in 1800. The white and coloured artificial marble, the gilded mouldings, marble borders on the walls painted in the manner of the grotesque ornamentation in the Vatican loggias created by Raphael and his pupils—all this imparts a formal stateliness to the New Study. Eight coloured engravings by

Temple of Friendship

Giovanni Volpato, set in the wall, are reproductions of the famous frescoes by Raphael and his pupils in the Papal chambers of the Vatican.

The pieces of bronze-inlaid mahogany furniture standing in the study were made by David Röntgen, a famous cabinet-maker, German by birth, who worked for the French court. These objects are a bureau and an escritoire-cum-reading-desk. On the desk stands a marble and bronze writing-set decorated with miniature mor-

tars, cannons and figures of children.

After the New Study comes the **Common Room** where Paul I's family often gathered. The walls of this room are hung with portraits painted by outstanding Russian and West European masters of the 18th and early 19th centuries. The mahogany furniture is in the Jacob style (after Georges Jacob, the French cabinet-maker who first began to adorn his furniture with fluted brass). In the centre of the room stands a bronze-inlaid mahogany bureau, the work of David Röntgen.

Next to the New Study is the **Old Study**, also called the **Crimson Study** because of the colour of the upholstery and draperies. Besides the mahogany bureau and tables made in 1784 by David Röntgen, there are a number of beautiful porcelain, bronze and ivory statuettes, little vases and other ornaments characteristic of wealthy 18th-century parlours.

You will notice the grandfather clock built with the assistance of David Röntgen. The bronze bas-relief under the face of this clock depicts Saturn; topping the case of the clock is a bronze Apollo with a lyre—the patron of the arts and the Muses. The clockwork is linked up with a miniature organ and a stringed musical instrument that reproduce the sounds of a harpsichord. A niche by the right-hand window is decorated with a fine mosaic picture of the Roman Coliseum, presented to the future Emperor Paul I in 1782 by Pope Pius VI.

An elongated **Hall** leads from the central building of the palace to its western wing, built by Giacomo Quarenghi and Andrei Voronikhin. Used as service quarters, this room had no artistic finish. The walls are hung with works by West European landscapists of the 18th and 19th centuries. Beyond it is the circular **Valet's Room**, where the valet (or secretary) on duty was stationed during official receptions.

From the Valet's Room you enter the **Pilaster Room** (architect Giacomo Quarenghi, 1800). The name derives from the golden-yellow artificial marble pilasters topped with Corinthian capitals. The traditions of Classicism are consistently observed in the décor of the room. Its walls are broken up into rectangular panels of white artificial marble, their corners are decorated with moulded, bronzed rosettes. The upper part of the walls is covered with moulded bas-reliefs the colour of

dark bronze, depicting Alexander the Great and his mother Olympia. The contrast between the white marble and golden pilasters with the dark bronze of the moulded bas-reliefs imparts a stately elegance to the room.

The mahogany furniture set in this room was designed by Voronikhin and made by Heinrich Gambs. The two jasper vases standing at both ends of the bureau were designed by Voronikhin and made at a lapidary factory in the Urals (1802).

The next room is one of the most charming in the palace. Called the **Lantern Room**, it was built to Voronikhin's plan in 1807. Part of this room is a glazed oriel jutting out, like a lantern (hence its name), into the garden. Its coffered vault rests on slender columns faced with artificial white marble. The coffers are covered with rosettes in the form of daisies. The arch dividing the oriel from the room proper is "supported" by caryatides, the work of the sculptor Vasily Demut-Malinovsky. The abundance of light creates an impression of airy lightness in the Lantern Room. Its black-and-gold furniture, designed by Voronikhin, excellently matches the architectural design of the room, intensifying the contrast between the light-flooded oriel and the shaded part.

Besides a writing table and some other pieces of furniture, the Lantern Room contains some remarkable works of applied art conceived by Voronikhin, notably, a round crystal table and a small three-legged table with a blue glass top. The writing-set and the numerous knick-knacks preserved here from the 19th century lend the room a "lived-in" appearance.

The Lantern Room communicates with the **Dressing-Room**, which was designed by Giacomo Quarenghi in 1800. One of the most outstanding features of this chamber is the plafond painted in the grisaille style by

Giovanni Baptiste Scotti. Also attractive are coloured glass and crystal articles designed by Voronikhin and made at the St. Petersburg glassworks. The 34-piece green porcelain toilet is a truly remarkable specimen of Russian workmanship.

Next comes the **Bedchamber** with its brightly painted walls and ceiling. The furniture for this room was designed by Voronikhin. However, part of it (the armchairs and the banquettes) was rebuilt anew by Soviet craftsmen. The restoration workers used the embroidered borders that were found among old textile fabrics in the palace storerooms.

The north-west suite on the ground floor ends with a small oval chamber, the **Marquee**. Its semi-circular couch, covered with embroidered upholstery, and the small work-tables indicate that the room was used for lounging and for needlework.

Your excursion through the rooms of the Grand Palace has come to an end. But before leaving Pavlovsk we suggest that you take a walk through its fine park and see some of its interesting sights.

As we already mentioned the park occupies an area of 600 hectares. Since it is simply impossible to cover the whole park in one day we shall tell you about the pavilions nearest to the palace that should be seen first of all.

The small **Private Garden** by the western façade of the Palace is laid out in the style of "regular" Dutch gardens. Its main adornment is the **Pavilion of the Three Graces**, built by Charles Cameron in 1800 on the very edge of the garden. The roof of the pavilion rests on 16 white Ionic columns and the pediments are decorated with bas-reliefs: Apollo with a lyre and other attributes of the arts, and the goddess of wisdom Minerva carrying symbols of Strength and Glory. In 1803, a sculptured group, carved out of a marble monolith by Paolo Triscorni, was placed in the centre of the pavilion. This group is the Three Graces—Euphrosyne (Joy), Thalia (Flowering), and Aglaia (Brilliance). The lovely graces support a vase decorated with an ornamental design and masks.

After the Private Garden, descend along the Great Stone Staircase to the bank of the Slavyanka. There are 64 steps in this staircase. At the top it is decorated with marble statues of lions; at the bottom, with wrought-iron ones.

Turn right along the bank of the Slavyanka and you will find yourself in front of another beautiful pavilion— the **Temple of Friendship**, built in 1782 by Charles Cameron. The name of the pavilion is associated with sentimentalism, a literary trend that prevailed in Russia at the close of the 18th century. On their estates the Russian nobility of that time built summer houses and pavilions with conspicuously sentimental names: Pavilion of Tears, Temple of Secluded Love, and so forth. The circular Temple of Friendship is surrounded by a Doric colonnade. Between the columns the architect placed moulded bas-reliefs that lend life to the blind inner wall. Under the cornice runs a moulded frieze on which are depicted wreaths and dolphins (dolphins being a symbol of friendship). A flat dome, its central part glassed-in, tops the pavilion.

The structure blends excellently with its surroundings; the columns are mirrored in the calm waters of the Slavyanka, the trees were planted in such a way so as not to screen the temple but link it with the surrounding landscape, so the pavilion is clearly visible even from outlying spots in the Pavlovsk Park.

Continuing along the bank of the Slavyanka, you come to an area that is called the **Old Sylvia** (Staraya Silvia). It was landscaped in 1793 by the architect Vincenzo Brenna. The symmetrical layout of the central part is called the **Twelve Paths**. Passing through a low stone gate, you come to a circle around which stand 12 bronze statues, cast from classical originals.

Beginning with the main path (leading from the stone gate), the statues stand in the following order, clockwise; Euterpe (muse of lyric poetry and music), Melpomene (muse of tragedy), Thalia (muse of comedy), Terpsichore (muse of dancing), Erato (muse of love poetry), Mercury (messenger of the gods, patron of commerce and travellers), Venus Callipyge (goddess of beauty and elegance), Polyhymnia (muse of sacred poetry), Calliope (muse of eloquence and epic poetry), Clio (muse of history), Urania (muse of astronomy), Flora (goddess of flowers). In the centre of the circle stands Apollo, god of the Sun and patron of the Muses. The statues were created in the 1790s in the foundries of the St. Petersburg Academy of Arts on the basis of models by sculptor Fyodor Gordeyev.

From the circular area twelve paths run radially. One of them leads westward to the pavilion called **Monument to My Parents**. In its centre, on a grey marble pedestal, stands a pyramid with a medallion on which the profiles of the parents of Paul I's wife are depicted.

Further you walk across a small footbridge to enter the **New Sylvia** (Novaya Silvia) area.

North of the little footbridge, on the other side of the Slavyanka, there stands a pavilion of unique design: a round tower crowned with a conical thatched roof. This is the so-called **Pil-Tower**, built in 1795. The artist Pietro Gonsago painted it to create the impression of ruined structure (such was the whim of the owners of the park). However, the interior was quite ornate; it was a luxurious hall decorated with mouldings and paintings, and furnished with a marble fireplace.

South of the Pil-Tower is the **Mausoleum of Paul I**, which is also entitled **To My Husband and Benefactor**. This pavilion is not actually a mausoleum, since the Emperor, who was assassinated by his courtiers, is not buried here, but in the Peter and Paul Fortress.

The Mausoleum was built in 1808–1809 to the design of the architect Thomas de Thomon in the style of an ancient Greek temple. The main façade consists of a pediment resting on four colums that form a half-open chamber. Around the walls runs a frieze of tragic masks with tears of grief. The interior of the mausoleum is faced with artificial marble; light comes in through two semicircular windows. Deep inside the chamber, opposite the entrance, stands a tall monument: a granite pyramid with a white marble medallion—a portrait of Paul I. In front of the pyramid, on a porphyry pedestal there is an urn before which stands a female figure bowed in grief—the dead emperor's widow. It must be pointed out that the "inconsolable grief" of the widowed empress was extremely hypocritical, since she was aware of the impending attempt upon the life of her husband. Their eldest son, the heir to the throne Alexander, also knew about the plan. He is depicted on the pedestal on the right. In front of Alexander stands his brother, Prince Konstantin, comforting him. Further are the two younger sons of Paul I, Nicholas and Mikhail. They are locked in an embrace "in order that they might bear their common grief together", as the court chronicler hypocritically said of the embracing brothers. On the left of the group are the emperor's daughters.

This composition was created by an eminent Russian sculptor, Ivan Martos, who, according to one of his contemporaries, could make even marble weep.

From the Mausoleum you return to the Old Silvia area, walk toward the palace and near it cross the Slavyanka by the **Centaur Bridge**. This bridge was built by the Russian stonemason Nikita Yakovlev. The builder added open-work railings to match the light contours of the bridge. In 1805, Andrei Voronikhin designed four marble centaurs for the four corners of the bridge; the work was executed by an Italian master. During the Nazi occupation the centaurs were destroyed. Today they have been replaced by copies cast in epoxy resin.

Near the Centaur Bridge, on the bank of the Slavyanka, stands a small pavilion, the **Cold Bath**, designed for ablutions in hot weather. Nearby is still another remarkable sight, the **Apollo Colonnade**, designed by Charles Cameron and built in 1783. Originally it was a closed ring formed by a double colonnade. After it was severely damaged by lightning during a thunderstorm in 1817 it was decided not to restore the ruined part of the structure but to place the fallen columns by the statue of the Apollo Belvedere; as a result the entire construction took on the appearance of an ancient ruin.

The colonnade is noted for its beautiful proportions, it seems to be permeated with light and air. Placed opposite the palace, clearly visible from the windows, the colonnade was intended to convey the idea of the royal family's patronage of the arts.

You have now become acquainted with the architectural ensembles and park of Pavlovsk, an outstanding monument of art and architecture of the second half of the 18th and beginning of the 19th centuries. For over a hundred years, while it remained the private property of the Romanov dynasty, the treasures of Pavlovsk were inaccessible to those who, together with the great architects and artists, put heart and soul into their creation, to those whose work and art continue to be a source of delight and admiration to us today.

Only the Great October Revolution of 1917 turned these treasures over to the people, opening up to them the palace and the vistas of the park. The people, in turn, take good care of Pavlovsk, one of the finest monuments in all of Europe.

RAZLIV

The township of Razliv first appeared at the beginning of the 20th century as a settlement for the workers of the Sestroretsk firearms factory. In July-August 1917 Lenin lived here in hiding from the sleuths of the Provisional Government.

As you have learned in previous chapters, a peaceful demonstration of Petrograd workers, sailors and soldiers was fired upon on the order of the bourgeois Provisional Government in July 1917, marking the beginning of a counter-revolutionary offensive. A particular target was the Bolshevik Party. The Provisional Government issued an order for the arrest of Lenin. The life of the leader of the Revolution was in danger. Therefore the Central Committee of the Party adopted a decision to hide Lenin from the spies of the Provisional Government in a secret retreat. From the 5th to the 9th (18-22) of July Lenin hid in secret flats in Petrograd, and on the night of July 10 (23) he arrived in the company of a Sestroretsk factory worker, Nikolai Yemelyanov, in Razliv, where he was lodged in a barn in Yemelyanov's backyard. At that time the Yemelyanov home was on the outskirts of the settlement. Passers-by could not see into the yard, screened as it was from the street by thick clusters of lilac bushes and rowan-trees. The loft of the barn was reached by a short but very steep ladder, and in this loft a bed was made up for Lenin and a table and some chairs placed.

While he lodged here Lenin worked very intensely. Every day he was supplied with copies of almost all the newspapers published in Petrograd. In his loft he was also visited by representatives of the Central Committee of the Bolshevik Party who brought information and received instructions.

In 1925, on the resolution of the Central Committee of the Party, the barn that was Lenin's hideaway was converted into a memorial museum. On the wall of the structure is a plaque with the inscription: "Vladimir Ilyich Lenin lived and worked here, in the loft of the barn, for several days, beginning with July 10 (23) 1917, in hiding from the persecution of the counter-revolutionary Provisional Government."

This memorial museum is carefully kept up. It was underpinned by a foundation, the walls and roof were impregnated with protective resins. In

1970, when the centenary of Lenin's birth was commemorated, a glass casing was erected over the historical barn to protect it from rain and snow.

The ground floor of the Barn museum has been restored to its 1917 appearance. The Yemelyanov family lived here, since their house was undergoing repairs then. By the wall stands a dining-table with dishes; in a corner—a Singer sewing machine used by the mistress of the house, Nadezhda Yemelyanova; an iron bedstead stands by the right-hand wall.

The furniture that stood in the loft for Lenin—the table and chairs—was turned over to the Leningrad branch of the Central Lenin Museum. Copies of these objects are exhibited in the Barn. But it also contains some authentic objects used by Lenin: four bent-wood chairs, a copper tea-kettle, a samovar. The small stove on which the Yemelyanovs prepared food for their lodger has also been preserved.

After you have viewed the Barn museum we advise you to have a look at the exposition arranged in the house opposite. Here you will see materials reflecting the situation that had developed in the country following the July 1917 events. Among them are photographs of the shooting-down of the demonstration of working people on July 4, 1917; of House No. 17, Tenth Rozhdestvenskaya Street, where Lenin hid out on July 7-9; of the Primorsky (Maritime) Railway Station (no longer in existence) from which Lenin departed for Razliv. On exposition is also a photocopy of Lenin's article *The Political Situation*, written on July 10 in the loft of the barn the day he arrived in Razliv. Having analyzed the political situation in the country, Lenin states in this article that the peaceful development of the Revolution is no longer possible, and that in order for the proletariat to win state power it is necessary to prepare for an armed uprising.

The article *The Political Situation*, as well as *On Slogans*, *Lessons of the Revolution*, and other works by Lenin served as the basis for the course towards an armed uprising adopted by the Sixth Congress of the Bolshevik Party.

The exposition contains numerous photo-documents, among them pictures taken of Lenin in the period when he went into hiding, of members of the Central Committee of the Bolshevik Party who visited their leader in Razliv—Felix Dzerzhinsky, Georgi Orjonikidze, Yakov Sverdlov, Lenin's wife Nadezhda Krupskaya. Krupskaya was photographed in attire unusual for her: the picture was taken for an identification card in the name of Agafya Atamanova, a woman worker at the Sestroretsk firearms factory. This fake document made it possible for Krupskaya to leave Petrograd and join Lenin in Finland. There are also photographs of the owners of the house, Nikolai and Nadezhda Yemelyanov, and of other persons connected with this period in Lenin's life.

Notwithstanding the strict secrecy, it was not safe for Lenin to remain for long in the loft of the barn. The area was teeming with sleuths of the Provisional Government, nearby there were summer residents (army officers, government officials), and quite a few overly inquisitive neighbours. Therefore Yemelyanov rented a meadow for haymaking beyond Lake Razliv (today it is called the Sestroretsk Razliv). The family told the neighbours that they had decided to buy a cow and therefore had to make hay for it. In order to get in as much hay as possible they had allegedly hired a Finnish mower. The future leader of the first workers' and peasants' state in the world, Lenin, was to be this "mower".

One day in July Nikolai Yemelyanov, with the consent of the Central Committee of the Bolshevik Party, rowed Lenin over to the far shore of Lake Razliv.

Lenin's Hut

The barn continued to serve for secret meetings; representatives of the Bolshevik Central Committee left information for Lenin there and received instructions from him.

Yemelyanov had put up a hut on the shore of the lake, and right next to the hut amidst the thick shrubs, he had cleared a small patch where he placed two blocks of wood, one larger, one smaller, to serve Lenin as table and chair. Outside the hut he made a kitchen: a pot over a campfire supported by two forked sticks. Yemelyanov mowed grass every morning to allay any suspicions on the part of people living in the neighbourhood.

In his "green study" Lenin wrote such works as *On Slogans*, *The Answer*, *The Beginning of Bonapartism* and *Lessons of Revolution*, works that were of tremendous importance for the victory of the coming socialist revolution and that have lost none of their abiding theoretical value to the present day. Here, too, Lenin began to work on his immortal *The State and Revolution*, in which the Marxist doctrine on the state is most fully and systematically expounded.

During the period when Lenin was staying beyond Lake Razliv the Sixth Congress of the Bolshevik Party was held in Petrograd (July 26–August 3). Even though Lenin was not present, he was elected honorary chairman of the Congress and his works and personal instructions determined the content of the most important resolutions passed at the Congress.

Lenin's illegal presence in the hayfield could not go on for long. Normal conditions had to be created for the life and work of the leader of the Revolution. The Central Committee of the Party decided to transfer him to Finland.

On August 8 Lenin left his hut and with Yemelyanov and other Party comrades walked a few kilometres through the marshes to the railway station Dibuny. A few days later he was in Finland.

Lake Razliv

Yemelyanov's Barn

In 1927, on the tenth anniversary of the October Revolution, the workers of Leningrad held a foundation-stone ceremony on the spot where Lenin's hut once stood; on July 15, 1928 the monument, designed by architect Alexander Gegello, was unveiled. An inscription on the granite wall of the "Hut" reads: "Here in July and August 1917 in a hut made of branches the leader of the October Revolution hid from the sleuths of the bourgeois government and wrote his book *The State and Revolution.* In memory of this event we have erected a granite hut. Workers of the City of Lenin. 1927."

In 1964, a new exposition pavilion built of granite, marble and glass was erected next to the "Hut" monument. To the right of the entrance there is an inscription on the wall. "Here, by Lake Razliv in July and August 1917 Vladimir Ilyich Lenin hid from the agents of the counter-revolutionary bourgeois Provisional Government. From here Lenin led the Bolshevik Party and prepared it for an armed up-

rising." Documents on exhibit in this pavilion reflect the theoretical and organisational work carried out by Lenin during his stay in Razliv. The exposition includes a copy of the statue you have already seen, *Lenin in Razliv,* by the sculptor Vladimir Pinchuk, photo-documents illustrating the events of the summer of 1917, Lenin's works written in Razliv and documents showing how Lenin led the Party while in hiding, particularly his guidance of the Sixth Congress of the Party. The most important exhibit is Lenin's work *The State and Revolution,* written during August-September of 1917. Particularly noteworthy is a copy of the "blue notebook" that Lenin took especial care of. It contains notes he took from the works of Karl Marx and Friedrich Engels on the state during his emigration in Switzerland, which he later used while writing his *The State and Revolution.*

Domestic objects associated with Lenin's stay by Lake Razliv are also on display in the pavilion. In glass showcases one sees a Russian blouse, a scythe, a rake, a tea-kettle and a pot. These are exact copies of the articles Lenin used here. The authentic articles are in the Central Lenin Museum in Moscow and in its Leningrad branch.

After viewing this memorial zone drive to Tarkhovka station, from there on again to the Primorskoye Highway that leads further out into the Karelian Isthmus, to the village of Repino.

REPINO

As you proceed along the Primorskoye Highway you can see, on the right-hand side behind a wooden fence, the glass turrets of Ilya Repin's country estate Penaty (the word comes from the Latin *penates*—the Roman household gods, the protectors of the home and family). The famous Russian painter, whose works were among the highest achievements of Russian realistic art, lived here for thirty years (from 1900 to 1930).

In Penaty Repin created many canvases that are gems in the world treasure-house of painting: *Meeting of the State Council, Bloody Sunday, Pushkin's Examination at the Lyceum*, portraits of the writers Lev Tolstoy and Maxim Gorky, the art historian Vladimir Stasov, the scientist Dmitri Mendeleyev, the singer Fyodor Chaliapin ... This hospitable house was often visited by outstanding figures of Russian literature, art, and science—the writer Vladimir Korolenko, the composer Alexander Glazunov, the physiologist Ivan Pavlov, the poet Vladimir Mayakovsky...

In 1940, the estate Penaty was turned into a museum. When the Great Patriotic War of 1941-1945 broke out many exhibits of the museum were taken away and carefully preserved far inside the country. The invaders wantonly destroyed Repin's Penaty. The Soviet troops who liberated the Karelian Isthmus in 1944 found, in place of the museum, only ruins—gutted remnants of stoves and the foundation of the former house. In many places in the park the trees had been felled, and the ponds had dried up and turned into a shrubby morass.

Restoration work on the estate was commenced after the war. The work was complicated by the fact that Repin's home initially had been a small, single-storey house that had gradually grown out and up—rooms, verandas, oriels and balconies were added to it. However, the restorers, with the help of the museum staff, succeeded in rebuilding the house; on June 14, 1962 the museum was opened for visitors.

A birch-lined walk leads from the gates to a ledge that Repin named Chuguyev Hill in honour of the town of Chuguyev in the Ukraine where he was born. Among flowers at the foot of the "hill", on a spot chosen by Repin himself, is the grave of the great painter. Over it stands his bust

Repin's estate **Penaty**

executed by the sculptor Nikolai Andreyev in Penaty in 1910.

Repin gave some parts of his estate rather pretentious appellations. Thus, Pushkin's Walk starts from the house, skirts a pond and leads to a green lawn—Homer's Sward. Here, on a hillock, is a wooden summer house with columns—the painter named it the Temple of Osiris and Isis. At the end of Pushkin's Walk there stands a 12-metre tower that was called Scheherazade's Tower.

And now let us have a look at the house-museum itself. Regrettably, when the Nazi troops were at the walls of Leningrad not all the museum pieces could be evacuated. A large couch from the painter's workshop, the round dining-table at which many outstanding visitors to Penaty sat, and some other exhibits of the museum were burned together with the house.

However, numerous photographs have been preserved that show the interior of Repin's house, the furniture

that stood there and various domestic articles. On the basis of these photographs the staff of the museum were able to duplicate the lost objects. This was not too difficult, for Repin, a modest person in his domestic requirements, did not have his furniture made to order, but usually bought it in furniture stores. There are also certain articles in Penaty that once belonged to Repin, but were not on expositiion here formerly, as they were in the possession of distant relatives of the painter in Leningrad. Such, for instance, are a small inlaid table depicted by Repin in his painting *The Negress* and a music-stand with Repin's autograph ...

The dining-table with a revolving centre piece was very precisely reproduced by the restorers with the aid of a drawing of this interesting item found in the Russian Museum together with a detailed description of its construction. In reproducing the stoves and fireplaces the restoration workers used drawings, pictures, and

Repin's studio

photographs showing guests at Penaty against the background of stoves or fireplaces. One of the Repin's pupils, Isaac Brodsky, painted a portrait of his teacher in Penaty against the background of the yellow fireplace in his studio. Brodsky was extremely accurate in reproducing details of this kind in his drawings, and so thanks to this portrait the fireplace was reconstructed in its original form.

Before you begin your tour of the museum we should like to inform you that every visitor to the museum can listen to a taped commentary on the exposition. There are several versions of these commentaries, including some in foreign languages. Additional information may be received from the staff researcher on duty. At the end of the exposition visitors can view a documentary film made up of the few stills depicting Ilya Repin in the final period of his life.

The excursion to the museum is preceded by a short talk on the basic works of the artist at various stages of his career. Large photographic copies of Repin's canvases hang in three rooms. Among them is a reproduction of his first major work, *Resurrection of Iair's Daughter*, painted on graduation from the Academy of Arts (for this work Repin was awarded the Greater Gold Medal). This painting was followed by *The Volga Boatmen*, *Religious Procession in Kursk Gubernia*, *Unexpected*, *The Zaporozhye Cossacks Writing a Letter to the Turkish Sultan*, *Rejection of Confession*, *Meeting of the State Council*... These canvases bear witness not only to Repin's outstanding talent, but also to the rise of Russian democratic pictorial art.

On display here are also biographical materials, among them a certificate stating that on July 24, 1844 in the town of Chuguyev a son, Ilya, was born to the soldier Yefim Vasilyevich Repin and his wife Tatyana Stepanovna. Here, too, the visitor learns about the people Repin associated with, about his friends, many of whom, like Repin himself, were the pride of Russian culture.

The excursion through the reconstructed rooms of Penaty starts with the small **Hall**. During Repin's life it was entered through a small porch. To the right of the door stands the Penaty flag which was hoisted above the house on Wednesdays, Repin's reception days. Upon entering the guests would strike a copper gong. A handwritten poster above the gong announces: "Self-service ... Take off your overcoat, your galoshes unaided ... Strike the gong smartly, merrily... Open the doors to the dining-room yourself ..." On a coat-rack hang Repin's outdoor clothes: a caped cloak, a brimmed felt hat and a beret. A leather trunk stands by a latticed window; the trunk was a wedding gift from Repin to his servant-girl Mina. In 1962, Mina's husband brought this trunk from Finland and presented it to the Penaty museum.

Note the leather travelling-bag, Repin's companion on his journeys. Here, too, are gardening implements the artist was fond of working with. The furnishing of the entrance hall reflects the modest domestic life of the great painter. He cleaned up his room himself, fed the stove himself and was very annoyed when anybody tried to help him to, say, put on his coat.

The next room is the **Study**. This was the last addition to the house, made in 1912. Here the artist wrote his memoirs, the book *So Far Away and Yet So Near* (Dalyokoye Blizkoye). Photographs, among them pictures of his parents, stand on the desk. The lump of green glass lying on the table served Repin as a paperweight. Another object is an optical device with a large magnifying glass for reading small type and examining photographs.

Under the windows there are low bookshelves on which stand, as Repin used to say, "statues of Russian giants in miniature"—sculptured portraits of the scientist Dmitri Mendeleyev, the composer Anton Rubinstein, the painter Vasily Surikov, the writer Lev Tolstoy ...

Having seen the Study, proceed into the **Drawing-Room**, where Repin's friends and admirers used to get together on Wednesdays. In this room is a moulded copy of the Venus de Milo, and works by Repin's pupils and friends. Over the grand piano hangs a landscape painting, *Moonlit Night*, by Isaac Brodsky.

After the Drawing-Room comes the **Winter Veranda**, an octagonal room—two-thirds of which is glassed in—with a glass tent-shaped roof; this is the lightest room in the house, the first extension built (1904) onto the original single-storey little house. At first it was the painter's studio; later he set up his easel in a new and larger studio on the upper floor. The Winter Veranda became the room where the Repins received their guests. In this light-filled room three sculptured portraits made by Repin stand in their former places: the famous Russian surgeon Nikolai Pirogov, the writer Lev Tolstoy, and the painter's second wife, Natalya Nordman-Severova. A noteworthy object is an armchair upholstered in blue velvet standing on a low dais. Sitting in this armchair, many of the famous visitors to the hospitable Penaty posed for Repin.

Next you enter the **Dining-Room**, a large room with a window opening onto the garden. On the walls hang many of Repin's portraits of his friends and family. A prominent place is occupied by a portrait of Natalya Nordman-Severova painted by Repin in 1905 during their journey to Italy. On the left of this picture is the portrait of two little girls, Repin's daughters Vera and Nadezhda, painted in 1877.

Lively, merry dinners were given by the painter for his friends from

St. Petersburg. Particularly noteworthy is the dinner-table. Repin's wife had it made to order in 1909. It seated twenty persons, and its specific feature was that its circular central part revolved. And so, when it was laden with various dishes the guests could help themselves, bringing the desired dish within reach by means of one of the several handles. The used dishes were placed in special drawers of the table. We have already mentioned that the present table is an exact copy of the one that stood here in Repin's time.

There were humorous rules to using the Round Table and violators were subject to a penalty: they had to deliver a speech from a special rostrum in a corner of the dining-room. Usually these impromptu speeches were very amusing. As Repin's wife, Natalya Nordman-Severova, was a vegetarian, the guests at Penaty were served dishes cooked with various greens and herbs. True, according to the testimonies of contemporaries, the chef knew his business and the guests heartily relished the food...

Towards the end of the 1920s, when the painter's strength was ebbing, this room was both his bedroom and his studio. On his 86th birthday, August 5, 1930, Repin received his guests here for the last time, and here he passed away on September 29, 1930 after a bout of pneumonia.

Finally, the last room in the exposition on the upper floor, is the **Studio**, where Repin, as he himself admitted, "spent the best hours of his life". From the Studio a door opens onto a balcony commanding a wonderful view of the park and the Gulf of Finland. Repin liked to sleep here both in summer and winter. Only when the frost was very severe would he sleep indoors.

By the balcony door, on an easel, is a sketch for the *Meeting of the State Council* (the painting itself is on exposition in the Russian Museum in Leningrad). Repin began this work in 1901 on a government commission. He demanded that all the members of the State Council pose for him in the meeting hall, rejecting the proposal to work from photographs.

On display here are also certain preparatory materials for the famous painting *Zaporozhye Cossacks Writing a Letter to the Turkish Sultan*. The artist depicted a company of free Cossacks, merry and roguish, capable of defending their native land and responding with a sharp (although far from diplomatic) rebuff to the groundless claims of the Turkish Sultan. While working on the sketches for this painting, Repin at times used clay instead of paints—he modelled clay figures of his merry heroes. Several of these sculptures may be seen on the little table near the couch.

We have already mentioned the big couch that could not be evacuated from Penaty at the beginning of the war. The couch now standing in the studio is a duplicate of the old one, which was known in Penaty as "Chaliapin's" because the famous Russian singer posed for Repin on this couch. Next to the couch, on an easel by the curtain, is Repin's last self-portrait, painted in 1920, when he was 76 years old. The painting is permeated with sadness. Repin depicted himself in an overcoat and hat, sitting by a table. This was a difficult time for the artist: his canvases found no buyers, cut off from his native country he suffered emotional distress and material hardships. There was no firewood, the house was unheated; to keep warm he had to wear a coat and hat. This hat lies on a stool, next to the self-portrait. Nearby hangs Repin's work smock.

A blue vase on a stand in front of the self-portrait holds the painter's brushes, on a stool lies a hang-up palette. At the end of the 1890s the muscles between the thumb and index finger of Repin's right hand became atrophied. The painter began to use his left hand, and his palette he hung on a strap.

His strength was ebbing. He had not completely realised all his plans. However, in the paintings Repin created he vividly reflected the liberation struggle of the people, their power and spiritual richness, their beauty, the hate for their oppressors, their patriotic aspirations. Owing to its profound ideological content, national spirit, humanism and realistic perception of life Repin's work is an outstanding contribution to Russian and world culture.

INFORMATION

Attention Pedestrians!

Remember that traffic moves **on the right** in the Soviet Union. **Cross only at marked crossing places.**

You should cross at the rear of buses and trolley-buses standing at stops, but you must walk **round the front** of a stationary tram.

"Zebra"-type crossings in the Soviet Union do not give the right of way to pedestrians.

When crossing at traffic lights, even if your signal is green, beware of vehicles making right-hand turns.

Take great care when crossing Leningrad streets, and remember, the use of horns is forbidden in the city.

When navigation starts on the Neva, bridges are raised at night to let ships pass. You should keep this in mind if you are planning to watch the sunrise on the Neva.

Here is a schedule showing when the largest Leningrad bridges are raised:

Aleksandra Nevskogo bridge—from 2.35 to 4.50 a.m.

Bolsheokhtinsky bridge—from 2.45 to 4.45 a.m.

Liteiny bridge—from 2.10 to 4.40 a.m.

Kirovsky bridge—from 2.00 to 4.40 a.m.

Volodarski bridge—from 2.05 to 3.45 a.m. and from 4.30 to 5.45 a.m.

Dvortsovy bridge—from 1.55 to 3.05 and from 3.15 to 4.45 a.m.

Leitenanta Schmidta bridge—from 1.55 to 2.55 a.m. and from 3.15 to 4.50 a.m.

Stroitelei bridge (Little Neva)—from 2.25 to 3.20 a.m. and from 3.40 to 4.40 a.m.

Tuchkov bridge (Little Neva)—from 2.20 to 3.10 a.m. and from 3.40 to 4.40 a.m.

On the days of national holidays—May 1 and 2 and November 7 and 8—the bridges are not raised.

Public Transport

Leningrad has an excellent public transport system, offering the facilities of buses and trams, Metro trains, trolley-buses and taxis.

Form of Transport	Hours of Operation	Fares (Single journey)
Trolley-bus	0600–0100	5 kop.
Bus	0600–0100	5 kop.
Tram	0530–0100	5 kop.
Metro	0535–0100	5 kop.
Taxi	24-hour service	20 kop. per kilometre plus 20 kop. on entry (irrespective of the number of passengers)
Taxibus	24-hour service	15 kop.

Since there are no conductors selling tickets on trolley-buses, buses and trams you can obtain a ticket-book to pay your fare from special dealers near trolley-bus, bus and tram stops as well as buy them at newsstands, tobacco stalls, etc. Do not forget to punch your ticket from the ticket book.

Taxis are identifiable by chequered stripes on the cab body, and the green light in the right-hand side of the windscreen means for hire. Taxis can be ordered through hotel service bureaus or simply hailed in the street—but don't forget that taxi-drivers are obliged to give preference to people waiting at taxi ranks.

Motor Tourists

A few words of advice for those who have brought their cars to Leningrad, or have rented cars from Intourist.

Two things to remember: traffic in the USSR moves on the right, and it is absolutely forbidden to drink and drive!

While driving around the city, take care, obey traffic signs and lights and follow any instructions given to you by the militia or other traffic officers.

In the interests of your safety and that of other people do not exceed the speed limit (60 kmph or 35 mph, except where otherwise indicated).

The use of horns is permitted only where this would prevent an accident, or outside the city limits.

Give the right of way to any vehicles displaying a blue flashing light or operating a siren (fire tenders, ambulances, etc.).

It is forbidden to drive in the left-hand lane, unless the lane, or lanes to the right are occupied.

Note that at intersections with four-signal traffic lights left- and U-turns are permitted only on a green light and a green arrow. You should wait at the Stop (СТОП) line.

It is forbidden to cross a continuous white line in the middle of a main road, and U-turns are only permitted at breaks in such a line, or where there is a U-turn road-sign.

Reduce speed at crossroads or when approaching "zebra"-type pedestrian crossings where there are no traffic lights.

In case of breakdown tourists should contact the service station at 5, Pervaya Staroderevenskaya Ulitsa, telephone numbers 239-22-31 or 239-20-30 (manager), which operates a tow-in and repair service.

Parking is free and permitted anywhere that there is no prohibitive sign or public transport stop. There are also specially protected parking lots with 24-hour service. (Charge: 30 kopecks per car per day and 50 kopecks per coach per day.)

Addresses of Recommended Parking Lots

Moskovsky Prospekt (near the Rossiya Hotel)
5, Pervaya Staroderevenskaya Ulitsa (the Vyborg Side of the city)
Torzhkovskaya Ulitsa (near the Vyborgskaya Hotel, next to Primorskoye Highway)

We recommend the service station near the Olgino camp site. Towing and repair services are provided. The station is equipped with spare parts for automobiles of Soviet make. A list of service charges is posted.

The Olgino and Repino camp sites on the Primorskoye Highway are open from May till August. Reservations should be made in advance.

A new Olgino Motel has been recently built on the Gulf of Finland. Guests staying at the Repino camp site can use the beach of the Dyuny Hotel.

Tourists can book a tent, a chalet, or a room. For those who prefer to do their own cooking, there are kitchens with gas stoves and refrigerators. There are post offices, telegraphs, newsstands (selling newspapers and magazines in Russian and foreign languages) as well as sports grounds, showers, and restaurants offering national dishes—all available at the camp site.

Eating Out in Leningrad

Some of Leningrad's restaurants will accept payment both in rubles and **in foreign currency**. These are to be found in the **Yevropeiskaya Hotel** (1/7, Ulitsa Brodskogo) and the **Leningrad Hotel** (5/2, Pirogovskaya Naberezhnaya). For Russian cuisine, try the **Sadko** restaurant (in the Yevropeiskaya Hotel at the corner of Nevsky Prospekt and Ulitsa Brodˌ skogo).

For a meal in exotic surroundings we recommend the **Kronwerk**, a restaurant on board a three-masted ship (a model of an ancient schooner) moored in the Kronwerk Strait by the walls of the Peter and Paul Fortress. A restaurant bearing the old name of **Austeria** is located inside the Peter and Paul Fortress by Peter's Gate.

Of the other restaurants in Leningrad, which take only Soviet currency, we specially recommend two—the **Baku** (12, Sadovaya Ulitsa) and **Fregat** (39/14, Bolshoi Prospekt, on Vasilyevsky Island). The Baku offers Caucasian food, while at the Fregat and Austeria you can sample dishes popular back in the days of Peter the Great.

Intourist Cultural Centre

Your hosts in Leningrad, Intourist, would like you to learn something of the contemporary cultural life of the USSR, and every year from June to October they run a special cultural centre for tourists. This is housed in the Palace of Culture, a beautiful modern building set up for employees of the Nevsky Machine Building Works.

At the Cultural Centre you can hear talks on the Soviet way of life; the domestic and foreign policies of the CPSU; Soviet women, their rights and duties; the nationalities policy of the CPSU; the Soviet social security system and many other topics. You can also see documentary, newsreel and feature films in a number of foreign languages and attend concerts by world-famous groups, such as the Omsk Folk Choir; Kabardinka, a Caucasian folk dance group; the Urals Folk Choir; and Zhok, a dance troupe from Moldavia.

The Cultural Centre is at 32, Prospekt Obukhovskoi Oborony, which can be reached by Metro (*Yelizarovskaya* Station), tram (Nos. 7, 17, 27, 38 or 44) or bus (Nos 8, 70), get off at Dvorets Kultury "Nėvsky".

Photography and Filming

Tourists in Leningrad are allowed to photograph or film objects of architectural interest, public buildings, theatres, dwellings, museum buildings, streets and squares. But, like other countries, the USSR has certain rules and practices concerning filming and photography which should be observed to avoid misunderstandings.

If you wish to photograph a person, do ask his permission first (not everyone takes kindly to being "snapped" by a stranger!). At industrial enterprises, farms, offices or educational establishments photographs and films can only be taken with the prior permission of the management.

It is forbidden to film or photograph: any military installations or equipment; seaports, airports, railway stations, bridges, tunnels, radio stations, etc.; from an aircraft.

Working Days,
Weekends and Holidays

Like other factories and offices throughout the Soviet Union, those in Leningrad work a five-day week.

Most enterprises and organisations are closed **on Saturdays and Sundays**.

The **working day** at offices and educational establishments is usually from nine o'clock in the morning to six in the evening with an hour lunchbreak.

Soviet Holidays: January 1—New Year's Day, March 8—International Women's Day, May 1 and 2—International Workers' Solidarity Day, May 9—Victory Day, October 7—Soviet Constitution Day, November 7 and 8—October Revolution Day.

All shops, including department stores, except those selling food, are closed on Sundays and holidays.

The Post Office,
Telegraph and Telephone

Post cards, stamps and envelopes are sold at newsstands and post offices. Blue post boxes are for mail being sent out of town or abroad, red post boxes are for local mail only.

Registered letters, parcels (small) and telegrams may be sent from the hotel post office or any other post office in the city.

The **Leningrad General Post Office** (9, Ulitsa Soyuza Svyazi). Open non-stop from 9 a.m. to 9 p.m., Sundays from 10 a.m. to 8 p.m.

Foreign postal and telegraph rates vary from country to country in accordance with agreements the Soviet Union has with these countries.

Telephone calls to other Soviet cities and abroad may be ordered through the service bureau of your hotel, and you can talk directly from your room. If you wish, you can place long-distance phone calls yourself at a call office; a full list of call offices is available at the hotel service bureau.

Shops

Of greatest interest to tourists are the **Beryozka shops**, which accept convertible currency.

Beryozka shops sell: Russian souvenirs—Matryoshka nest dolls, Khokhloma ware, lacquer boxes from Palekh, Fedoskino, Mstyora and Kholui; Russian furs, samovars, balalaikas, amber and crystal, watches, jewelry, cameras, transistors, caviar, tinned crab, vodka, wines, brandies, cigarettes, tobacco and cigars.

Where to Find the Beryozka Shops

Hotel Leningrad	—5/2, Pirogovskaya Naberezhnaya
Hotel Oktyabrskaya	—10, Ligovsky Prospekt
Hotel Pribaltiiskaya	—14, Ulitsa Korablestroitelei
Hotel Sovietskaya	—43, Lermontovsky Prospekt
Hotel Yevropeiskaya	—1/7, Ulitsa Brodskogo
Beryozka Shop	—26, Ulitsa Gertsena and at Pulkovo Airport (Ploshchad Pobedy)

A Few Large Department Stores
(Soviet currency only):

Dom Leningradskoi Tor- govli	—21-23, Ulitsa Zhelyabova
Frunzensky Univermag	—60, Moskovsky Prospekt
Gostiny Dvor	—35, Nevsky Prospekt
Kirovsky Univermag	—9, Ploshchad Stachek
Moskovsky Univermag	—205 and 220, Moskovsky Prospekt
Narvsky Univermag	—12, 20, 24, 26, 30 and 34, Prospekt Geroyev
Passazh (ladies' goods)	—48, Nevsky Prospekt
Sintetika	—4, Novoizmailovsky Prospekt

There are also a number of shops specialising in various types of goods: **Ties** (Galstuki)—22-24, Nevsky Prospekt; **Records** (Gramplastinki)—32-34, Nevsky Prospekt; **Varnish and Paint** (Laki i kraski)—96, Nevsky Prospekt; **Sheet Music** (Noty)—13, Ulitsa Zhelyabova; **Television Sets** (Televizory)—94, Bolshoi Prospekt, Petrogradskaya Storona; 4 Ulitsa Nekrasova; 20, Nevsky Prospekt; **Travel Goods** (Tovary v dorogu)—114, Nevsky Prospekt; **Photography Goods** (Fototovary)—61, Liteiny Prospekt; 92, Nevsky Prospekt; **Paintings, sculptures, objects of applied art**—8 and 45, Nevsky Prospekt.

Bookshops: **Akademkniga** (run by the USSR Academy of Sciences)—57, Liteiny Prospekt; **Dom Knigi**—28, Nevsky Prospekt; **Mir** (books published by the socialist countries)—13, Nevsky Prospekt; **Leningrad** (books about Leningrad)—50, Nevsky Prospekt; **Books on civil construction**—3, Bolsheokhtinsky Prospekt; **Meditsinskaya Literatura** (books on medicine)—70/72, Bolshoi Prospekt, Petrogradskaya Storona; **Globus** (Philately)—78, Nevsky Prospekt; **Prints, reproductions**—72, Nevsky Prospekt; **Books on mining, geology and meteorology**—45, Sredny Prospekt, Vasilyevsky Ostrov.

Kosmos (watches)—57, Nevsky Prospekt; **Krasnaya Shapochka** (toys)—32, Sadovaya Ulitsa.

Jewelry: **Yakhont**—24, Ulitsa Gertsena; **Beryozka**—7/9, Nevsky Prospekt; 47, Sadovaya Ulitsa.

Foreign currency may be exchanged at the airport, the Maritime Port and in the Astoria, Yevropeiskaya, Karelia, Leningrad, Moskva and Pribaltiiskaya hotels daily from 9 a.m. to 8 p.m. (closed during lunch hour—2-3 p.m.). You may change back any unspent money at the airport or the Maritime Port.

Museums

Museums of the History of the Revolution

Leningrad museums are usually open from 11 a.m. to 7 p.m.
Leningrad branch of the Central Lenin Museum—5/1, Ulitsa Khalturina
Lenin Flat-Museum—7, Pereulok Ilyicha
Lenin Flat-Museum—52, Ulitsa Lenina
Lenin Flat-Museum—17, Desyataya Sovetskaya Ulitsa
Lenin Flat-Museum—1, Serdobolskaya Ulitsa
Lenin Flat-Museum—32, Naberezhnaya Reki Karpovki

Lenin Flat-Museum—5, Khersonskaya Ulitsa
Lenin Flat-Museum—Ploshchad Proletarskoi Diktatury, the Smolny building
"Barn" Museum—3, Ulitsa Yemelyanova, Sestroretsk
"Hut" Museum—Tarkhovka Station, Sestroretsk
Lenin House-Museum at Ilyichovo—Zelenogorsk Station, Posyolok Ilichovo
Lenin House-Museum at Vyborg—15, Rubezhnaya Ulitsa, Vyborg
Leningrad branch of the Museum of the Great October Socialist Revolution—1/2, Prospekt Maxima Gorkogo
Kirov Museum—26/28, Kirovsky Prospekt
Cruiser Aurora (Branch of the Central Naval Museum)—Petrogradskaya Naberezhnaya, Bolshaya Nevka

History Museums

History of Leningrad—44, Naberezhnaya Krasnogo Flota
Peter and Paul Fortress (Branch of the Museum of the History of Leningrad)—Ploshchad Revolutsii
Museum of the History of Religion and Atheism (Kazansky Cathedral)—2, Kazanskaya Ploshchad
St. Isaac's Cathedral—1, Isaakiyevskaya Ploshchad
Peter the Great's Cottage—6, Petrovskaya Naberezhnaya
Menshikov Palace—15, Universitetskaya Naberezhnaya
Central Naval Museum—4, Ploshchad Pushkina
Artillery, Military Engineering and Signals Museum—7, Park Lenina
Suvorov History of the Armed Forces Museum—43, Ulitsa Saltykova-Shchedrina
Museum of Army Medical Corps—2, Lazaretny Pereulok
Piskaryovskoye Memorial Cemetery—74, Prospekt Nepokoryonnykh

Art Museums and Galleries

Hermitage—34, Dvortsovaya Naberezhnaya
Russian Museum—4/2, Inzhenernaya Ulitsa
Peter the Great's Summer Palace—Naberezhnaya Kutuzova, Letny Sad
USSR Academy of Arts Scientific Research Museum—17, Universitetskaya Naberezhnaya
Museum of Applied Art (Mukhina School of Industrial Art)—13, Solyanoi Pereulok
Museum of Urban Sculpture—1, Ploshchad Alexandra Nevskogo
State Museum of Theatrical Art—6a, Ploshchad Ostrovskogo
Museum of Musical Instruments—5, Isaakievskaya Ploshchad

Literary Museums

Museum of Literature—4, Naberezhnaya Makarova
All-Union Pushkin Museum—2, Komsomolskaya Ulitsa, Gorod Pushkin

Ethnographical Museums

Peter the Great Museum of Anthropology and Ethnography—3, Universitetskaya Naberezhnaya
Museum of Ethnography of the Peoples of the USSR—4/1, Inzhenernaya Ulitsa

Natural History Museums

Zoology Museum—1, Universitetskaya Naberezhnaya
Botany Museum—2, Ulitsa Professora Popova
Dokuchayev Central Soil Science Museum—6, Birzhevoi Proyezd, Vasilyevsky Ostrov
Mining Museum (excursions by prior arrangement)—2, Dvadtsat Pervaya Liniya, Vasilyevsky Ostrov
Museum of the Arctic and the Antarctic—24a, Ulitsa Marata
Museum of Public Health—25, Ulitsa Rakova

Museums of Technology

Popov Central Communications Museum—7, Ulitsa Soyuza Svyazi
Railway Museum—50, Sadovaya Ulitsa

Memorial Museums

Pushkin Flat-Museum—12, Naberezhnaya Reki Moiki
Lyceum where Pushkin studied—1, Komsomolskaya Ulitsa, Gorod Pushkin
Pushkin's Country House (the former Kitayeva's house)—2, Pushkinskaya Ulitsa, Gorod Pushkin
Nekrasov Flat-Museum—36, Liteiny Prospekt
Dostoyevsky Literary-Memorial Museum—5/2, Kuznechny Pereulok
Brodsky Flat-Museum—3, Ploshchad Iskusstv
Penaty, Repin Estate-Museum—63, Ulitsa Repina, Posyolok Repino
Shevchenko Museum-Studio—17, Universitetskaya Naberezhnaya
Rimsky-Korsakov Flat-Museum—28, Zagorodny Prospekt
Pavlov Flat-Museum—2, Sedmaya Liniya, Vasilyevsky Ostrov
Pavlov Museum-Laboratory at the Institute of Experimental Medicine—12, Ulitsa Akademika Pavlova
Lomonosov Museum—3, Universitetskaya Naberezhnaya
Mendeleyev Flat-Museum—7/9, Universitetskaya Naberezhnaya
Popov Museum at the Ulyanov Electrotechnical Institute (excursions by prior arrangement)—5, Ulitsa Professora Popova

Leningrad Branches of the Unions of Creative Workers

USSR Union of Architects—52, Ulitsa Gertsena
USSR Union of Journalists—70, Nevsky Prospekt
USSR Union of Cinematic Workers—12, Ulitsa Tolmachova
USSR Union of Composers—45, Ulitsa Gertsena
RSFSR Union of Writers—18, Ulitsa Voinova
RSFSR Union of Artists—38, Ulitsa Gertsena

Theatres and Concert Halls

Do not be late for plays, operas or concerts—there is no admission to the auditorium once the performance has begun. Evening performances of plays in Leningrad theatres normally start at 7.30 p.m. and concerts begin at 8.00 p.m. In any case the time of the performance is indicated on your tickets.

Do not wear or carry your overcoat or raincoat into the auditorium—check it at the cloakroom (no charge) where you can also hire opera-glasses for 40-50 kopecks.

Oktyabrsky Concert Hall—6, Ligovsky Prospekt
Gorky Academic Bolshoi Drama Theatre—65, Naberezhnaya Reki Fontanki
Pushkin Academic Drama Theatre—2, Ploshchad Ostrovskogo
Glinka Academic Capella—20, Naberezhnaya Reki Moiki
Comedy Theatre—56, Nevsky Prospekt
Maly Academic Theatre of Opera and Ballet—1, Ploshchad Iskusstv
Kirov Academic Theatre of Opera and Ballet—1, Teatralnaya Ploshchad
Lenin Sports and Concert Complex—8, Prospekt Gagarina
Komissarzhevskaya Drama Theatre—19, Ulitsa Rakova
Komsomol Theatre—4, Park Imeni Lenina
Lensoviet Theatre—12, Vladimirsky Prospekt
Puppet Theatre—10, Ulitsa Nekrasova
Theatre of Musical Comedy—13, Ulitsa Rakova
Children's Theatre—1, Pionerskaya Ploshchad
Leningrad Philharmonia—2, Ulitsa Brodskogo
State Circus—3, Naberezhnaya Reki Fontanki
Maly Theatre of Drama—18, Ulitsa Rubinshteina
Rimsky-Korsakov Conservatoire (Opera Studio)—3, Teatralnaya Ploshchad

Cinemas

As a rule Leningrad film showings begin between 9 and 10 in the morning, and continue all day. Tickets for showings before 4.00 p.m. are half price. You may only take your seats in the interval between showings. Smoking is not permitted!

Showings usually last about 1 hour 40 minutes. Tickets are stamped with the row and seat number. Do not remove your coats: in cinemas there is no cloakroom. Cinema tickets can be bought at the cinema ticket office or through hotel service bureaus.

Avrora—60, Nevsky Prospekt
Baltika—34, Sedmaya Liniya, Vasilyevsky Ostrov
Gigant—44, Kondratyevsky Prospekt
Khudozhestvenny—67, Nevsky Prospekt
Kolizei—100, Nevsky Prospekt
Kosmonavt—24, Bronnitskaya Ulitsa
Leningrad—4, Potyomkinskaya Ulitsa
Meridian—48, Novo-Izmailovsky Prospekt
Moskva—6, Prospekt I. Gaza
Narvsky—32, Bulvar Novatorov
Nevsky—4, Narodnaya Ulitsa
Oktyabr—80, Nevsky Prospekt
Rodina—12, Ulitsa Tolmachova

Sovremennik—25, Prospekt Nauki
Spartak—8, Ulitsa Saltykova-Shchedrina
Titan—47, Nevsky Prospekt
Zenit—5, Ulitsa Gastello

Stadiums and Sport Centres

Jubilee Palace of Sports—18, Prospekt Dobrolyubova
Sports Palace—9, Ulitsa Butlerova
Lenin Stadium—2, Petrovsky Ostrov
Kirov Stadium—35, Morskoi Prospekt, Krestovsky Ostrov
Winter Stadium—11, Inzhenernaya Ulitsa
Dynamo Sports Complex—Krestovsky Ostrov
Lenin Sports and Concert Complex—8, Prospekt Gagarina

Hotels

Astoria—39, Ulitsa Gertsena. Nearest Metro Station *Nevsky Prospekt*
Baltiiskaya—57, Nevsky Prospekt. Nearest Metro Station *Mayakovskaya*
Druzhba—4, Ulitsa Chapygina. Nearest Metro Station *Petrogradskaya*
Karelia—27/2, Ulitsa Tukhachevskogo
Kievskaya—49, Dnepropetrovskaya Ulitsa
Ladoga—26, Prospekt Shahumyana
Leningrad—5/2, Pirogovskaya Naberezhnaya. Nearest Metro Station *Ploshchad Lenina*
Mir—17/19, Ulitsa Gastello. Nearest Metro Station *Park Pobedy*
Moskva—2, Ploshchad Alexandra Nevskogo. Nearest Metro Station *Ploshchad Alexandra Nevskogo*
Moskovskaya—43/45, Ligovsky Prospekt. Nearest Metro Station *Ploshchad Vosstaniya*
Oktyabrskaya—10, Ligovsky Prospekt. Nearest Metro Station *Ploshchad Vosstaniya*
Pribaltiiskaya—14, Ulitsa Korablestroitelei. Nearest Metro Station *Primorskaya*
Pulkovskaya—1, Ploshchad Pobedy. Nearest Metro Station *Moskovskaya*
Rossia—163, Moskovsky Prospekt. Nearest Metro Station *Park Pobedy*
Sovietskaya—43, Lermontovsky Prospekt. Nearest Metro Station *Baltiisky Vokzal*
Sputnik—34, Prospekt Morisa Toreza
Vyborgskaya—3, Torzhkovskaya Ulitsa
Yevropeiskaya—1/7, Ulitsa Brodskogo. Nearest Metro Station *Nevsky Prospekt*
Zarya—40, Kurskaya Ulitsa

Some State and Public Organisations and Agencies Dealing with Foreign Visitors

Leningrad branch of the USSR Bank for Foreign Trade (Vneshtorgbank)—29, Ulitsa Gertsena
Intourist (Leningrad branch)—11, Isaakievskaya Ploshchad. Tel. (Secretariat) 211-51-23
Insurance for tourists "Ingosstrakh"—17, Ulitsa Kalyayeva
Leningrad Region Peace Committee—21, Naberezhnaya Reki Fontanki

Leningrad Red Cross Committee—25, Ulitsa Rakova

Soviet War Veterans' Committee, Leningrad branch—22, Naberezhnaya Kutuzova

Union of Societies for Friendship and Cultural Relations with Foreign Countries, Leningrad branch—21, Naberezhnaya Reki Fontanki

Committee of Soviet Women, Leningrad Regional branch—21, Naberezhnaya Reki Fontanki

Sputnik Youth Travel Agency, Leningrad Office—4, Ulitsa Chapygina

PHRASE-BOOK

Arrival

Porter!	Nasee'l'shchik!
Where can I get a taxi, please?	Skazhee't'e, pazhah'lsta, gd'e stayah'nka taksee'?
Where is the Intourist representative (office)?	Gd'e pretstavee'tel' (otd'ele'neeye) "Eentooree'sta"?
Where is the ... hotel?	Kahk praye'khat' v gastee'neetsoo?
I am a foreigner.	Yah eenastrah'nets/eenastrah'nka.*
I am a tourist.	Yah tooree'st.

Customs

I have nothing to declare.	Oo min'yah' n'et neechevo' shto padlezhi't po'shleennoy aplah't'e.
These things are for personal use.	E'ta ve'shchee lee'chnava po'l'zavaneeya.
Here is my money.	Vot mayah' val'oo'ta.
This is all my baggage.	Ves' e'tat bagah'sh moy.
Where do I go through customs?	Gd'e boo'det tamo'zhennoye afarmle'neeye?
This is my suitcase.	E'ta moy cheemadah'n.
This is someone else's suitcase.	E'ta choozhoi' cheemadah'n.
How much duty do I have to pay?	Kakoo'yoo po'shleenoo yah do'lzhen ooplatee't'?
Is the inspection finished?	Dasmo'tr ako'nchen?
Is my baggage overweight?	Yest' lee lee'shneey v'es?
How much must I pay for overweight baggage?	Sko'l'ka yah do'lzhen ooplatee't' zah lee'shneey v'es?

Hotel Accommodations

I want a single room with bath/shower.	Mn'e noo'zhen no'mer dlyah adnavo' chelave'ka s vah'nnoy (s doo'shem).
My wife and I would like a double room.	Nahm s zhenoy' noo'zhen adee'n no'mer nah dvaee'kh.
May I have the key to my room?	Dai't'e mn'e, pazhah'lsta, klyooch at no'mera.
Please take my baggage to my room.	Dastah'vt'e, pazhah'lsta, moy bagah'sh v no'mer.

_____

* In instances where two forms are given, the latter is the feminine equivalent.

What is my room number?	Kakoy' no'mer mayey' ko'mnaty?
Where can I have breakfast (lunch, dinner)?	Gd'e yah magoo' pazah'vtrakat' (paabe'dat', paoo'zheenat')?
Where can I buy foreign newspapers?	Gd'e yah magoo' koopee't' eenastrah'nniye gaz'e'ty?
Please wake me at ... o'clock.	Razboodee't'e min'yah', pazhah'lsta, v ... chaso'f ... minoo't
Where is the elevator (service bureau, restaurant, café)?	Gd'e nakho'deetsa leeft (biooro' apsloo'zheevaneeya, restarah'n, kafe')?
I am staying at the ... hotel.	Yah astanavee'ls'a v gastee'neetse ...
I live in room ... on the ... floor.	Yah zheevoo' v no'mere ... nah ... etazhe'
Wait a minute!	Adnoo' meenoo'too!
Come in.	Vaidee'te!
Can I change money here?	Mo'zhna lee zd'es' abmenyah't' val'oo'too?
Where can I make a phone call?	Gd'e mo'zhna pazvanee't' pa telefo'noo?
Please buy me a ticket (two tickets) to the theatre for tomorrow's performance of ...	Koopee't'e, pazhah'lsta, mn'e beele't (dvah beele'ta) v teah'tr nah zah'ftra, na spektah'kl' ...
Is there any mail for me?	N'et lee dlyah minyah' karrespanden'tsii?

At the Bank

Where is the nearest bank?	Gde nakho'deetsa bleezhai'sheey bank?
I should like to change some money and one traveller's cheque.	Yah khatel' bih abmenyah't' val'oo'too ee adee'n chek.
What documents do I need to change money?	Kakee'ye tre'booy'ootsa dakoome'nti, shto'bi abmenyah't' val'oo'too?
Can you change a ten-ruble (a five-ruble, a three-ruble) note?	Razmen'ai'te, pazhah'lsta, des'at' (p'aht') rooblei' (tree roobl'ah').

Greetings, Getting Acquainted, Relations, Professions

Hello!	Zdrah'stvooite!
Good morning!	Do'broye oo'tro!
Good afternoon!	Do'briy d'en!
Good evening!	Do'briy ve'cher!
Goodbye!	Da sveedah'neeya!
Mr.	Gaspadee'n
Mrs./Miss	Gaspazhah'
Comrade	Tavah'reeshch
Let me introduce myself.	Razreshee'te pretstah'veetsa.
My name is ...	Men'ah' zavoo't ...
What's your name?	Kahk vahs zavoo't?
How old are you?	Sko'l'ka vahm l'et?
I am from ...	Yah preeye'khal eez ...

Father	Ate'ts
Mother	Maht'
Brother	Braht
Sister	Sestrah'
Son	Sin
Daughter	Doch
Boy	Mah'l'cheek
Little girl	De'vachka
Girl	De'vooshka
Man	Moozhshchee'na
Woman	Zhe'nshcheena
Husband, spouse	Moozh, sooproo'k
Wife, spouse	Zhenah', sooproo'ga
Worker	Rabo'cheey/rabo'tneetsa
Peasant	Krest'a'neen/krest'ah'nka
Office or professional worker	Sloo'zhashchey
Public figure	Apshche'stvenniy de'yatel'
Journalist	Zhoornalee'st
Writer	Peesah'tel'
Teacher	Oochee'tel'/oochee'tel'neetsa
Actor/actress	Akt'or'/aktr'ee'sa
Student	Stood'e'nt/stood'e'ntka
Engineer	Eenzhene'r
Doctor	Vrahch
Miner	Shakht'o'r
Mechanic	Mekhah'neek
Artist	Khoodo'zhn'eek
Interpreter	Perevo'tcheek
Group	Groo'pa
Excursion	Ekskoo'rseeya

Requests, Expression of Gratitude, Apologies, Wishes

Please get an interpreter/Please help me!	Pazavee'te, pazhah'lsta, per'evo'tcheeka/Pamaghee'te, pazhah'lsta!
Please take me to ... (meet me at) ...	Prahshoo' vahs pravadee't' (fstr'e'teet') menyah'
I am very grateful to you!	Blagadar'oo' vahs!
Thank you!	Spasee'ba!
Excuse me!	Eezveenee'te, pazhah'lsta!
I want to rest (to eat, to drink, to sleep).	Yah khachoo' atdakhnoo't' (yest', peet', spaht').

I'd like to see the city (exhibition, museum).	Yah khachoo' asmatre't' go'rot (vis'tafkoo, moozey').
I'd like to go to the theatre (to the cinema, to a park).	Yah khachoo' paitee' f teah'tr (f keeno', f pahrk).
I would like to buy a souvenir.	Yah khachoo' koopee't' shto'-neebood' nah pah'myat'.
I agree.	Yah saglah'sen/saglah'sna.
I don't object.	N'e vazrazhah'yoo.
Yes, of course!	Dah, kane'shna!
With pleasure!	S oodavo'l'stveeyem!
I don't want to.	Yah ne khachoo'.
I can't.	Yah ne magoo'!
No, thank you!	N'et, spasee'ba!
Unfortunately, I am busy.	K sazhale'neeyoo, yah zah'n'at/zah'n'ata.
I don't agree with you.	Yah n'e saglah'sen/n'e saglah'sna s vah'mee.
Congratulations!	Pazdravl'ah'yoo vahs!
To your good health!	Zah vah'she zdaro'vye!
I wish you happiness (health, success).	Zhelah'yoo shchah'stya (zdaro'vya, oospe'kha).
I don't understand you.	Yah ne poneema'yoo vahs.
I (only) speak …	Yah gavar'oo' (to'l'ka) pa …
Please repeat what you said.	Paftaree't'e, pazhah'lsta, yeshcho' rahs.
Please speak a little slower.	Gavaree'te, pazhah'lsta, me'dlenn'eye.

Days of the Week, Months and Seasons

What day of the week is it today?	Kakoi' seevo'dnya den'?
Monday	Poneede'l'nik
Tuesday	Vto'rnik
Wednesday	Sreda'
Thursday	Chetve'rk
Friday	P'a'tn'itsa
Saturday	Sooboh'ta
Sunday	Voskresen'ye
Working day (day off)	Raboh'cheey (neraboh'cheey) den'
Week	Nehdeh'l'a
Month	Meh's'ats
January	Yanvahr'
February	Fevral'
March	Mahrt
April	Aprel'

May	Mai
June	Iyoo'n'
July	Iyoo'l'
August	Av'goost
September	Sent'a'br'
October	Okt'a'br'
November	Noya'br'
December	Dekah'br'
Winter	Zeemah'
Spring	Veesnah'
Summer	L'eh'to
Autumn	Oh'sen'
Holiday	Prahz'nik
New Year	Noh'viy Gohd

Time

What time is it?	Kato'riy chahs?
Nine a.m. (p.m.)	Dev'at' chasof' ootrah' (ve'chera)
Nine-thirty	Palavee'na des'ah'tava
At ... hours ... minutes	V ... chaso'f ... m'eenoo't
Morning, in the morning	Ootra', oo'tram
Evening, in the evening	Ve'cher, ve'cheram
Afternoon, in the afternoon	Den', dn'om
Night, at night	Noch, no'chyoo
Minute	M'eenoo'ta
Hour	Chahs
Half-hour	Polchasah'
Today	Sevo'dn'a
Tomorrow	Zah'ftra
Yesterday	Fcherah'
The day before yesterday	Pozafcherah'
The day after tomorrow	Poslezah'ftra
Last (next) week	Nah pro'shloy (sle'dooshchei) nede'le
Next month (year)	V boo'dooshchem me's'atse (godoo')

Counting

How much (many)?	Skol'ka?
1 – one	1 – adee'n
2 – two	2 – dvah
3 – three	3 – tree

4 – four	4 – cheti're
5 – five	5 – p'aht'
6 – six	6 – shest'
7 – seven	7 – sem'
8 – eight	8 – vo'sem'
9 – nine	9 – de'vat'
10 – ten	10 – de's'at'
11 – eleven	11 – adee'nnatsat'
12 – twelve	12 – dvenah'tsat'
13 – thirteen	13 – treenah'tsat'
14 – fourteen	14 – cheti'rnatsat'
15 – fifteen	15 – p'atnah'tsat'
16 – sixteen	16 – shesnah'tsat'
17 – seventeen	17 – semnah'tsat'
18 – eighteen	18 – vasemnah'tsat'
19 – nineteen	19 – dev'atnah'tsat'
20 – twenty	20 – dvah'tsat'
30 – thirty	30 – tree'tsat'
40 – forty	40 – so'rok
50 – fifty	50 – p'ades'ah't
60 – sixty	60 – shezdes'ah't
70 – seventy	70 – se'm'des'at
80 – eighty	80 – vo'sem'des'at
90 – ninety	90 – deveno'sta
100 – one hundred	100 – sto
200 – two hundred	200 – dve'stee
300 – three hundred	300 – tree'sta
400 – four hundred	400 – cheti'resta
500 – five hundred	500 – p'at'so't
600 – six hundred	600 – shesso't
700 – seven hundred	700 – semso't
800 – eight hundred	800 – vosemso't
900 – nine hundred	900 – devetso't
1000 – one thousand	1000 – ti's'acha

Money, Prices

1 (one) kopeck	1 (adnah') kapey'ka
2 (two) kopecks	2 (dv'e) kapey'kee
3 (three) kopecks	3 (tr'ee) kapey'kee
5 (five) kopecks	5 (p'at') kapey'ek

10 (ten) kopecks	10 (de's'at') kapee'yek
15 (fifteen) kopecks	15 (p'atnah'tsat') kapee'yek
20 (twenty) kopecks	20 (dvah'tsat') kapee'yek
1 (one) ruble	1 (adee'n) roobl'
3 (three) rubles	3 (tr'ee) roobl'ah'
5 (five) rubles	5 (p'at') roobley'
10 (ten) rubles	10 (d'es'at') roobley'
25 (twenty-five) rubles	25 (dvah'tsat' p'at') roobley'
50 (fifty) rubles	50 (p'ades'at') roobley'
100 (one hundred) rubles	100 (sto) roobley'
How much does it cost?	Sko'l'ka sto'eet?
Please write down the price	Nap'eeshee't'e, pazhah'lsta, tse'noo
Change	Zdah'cha

Signs

Attention!	Vneemah'n'eeye!
Stop!	Stop!
Crossing	Perekho't
Bus (trolley-bus, tram) stop	Astano'fka afto'boosa (traley'boosa, tramva'hya)
Look out for cars!	Bereghee's' aftamabee'l'a!
Taxi stand	Stayah'nka taks'ee'
Phone box	Telefo'n-aftamah't
Information bureau	Sprah'vachnoye b'ooro'
Lavatory (Gents, Ladies)	Tooal'et
Chemist's	Apte'ka
Post office. Telegraph office	Po'chta. Telegraf'
Beauty parlour, barber's shop	Pareekmah'kherskaya
Box office (for a theatre)	Teatrah'lnaya kah'ssa
Restaurant	Restarah'n
Café	Kafe'
Bakery	Boo'lachnaya
Confectionery	Kondee'terskaya
Grocery store	Gastrano'm
Grocery shop (for dry goods: flour, sugar, grains, etc.)	Bakale'ya
Meat/fish	M'ah'sa-ri'ba
Closed	Zakri'ta
Open	Atkri'ta
Dinner break	Pereri'f na abe't

Self-service	Samaapsloo'zheevaneeye
Entrance (exit)	Fkhot (vi'khot)
Milk	Malako'
Beer/soft drinks	Pee'va-vo'di
Fruit and vegetable juices/mineral water	So'kee-vo'di
Wines/liqueurs, alcoholic drinks	Vee'na-leek'o'ri, alkogo'l'niye napee'tkee
Vegetables/fruit	O'vashchi-froo'kti
Florist's	Tsveti'
Perfumery	Parfoome'reeya
Tobacconist's	Papeero'si-tabahkee', seegare'ti
Bookshop	Knee'ghee
Articles for cultural and recreational needs	Kool'ttavah'ri
Furniture store	Me'bel'
Clothing store	Ade'zhda
Shoe store	O'boof'
Hats	Galavni'e oobo'ri
Haberdasher's	Galantere'ya
Detsky Mir (a store selling goods for children)	De'tskeey mee'r
Department store	Ooneevermah'k

The Metro (M)

Entrance	Fkhot
Exit	Vi'khot (vi'khot v go'rot)
No exit	Vi'khada net
Ticket office	Kah'ssi
Drop 5 kopecks in the slot.	Apoost'ee'te 5 kapey'ek.
Stand to the right, pass through on the left side.	Stoy'te sprah'va, prakhadee't'e sle'va.
To the trains	K payezdah'm
Transfer to ... line	Peresah'tka nah ...

Shopping

Where is the nearest ... shop/store?	Gde bleezhay'shiy magazee'n?
I would like to see ... please.	Pakazhee't'e, pazhah'lsta!
Do you have ...?	Oo vahs yest'...?
Another colour.	Droogo'va tsve'ta.
Another style.	Droogo'i faso'n.
A larger (smaller) size.	Bol'sheey (men'sheey) razme'r.
I'll take that.	Yah e'ta koopl'oo'.
Where can I pay for this?	Gd'e yah magoo' aplatee't' pakoo'pkoo?

Medical Aid

I am unwell.	Yah nezdaro'f/nezdaro'va.
I don't feel well.	Yah plo'kha seb'ah' choo'stvooyoo.
Please call a doctor (first aid).	Vi'zaveete, pazhah'lsta, vrachah' (sko'rooyoo po'moshch).
I have a temperature.	Oo men'ah' temperatoo'ra.
My head (heart, stomach, throat, eye, hand, arm, leg) hurts/aches.	Oo men'ah bolee't galavah' (se'rtse, zheloo'dak, go'rla, glahs, rookah', nagah').
Do you have something for a cold?	Yest' lee oo vahs shtoneeboo'd' at prastoo'di?

Dining Out

Please bring me a menu.	Dait'e, pazhah'lsta, men'oo'!
Please bring me one serving (two servings) of ...	Preenesee'te, pazhah'lsta, adnoo' po'rtsiyoo (dv'e po'rtsii) ...
Please bring me some beer (wine, mineral water, cognac, champagne, vodka).	Prenesee'te, pazhah'lsta, p'ee'va (v'eenah', minerah'l'noi vodi', kanyakoo', shampah'nskava, vo'tkee).
Glass	Stakah'n
Wine-glass	R'oo'mka
Plate	Tare'lka
Knife	Nosh
Fork	Vee'lka
Spoon	Lo'shka
Napkin	Salfe'tka
Tablecloth	Skah'tert'
Salt	Sol'
Pepper	Pe'rets
Mustard	Garchee'tsa
Butter	Sl'ee'vachnaye mah'sla
Sugar	Sah'khar
Cigarettes	S'eegare'ti
Matches	Spee'chkee
Please give me the bill.	Dai'te, pazhah'lsta, shchot!

On the Street

Can you tell me how to get to the ... hotel?	Skazhee'te, pazhah'lsta, kahk proitee' k gastee'neetse ...?
Straight ahead, to the right, to the left, ahead, back	Pr'ah'ma, naprah'va, nal'eva, fperyo't, nazah't
Street, square, alley, crossroads, avenue, highway	Oo'leetsa, plo'shchat', pereoo'lak, perekro'stak, praspe'kt, shase'

Can you tell me what bus (trolley, tram) I should take to get to the city centre (to ... hotel ... station)?

Skazhee'te, pazhah'lsta, kakee'm afto'boosam (traley'boosam, tramva'em) yah magoo' daye'khat' do tse'ntra go'rada (gastee'neetsi, vokzah'la)?

Where is the trolley stop, please?

Skazhee't'e, pazhah'lsta, gde astano'fka traley'boosa?

Where is a taxi stand?

Gde stayah'nka taksee'?

Please show me on the map where I am.

Pokazhee'te, pazhah'lsta, na kah'rte gde yah nakhazhoo's'.

I am lost.

Yah zabloodee'lsa/zabloodee'las'.

Militiaman

Meeleetsiane'r

How can I get (in a vehicle) to ...?

Kahk mne daye'khat' da ...?

Where is the transfer for ...?

Gde peresah'tka nah ...?

How many stops to ...?

Sko'l'ka astano'vak da ...?

Departure

I am leaving tomorrow at ... o'clock

Yah ooyezhah'yoo zah'ftra v ... chaso'f

Please have my bill ready to be paid.

Preegato'f'te mne, pazhah'lsta, shchot.

When does the train for ... leave?

Kagdah' atkho'deet po'yest nah ...?

Where can I look at a train (plane, boat) timetable?

Gd'e mo'zhna pasmatre't' raspeesah'neeye payezdo'f (samal'o'tof, parakho'dof)?

When does the flight ... for ... leave?

Kagdah' vi'let samal'o'ta nah ... reis ...?

Please call me a taxi!

Vi'zaveete, pazhah'lsta, taksee'!

Where do I board the train ... for ...?

Gde pasah'tka nah po'yest no'mer ... da ...?

Where do I board the flight ... for ...?

Gde pasah'tka nah samalo't no'mer ... da ...?

What platform does the train ... for ... leave from?

S kakoi' platfo'rmi atkho'deet po'yest no'mer ... da ...?

SUBJECT INDEX

MONUMENTS

ARCHITECTURAL ENSEMBLES

CERTAIN OTHER SIGHTS

NAME INDEX

STATE, PARTY, ARMY AND NAVAL LEADERS

MASTERS OF APPLIED ARTS

COMPOSERS

Berlioz, Hector— 187
Degeyter, Pierre— 66
Glazunov, Alexander— 351
Kui, Tsesar— 167
Liszt, Franz— 187
Monsigny, Pierre-Alexander— 338
Mravinsky, Yevgeni— 191
Musorgsky, Modest— 157, 167, 206
Rimsky-Korsakov, Nikolai— 157, 167, 206

Rubinstein, Anton— 157, 191
Shostakovich, Dmitry— 26, 157, 191-92
Solovyov-Sedoi, Vasily— 205
Strauss, Johann— 187
Tchaikovsky, Pyotr— 26, 157, 178, 191, 206
Wagner, Richard— 187

PERSONALITIES IN THEATRE, OPERA AND BALLET

Akimov, Nikolai— 109
Balanchin, George— 199
Chabukiani, Vakhtang— 157, 199
Chaliapin, Fyodor— 86, 157
Eliasberg, Karl— 26, 191
Fokin, Mikhail— 199

Komissarzhevskaya, Vera— 193
Mravinsky, Yevgeni— 191
Pavlova, Anna— 157, 199
Vaganova, Agrippina— 199
Ulanova, Galina— 157, 199, 220

SCIENTISTS, INVENTORS, EXPLORERS

Euler, Leonard— 111
Dashkova, Yekaterina— 197, 213
Graftio, Heinrich— 86
Grabovsky, Boris— 147
Grot, Yakov— 111
Hertz, Heinrich— 83
Heyerdahl, Thor— 84
Fersman, Alexander— 111
Ioffe, Abram— 8
Kant, Immanuel— 197
Karpinsky, Alexander— 111
Kibalchich, Nikolai— 79
Korolyov, Sergei— 79
Krachkovsky, Ignaty— 111
Krusenstern, Ivan— 111
Krylov, Alexei— 8
Kulibin, Ivan— 60, 240
Lebedev, Sergei— 57
Lesgaft, Pyotr— 158
Lodygin, Alexander— 59
Lomonosov, Mikhail— 57, 100, 101, 111, 206, 240, 243, 267

Mendeleyev, Dmitry— 104-05, 159, 217
Michurin, Ivan— 267
Orbeli, Joseph— 298
Orbeli, Leon— 83
Pavlov, Ivan— 83, 86, 111, 267
Pirogov, Nikolai— 83, 164
Popov, Alexander— 83, 147, 267
Przhevalsky, Nikolai— 96
Semyonov-Tien-Shansky, Pyotr— 8
Struve, Vasili— 8
Tsander, Friedrich— 79
Tsiolkovsky, Konstantin— 79
Timiryazev, Kliment— 267
Ushinsky, Konstantin— 181
Vavilov, Nikolai— 26, 177
Vinogradov, Alexander— 220
Yablochkov, Pavel— 59, 124
Yakobi, Boris— 147
Zhukovsky, Nikolai— 79
Zeiss, Carl— 81

WRITERS

Balzac, Honoré de— 126
Belinsky, Vissarion— 203
Béranger, Pierre Jean— 197

Berggolts, Olga— 22, 259
Blok, Alexander— 97, 115, 159
Bryusov, Valery— 255

ARTISTS

SCULPTORS

ARCHITECTS

Request to Readers

Planeta Publishers would be glad to have your opinion of this book, its translation and design and any suggestions you may have for future publications. Please send all your comments to 8/11, Petrovka Street, Moscow 103031, USSR.

Заведующая редакцией Т. В. Гуськова
Редактор русского текста Я. Бродский
Контрольный редактор А. Буяновская
Художник Э. Симанович
Художественный редактор А. Томчинская
Технический редактор Т. Гисаева

ИБ № 3989

Сдано в набор и подписано в печать 02.03.89.
Формат 84 × 108/32. Изд. 11/3-8922.
Бумага мелованная. Гарнитура Максима. Печать офсет.
Усл. п. л. 20,16.
Усл. кр.-отт. 122,22. Уч.-изд. л. 28,868. Тираж 72 900 экз.
Заказ 005025/1
Цена 5 р. 10 к.

Издательство "Планета". 103031. Москва, Петровка, 8/11

Отпечатано при посредстве В/О "Внешторгиздат"

"Интердрук" головное полиграфическое предприятие
г. Лейпциг, ГДР

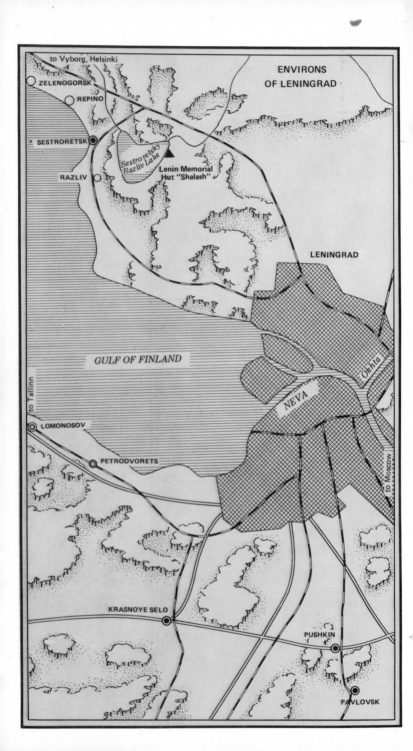